COUNTRY LIVING
M A G A Z I N E

# GUIDE TO RURAL ENGLAND

## EAST ANGLIA

D1579275

By Barbara Vesey

© Travel Publishing Ltd.

Published by:
Travel Publishing Ltd
7a Apollo House, Calleva Park
Aldermaston, Berks, RG7 8TN
ISBN 1-904-43408-8
© Travel Publishing Ltd

Country Living is a registered trademark of The National
Magazine Company Limited.

First Published:   2001        Second Edition:   2004

## COUNTRY LIVING GUIDES:

East Anglia                                    Scotland
Heart of England                               The South of England
Ireland                                        The South East of England
The North East of England                      The West Country
The North West of England                      Wales

## PLEASE NOTE:

All advertisements in this publication have been accepted in good faith by Travel
Publishing and they have not necessarily been endorsed by *Country Living*
Magazine.

All information is included by the publishers in good faith and is believed to be
correct at the time of going to press. No responsibility can be accepted for errors.

Editor:          Barbara Vesey

Printing by:     Scotprint, Haddington

Location Maps:© Maps in Minutes ™ (2003)   © Crown Copyright, Ordnance Survey 2003

Walks:           Walks have been reproduced with kind permission of the internet
                 walking site www.walkingworld.com

Walk Maps:       Reproduced from Ordnance Survey mapping on behalf of the
                 Controller of Her Majesty's Stationery Office, © Crown Copyright.
                 Licence Number MC 100035812

Cover Design:    Lines & Words, Aldermaston

Cover Photo:     Hunsett Mill, Norfolk © www.britainonview.com

Text Photos:     Text photos have been kindly supplied by the Britain on View photo library
                 © www.britainonview.com

# Foreword

From a bracing walk across the hills and tarns of The Lake District to a relaxing weekend spent discovering the unspoilt hamlets of East Anglia, nothing quite matches getting off the beaten track and exploring Britain's areas of outstanding beauty.

Each month, *Country Living Magazine* celebrates the richness and diversity of our countryside with features on rural Britain and the traditions that have their roots there. So it is with great pleasure that I introduce you to the *Country Living Magazine Guide to Rural England* series. Packed with information about unusual and unique aspects of our countryside, the guides will point both fair-weather and intrepid travellers in the right direction.

Each chapter provides a fascinating tour of the East Anglia area, with insights into local heritage and history and easy-to-read facts on a wealth of places to visit, stay, eat, drink and shop.

I hope that this guide will help make your visit a rewarding and stimulating experience and that you will return inspired, refreshed and ready to head off on your next countryside adventure.

*Susy Smith*

Susy Smith
Editor, Country Living magazine

PS To subscribe to *Country Living Magazine* each month, call 01858 438844

# Introduction

This is the second edition of the *Country Living Guide to Rural England - East Anglia* and is full of information on the tradtional English countryside in Norfolk, Suffolk, Cambridgeshire and Essex. It is over 2 years since publication of the very popular first edition and we hope you enjoy this thoroughly updated version just as much. Barbara Vesey, the editor, is an experienced travel writer and editor who has worked extensively for travel publishers such as Fodor's and the AA. Born in New York and educated at Oberlin College in the U.S.A., Barbara moved to the U.K. in 1987. She and her family now live in South Yorkshire. Since joining our editorial team in 1997 she has edited many Travel Publishing titles.

The guide is packed with vivid descriptions, historical stories, amusing anecdotes and interesting facts on hundreds of places in East Anglia. *Norfolk* is famous for the Norfolk Broads but has a rich and interesting past, gentle hills as well as expansive horizons, delightful pastoral scenes, a beautiful coastline rich in wildlife and many interesting hidden places to visit. *Suffolk* was made famous by the brush of John Constable and is blessed with incomparable rural beauty which encompasses wide open spaces broken by gentle hills and tidal rivers meandering from a coastline teeming with birdlife. *Cambridgeshire* is famous for its ancient university and being the birthplace of Oliver Cromwell and Samuel Pepys but offers a wealth of peaceful and attractive countryside with many towns and villages steeped in history. *Essex*, containing England's oldest recorded town (Colchester), has a strong maritime tradition, pretty villages, a coastline with attractive estuaries and a rich history going back to Roman times.

The coloured advertising panels within each chapter provide further information on places to see, stay, eat, drink, shop and even exercise! We have also selected a number of walks from *walkingworld.com* (full details of this website may be found to the rear of this guide) which we highly recommend if you wish to appreciate fully the beauty and charm of the varied rural landscapes of East Anglia.

The guide however is not simply an "armchair tour". Its prime aim is to encourage the reader to visit the places described and discover much more about the wonderful towns, villages and countryside of East Anglia. In this respect we would like to thank all the Tourist Information Centres who helped us to provide you with up-to-date information. Whether you decide to explore this region by wheeled transport or by foot we are sure you will find it a very uplifting experience.

We are always interested in receiving comments on places covered (or not covered) in our guides so please do not hesitate to use the reader reaction form provided at the rear of this guide to give us your considered comments. This will help us refine and improve the content of the next edition. We also welcome any general comments which will help improve the overall presentation of the guides themselves.

Finally, for more information on the full range of travel guides published by Travel Publishing please refer to the details and order form at the rear of this guide or log on to our website at www.travelpublishing.co.uk

Travel Publishing

# Locator Map

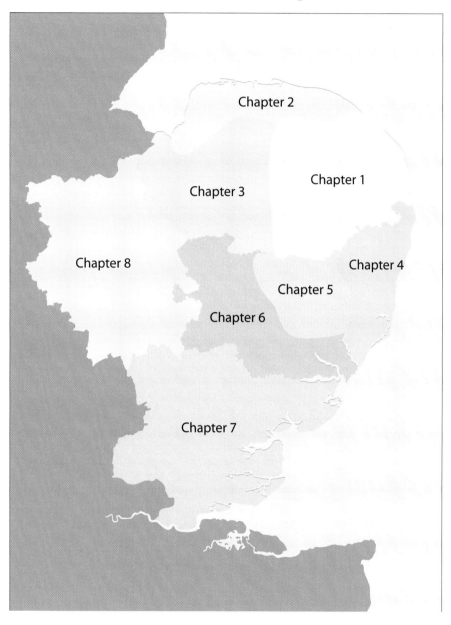

# Contents

FOREWORD    III

INTRODUCTION    V

REGIONAL MAP    VI

CONTENTS    VII

GEOGRAPHICAL AREAS:

Chapter 1:    South Norfolk and the Broads   3
Chapter 2:    North Norfolk Coast   37
Chapter 3:    King's Lynn and West Norfolk   79
Chapter 4:    The Suffolk Coast   107
Chapter 5:    Central Suffolk   155
Chapter 6:    South and West Suffolk   175
Chapter 7:    Essex   225
Chapter 8:    Cambridgeshire   301

INDEXES AND LISTS:

Tourist Information Centres   343
Alphabetic List of Advertisers   348
List of Walks   353
Order Form   358
Reader Comment Forms   359
Index of Towns, Villages and Places of Interest   365

# LOCATOR MAP

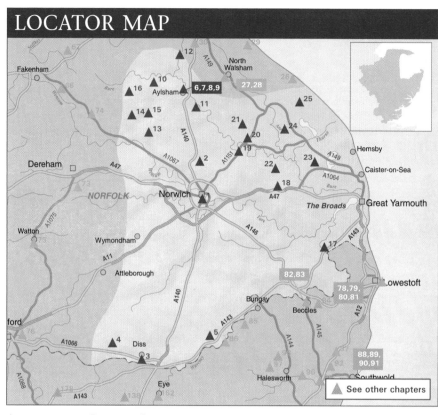

Fakenham
North Walsham
12
10
16 Aylsham
6,7,8,9
27,28
25
14 15
11
13
21
24
20
19
Dereham
2
23
Hemsby
22
Caister-on-Sea
18
NORFOLK
Norwich
A47
The Broads
Great Yarmouth
Watton
Wymondham
17
Attleborough
82,83
78,79, 80,81
Lowestoft
Bungay
Beccles
ford
4
Diss
5
3
88,89, 90,91
Eye
Halesworth
Southwold

▲ See other chapters

ADVERTISERS AND PLACES OF INTEREST

| | | |
|---|---|---|
| 1 | Dragon Hall, Norwich | Page 8 |
| 2 | City of Norwich Aviation Museum, Norwich | Page 9 |
| 3 | Walcot Green Farm Cottage, Diss | Page 12 |
| 4 | Bressingham Gardens, Bressingham | Page 13 |
| 5 | The Cheeseboard, Harleston | Page 14 |
| 6 | Bure Valley Railway, Aylsham | Page 14 |
| 7 | Black Sheep Ltd, Aylsham | Page 15 |
| 8 | Artstop. Biz., Aylsham | Page 16 |
| 9 | Dyes House Gallery, Aylsham | Page 16 |
| 10 | Blickling Hall, Blickling | Page 17 |
| 11 | The Plough Inn, Marsham | Page 18 |
| 12 | Charles Matts, Thurgarton, Norwich | Page 19 |
| 13 | The Romantic Garden Nursery, Swannington, Norwich | Page 22 |
| 14 | Very Nice Things, Reepham | Page 22 |
| 15 | Broadland Wineries, Cawston, Norwich | Page 22 |
| 16 | The Knot Garden, Wood Dalling, Norwich | Page 23 |
| 17 | Fritton Lake Countryworld, Fritton, Great Yarmouth | Page 26 |
| 18 | British Wildflower Plants, North Burlingham | Page 28 |
| 19 | Kingfisher Lodge, Wroxham, Norwich | Page 29 |
| 20 | Eric Bates & Sons Ltd, Hoveton, Wroxham | Page 30 |
| 21 | Tunstead Old Farm Cottages, Tunstead, Norwich | Page 31 |
| 22 | Fairhaven Woodland & Water Garden, South Walsham, Norwich | Page 33 |
| 23 | Clippesby Hall, Clippesby, Great Yarmouth | Page 34 |
| 24 | Grove Farm Gallery & Studio, Catfield, Great Yarmouth | Page 34 |
| 25 | The Treasure Box, Hickling, Norwich | Page 35 |

# SOUTH NORFOLK AND THE BROADS 1

The area that lies between the county capital of Norwich and the border with Suffolk is effectively a plateau, where the gentle contours never rise or fall more than a few metres. The valleys of the Rivers Nar and Wensum display some of the most enchanting scenery in the county, and the area boasts one of the finest Gothic parish churches in England, at Cawston. In prehistoric times this was the most wooded part of Norfolk, and a good number of medieval natural woods still remain, a feature which adds another visual attraction to this pastoral area of the country. Dotted throughout these rural pleasures is a wealth of quiet, unspoilt villages hidden away on minor roads.

*Sunset over the Broads*

The major centres of population include Diss, an old market town with a mix of Tudor, Georgian and Victorian houses, and Wymondham, with its timber-framed houses, picturesque market place and an Abbey church that stands up well to comparison even with the majestic Norwich Cathedral. Norwich, once an important centre of the worsted trade, retains many medieval buildings, a number of which now serve as museums relating the fascinating history of the region.

The area to the east of this fine city contains the unique Norfolk Broads, beautiful stretches of shallow water, most of them linked by navigable rivers and canals. Visitors who want to experience a bird's-eye view that encompasses the essence of the Broads should climb the tower of the 'Cathedral of the Broads', the Church of St Helen's at Ranworth. Spread out below lies a panorama of glittering waterways, acres of marshland dotted with windmills, reed beds which are still harvested for thatch, grand medieval churches, and farmhouses of warm, red brick.

*Rollesby*

This is Britain's finest wetland area, a National Park in all but name. Broadland covers some 220 square miles in a rough oval to the northwest of Great Yarmouth. Three main rivers – the Ant, the Thurne and the Bure – thread their way through the marshes, providing some 120 miles of navigable waterways. The Broads, long popular for restful, relaxing holidays, remain none the less a refuge for many species of endangered birds and plants, and during the spring and autumn they are a favourite stopping-off place for migrating birds.

On the coast due east of Norwich is the old port and modern holiday resort of Great Yarmouth, where the visitor will find miles of sandy beaches, a breezy promenade, two grand old traditional piers and all the fun of the fair, as well as a rich maritime heritage that lives on to this day.

# NORWICH

'Norwich has the most Dickensian atmosphere of any city I know,' declared J B Priestley in his *English Journey* of 1933. 'What a grand, higgledy-piggledy, sensible old place Norwich is!' More than half a century later, in a European Commission study of 'most habitable' cities, Norwich topped the list of British contenders, well ahead of more favoured candidates such as Bath and York. The political, social and cultural capital of Norfolk, Norwich has an individual charm that is difficult to define, a beguiling atmosphere created in part by its prodigal wealth of sublime buildings, and partly by its intriguing dual personality as both an old-fashioned Cathedral town and a vibrant, modern metropolis. Back in prehistoric times, there were several settlements around the confluence of the Rivers Wensum and

Yare. By the late fourth century, one of them was important enough to have its own mint. This was *Northwic*. By the time of the *Domesday Book* 700 years later, Northwic/Norwich, had become the third-most populous city in England, only outnumbered by London and York. To the Norman conquerors, such a major centre of population (about 5,500 residents) needed a **Castle** to ensure that its Saxon inhabitants could be kept in order.

The first castle structure, in wood, was replaced in the late 1100s by a mighty fortress in stone which, unlike most blank-walled castles of the period, is decorated with a rich façade of blind arcades and ornamental pilasters. This great fort never saw any military action, and as early as the 13th century was being used as the county gaol, a role it continued to fill until 1889. From its walls, in December 1549, the leader of

*Castle Museum*

from the artistic quality of their works, they have left a fascinating pictorial record of early 19th century Norfolk.

The **Bulwer and Miller** collection of more than 2,600 English china teapots makes its home in a brand new gallery called the Twinings Gallery, while the museum's Langton collection of around 100 cats fashioned in porcelain, ivory, bronze, glass and wood, originating from anywhere between Derbyshire and China,

the rebellion against land enclosures, Robert Kett, was hung in chains and left to starve to death.

The Castle is now home to the **Castle Museum and Art Gallery**, home to some of the most outstanding regional collections of fine art, archaeological exhibits and natural history displays. The former dungeons contain a forbidding display of instruments of torture, along with the death masks of some of the prisoners who were executed here. Among the countless other fascinating exhibits are those devoted to Queen Boudicca, which features the life of the Iceni tribe with an interactive chariot ride, the Egyptian gallery with its mummy Ankh Hor, and new and interactive displays in the Castle keep and keep basement, recently made accessible to the public.

The Art Gallery has an incomparable collection of paintings by the celebrated Norwich artist, John Sell Cotman (1782-1842), and others in the group known as the Norwich School. Their subjects were mostly landscape scenes, such as John Crome's *The Poringland Oak*. Quite apart

and Margaret Elizabeth Fountaine's mind-boggling accumulation of 22,000 butterflies which she had personally netted during her travels around the world, are available to view by appointment at the Shirehall Study Centre, next door to the Royal Norfolk Regimental Museum on Market Avenue.

The great open space of the Market Square, where every weekday a colourful jumble of traders' stalls can be found, offers just about every conceivable item for sale. Dominating the western side of the Market Square is **City Hall**, modelled on Stockholm City Hall and opened by King George VI in 1938. Opinions differ about its architectural merits, but there are no such doubts about the nearby **Guildhall**, a fine example of 15th century flintwork that now houses a tea room.

Around the corner from London Street, in Bridewell Alley, is the **Bridewell Museum**, a late 14th century merchant's house now dedicated to Norfolk's crafts and industries. Another museum/shop, this one located in the **Royal Arcade**, a tiled riot of Art Nouveau fantasy, celebrates the county's great contribution to world cuisine: mustard. Back in the early 1800s, Jeremiah Colman perfected his blend of mustard flours and spice to produce a condiment that was smooth in texture and tart in flavour. Together with his nephew James he founded J & J Colman in 1823; 150 years later **The Mustard Shop** was established to commemorate the company's history. The shop has an appropriately late-Victorian atmosphere and a fascinating display of vintage containers and advertisements, some of them from 'Mustard Club' featuring such characters as Lord Bacon of Cookham and Miss Di Gester, created by no less distinguished a writer than Dorothy L Sayers. All in all, a most appetising exhibition.

Millennium Plain just off Theatre Street is where visitors will find **The Forum**, an architecturally stunning new building designed by Sir Michael Hopkins. Combining a unique horseshoe shape with an all-glass façade, this spectacular structure has, at its heart, the **Atrium** and **Bridge**, meeting places where you can enjoy a meal or drink anytime through to midnight, seven days a week. At the **Origins** Visitor Centre, an attractive multi-media display on three floors affords the opportunity to experience the life and times of Norwich and the wider Norfolk region. Here can also be found the Tourist Information Centre. The new **Norfolk & Norwich Millennium Library** houses 120,000 books and offers the best in information and communication technology.

**The Assembly House** in Theatre Street is one of the city's finest historical houses and also a leading venue for the arts. With two concert halls, three galleries featuring changing exhibitions and a restaurant and tea rooms, this

*Royal Arcade, Norwich*

magnificent Georgian home must be included in any visit to the city.

While the Castle has been used for many purposes over the years, the **Cathedral** remains what it has always been: the focus of ecclesiastical life in the county. It's even older than the castle, its service of consecration taking place over 900 years ago, in 1101. This peerless building, its flint walls clad in creamy-white stone from Caen is, after Durham, the most completely Norman cathedral in England, its appeal enhanced by later Gothic features such as the flying buttresses. The Norman cloisters are the largest in the country and notable for the 400 coloured and gilded bosses depicting scenes from medieval life. Another 1,200 of these wondrous carvings decorate the glorious vaulted roof of the nave.

It's impossible to list all the Cathedral's treasures here, but do seek out the **Saxon**

*Cathedral and Close, Norwich*

**Bishop's Throne** in the Presbytery, the lovely 14ᵗʰ century altar painting in St Luke's Chapel, and the richly carved canopies in the Choir.

Outside, beneath the slender 315-foot spire soaring heavenwards, the **Cathedral Close** is timeless in its sense of peace. There are some 80 houses inside the Close, some medieval, many Georgian, their residents enjoying an idyllic refuge free from cars. At peace here lie the remains of Nurse Edith Cavell. A daughter of the rector of Swardeston, a few miles south of Norwich, Nurse Cavell worked at a Red Cross hospital in occupied Brussels during the First World War. She helped some 200 Allied soldiers to escape to neutral Holland before being detected and court-martialled by the Germans. As she faced execution by firing squad on 12 October 1915, she spoke her own resonant epitaph: 'Standing as I do, in the view of God and eternity, I realise that patriotism is not enough. I must have no hatred or bitterness towards anyone.'

A stroll around the Close will take you to **Pull's Ferry** with its picturesque flint gateway fronting the River Wensum. In medieval times a canal ran

inland from here so that provisions, goods and, in the earliest days, building materials, could be moved direct to the Cathedral. A short stroll along the riverside walk will bring you to **Cow Tower**, built around 1378 and the most massive of the old city towers.

At the western end of the Cathedral Close is the magnificent **Erpingham Gate**, presented to the city in 1420 by a hero of the Battle of Agincourt, Sir Thomas Erpingham. Beyond this gate, in Tombland (originally Toom or wasteland), is **Samson and Hercules**

*Pull's Ferry*

## DRAGON HALL

115-123 King Street, Norwich NR1 1QE
Tel: 01603 663922

**Dragon Hall** is a magnificent medieval merchant's hall with an outstanding timber-framed structure. The 15th century Great Hall has a crown post roof with an intricately carved and painted dragon.

Opening times: 2nd January to 31st March, Monday to Friday 10am-4pm; 1st April to 31st October, Monday to Saturday 10am-4pm; 1st November to 20th December, Monday to Friday 10am-4pm. Closed 21st December to 1st January and Bank Holidays.

Admission prices and further information can be obtained from the telephone number above.

**House**, its entrance flanked by two 1674 carvings of these giants. Diagonally opposite stands the 15th century Maid's Head Hotel. A 14th century door within a 15th century opening on King Street leads to the only medieval merchants trading halls known to survive in Western Europe. **Dragon Hall** was built for the merchant Robert Toppes in the mid 15th century (see panel above).

Norwich is home to some 32 medieval churches in all, every one of them worth attention, although many are now used for purposes other than worship. Outstanding among them are **St Peter Mancroft**, a masterpiece of Gothic architecture built between 1430-55 (and the largest church in Norwich), and **St Peter Hungate**, a handsome 15th century church standing at the top of **Elm Hill**, a narrow, unbelievably picturesque lane where in medieval times the city's wool merchants built their homes, close to their warehouses beside the River Wensum.

St Gregory's Church in Pottergate is another Norwich church to have been deconsecrated, and its fate might well have been a sad one. Happily, it is now the home to an arts centre where local artists, actors, musicians, dancers and other arts groups stage a variety of performances and exhibitions throughout the year.

When the basic structure of the present St Gregory's was built in the late 14th century, the general rule seems to have been that any parish of around 1,000 people would have its own place of worship. St Gregory's was founded on the site of a Saxon church in 1210 and rebuilt in its present form in 1394. The church takes it name from Gregory the Great, the 6th century Pope best known for his campaign to convert the heathen Anglo-Saxons of 'Angle-land' to Christianity, despatching a party of 40 monks to Angle-land in AD596, led by Augustine, whom the Pope consecrated as the first Archbishop of Canterbury.

The **Inspire Discovery Centre**, housed in the medieval church of St Michael in Coslany Street, just across the Wensum northeast of the city centre, is full of exciting hands-on displays and activities that make scientific enquiry come to life.

There are also a large number of beautiful and well-maintained parks in the city, some of which offer chess, lawn tennis and hard tennis courts, bowls, pitch and putt, rowing and more, together with a programme of entertainments ranging from theatre to concerts. One worth particular mention is The Plantation Garden in Earlham Road, three acres of Victorian plantings restored after having fallen into disrepair, and thought to be the only one in the nation with a Grade II listing.

On the western edge of the city stands the **University of East Anglia**. It's well worth making your way here to visit the **Sainsbury Centre for Visual Arts**. Housed in a huge hall of aluminium and glass designed by Norman Foster, the Centre contains the eclectic collection of a 'passionate acquirer' of art, Sir Robert Sainsbury. For more than 50 years, Sir Robert purchased whatever works of art took his fancy, ignoring fashionable trends. Thus the visitor finds sculptures and pictures by Henry Moore, Bacon and Giacometti, along with African and pre-Columbian artefacts, Egyptian, Etruscan and Roman bronzes, works by Native Americans and Inuit Eskimos, and sculptures from the Cyclades, the South Seas, the Orient and medieval Europe. This extraordinary collection was donated to the University by Sir Robert and Lady Lisa Sainsbury in 1973; their

son David complemented his parents' generosity by paying for the building in which it is housed.

To the south of Norwich in the village of Caistor St Edmund are the remains of **Venta Icenorum**, the Roman town established here after Boudicca's rebellion in AD61. Unusually, this extensive site has not been disturbed by later developments, so archaeologists have been able to identify the full scale of the original settlement. Sadly very little remains above ground, although in dry summers the grid pattern of the streets show up as brown lines in the grass. Most of the finds discovered during excavations in the 1920s and 1930s are now in **Norwich Castle Museum**, but the riverside site still merits a visit.

Just to the north of the city, on the Cromer road, lies the **City of Norwich Aviation Museum**. (see panel below)

## CITY OF NORWICH AVIATION MUSEUM

Old Norwich Road, Horsham St Faiths, Norwich, Norfolk NR10 3JF
Tel: 01603 893080

Follow the brown tourist signs from the A140 Norwich-Cromer road to find the **City of Norwich Aviation Museum**, a museum dedicated to keeping Norfolk's aviation heritage alive. Dominating the museum's collection is a massive Avro Vulcan bomber, a veteran of the Falklands War of 1982.

Eight other military and civilian aircraft are on show, and although they are the main attraction for many visitors, the most fascinating feature is the display within the main exhibition building showing the development of aviation in Norfolk. From the pioneering days of aviation to present-day civilian and military operations, every aspect is covered in a number of displays that are constantly being revised and expanded. The major roles played by Norfolk-based aircraft during the great air battles of World War II are remembered by exhibitions on the USAAF 8th Air Force and the role of the Royal Air Force in this conflict.

A special section is dedicated to the operations of RAF Bomber Command's 100 Group which flew on electronic counter measure, deception and night intruder missions from a number of Norfolk airfields.

# AROUND NORWICH

## Poringland
### 6 miles SE of Norwich on the B1332

The name of this sizable village will be familiar to those who love the paintings of the Norwich artist John Crome (1794-1842) whose arcadian painting of *The Poringland Oak* hangs in the Tate Gallery.

To the southwest of Poringland is **The Playbarn**, an indoor and outdoor adventure centre specially designed for the under-sevens. All the play equipment is based on a farmyard theme, with a miniature farm, bouncy tractors, soft play sheep pens, and donkey rides among the attractions. Refreshments and light lunches are available, or you can bring along your own picnic.

## Wymondham
### 9 miles SW of Norwich off the A11

The exterior of **Wymondham Abbey** presents one of the oddest ecclesiastical buildings in the county; the interior reveals one of the most glorious. The Abbey was founded in 1107 by the Benedictines - or Black Monks, as they were known because of the colour of their habits. The richest and most aristocratic of the monastic orders, the Black Monks apparently experienced some difficulty in respecting their solemn vows of poverty and humility. Especially the

latter. Constantly in dispute with the people of Wymondham, the dissension between them grew so bitter that in 1249 Pope Innocent IV himself attempted to reconcile their differences. When his efforts failed, a wall was built across the interior of the Abbey, dividing it into an area for the monks and another for the parishioners. Even this drastic measure failed to bring peace, however. Both parties wanted to ring their own bells, so each built a tower. The villagers erected a stately rectangular tower at the west end; the monks an octagonal one over the crossing, thus creating the Abbey's curious exterior appearance.

Step inside and you find a magnificent Norman nave, 112 feet long. (It was originally twice as long, but the eastern end, along with most of the Abbey buildings, was demolished after the Dissolution of the Monasteries.) The superb hammerbeam roof is supported by 76 beautifully carved angels. There's also an interesting 16th century tomb, of the last Abbot, in delicate terracotta work, and a striking modern memorial: a gilded and coloured reredos and tester

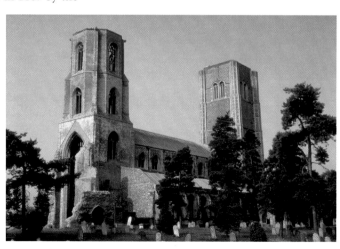

*Wymondham Abbey*

commemorating the local men who lost their lives in the First World War.

The rectangular western tower of the Abbey was the setting for one of the last acts in the ill-fated Kett's Rebellion of 1549. From its walls, William Kett was hung in chains and left to die: his brother Robert, the leading figure in the uprising, suffered the same fate at Norwich Castle.

Although many of Wymondham's oldest houses were lost in the fire of 1615, when some 300 dwellings were destroyed, there are still some attractive Elizabethan buildings in the heart of the town. The **Market Place** (Friday is market day, and on the first Friday of every month there's an antiques and collectors' fair held in Central Hall) is given dignity by the picturesque octagonal Market Cross, rebuilt two years after the fire. Crowned by a pyramid roof, this appealing timber-framed building is open on all sides on the ground floor, and its upper floor is reached by an outside stairway. Also of interest is **Becket's Chapel**, founded in 1174 and restored in 1559. In its long history it has served as a pilgrim's chapel, grammar school, and coal store. Currently, it houses the town library. The **Bridewell**, or House of Correction, in Bridewell Street was built as a model prison in 1785 along lines recommended by the prison reformer, John Howard, who had condemned the earlier gaol on the site as 'one of the vilest in the country'. Wymondham's Bridewell is said to have served as a model for the penitentiaries established in the United States. Now owned by the town's Heritage Society, Bridewell is home to several community projects, including the **Wymondham Heritage Museum**.

Railway buffs will also want to visit the historic **Railway Station**, built in 1845 on the Great Eastern's Norwich-Ely line.

At its peak, the station and its section employed over 100 people. Still providing a rail link to Norwich, London and the Midlands, the station has been restored, and its buildings house a railway museum, restaurant and tea room, and a piano showroom.

# Diss
## 20 miles S of Norwich on the A1066

The late Poet Laureate, John Betjeman, voted Diss his favourite Norfolk town, and it's easy to understand his enthusiasm. The River Waveney running alongside forms the boundary between Norfolk and Suffolk, but this attractive old market town – winner of Best Kept Market Town in Norfolk, whose town centre is now a designated conservation area - keeps itself firmly on the northern bank of the river. The town is a pleasing mixture of Tudor, Georgian and Victorian houses grouped around **The Mere**, which gives the town its name, derived from the Anglo-Saxon word for 'standing water'.

The old town grew up on the hill above The Mere, perhaps because, as an 18th century resident observed, 'all the filth of the town centring in the Mere, beside the many conveniences that are placed over it, make the water very bad and altogether useless ... it stinks exceedingly, and sometimes the fish rise in great numbers, so thick that they are easily taken; they are chiefly roach and eels.' A proper sewerage system was finally installed in 1851.

There's a public park beside the six-acre Mere, and from it a narrow street leads to the small **Market Place**. This former poultry market is dominated by the somewhat over-restored **St Mary's** church. The oldest parts date back some 700 years, and the St Nicholas Chapel is particularly enjoyable with its wonderful corbels, angels in the roof, and gargoyles.

## WALCOT GREEN FARM COTTAGE

Burston Road, Diss, Norfolk IP22 5SU
Tel/Fax: 01379 652806
e-mail: n.catchpole.wgf@virgin.net
website: www.walcotgreenfarm.co.uk

**Walcot Green Farm Cottage** is a tastefully converted cottage in the grounds of a working farm run by owners Ken and Nannette Catchpole, who are Norfolk-born and -bred and have been arable farmers throughout their working lives.

This handsome self-catering cottage is large and

welcoming, with three bedrooms – one family room, two singles – and boasts such luxuries as an indoor heated swimming pool and a spacious lawned garden, patio with barbecue and garden furniture. The cottage boasts a fully-equipped kitchen and is clean and comfortable throughout. Set amid peaceful and idyllic countryside close to the pleasant market town of Diss, this welcoming establishment makes an excellent base from which to explore sights and attractions such as Banham Zoo, the Steam Museum and Gardens at Bressingham, Minsmere Nature Reserve, Cambridge, the Otter Trust at Earsham, Newmarket, Thetford and Norwich. No pets and no smoking. Children welcome. 4 Stars ETB.

In the early 1500s, the Rector here was John Skelton, Court poet and tutor to Prince Henry, later Henry VIII. A bitter, quarrelsome man, Skelton was appointed Poet Laureate through the patronage of Cardinal Wolsey, despite the fact that most of Skelton's output has been described as 'breathless doggerel'. Appointed Rector of Diss in 1502, he appears to have been suspended nine years later for having a concubine. Not far from his church is the delightful Victorian **Shambles** with a cast-iron veranda and a small museum inside.

### BRESSINGHAM

#### 5 miles W of Diss off the A1066

**Bressingham Gardens and Steam Museum** (see panel opposite) boasts one of the world's finest collections of British and Continental locomotives, amongst them the famous 'Royal Scot'. A number of the locomotives on display here are

on loan from the National Railway Museum at York. All are housed under cover in the museum's extensive locomotive sheds, which also contain many steam-driven industrial engines, traction engines, and **The Fire Museum**, whose collection of fire engines and fire-fighting equipment could form a complete museum in its own right. Visitors can view the interior of the Royal Coach and ride along five miles of track through the woods and gardens.

The six acres of landscaped grounds are notable in themselves, since they are planted with more than 5,000 alpine and other types of plants. A two-acre plant centre adjoins the gardens and here there are thousands of plant specimens, many of them rare, available for purchase. Bressingham is renowned for its special 'Steam Days' when the engines can be seen in full steam on the three narrow-gauge lines, and talks and

## BRESSINGHAM GARDENS

Bressingham, Norfolk IP22 2AB
Tel: 01379 688585  Fax: 01379 688490
website: www.blooms-online.com/about/bressingham.php

A day to remember is guaranteed at **Bressingham**, where gardeners will be in paradise and children past and present can experience the thrill of the golden age of steam. Alan Bloom, one of the

most respected plantsmen of his age, created the Dell Garden and its famous Island Beds between 1955 and 1962, and his garden is now world-renowned for its collection of nearly five thousand species and varieties of hardy perennials. The Garden Centre has a comprehensive collection of hardy perennials including the Blooms Heritage Collection, plus plants for the house and conservatory and all sorts of gardening gifts and accessories, as well as a café and bookshop.

Alan's son-in-law Jaime Blake carries on the family tradition as Curator of Dell Garden, while son Adrian has created a garden for all seasons at nearby Foggy Bottom, where trees, conifers and shrubs provide a backdrop which is enhanced by plantings of perennials and ornamental grasses. The two gardens are open from April to October, the Garden Centre and Steam Experience all year round. There's a full programme of special events, lectures, talks and demonstrations. This really is a place to linger, and Alan Bloom offers B&B accommodation at his Georgian home, Bressingham Hall.

footplate rides are given on the standard-gauge locomotives.

## SCOLE

### 2 miles E of Diss on the A140

Scole's history goes back to Roman times, since it grew up alongside the Imperial highway from Ipswich to Norwich at the point where it bridged the River Waveney. Traffic on this road (the A140) became

unbearable in the 1980s, but a bypass has now mercifully restored some peace to the village. There are two hostelries of note: a coaching inn of 1655, built in an extravagant style of Dutch gables, giant pilasters and towering chimney stacks, and the Crossways Inn, which must have a good claim to being the prettiest pub in the county.

## LANGMERE

### 6 miles NE of Diss on minor road off the A140 (through Dickleburgh)

Veterans of the Second World War and their families and friends will be interested in the **100th Bomb Group Memorial Museum**, a small museum on the edge of Dickleburgh Airfield (now disused). The Museum is a tribute to the US 8th Air Force which was stationed here during the war, and includes displays of USAAF decorations and uniforms, equipment, combat records and other memorabilia. Facilities include refreshments, a museum shop, visitor centre and a picnic area.

## HARLESTON

### 7 miles NE of Diss off the A143

This pretty market town with some notable half-timbered and Georgian houses, and a splendid 12th century coaching inn, was a favourite of the renowned architectural authority, Nikolaus Pevsner, who particularly admired the early Georgian Candlers House at the northern end of the town. Another writer has described the area around the marketplace as 'the finest street scene in East Anglia'. The town lies in the heart of the Waveney Valley, a lovely area which inspired many

## THE CHEESEBOARD

5 Market Place, Harleston, Norfolk IP20 9AD
Tel: 01379 852229  Fax: 01379 854700
e-mail: alanejarvis@supanet.com

Good things most definitely come in small packages: **The Cheeseboard** is filled to the brim with a vast array of cheeses from Norfolk, throughout Britain and from Europe. Goat's and sheep's milk cheeses – up to 15 at any one time – are a speciality, together with popular favourites such as Cheddar and Stilton, French Bries, home-grown Buffalo milk cheeses and more. There is also a selection of chilled deli items such as pâté and ham on the bone, local chutneys, salad dressings and more. Open: Tuesday and Wednesday 9-3; Thursday 9-1; Friday and Saturday 8.30-3.

paintings by the locally-born artist, Sir Alfred Munnings.

## COLTISHALL

**8 miles N of Norwich on the B1150/B1354**

This charming village beside the River Bure captivates visitors with its riverside setting, leafy lanes, elegant Dutch-gabled houses, village green and thatched church. Coltishall has a good claim to its title of 'Gateway to Broadland', since for most cruisers this is the beginning of the navigable portion of the Bure. Anyone interested in Norfolk's industrial heritage will want to seek out the **Ancient Lime Kiln**, next door to the Railway Tavern in Station Road. Lime, formerly an important part of Norfolk's rural economy, is obtained by heating chalk to a very high temperature in a kiln. Most of the county sits on a bed of chalk, but in the area around Coltishall and

## BURE VALLEY RAILWAY

Aylsham Station, Norwich Road, Aylsham, Norfolk NR11 6BW
Tel: 01263 7338585  Fax: 01263 733814
e-mail: info@bvr.co.uk website: www.bvrw.co.uk

Norfolk's longest narrow gauge heritage railway is a 15" gauge line operating between the old market town of Aylsham and Wroxham, a distance of nine miles. The line was built in 1989-1990 on the track bed of the former East Norfolk Railway, which opened in 1880. The Bure Valley Narrow Gauge Railway was opened in July 1990 with new station buildings and workshops at Aylsham and a new station adjacent to Hoveton and Wroxham station. Unstaffed stations are at Coltishall (the famous RAF Battle of Britain station), Buxton and Brampton. The railway is operated primarily by steam locomotives, of which there are four. Passengers are carried in 22 fully enclosed and luxuriously upholstered coaches. During 1998 two new wheelchair accessible coaches were completed at Aylsham. These can each carry four wheelchairs with their carers. The journey time is 45 minutes.

The Bure Valley Railway specialises in joint operations with other attractions. There is a regular boat train facility from Aylsham connecting with cruises on the Broads from Wroxham. Combined train and boat fares are available, and after arriving at Wroxham passengers take a short stroll to Wroxham Bridge, where the Broad Tours boat will be waiting. After the cruise, normally an hour and a half in duration, passengers are free to return to Aylsham by any train, allowing time to explore the village of Wroxham. In off-peak periods the Railway operates Steam Locomotive Driving Courses for beginners and the more experienced. The railway operates regular services from April to October, Santa Specials towards Christmas and Day out with Thomas the Tank Engine events in May and September. The Railway is paralleled along its whole length by the scenic Bure Valley Walk and cycle path.

Horstead it is of a particularly high quality. The kiln at Coltishall, one of the few surviving in the country, is a listed building of finely finished brickwork, built in a style unique to Norfolk.

The top of the tapered kiln pot is level with the ground, and down below a vaulted walkway allowed access to the grills through which the lime was raked out. This was uncomfortable and even dangerous work since fresh lime, when it comes into contact with a moist surface, such as a human body, becomes burning hot. The lime had to be slaked with water before it could be used as a fertiliser, for mortar or as whitewash. Access to the kiln is by way of the Railway Tavern, but during the months from October to March you may find that the building has been taken over by a colony of hibernating bats which, by law, may not be disturbed.

A couple of miles south of Coltishall,

on the B1150, is another animal refuge, the **Redwings Horse Sanctuary**, founded in 1984 to provide a caring and permanent home for horses, ponies, donkeys and mules rescued from neglect and slaughter. The Sanctuary cares for more than 1,000 animals at any one time, and there are no indications that this number is likely to diminish. Even with the help of many volunteers, the work is expensive. To raise funds, the Sanctuary holds regular Open Days, has a gift shop with many horse-related items on sale, and also runs an Adopt-a-Horse scheme.

## Aylsham

**14 miles N of Norwich on the A140**

The attractive little town of Aylsham is set beside the River Bure, the northern terminus of the **Bure Valley Railway** (see panel on page 14). It has an unspoilt **Market Place**, surrounded by late 17th

### Black Sheep Ltd

9 Penfold Street, Aylsham, Norfolk NR11 6ET
Tel: 01263 733142/732006  Fax: 01263 735074
e-mail: email@blacksheep.ltd.uk
website: www.blacksheep.ltd.uk

With classic countrywear – tweed jackets and coats, heavyweight knitted jerseys and lightweight sweaters, cardigans, scarves, hats, gloves, socks and more – **Black Sheep Ltd** is the place to shop for superb quality woollens. Natural, dyed and undyed wools are used to create an excellent and extensive collection of traditional clothing. All knitwear bearing the Black Sheep brand is British made from sheep reared in the UK. In addition, this excellent shop stocks an extensive range of summer and winter casual wear

from deck shirts and sweatshirts by makers such as Chatham, Sebago and Weird Fish to coats and jackets by Chrysalis and Gurteen.

Together with this there's a good selection of gift items such as sheepskins, bags, picnic sets and much more on hand in this spacious, smart shop. Aylsham was famous in the 17th and 18th century for woollen knitted goods, and this fine shop - occupying a handsome Grade II listed building – continues this proud tradition by offering quality clothing that cannot be found in the usual High Street shops. The knowledgeable staff are always friendly and helpful.

## Artstop.biz

29 Red Lion Street, Aylsham, Norfolk NR11 6ER
Tel: 01263 734571  Fax: 01263 735804
e-mail: art@artstop.biz  website: www.artstop.biz

**Artstop.biz** is a one-stop shop for a comprehensive selection of art supplies, creative framing and contemporary works of art. Run by Meg and Charles Foster – Meg is a nationally and internationally known artist in mixed media, Charles has a background in boat-building and now crafts bespoke, hand-finished frames – this fine gallery cum artists' supply shop features exciting, innovative art and sculpture from local and national artists. Many more pieces are displayed at the Fosters' dedicated gallery space at Dyes House, which opened in 2003.

The stock of fine art materials is extensive – acrylics, watercolours, oils, gouache and inks, pigments, pastels, easels, canvas and stretchers, charcoals, pencils and more – and includes some of the more unusual hand-made paints and papers. The framing service caters for all types of art, and the knowledgeable and experienced owners can offer advice on all types of framing from simple mouldings to gilded and hand-painted frames and mounts. As members of the Fine Art Trade Guild, they are also qualified to offer advice on conservation. Workshops and demonstrations are held regularly on the premises and at nearby Blickling Hall.

## Dyes House Gallery

Market Place, Aylsham, Norfolk NR11 6EH
Tel/Fax: 01263 735577
e-mail: art@dyeshousegallery.co.uk
website: www.dyeshousegallery.co.uk

**Dyes House Gallery**, located just off the Market Square in Aylsham, is the home of owners Meg and Charles Foster, who have devoted one spacious room to creating a dedicated gallery space to house the work of artists featured at their Artstop.biz shop nearby.

The gallery, which opened in November of 2003, features a range of spirited and innovative contemporary work, with constantly changing exhibitions by local and international artists who create work in many media including photography, limited-edition prints and hand-crafted greeting cards designed and produced by the featured artists.

Set in a Grade II listed building, this timber-framed house with Georgian façade has been tastefully and sympathetically converted to provide the best showcase for the work on display.

Original works include oil paintings, watercolours, sculpture fashioned in wood and bronze, hand-made silver and gold jewellery, exquisitely crafted glassware and more.

and early 18<sup>th</sup> century houses, reflecting the prosperity the town enjoyed in those years from the cloth trade, and a 14<sup>th</sup>/15<sup>th</sup> century church, St Michael's, said to have been built by John O'Gaunt. In the churchyard is the tomb of one of the greatest of the 18<sup>th</sup> century landscape gardeners, Humphrey Repton, the creator of some 200 parks and gardens around the country.

One of Repton's many commissions was to landscape the grounds of **Blickling Hall** (National Trust - see panel below), a 'dream of architectural beauty'

which stands a mile or so outside Aylsham. Many visitors have marvelled at their first sight of the great Hall built for Sir Henry Hobart in the 1620s. 'No-one is prepared on coming downhill past the church into the village, to find the main front of this finest of Jacobean mansions, actually looking upon the road, unobstructedly, from behind its velvet lawns' enthused Charles Harper in 1904. 'No theatrical manager cunning in all the artful accessories of the stage could devise anything more dramatic.'

Inside, the most spectacular feature is

**SOUTH NORFOLK AND THE BROADS**

## BLICKLING HALL

Garden and Park, Blickling, Norwich NR11 6NF
Tel: 01263 738030  Fax: 01263 738035

Situated outside Aylsham in Norfolk, Blickling was built in the early seventeenth century. One of England's great Jacobean houses, it is famed for its spectacular long gallery, superb plasterwork ceilings and fine collections of furniture, pictures, books and tapestries.

Built by Sir Henry Hobart, the key elements of some of his rooms survive and nowhere can be seen a better Jacobean plaster ceiling than the long gallery with its great cycle of heraldry and emblems. The library of more than 12,000 books is one of the most distinguished in any English house.

Ancient yew hedges draw every eye towards the front of the house, but there is more to this National

© NTPL

Trust property than just the Jacobean mansion. It lies at the heart of the richly planted garden and the parterre with its distinctive topiary and spectacular herbaceous borders. The sweeping parkland and a traditional working estate of almost 5000 acres attracts wildlife of many kinds. The gardens are full of colour throughout the year and the extensive parkland features a lake and series of beautiful woodland and lakeside walks.

© NTPL

the Long Gallery, which extends for 135 feet and originally provided space for indoor exercise in bad weather. Its glory is the plaster ceiling, an intricately patterned expanse of heraldic panels bearing the Hobart arms, along with others displaying bizarre and inscrutable emblems such as a naked lady riding a two-legged dragon.

Other treasures at Blickling include a dramatic double-flight carved oak staircase, the Chinese Bedroom lined with 18th century hand-painted wallpaper, and the dazzling Peter the Great Room. A descendant of Sir Henry Hobart, the 2nd Earl of Buckinghamshire, was appointed Ambassador to Russia in 1746, and he returned from that posting with a magnificent tapestry, the gift of Empress Catherine the Great. This room was redesigned so as to display the Earl's sumptuous souvenir to its full effect, and portraits of himself and his Countess by Gainsborough were added later.

The Earl was a martyr to gout, and his death in 1793 at the age of 50 occurred when, finding the pain unbearable, he thrust his bloated foot into a bucket of icy water, and suffered a heart attack. He was buried beneath the idiosyncratic Egyptian Pyramid in the grounds, a 45-foot high structure designed by Ignatius Bonomi that combines Egyptian and classical elements to create a mausoleum which, if nothing else, is certainly distinctive.

Within a few miles of Blickling Hall are two other stately homes, both the properties of Lord and Lady Walpole. **Mannington** Gardens and Countryside are set around a medieval moated manor house and feature a wide variety of plants, trees and shrubs, including thousands of roses, and particularly classic varieties. The Heritage Rose Garden and Twentieth-century Rose Garden are set in small gardens reflecting their period of origin. There are also Garden Shops, with plants, souvenirs and crafts, and tea rooms. The Hall itself is open by appointment, while the grounds are open Sundays between May-September and also Wednesdays-Fridays from June-August.

**Wolterton Park**, the stately 18th century Hall built for Horatio Walpole, brother of Sir Robert, England's first Prime Minister, stands in grounds landscaped by Humphrey Repton. Here can be found walks and trails, orienteering, an adventure playground and various special events are held throughout the year. The Hall is open for

## THE PLOUGH INN

Norwich Road, Marsham, Norfolk NR10 5PS
Tel: 01263 735000   Fax: 01263 735407
e-mail: enquiries@ploughinnmarsham.co.uk
website: www.ploughinnmarsham.co.uk

At **The Plough Inn**, the award-winning restaurant boasts an impressive menu of tempting dishes, which can be accompanied by the superior choice of wines. The 13 en suite guest bedrooms (11 twin/doubles, 2 family) are a taste of luxury – beautifully and tastefully furnished and decorated – and offer full facilities. Many offer excellent views over the surrounding countryside. Located eight miles from Norwich and three from Aylsham, it makes a good touring base for the many sights and attractions of the region. Children welcome. 3 Diamonds ETB.

*Mannington Hall and Gardens*

Holt circular walk. Just north of Mannington Hall stands the village of **Little Barningham**, where St Mary's Church is a magnet for collectors of ecclesiastical curiosities. Inside, perched on the corner of an ancient box pew, stands a remarkable wood-carved skeletal figure of the Grim Reaper. Its fleshless skull stares hollow-eyed at visitors with a defiant, mirthless grin: a scythe gripped in one clutch of bones, and an hour-glass in the other, symbolise the inescapable

tours every Friday from April.

Over 20 miles of waymarked public footpaths and permissive paths around Mannington and Wolterton link into the Weavers Way long-distance footpath and

## CHARLES MATTS

Manor Farm, School Road, Thurgarton, Norwich, Norfolk NR11 7PG
Tel: 01263 761422
e-mail: candm.matts@virgin.net

**Charles Matts** in Thurgarton specialises in quality furniture made from local trees, to both individual and traditional designs. Charles lived in an ancient timber house in New Zealand for seven years, and became interested in hard woods. In 1969, two years after he returned to England, he formed this company; then in 1975 he bought Manor Farm and renovated the barns into workshops. Oak, elm, ash, wild cherry, yew, tiger oak and walnut are used to

create beautifully crafted sideboards, dining tables and chairs, bookshelves, chests of drawers, desks and more.

All pieces are made on-site by Charles and his staff of three, whom he has trained personally. In addition to the superlative range of furniture, pieces can be made to customers' own specifications, designs and styles. Charles also offers a delivery service to all customers. Pieces produced here can also be seen in a shop at 11 Fish Hill in Holt, and in a showroom in the Alby Crafts complex at Erpingham on the A140 near Aylsham.

# Alderford Common

**Distance:** 3.1 miles (4.83 kilometres)

**Typical time:** 90 mins

**Height gain:** 20 metres

**Map:** Explorer 238

**Walk:** www.walkingworld.com
ID:1504

**Contributor:** Joy & Charles Boldero

## Access Information:

There is no bus route to the car parking area, however there is a bus route to Swannington and the walk could be started at * at Point 7. The car park is on Alderford Common which is situated on the Reepham to Hellesdon road 3 miles southeast of Reepham.

## Description:

This is a nice easy short rural walk not far from Norwich. The route is through woodland, along tracks, across meadows and through the rural village of Swannington.

## Additional Information:

Alderford Common is a haven for wild life. Parts of it have been listed as a site of Special Scientific Interest since 1957. On the south side there is an overgrown Bronze Age barrow. In 1988, the National Nightingale survey stated that this area had more pairs of nightingales than any other in east Norfolk.

Swannington Hall was probably built in the late 1500's for a family named, Richers. Some years ago it became a popular 'pub' but now it is again a private house; part of the old moat can still be seen. St Margaret's Church has stood here since the 13th century and inside the font is of that age too.

## Features:

Church, StatelyHome, Wildlife, Birds, Flowers, Great Views, Butterflies

## Walk Directions:

1 From the car park turn right along the road.

2 Turn left at the finger post sign into a woodland path. It goes through the bracken then across open spaces, at the second of which the path keeps to the top of the bank. The path then goes up and down finally going up steps.

3 Turn left at the road then after about 10 paces turn right at the fingerpost along track.

4 Turn right along a country lane. Opposite the footpath in Upgate turn left across grass to a yellow marker in the far hedgeline. Go over a plank bridge, up the bank and continue along the field edge.

5 Turn right at the yellow marker signs, over a bridge and through a gate. Turn left along a meadow, go through a gate and diagonally right under wires to the next gate. Cross the next meadow to a gate ahead.

6 Turn left along a tarmac lane.

7 Turn left along a country lane, by a church walking through Swannington. Keep along The Street then bear right along Broad Lane (Near here is the bus stop *).

8 At the bend turn right at the fingerpost along a track.

9 At a footpath marker on the ground turn left through a hedge gap. Take the path southwestwards across the two fields. Cross the road to the car park.

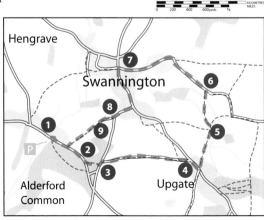

fate that awaits us all. This gruesomely powerful *memento mori* was donated to the church in 1640 by one Stephen Crosbie who, for good measure, added the inscription: 'As you are now, even so was I, Remember death for ye must dye.' Those words were a conventional enough adjuration at that time, but what is one supposed to make of Stephen's postscript inscribed on the back of the pew: 'For couples joined in wedlock this seat I did intend'?

## GREAT WITCHINGHAM
**11 miles NW of Norwich off the A1067**

**Norfolk Wildlife Centre & Country Park** is home to an interesting collection of rare, or ancient, breeds of farm livestock such as white-faced woodland and Shetland sheep, pygmy goats and Exmoor ponies. Set in 40 acres of peaceful parkland, the Centre also has reindeer, otters and badgers, pools teeming with wildfowl and a huge colony of wild herons nesting in the trees. There are also 'Commando' and Adventure Play Areas, one of the finest collection of trees and flowering shrubs in the county, a café and gift shop. The Centre is also home to **Wings Raptor**, the most spectacular birds-of-prey flying display in Norfolk.

A little further southeast, the **Dinosaur Adventure Park** near Lenwade doesn't have any living creatures, but as you wander through the woods here you will come across some startlingly convincing life-size models of dinosaurs. One of them, the 'Climb-a-Saurus', is a children's activity centre. A woodland maze, picnic area with gas-fired barbecues, a play area for toddlers, a restaurant and a 'Dinostore' offering a wide variety of dinosaur models, books and gifts are among the park's other attractions.

Anyone who has ever read Parson Woodforde's enchanting *Diary of a Country Parson* will want to make a short diversion to the tiny village of **Weston Longville**, a mile or so south of the Dinosaur Park. The Revd James Woodforde was vicar of this remote parish from 1774 until his death in 1803, and throughout that time he conscientiously maintained a daily diary detailing a wonderful mixture of the momentous and the trivial. 'Very great Rebellion in France' he notes when, 10 days after the Fall of the Bastille, the dramatic news eventually arrived at Weston Longville. More often he records his copious meals ('We had for dinner a Calf's head, boiled Fowl and Tongue, a saddle of Mutton roasted on the side table, and a fine Swan roasted with Currant Jelly Sauce for the first Course. The Second Course a couple of Wild Fowl, Larks, Blamange, Tarts etc. etc.'), the weather (during the winter of 1785, for example, the frost was so severe that it froze the chamberpots under the beds), and his frequent dealings with the smuggler Andrews, who kept the good parson well-supplied with contraband tea, gin and cognac.

Inside the simple village church there's a portrait of Parson Woodforde, painted by his nephew, and across the road the inn has been named after this beguiling character.

## SWANNINGTON
**11 miles NW of Norwich off the A1067/B1149**

The gardens of **Swannington Manor** are famous for the 300-year-old yew and box topiary hedge. Other features of this small town are the 13th century St Margaret's church, Swannington Hall – where can be seen the remains of the former moat – and the charming thatched village water pump.

## THE ROMANTIC GARDEN NURSERY

Swannington, Norwich, Norfolk NR9 5NW
Tel: 01603 261488   Fax: 01603 864231
e-mail: enquiries@romantic-garden-nursery.co.uk
website: www.romantic-garden-nursery.co.uk

The Romantic Garden Nursery is a specialist nursery with
one of the finest selection of topiary, ornamental standards
and specimen trees and shrubs in the region. The impressive
range includes box, holly, yew, bamboo, betula and cupressus,
as well as topiary shears and a selection of wire frames, stone and hand-thrown terracotta pots, wooden
versailles cases and lead planters. The experienced staff can advise on plants and plantings, and put
you in touch with garden designers. Topiary and specimen plants available for hire. *Open:* Wednesdays,
Fridays, Saturdays and Bank Holiday Mondays 10 – 5.

## VERY NICE THINGS

Market Place, Reepham, Norfolk NR10 4JJ
Tel: 01603 873390

Beautiful, interesting, locally-made gifts are the byword
at **Very Nice Things**, a large and charming shop situated
in the old marketplace in Reepham alongside the parish
church. Originally a house, it retains a relaxed and
welcoming atmosphere, and the extensive range of items
– decorative hand-painted pottery, kitchenware, teapots,
silk scarves, soft furnishings, hand-made soaps made from
natural (non-animal) ingredients, silver jewellery, blankets, candles, a vast selection of lovely cards,
and more – are expertly displayed. Customers are sure to find a unique gift here, for every occasion.

## BROADLAND WINERIES LTD.

The New Winery, Cawston, Norwich, Norfolk
Tel: 01603 872474   Fax: 01603 871312
e-mail: broadland-wineries@supanet.com  website: www.broadland-wineries.co.uk

**Broadland Wineries** is a family-owned business which was founded in 1965.  It is home to a four-acre
site, bottling 22million
litres of wine a year from
countries such as Australia,
Argentina, Chile, California,
Hungary, France, Spain,
Italy and South Africa.  It is
also well known for its
own Perrys and extensive
range of Fruit & Country
Wines including, amongst
others, apple, damson,
blackcurrant,    cherry,
strawberry, ginger, sloe and
cranberry, as well as many
more.  These are on sale
across the UK and can also
be purchased on site in the
Winery shop.

Swannington's Ketts Lane was named after Robert Kett, leader of the peasants' revolt, who reputedly was captured in a barn nearby.

## REEPHAM

**12 miles NW of Norwich on the B1145**

Reepham is an attractive town set in the rich countryside between the Wensum and Bure Valleys. Lovely 18th century houses border the Market Place, and there is delightful walking along the **Marriott's Way** cycle path. Market day is Wednesdays, and regular antiques fairs are held at the Old Reepham Brewery.

## CAWSTON

**12 miles NW of Norwich on the B1145**

'Lovers of the Norfolk churches can never agree which is the best,' wrote Sir John Betjeman. 'I have heard it said that you are either a Salle man or a Cawston man.' In this county so rich in exceptionally beautiful churches, Salle and Cawston are indeed in a class of their own. **St Agnes Church** in Cawston, among many other treasures, boasts a magnificent double hammerbeam roof, where angels with protective wings 8 feet across float serenely from the roof, and a gorgeous 15th century rood screen embellished with lovely painted panels of saints and Fathers of the Church. The two churches are just a couple of miles apart, so you can easily decide for yourself whether you are 'a Salle man or a Cawston man'. Surprisingly for such a genial character, Sir John seems to have overlooked the possibility that other visitors to these two remarkable churches might define themselves as either 'a Salle woman or a Cawston woman'.

On the edge of Cawston village is **Broadland Wineries**, a family-owned business established in 1965, which moved to this 4.5 acre site in 1971.

## THE KNOT GARDEN

Heydon Lane, Wood Dalling, Norwich,
Norfolk NR11 6SA
Tel/Fax: 01263 587501 (nursery)
e-mail: clarka@btconnect.com
website: www.theknotgarden.co.uk

**The Knot Garden** in Wood Dalling is an extensive and imaginatively designed specialist plant nursery stocking a host of beautiful established trees, specimen plants and shrubs, tree ferns, bamboos, grass trees, topiary and imported exotica. Rhododendrons, azaleas, acers, photinias, pines and numerous other species provide a great variety of choice for any planting scheme. All plants are treated with loving care and attention, to provide customers with the finest quality, backed up by excellent service.

All stock is in containers and reared in ideal growing conditions, care for by hand using traditional methods to ensure an ideal environment suited to every species. This family-owned business is run by keen gardeners Ann and Barry Clark, their son Charles and their daughter Alex (a qualified horticulturist). Their initial interest in creating a spacious water garden, which included sourcing semi-tropical plants for the conservatory, led in 1998 to the establishment of this unique six-acre nursery site. All the staff can offer good advice and planning help. Delivery and a planting service available.

# GREAT YARMOUTH

The topography of Great Yarmouth is rather curious. Back in Saxon times, it was actually an island, a large sandbank dotted with fishermen's cottages. Later, the narrow estuary of the River Bure at the northern end was blocked off, causing it to flow down the western side of the town. It runs parallel to the sea for two miles before joining the larger River Yare, and then their united waters curve around the southern edge of the town for another three miles before finally entering the sea.

So Yarmouth is now a promontory, its eastern and western sides displaying markedly different characters. The seaward side is a 5-mile stretch of sandy beaches, tourist attractions and countless amusements, with a breezy promenade from which one can watch the constant traffic of ships in Yarmouth Roads. There are two fine old traditional piers, the Britannia (810 feet long) and the Wellington (600 feet long), as well as The Jetty, first built in the 16th century for landing goods and passengers. A host of activities are on offer for families: **The Sealife Centre** with many kinds of

marine life including octopus and seahorses, and an underwater viewing channel passing through shark-infested 'oceans'; **Amazonia**, an indoor tropical paradise featuring the largest collection of reptiles in Britain; **Merrivale Model Village** which offers an acre of attractive landscaped gardens with over 200 realistic models of town and country in miniature, which are illuminated at dusk, and the **Pleasure Beach**, featuring over 70 rides and attractions combining all the thrills of modern high-tech amusement park rides with the fun of traditional fairground attractions.

For heritage enthusiasts, Great Yarmouth has a rich and proud maritime history. The **Norfolk Nelson Museum** on South Quay features displays, paintings and contemporary memorabilia relating to the life and times of Horatio Lord Nelson. Also on South Quay is the **Elizabethan House Museum**, built by a wealthy merchant and now a museum of domestic life, with 16th century panelled rooms and a functional Victorian kitchen. In Row 117, South Quay, the **Old Merchant's House** is an excellent example of a 17th century dwelling and a showplace for local wood and metalwork. Nearby is **The Tollhouse**, originally built in 1262 as a gaol and later used as a courthouse. It is now a museum with original dungeons.

At South Denes the 144-foot high **Nelson's Monument** crowned by a statue, not of Norfolk's most famous son, but of Britannia.

Most of Yarmouth's older buildings are concentrated in the western, or riverside, part

*Great Yarmouth Harbour*

of the town. Here you will find **The Quay**, which moved Daniel Defoe, in 1724, to describe it as 'the finest quay in England, if not Europe'. It is more than a mile long and in places 150 yards wide. The **Town Hall** is well known for its grand staircase, Court Room and Assembly Room; the building itself is in use by the Local Authority. **The Rows**, a medieval network of tiny courtyards and narrow alleys, are a mere 2 feet wide in places. Badly damaged during a bombing raid in 1942, enough remains to show their unique character. There were originally 145 of these rows, about 7 miles in total, all of them built at right angles to the sea and therefore freely ventilated by onshore breezes which, given the urban sanitary conditions of those times, must have been extremely welcome.

The bombing raid of 1942 also completely destroyed the interior of **St Nicholas'** church, but left its walls standing. Between 1957 and 1960 this huge building - the largest parish church in England - was completely restored and furnished in traditional style largely by using pieces garnered from redundant churches and other sources. The partly Norman font, for example, came from Highway church in Wiltshire, the organ from St Mary-the-Boltons in Kensington.

Just south of the church, off the Market Place, is the half-timbered **Anna Sewell House**, built in 1641, in which the author of *Black Beauty* lived. Sewell was born in the town in 1820, but it was only when she was in her late fifties that she transmuted her concern for the more humane treatment of horses into a classic and seemingly timeless novel. Anna was paid just £20 for the rights to a book which, in the five months that elapsed between its publication and her death in 1878, had already sold an incredible 100,000 copies.

Another famous author associated with the town is Charles Dickens, who stayed at the Royal Hotel on Marine Parade in 1847-48 while writing *David Copperfield*. Dickens had visited the town as a child and had actually seen an upturned boat on the beach being used as a dwelling, complete with a chimney emerging from its keel. In his novel, this becomes Peggotty's house to which young Copperfield is brought following the death of his mother. 'One thing I particularly noticed in this delightful house,' he writes, 'was the smell of fish; which was so searching, that when I took out my pocket-handkerchief to wipe my nose, I found it smelt exactly as if it had wrapped up a lobster.'

In fact, the whole town at that time was pervaded with the aroma of smoked herring, the silvery fish that were the basis of Yarmouth's prosperity. Around the time of Dickens' stay here, the author of the town's directory tried to pre-empt any discouraging effect this might have on visitors by claiming that 'The wholesome exhalations arising from the fish during the operation of curing are said to have a tendency to dissipate contagious disorders, and to be generally beneficial to the human constitution which is here sometimes preserved to extreme longevity.'

Across the town, some 60 curing houses were busy gutting, salting and spicing herrings to produce Yarmouth's great contribution to the English breakfast, the kipper. The process had been invented by a Yarmouth man, John Woodger: a rival of his, a Mr Bishop, developed a different method which left the fish wonderfully moist and flavoursome, and so created the famous Yarmouth bloater.

For centuries, incredible quantities of herring were landed, nearly a billion in 1913 alone. In earlier years the trade had involved so many fishermen that there were more boats (1,123) registered at Yarmouth than at London. But the scale of the over-fishing produced the inevitable result: within the space of two decades Yarmouth's herring industry foundered, and by the late 1960s found itself dead in the water. Luckily, the end of that historic trade coincided with the beginning of North Sea oil and gas exploitation, a business which has kept the town in reasonably good economic health up to the present day.

## AROUND GREAT YARMOUTH

### Caister-on-Sea
**3 miles N of Great Yarmouth off the A149**

In Boudicca's time, this modern holiday resort with its stretch of fine sands was an important fishing port for her people, the Iceni. After the Romans had vanquished her unruly tribe, they settled here sometime in the 2nd century and built a *castra*, or castle, or Caister, of which only a few foundations and remains have yet been found. **Caister Castle**, which stands in a picturesque setting about a mile to the west of the

town, is a much later construction, built in 1432-5 by the legendary Sir John Fastolf with his spoils from the French wars in which he had served, very profitably, as Governor of Normandy and also distinguished himself leading the English bowmen at the Battle of Agincourt. Academics have enjoyed themselves for centuries disputing whether this Sir John was the model for Shakespeare's immortal rogue, Falstaff. Certainly the real Sir John was a larger-than-life character, but there's no evidence that he shared Falstaff's other characteristics of cowardliness, boastfulness or general over-indulgence.

Caister Castle was the first in England to be built of brick, and is in fact one of the earliest brick buildings in the county. The 90-foot tower remains, together with much of the moated wall and gatehouse, now lapped by still waters and with ivy relentlessly encroaching. The castle is open daily from May to September and, as an additional attraction, there is a Car Collection in the grounds which features an impressive collection of veteran, Edwardian and vintage cars, an antique fire engine, and the original car used in the film of Ian Fleming's *Chitty Chitty Bang Bang*.

### Fritton Lake Countryworld

Church Lane, Fritton, Great Yarmouth, Norfolk NR31 9HA
Tel: 01493 488288/488208  Fax: 01493 488355
website: www.frittonlake.co.uk

For an enjoyable day out in the country, **Fritton Lake Countryworld** has few rivals. The beautiful grounds offer a splendid contrast between natural woodland and formal Victorian gardens, and

Fritton Lake, with fishing and boating both available, is one of the loveliest stretches of water in East Anglia. A miniature railway runs by the lake, and among the many new attractions introduced for 2001 are a family cycle trail, an orienteering course and giant outdoor board games. Also on site are a 9 hole par 3 golf course and an 18-hole putting green, displays of falconry and basket-making, a growing collection of waterfowl, a children's farm and a heavy horse centre with working Suffolk Punches and Shires.

About three miles west of Caister Castle, the pleasantly landscaped grounds surrounding an 1876 Victorian mansion have been transformed into the **Thrigby Hall Wildlife Gardens**, home for a renowned collection of Asian mammals, birds and reptiles. There are snow leopards and rare tigers; gibbons and crocodiles; deer and otters; and other attractions include a tropical house, aviaries, waterfowl lake, willow pattern garden, gift shop and café. The Gardens are open every day, all year round.

### FRITTON

**6 miles SW of Great Yarmouth off the A143**

At **Fritton Lake Countryworld** (see panel opposite), visitors will find a large undercover falconry centre with birds-of-prey flying displays twice daily. There are also heavy horse stables and a children's farm, 9-hole golf and 18-hole putting courses, lakeside gardens, boating and a large adventure playground. Open end-March to end-September every day, and weekends and half-term in October.

## THE BROADS

The Broads area covers more than 33 square kilometres that include 200 kilometres of waterways. The broads themselves are shallow lakes formed in medieval times when peat was dug out to provide fuel and over the years the diggings became flooded as the water level rose. These waterways have always been important transport routes, and each village had its own staithe, or quay, many of which are still in use.

The traditional Broads boat, originally used for commercial purposes, was the wherry, a large, single-sail vessel of shallow draught which plied the broads with cargoes of corn, coal and reed. As

*The Broads*

rail and road transport gradually took over and the holiday trade began to boom, the wherry's original role was lost and many were converted for leisure use or purpose-built for that purpose, with all mod cons. A few - perhaps no more than half a dozen - still survive, available for regular tours or for private charter, and there really is no finer way to savour the delights of the Broads than from the deck of a wherry.

The Broads, with their wonderful mixture of open water, woodland, fen and marsh, have virtually the status of a National Park; they are protected by the Broads Authority, which is responsible for conservation, recreation and navigation in this unique part of the world. Besides providing peaceful waterborne holidays the area offers great opportunities for walking and cycling, and there are many points from which fishing is permitted. Some of the individual broads are nature reserves, and the waterways are home to an amazing variety of bird, fish and plant life.

## REEDHAM

**8 miles SW of Great Yarmouth off the B1140**

Here in Reedham is the single remaining car and passenger ferry in the Broads. There's also an interesting craft showroom at the Old Brewery, and a great pub in The Reedham Ferry Inn.

## BURGH CASTLE

**4 miles W of Great Yarmouth off the A12 or A143**

When the Romans established their fortress of *Garionnonum*, now known as Burgh Castle, the surrounding marshes were still under water. The fort then stood on one bank of a vast estuary, commanding a strategic position at the head of an important waterway running

into the heart of East Anglia. The ruins are impressive, with walls of alternating flint and brick layers rising 15 feet high in places, and spreading more than 11 feet wide at their base. The Romans abandoned Garionnonum around AD 408 and some two centuries later the Irish missionary St Fursey (or Fursa) founded a monastery within its walls. Later generations cannibalised both his building, and much of the crumbling Roman castle, as materials for their own churches and houses.

## ACLE

**10 miles W of Great Yarmouth off the A47**

A thousand years ago, this small market town, now 10 miles inland, was a small fishing port on the coast. Gradually, land has been reclaimed from the estuaries of the Rivers Bure, Waveney and Yare, so that today large expanses of flat land stretch away from Acle towards the sea.

## BRITISH WILD FLOWER PLANTS

Burlingham Gardens, 32 Main Road, North Burlingham, Norfolk NR13 4TA
Tel/Fax: 01603 716615
e-mail: linda@wildflowers.co.uk
website: www.wildflowers.co.uk

**British Wild Flower Plants** is a family-run specialist nursery established in 1986. With a list of over 400 native species, the site occupies six acres and boasts an established nursery of greenhouses and gardens. All species are grown from known provenance native origins, many from their own seed collections, and are available most of the year as plugs and/or 7-cm/9-cm pots. Seed is

collected on contract from many regioins of Britain, allowing customers to choose from species such as Welsh poppies from Glamorgan, Jersey Thrift and Marsh Cinquefoil from Shropshire. The excellent brochure groups plants by situation (for sunny sites, coastal sites, semi-shade, etc.).

Using peat-free compost which is specially formulated for British Wild Flower Plants and contains artificial slow-release fertilisers to get the plants off to a good start, pest control is, wherever possible, biological, relying on frogs, birds and hedgehogs to control slugs and other pests. Delivery available. Open to the public from 1st March Monday to Thursday, 10 – 4; Fridays 10 – 2.30. Other times by appointment. A recent addition is the holiday bungalow onsite, with access to the garden and wildlife habitats over the six-acre site, which sleeps six. Please ring for details.

The town's importance as a boating centre began in the 19th century with boat-building yards springing up beside the bridge. When Acle's first Regatta was held in 1890, some 150 yachts took part. The town became known as the 'Gateway to the Broads' and also as the gateway to 'Windmill Land', a picturesque stretch of the River Bure dotted with windmills. The medieval bridge that formerly crossed the

*Wroxham Broad*

Bure at Acle has less agreeable associations, since it was used for numerous executions with the unfortunate victims left to dangle over the river.

Acle was granted permission for a market in 1272, and it's still held every Thursday, attracting visitors from miles around. Others come to see the unusual church of **St Edmund** with its Saxon round tower, built some time around AD 900, crowned with a 15th century belfry

from which eight carved figures look down on the beautifully thatched roof of the nave. The treasures inside include a superbly carved font, 6 feet high, and inscribed with the date 1410, and a fine 15th century screen.

## WROXHAM

**8 miles NE of Norwich on the A1151**

This riverside village, linked to its twin, Hoveton, by a hump-backed bridge over the River Bure, is the self-styled 'capital'

---

### KINGFISHER LODGE

Riverside Road, Wroxham, Norwich, Norfolk NR12 8UD
Tel: 01603 782309 Fax: 01603 784838
e-mail: steve@fineway.freeserve.co.uk
website: www.finewayleisure.co.uk

**Kingfisher Lodge** is a modern and attractive chalet set just off the main river in a quiet backwater. Sleeping up to six, this charming and peaceful place is tastefully and comfortably furnished and decorated, with every amenity including dishwasher, washer and dryer and fully fitted kitchen. There are ground-floor and first-floor bedrooms, and local shops, pubs and more are within two minutes' walk. Open all year round. The price for the lodge includes a dinghy with an outboard engine. Dayboats – diesel or electric, seating up to 11 – are available at special prices to lodge guests for hourly or weekly hire.

## ERIC BATES & SONS LTD

Horning Road West, Hoveton, Wroxham, Norfolk NR12 8QJ
Tel: 01603 781771    Fax: 01603 781773
e-mail: furniture@ebates.fsnet.co.uk
website: www.batesfurniture.co.uk

Founded 30 years ago, **Eric Bates & Sons Ltd** is widely known
for its high-quality dining room suites, Victorian chaises
longues, sideboards, bookcases, lowboys and more, crafted in a
range of traditional English and French styles. Eric – together
with his son Graham and grandson James – uses traditional
methods to hand-craft period-style furniture. The business also
deals in beautiful antiques and provides a superior restoration service. Employing over 40 skilled staff,
there's over 15,000 square feet of showroom with an additional 37,000 square feet of on-site workshops
and warehousing.

of the Norfolk Broads and as such gets
extremely busy during the season. The
banks of the river are chock-a-block with
boatyards full of cruisers of all shapes
and sizes, there's a constant traffic of
boats making their way to the open
spaces of **Wroxham Broad**, and in July
the scene becomes even more hectic
when the annual Regatta is under way.

Wroxham is also the southern terminus
of the **Bure Valley Railway** (see panel on
page 14), a nine-mile long, narrow-gauge
(15-inch) steam train service that closely
follows the course of the River Bure
through lovely countryside to the market
town of Aylsham. It runs along the
trackbed of the old East Norfolk Railway,
has two half-scale locomotives, and
specially constructed passenger coaches
with large windows to provide the best
possible views.

A couple of miles north of Wroxham is
**Wroxham Barns**, a delightful collection
of beautifully restored 18th century barns
set in 10 acres of countryside, and
housing a community of craftspeople.
There are 13 workshops, producing
between them a wide range of crafts,
from stained glass to woodturning,
stitchcraft to handmade children's
clothes, pottery to floral artistry, and
much more. The complex also includes a
cider-pressing centre, a junior farm with

lots of hands-on activities, a traditional
Family Fair (with individually priced
rides), a gift and craft shop, and a
tearoom.

A mile or so east of Wroxham Barns,
**Hoveton Hall Gardens** offer visitors a
splendid combination of plants, shrubs
and trees, with rare rhododendrons,
azaleas, water plants and dazzling
herbaceous borders within a walled
garden. There are woodland and lakeside
walks, plant sales, gardening books and
a tearoom.

Anyone interested in dried flower
arrangements should make their way to
the tiny hamlet of **Cangate**, another
couple of miles to the east, where
**Willow Farm Flowers** provides an
opportunity of seeing the whole process,
from the flowers in the field to the final
colourful displays. The farm shop has an
abundance of dried, silk, parchment and
wooden flowers, beautifully arranged,
and more than 50 varieties of dried
flowers are available in bunches or made
into arrangements of all shapes and
sizes, or to special order. Willow Farm
also has a picnic and play area, a guided
farm walk, lays on flower arranging
demonstrations and also runs one day
classes for those interested in learning
more about mastering this delicate-
fingered skill.

## TUNSTEAD OLD FARM COTTAGES

Old Farm, Tunstead, Norwich, Norfolk NR12 8HS
Tel/Fax: 01692 536612
e-mail: mail@oldfarmcottages.fsnet.co.uk  website: www.oldfarmcottages.com

There are six spacious and comfortable cottages at **Tunstead Old Farm Cottages** in tranquil Broadland. At this small group of superb farm building conversions, each characterful cottage makes a wonderful home from home while exploring the many sights and attractions of the region: the Broads, Wroxham, How Hill Trust Nature Reserve, Blickling Hall, Felbrigg Hall, beaches at Sea Palling and Waxham, Norwich and more. Walking, birdwatching, golfing, cycling and boating are all available in the area.

The cottages are tastefully and comfortably furnished and decorated. Three sleep four people, one sleeps five, and two sleep six. Each one has original features such as the exposed beams and retains a

rural charm in its pine furnishings. One has a four-poster bed. All have private enclosed patio and barbecue area. Among the excellent facilities are the indoor swimming pool, fitness room, spa bath, solarium, games room and children's play area. Pets are welcome.

### SOUTH WALSHAM

**9 miles E of Norwich on the B1140**

This small village is notable for having two parish churches built within yards of each other. Just to the north of the village is the **Fairhaven Woodland and Water Garden** (see panel on page 33), an expanse of delightful water gardens lying beside the private **South Walsham Inner Broad**. Its centrepiece is the 900-year-old King Oak, lording it over the surrounding displays of rare shrubs and plants, native wild flowers, rhododendrons and giant lilies. There are tree-lined walks, a bird sanctuary, plants for sale, and a restaurant. A vintage-style riverboat runs trips every half-hour around the Broad.

The best way to see the remains of **St Benet's Abbey** is from a boat along the River Bure (indeed, it's quite difficult to reach it any other way). Rebuilt in 1020 by King Canute, after the Vikings had

destroyed an earlier Saxon building, St Benet's became one of the richest abbeys in East Anglia. When Henry VIII closed it down in 1536 he made an unusual deal with its last Abbot. In return for creating the Abbot Bishop of Norwich, the Cathedral estates were to be handed over to the King, but St Benet's properties could remain in the Abbot/Bishop's possession. Even today, the Bishop of Norwich retains the additional title of Abbot of St Benet's, and on the first Sunday in August each year travels the last part of the journey by boat to hold an open-air service near the stately ruins of the Abbey gatehouse.

### RANWORTH

**9 miles E of Norwich off the B1140**

This beautiful Broadland village is famous for its church and its position on Ranworth Broad. From the tower of **St Helen's** church it is possible to see five

# Ludham Marshes

**Distance:** 3.5 miles (5.5 kilometres)

**Typical time:** 90 mins

**Height gain:** 0 metres

**Map:** Outdoor Leisure 40 The Broads

**Walk:** www.walkingworld.com
ID:800

**Contributor:** Stephanie Kedik

### Access Information:

Ludham can be reached by car from Norwich (A1151/A1062) or by bus (tel: Norfolk Bus Information 0845 300 6116)

### Description:

Ludham is a beautiful, peaceful village at the heart of the Norfolk Broads. A teashop, small restaurant and pub provide a choice of refreshments. The pub with beer garden and children's outside play area, caters for families with young children. The walk takes you from the village centre, down a lane and past a small marina where day boats can be hired. Further down you enter Ludham Marshes Nature Reserve on the edge of the River Thurne. In the summer months the air is buzzing with insects and butterflies and many varieties of birds are to be seen all year round. Deer can also sometimes be spotted in the nearby wood, while on the river, you will see

sailing craft and water birds. The undergrowth can get quite high along the riverbank in the summer, so leg covering is recommended. Short enough for a gentle afternoon stroll, this walk offers something for everyone.

### Features:

River, Pub, Toilets, Play Area, Church, Wildlife, Birds, Flowers, Butterflies, Gift Shop, Food Shop, Good for Kids, Nature Trail, Tea Shop

### Walk Directions:

**1** After arriving in the centre of Ludham, take the Yarmouth Road, past the Ludham village sign at Bakers Arms Green. Further down, on your right is a little path leading off and alongside the road. Follow this until you get to a right turn where Horse Fen Road meets the main Yarmouth Road.

**2** Turn right, into Horse Fen Road. Continue along the lane, past Womack Staithe boat hire and camping site.

**3** Follow the public bridleway down onto Ludham Marshes National Nature Reserve. As you take the path round the corner and into the reserve, first a garden and then a wood will be on your left beyond the drainage ditch. Deer can sometimes be seen in these woods. On your right, the marshes stretch out across to the River Thurne.

**4** Follow the footpath through the reserve. Where you meet the gravel track, take a turn to the right through the gate (that says 'Danger unstable road!'). Continue along this track and through another gate. At Horse Fen pumping station, turn right to follow the green footpath sign.

**5** Across the bridge, follow the footpath along the river, keeping the river on your left. This stretch can be a bit overgrown in summer, although it is compensated for by the views of the river. This footpath will take you back from the river, up the creek (!) and out of the reserve at the side of Hunters Yard.

**3** Walk back up Horse Fen Road, past Womack Staithe and the boatyard.

**2** At the top of Horse Fen Road, turn left and onto the road leading back into Ludham.

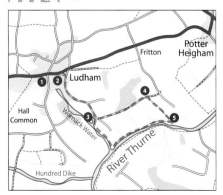

Norfolk Broads, Horsey Mill, the sea at Great Yarmouth and, on a clear day, the spire of Norwich Cathedral. Inside, the church houses one of Norfolk's greatest ecclesiastical treasures, a breathtaking early 15th century Gothic choir screen, the most beautiful and the best preserved in the county. In glowing reds, greens and golds, gifted medieval artists painted a gallery of more than 30 saints and martyrs, inserting tiny cameos of such everyday scenes as falcons seizing hares, dogs chasing ducks and, oddly for Norfolk, lions. Cromwell's men, offended by such idolatrous images, smothered them with brown paint - an ideal preservative for these wonderful paintings, as became apparent when they were once again revealed during the course of a 19th century restoration of the church.

Just to the north of the village is the **Broadland Conservation Centre** (Norfolk Naturalists Trust), a thatched building floating on pontoons at the edge of Ranworth Broad. It houses an informative exhibition on the history of the Broads, and there's also an interesting Nature Trail which shows how these wetlands gradually developed over the centuries.

## FAIRHAVEN WOODLAND & WATER GARDEN

South Walsham, Norwich, Norfolk NR13 6EA
Tel/Fax: 01603 270449
website: www.norfolkbroads.com/fairhaven

Nine miles north of Norwich on the B1140, this delightful and unique natural garden is environmentally managed for the benefit of all wildlife. A harmonious mix of wild and cultivated plants grow together, and the natural food chain takes care of any pests. It is a haven of peace and tranquillity, with three miles of paths under trees, over bridges and through sunny glades .

In winter and early spring there are snowdrops, followed by carpets of wild primroses, daffodils, skunk cabbage, butterbur, camellias and early rhododendrons in March and April. May sees the garden's spectacular Candelabra primulas, the largest naturalised collection in England, and the breathtaking blue of the wild bluebells. In June, July and August there are hostas, ligularia, astilbes, hydrangeas, foxgloves and wild flowers such as mullein and meadowsweet providing nectar for a variety of colourful butterflies. In autumn the glow of russet, red and gold leaves and bright berries provide the colour, while in winter the bare trees reveal views of the private Inner Broad that are hidden in other seasons.

Christmas trees and wreaths are on sale in December, and Father Christmas calls in on the three weekends before Christmas. Ninety-two species of garden, woodland and water birds have been recorded here over the seasons, including all three of the native British woodpeckers. The garden is accessible to wheelchairs except in wet weather; the tea room and toilet are also accessible, but visitors need to be able to board on foot the Edwardian-style river boat Beatrice for the Water Trail trip. The garden is open from 10am to 5pm all year and until 9 o'clock on Wednesday and Thursday evenings in May, June, July and August.

## HORNING

**12 miles NE of Norwich off the A1062**

The travel writer Arthur Mee described Horning as 'Venice in Broadland', where 'waterways wandering from the river into the gardens are crossed by tiny bridges.' With its pretty reed-thatched cottages lining the bank of the River Bure and its position in the heart of the Broads, there are few more attractive places from which to explore this magical area.

## CLIPPESBY HALL

Clippesby, Great Yarmouth, Norfolk NR29 3BL
Tel: 01493 367800  Fax: 01493 367809
e-mail: holidays@clippesby.com
website: www.clippesby.com

**Clippesby Hall** encompasses beautiful holiday lodges, cottages and a touring park for caravans. Located off the B1152 not far from Acle, Norwich and Great Yarmouth, this superb award-winning site provides the ideal base for exploring the Broads National Park and the Norfolk Coast. This area of outstanding natural beauty provides many opportunities for a range of activities including birdwatching, boating, cycling, fishing and more. There is accommodation to suit everyone, from charming pine lodges – airy and light in summer, cosy and warm in winter – to a range of apartments set around the old coaching yard and lovely cottages

surrounded by spacious lawns and woodland.

All the accommodation offers a high standard of comfort and convenience – many have easy access for people with disabilities. Lying in the heart of the Broads National Park, Clippesby occupies a charming countryside setting with pine woods, heated outdoor swimming pool, café and shop, family golf course, pub, tennis court, football pitch, treehouse and play area – everything required for a memorable, fun and relaxing holiday.

## GROVE FARM GALLERY & STUDIO

Sharp Street, Catfield, Great Yarmouth,
Norfolk NR29 5AF
Tel: 01692 670679
e-mail: grovefarmgallery@sagainternet.co.uk

Set in two acres of mature water gardens reclaimed from an overgrown bogland and landscaped in a Broadlands theme, **Grove Farm Gallery & Studio** is well worth seeking out, not just for its lovely location but for its fine collection of oil and watercolour paintings and

fine clay figurine sculptures crafted by local artists. Purpose-built in traditional style in 1992, the gallery has tall windows to the front and side to allow maximum natural light, and boasts a light and airy atmosphere that offsets the many fine pieces on display.

It is the gallery and home of Sid Clarke, whose paintings are displayed here and who has lived and farmed here with his wife Jean since 1971. Sid's work captures the unique flavour of the Norfolk countryside. He is a member of the Fine Art Trade Guild and is now in his twelfth year at the Gallery and extends a warm welcome to all visitors.

## POTTER HEIGHAM

**14 miles NE of Norwich off the A149**

Modern Potter Heigham has sprung up around the medieval bridge over the River Thurne, a low-arched structure with a clearance of only 7 feet at its highest, a notorious test for novice sailors. The Thurne is a major artery through the Broads, linking them in a continuous waterway from Horsey Mere in the east to Wroxham Broad in the west. Generally regarded as one of the liveliest of the Broadland boating centres, Potter Heigham is also home to the **Museum of the Broads**, located in boat sheds in the historic Herbert Woods boat yard. Among the museum's many intriguing exhibits are the only concrete dinghy ever constructed, an ice yacht, tools from traditional Broads industries such as eel catching, gun punts for duck-shooting (complete with incredibly long guns), and a display featuring one of Broadland's most destructive pests, the coypu.

A pleasant excursion from Potter Heigham is a visit to **Horsey Mere**, about six miles to the east, and **Horsey Windpump** (both National Trust). From this early 20th century drainage mill, now restored and fully working, there are lovely views across the Mere. A circular walk follows the north side of Horsey Mere, passes another windmill, and returns through the village. There's a small shop at the Windpump, and light refreshments are available.

## WORSTEAD

**12 miles NE of Norwich off the A149/B1150**

Hard to imagine now, but Worstead was a busy little industrial centre in the Middle Ages. The village lent its name to the hard-wearing cloth produced in the region, and many of the original weavers' cottages can still be seen in the narrow side-streets. Worsted cloth, woven from tightly-twisted yarn, was introduced by Flemish immigrants and became popular throughout England from the 13th century onwards. The Flemish weavers settled happily into the East Anglian way of life and seem to have influenced its architecture almost as strongly as its weaving industry.

The lovely 14th century church of **St Mary** provides ample evidence of Worstead's former prosperity. Its many treasures include a fine hammerbeam roof, a chancel screen with a remarkable painted dado, and a magnificent traceried font complete with cover.

The village stages an annual weekend of events in July to raise money for the restoration of the church. The festival started up some 35 years ago, attracting more than 35,000 visitors in 1999. The memory of Worstead's days of glory is kept alive by a still-functioning Guild of Weavers. The Guild has placed looms in the north aisle of St Mary's, and from time to time there are demonstrations of the ancient skill of weaving.

## THE TREASURE BOX

The Green, Hickling, Norwich, Norfolk NR12 0XN
Tel: 01692 598291  Fax: 01692 598745
e-mail: info@treasurebox.com website: www.treasurebox.com

A village shop with an important difference, **The Treasure Box** is the hub of the community of the village of Hickling. A treasure-trove indeed, its shelves are filled with hand-made arts and crafts – carved boxes, ceramics, jewellery, glassware and more – and the shop also specialises in home-made fudge and chocolates, tempting rolls and sandwiches, cakes, honeys, preserves and teas and coffees. A separate art gallery features the work of local artists.

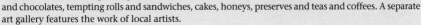

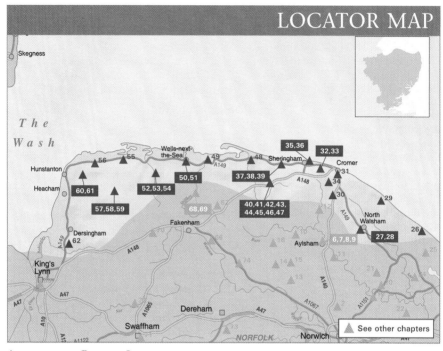

ADVERTISERS AND PLACES OF INTEREST

| | | |
|---|---|---|
| 26 | Manor Barn, Happisburgh | Page 38 |
| 27 | North Walsham Garden Centre, North Walsham | Page 41 |
| 28 | The Country Shop, North Walsham | Page 42 |
| 29 | The C21 Shop, Mundesley | Page 43 |
| 30 | Grove Farm, Roughton | Page 44 |
| 31 | Cromer Museum, Cromer | Page 45 |
| 32 | Mirabelle Restaurant & Bistro, West Runton, Cromer | Page 45 |
| 33 | The Norfolk Shire Horse Centre, West Runton, Cromer | Page 46 |
| 34 | Felbrigg Hall, Felbrigg, Norwich | Page 47 |
| 35 | Westcliffe Gallery, Sheringham | Page 48 |
| 36 | Crowes, Sheringham | Page 48 |
| 37 | Weybourne Forest Lodges, Weybourne, Holt | Page 50 |
| 38 | Bolding Way Holiday Cottages, Weybourne, Holt | Page 51 |
| 39 | The Muckleburgh Collection, Weybourne | Page 52 |
| 40 | The Stables, Holt | Page 52 |
| 41 | Countryside Cottages, Holt | Page 53 |
| 42 | Wood 'N' Things, Holt | Page 54 |
| 43 | Art - e - Fax, Holt | Page 54 |
| 44 | the passion of flowers, Holt | Page 55 |
| 45 | Doodle Pots, Holt | Page 55 |

| | | |
|---|---|---|
| 46 | Meadow Dairies, Holt | Page 56 |
| 47 | Emcy Garden & Leisure, Holt | Page 56 |
| 48 | Cley Smokehouse, Cley-next-the-Sea, Holt | Page 57 |
| 49 | Stiffkey Antiques, Stiffkey, Wells-next-the-Sea | Page 61 |
| 50 | The Wells Deli Company, Wells-next-the-Sea | Page 62 |
| 51 | Holkham Hall & Bygones Museum, Wells-next-the-Sea | Page 64 |
| 52 | Whitehall Farm, Burnham Thorpe | Page 65 |
| 53 | House Bait II, Burnham Market | Page 66 |
| 54 | The Lord Nelson, Burnham Thorpe | Page 67 |
| 55 | Staithe Antiques, Brancaster Staithe | Page 68 |
| 56 | The Titchwell Manor Hotel, Brancaster, King's Lynn | Page 69 |
| 57 | Norfolk Barn, Docking | Page 69 |
| 58 | Pilgrims Reach Restaurant & Freehouse, Docking | Page 70 |
| 59 | Holland House, Docking | Page 71 |
| 60 | The Gin Trap Inn, Ringstead, Hunstanton | Page 72 |
| 61 | Ringstead Gallery, Ringstead, Hunstanton | Page 73 |
| 62 | Sandringham House, Sandringham | Page 76 |

Miles of sandy beaches, spectacular sea views and fresh sea air are the rewards awaiting visitors to the Norfolk coast, which stretches from Great Yarmouth in the east up to Cromer on the edge of the county and west to Sheringham, Hunstanton and beyond. The northeast coast includes what are sometimes known as 'the Highlands of Norfolk' - the Cromer Ridge, which rise to the not-so-dizzy heights of 330 feet above sea level.

Substantial stretches of the coast are, happily, in the care of the National Trust, including the highest point in the county at West Runton, and the North Norfolk coast is also of major importance for its birdlife. Morston Marshes and Stiffkey Marshes are sanctuaries to a wide variety of seabirds, and the birds and the seals at Blakeney Point are favourite tourist attractions. All these places are National Trust locations, as are Brancaster – an area of salt marsh and mud flats that includes the site of a Roman fort – and Felbrigg Hall, a superb 17th century house with Grand Tour paintings and marvellous grounds. The house is near Cromer, a charming resort with a 100-year-old pier and a proud fishing tradition: Cromer crabs are known far and wide.

The shoreline along Norfolk's northwest coast changes from salt marshes threaded by winding creeks, and windswept dunes barely held in place by marram grass, to the perfect sands at Hunstanton. It's an exhilarating coast, with huge skies, ozone-tangy breezes sweeping in from the North Sea, and an abundance of wildlife. There are three separate Nature Reserves within an eight-mile stretch, including the huge National Trust-owned bird sanctuary of Scolt Head Island. An admirable way to experience the area to the full is to walk all or part of the Coastal Footpath which follows the coastline for some 36 miles from Cromer in the east to Holme-next-the-Sea, for most of its route well away from any roads.

Although the whole of Norfolk lies on a foundation of chalk, 1,000 feet deep in places, it is only in its northwest corner that the chalk lies close enough to the surface to have been used as a building material. Once exposed to the air, the chalk, or 'clunch' as it is known, becomes a surprisingly

*Salthouse Church*

durable material. It was widely used in medieval buildings and can still be found in many barns, farmhouses and cottages in the area. Chalk was also quarried and then burnt to produce lime, prodigious quantities of which were used in building the sublime churches of the Middle Ages. The most important town on the northwest coast is the busy seaside resort of Hunstanton, which has cliffs comprising red, white and brown geological layers. Another curious thing about Hunstanton: it is the only east coast resort that actually faces west!

## MANOR BARN

Happisburgh, Norfolk NR12 0SA
Tel: 01692 651262  Fax: 01692 650220
e-mail: manorathappisburgh@hotmail.com
website: www.northnorfolk.co.uk/manorbarn

Just half a mile from the seaside village of Happisburgh with its famous lighthouse and beach, **Manor Barn** offers guests superb accommodation in a beautifully restored historic building. A 16th century thatched, Grade II listed barn, it was saved from dereliction by owners David and Rosie Eldridge, who have sensitively and carefully converted and refurbished it to provide supremely comfortable and attractive accommodation. There are three luxurious en suite bedrooms (two doubles and one double/twin), one on the ground floor and one with views to the lighthouse.

The beautiful vaulted sitting room has an open fire. The hearty and delicious breakfast is served in the Manor Farmhouse, just a few steps away from the barn. Excellent three-course evening meals are available by arrangement. Relaxing and welcoming, it makes an ideal base for exploring the many sights and attractions of the region – the Broads, the coast, Norwich and more – and this wonderful accommodation is available all year round. No smoking. ETC 4 Diamonds.

# HAPPISBURGH TO CROMER

## HAPPISBURGH
**14 miles SE of Cromer on the B1159**

The coastal waters off Happisburgh (or 'Hazeborough', to give the village its correct pronunciation), have seen many a shipwreck over the centuries, and the victims lie buried in the graveyard of **St Mary's** church. The large grassy mound on the north side of the church contains the bodies of the ill-fated crew of HMS *Invincible*, wrecked on the treacherous sandbanks here in 1801. The ship was on its way to join up with Nelson's fleet at Copenhagen when the tragedy occurred, resulting in the deaths of 119 sailors. Happisburgh's distinctive Lighthouse, built in 1791 and striped like a barber's pole, certainly proved ineffectual on that occasion; as did the soaring 110-foot tower of the church itself, which could normally be relied on as a 'back-up' warning to mariners.

Inside the Church is a splendid 15th century octagonal font carved with the figures of lions, satyrs and 'wild men'; embedded in the pillars along the aisle are the marks left by shrapnel from German bombs dropped on the village in 1940.

## LESSINGHAM
**14 miles SE of Cromer off the B1159**

From this small village a lane winds down through spectacular dunes to the sands at Eccles Beach and, a little further north, to Cart Gap with its gently sloping beach and colourful lines of beach huts.

About four miles south of Lessingham stands a windmill that is not just the tallest in Norfolk, but in the whole of England. Eighty feet high, **Sutton Windmill** was built in the year of the French Revolution, 1789, and its millstones only finally ground to a halt in 1940. Chris Nunn bought the mill in 1976, and since then he has devoted himself to renovating this glorious nine-storey building with the ultimate aim of restoring it to working order. During those years, Chris and his family have also built up a fascinating private collection of artefacts which reflect the social history of Norfolk over the past 150 years or so. These are on display in the family's privately-owned **Broadlands Museum**, a magpie's nest in which you'll find anything from vintage kitchen and veterinary tools to a reconstructed Pharmacy Shop of the 1880s, complete with a fine collection of patent medicines, ointments and pills.

## NORTH WALSHAM
**9 miles SE of Cromer on the A149**

This busy country town with its attractive **Market Cross** of 1600 has some interesting historical associations. Back in 1381, despite its remoteness from London, North Walsham became the focus of an uprising in support of Wat Tyler's Peasants' Rebellion. These North Norfolk rebels were led by John Litester, a local dyer, and their object was the abolition of serfdom. Their actions were mainly symbolic: invading manor houses, monasteries and town halls and burning the documents that recorded their subservient status. In a mass demonstration they gathered on Mousehold Heath outside Norwich, presented a petition to the King, and then retreated to North Walsham to await his answer. It came in the form of the sanguinary Bishop of Norwich, Henry Despenser, who, as his admiring biographer recorded, led an assault on the rebels, 'grinding his teeth like a wild boar, and sparing neither himself nor his enemies ... stabbing some, unhorsing

# Bacton Woods

**Distance:** 3.1 miles (4.83 kilometres)

**Typical time:** 90 mins

**Height gain:** 20 metres

**Map:** Explorer 25

**Walk:** www.walkingworld.com
ID:1208

**Contributor:** Joy & Charles Boldero

### Access Information:

Free car parking at the woodland car/picnic site. Go along the B1150 east from North Walsham and then follow the signs, 'Bacton Wood' and 'picnic centre' to the car park.

### Additional Information:

There has been a woodland here since Saxon times. It is thought that because the soil is so poor it is the reason the area was not converted to agriculture. The Forestry Commission bought the wood in the 1950's. In the larch woodlands goldcrests and warblers can be spotted. There are two sessile oaks standing, they have been there for over 200 years. The sessile and the English oak are true native species. The sessile oak was planted like a crop in centuries past because the wood is so good for making charcoal. Oak bark of course was used for the tanning of leather before manmade chemicals were used. Mountain cycling is permitted, also horse riding by permit.

There is a Permanent Orienteering course, maps for this and permits are obtained from the Countryside Project Officer at North Norfolk District council 01263 513811

### Description:

This walk is mostly around the ancient Bacton woodland although the route has a short section along a country lane.

### Features:

Wildlife, Birds, Flowers, Great Views, Butterflies, Woodland

### Walk Directions:

**1** Go to the notice board. Turn left along the path with a red and yellow band on a small post.

**2** At the left hand bend turn right through two small posts and along a narrow path. Turn left along a wider path ignoring all paths off it.

**3** At the T junction turn right along a track.

**4** At a country lane turn left.

**5** At Wood Mill Farm track turn left along the bridleway. This leads into the wood. Ignore all the paths off it. Keep along it until you reach the road, then the path curves left still in woodland beside the road.

**6** Turn left, the path takes you back into the wood again.

**7** Take the right fork.

**8** At the T junction turn left, following red marker posts. Turn right. Turn left downhill. Cross the track and go up the bank opposite and back to the car park.

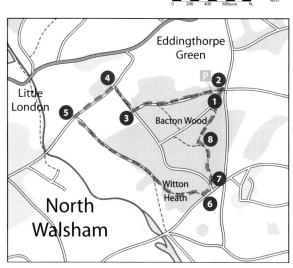

*Paston School, North Walsham*

A more glorious fate awaited the town's most famous resident, Horatio Nelson, who came to the Paston School here in 1768 as a boy of ten. Horatio was already dreaming of a naval career and, three years later when he read in the county newspaper that his Uncle Maurice had been appointed commander of a warship, he prevailed on his father to let him join the *Raisonnable*.

The **Paston School** had been founded in 1606 by Sir William Paston. His ancestors were the writers of the extraordinary collection of more than a thousand letters, written between 1422 and 1509, which present an astonishingly vivid picture of East Anglian life at the end of the turbulent Middle Ages. Sir William himself is

others, hacking and hewing'. John Litester was captured, summarily executed and, on the orders of the Bishop, 'divided into four parts, and sent throughout the country to Norwich, Yarmouth, Lynn and to the site of his own house.'

## NORTH WALSHAM GARDEN CENTRE

Norwich Road, North Walsham, Norfolk NR28 0DR
Tel: 01692 402591 Fax: 01692 407588
website: www.northwalshamgardencentre.com

Found just 15 miles east of Norwich off the A149, **North Walsham Garden Centre** is a modern centre with a comprehensive selection of everything needed to create or maintain gardens of every shape, size and style.

The centre stocks 300 varieties of roses, including floribundas, hybrid teas, climbers and celebration roses, a wide selection of fruit trees including unusual local varieties such as Norfolk Beefing and Norfolk Royal, 300 different shrub varieties, herbaceous plants, perennials, rockery plants, seasonal bedding plants, heathers, rhododendrons, hanging baskets, indoor plants and more. To complement this selection there is a full range of gardening tools, equipment and machinery. In addition we also have an extensive gift area where you will find that unusual gift. The professional garden design and landscaping service will help you to create the garden of your dreams. To make your day complete why not have lunch or a light snack in Ramblers Restaurant with its wide selection of home cooked meals and cakes or simply relax with a coffee in our patio area while deciding which of our vast range of plants suit your garden best.

## THE COUNTRY SHOP

10 Market Street, North Walsham, Norfolk NR28 9BZ
Tel: 01692 406403 Fax: 01692 400900
website: www.thecountryshop.co.uk

Specialising in outdoor leisurewear, **The Country Shop** stocks an excellent range of clothing, walking boots, wellingtons and more, for both men and women, from the likes of Barbour, Aigle and other famous names. This fine shop, located just minutes from the centre of town, also features a choice selection of camping gear – small tents, backpacks, compasses, kettles, gas lamps, torches, tools – and an online shop for internet purchases.

buried in the parish church where he personally supervised (and paid for) the construction of the impressive marble and alabaster monument he desired to be erected in his memory.

About four miles east of North Walsham, near the village of Erpingham on the A140, **Alby Crafts & Gardens** has a Crafts Gallery promoting the excellence of mainly East Anglian and British craftsmanship - lacework, woodturning, jewellery, canework and much more. The 'Plantsman's Garden' displays a fine collection of unusual shrubs, plants and bulbs in a 4-acre site; there are also workshops where you can watch craftsmen at work, a Bottle Museum (small charge for admission) and a tearoom.

### PASTON

**9 miles SE of Cromer on the B1159**

It was in this small village that the Paston family entered historical record. The vivid collection of letters they wrote to each other during the years that England was being wracked by the Wars of the Roses has already been mentioned, and the village boasts another magnificent legacy from this remarkable family. In 1581, Sir William Paston built a cavernous tithe-barn here with flint walls and a thatched roof. It still stands, its roof still thatched: 160 feet long, almost 60 feet high - the longest, most

imposing barn in Norfolk. In the nearby church, the most striking of the family memorials is the one dedicated to Katherine Paston. Sculpted in alabaster by Nicholas Stone in 1628, Katherine lies dressed to kill in her Jacobean finery of starched ruff, embroidered bodice, puffed sleeves and pearl necklaces. The monument cost £340, a staggering sum of money at that time.

### MUNDESLEY

**7 miles SE of Cromer on the B1159**

'The finest air in the kingdom has been wasted for centuries,' said a speaker celebrating the arrival of the railway at Mundesley in 1898, 'because nobody had the courage to bring the people to the district.' The railway has been and gone, but the fresh breezes off the North Sea remain as invigorating as ever.

After the hazards of the coastline, immediately to the north where cliffs, fields and houses have all been eroded by the relentless sea, it's a pleasure to arrive at this unassuming holiday resort with its superb sandy beach, considered by many the very best in Norfolk. Mundesley village is quite small (appropriately, its Maritime Museum is believed to be the smallest museum in the country), but it provides all the facilities conducive to a relaxing family holiday. Best of all, there is safe swimming in the sea, and when the tide is out children

## THE C21 SHOP

38 High Street, Mundesley, Norfolk NR11 8LH
Tel: 01263 720473

Contemporary art by both local and national artists can be found at **The C21 Shop**, owned and run by Jenny Rumens and Sally Wallace. Opened in 2001, this spacious gallery, encompassing a large front room and smaller gallery to the rear, showcases a tasteful display of original pieces in various media, including ceramics, Jenny's sculpture and driftwood furniture, and a range of hand-made pieces including jewellery, paper, greetings cards and more. Open: Wednesday to Sunday 10 – 5.

can spend many a happy hour exploring the many 'lowes', or shallow lagoons, left behind.

# CROMER

As you enter a seaside town, what more reassuring sight could there be than to see the pier still standing? **Cromer Pier** is the genuine article, complete with Lifeboat Station and the Pavilion Theatre, which still stages traditional end-of-the-pier shows. The Pier's survival is all the more impressive since it was badly damaged in 1953 and 1989, and in 1993 sliced in two by a drilling rig which had broken adrift in a storm.

Cromer has been a significant resort since the late 1700s and in its early days even received an unsolicited testimonial from Jane Austen. In her novel *Emma* (1816), a character declares that 'Perry was a week at Cromer once, and he holds it to be the best of all the sea-bathing places.' A succession of celebrities, ranging from Lord Tennyson and Oscar Wilde to Winston Churchill and the

German Kaiser, all came to see for themselves.

The inviting sandy beach remains much as they saw it (horse-drawn bathing machines aside), as does the Church of **St Peter & St Paul**, which boasts the tallest tower in Norfolk, 160 feet high. And then as now, Cromer Crabs were reckoned to be the most succulent in England. During the season, between April and September, crab-boats are launched from the shore (there's no harbour here), sail out to the crab banks about 3 miles offshore, and there the two-man teams on each boat deal with some 200 pots.

The **Lifeboat Museum**, however, is a fairly recent addition. Housed in the

*Cromer Beach*

*Fishing Boats, Cromer*

those years his boat, the *H F Bailey*, was called out 128 times and saved 518 lives. In 1991, the H F Bailey was purchased by Peter Cadbury of the chocolate manufacturing family and presented to the Museum as its prime exhibit.

Also well worth visiting is the **Cromer Museum** (see panel opposite), housed in a row of restored fishermen's cottages near the church, where you can follow the story of Cromer from the days of the dinosaurs, some of whose bones were found nearby, up to the present, and access the computer for thousands of pictures and facts about this attractive town.

former Lifeboat Station, it tells the dramatic story of the courageous men who manned the town's rescue service. Pre-eminent among them was Harry Blogg who was coxswain of the lifeboat for 37 years, from 1910 to 1947. During

## GROVE FARM

Roughton, Norfolk NR11 8QR
Tel: 01263 761594  Fax: 01263 761605
e-mail: grovefarm@homestay.co.uk  website: www.grove-farm.com

Located in an ideal rural setting, **Grove Farm** dates back to 1620, when if was part of the Felbrigg Estate. Extended during the 18th and 19th centuries, the farm buildings now form a secluded courtyard.

Owner Clare Wilson bought the farm in 1999, when it was derelict, and tastefully renovated the main farmhouse and adjoining barn to open, in 2000, a cosy, charming and welcoming home. There are two guest rooms – The Green Room is a dramatic double with a vaulted ceiling, while The Theatre Room is a ground floor suite with bedroom and sitting area. Both are en suite.

Clare will provide dinner by arrangement, making use of homegrown and local produce whenever possible. The gardens are pristine and welcoming, while Roughton is just 3 miles from Cromer and the coast, and within easy reach of King's Lynn, Peterborough and the many sights and attractions of this part of Norfolk. Pets accommodated by arrangement.

## CROMER MUSEUM

East Cottages, Tucker Street, Cromer, Norfolk NR27 9HB
Tel: 01263 513543
e-mail: cromer.museum@norfolk.gov.uk
website: www.norfolk.gov.uk/leisure/museums/cromer.htm

A row of restored fisherman's cottages houses **Cromer Museum**, where the look and feel of a fishermans' home life 100 years ago is enhanced by the gentle glow of real gas lights. The rooms in the cottages tell the story of Cromer and the area from the bones of prehistoric animals that once roamed this part of the world to the development of the town, the coming of the railway and the building of the grand Victorian hotels. Thousands of pictures of old Cromer are stored in the Museum's computer, and visitors can find out about the geology and natural history of the local beaches in the Beachcombers' Shed. The Museum has a small, well-stocked shop.

# WEST OF CROMER

## WEST RUNTON

**3 miles W of Cromer on the A149**

The parish of West Runton can boast that within its boundaries lies the highest point in Norfolk - **Beacon Hill**. This eminence is 330 feet high, so you won't be needing any oxygen equipment to reach the summit, but there are some excellent views. Nearby is the Roman Camp (National Trust), a misleading name since there's no evidence that the Romans ever occupied this 70 acres of heathland. Excavations have shown, however, that in Saxon and medieval times this was an iron-working settlement.

West Runton's major tourist

## MIRABELLE RESTAURANT & BISTRO

Station Road, West Runton, Cromer,
Norfolk NR27 9QD
Tel: 01263 837396

For over 30 years, Austrian-born Manfred Hollwöger has been chef and proprietor of the distinguished **Mirabelle Restaurant and Bistro**. Food-lovers from all over Norfolk and beyond come here to sample the delights of the excellent menus and extensive wine list. Only the freshest, finest ingredients – including locally-caught seafood – are used to create the range of delicious

dishes that are expertly prepared, cooked to order and presented with flair.

In the relaxed and informal Bistro, guests can enjoy ribeye steak au poivre, baked halibut, wild mushroom stroganoff and supreme of chicken with Boursin and herbs, to name but a few of the dishes. In the Mirabelle, the cuisine features mouth-watering dishes such as whole roast grouse garnie, roast Norfolk duck, lobster thermidor, Dover sole Meunière, fillet steak and roast rack of lamb. The décor and furnishing are classic and tasteful; guests' comfort is assured. Open for lunch and dinner Tuesday – Sunday, 12.30-2 and 7-9.15 (closed Sunday evenings from November to May).

## THE NORFOLK SHIRE HORSE CENTRE

West Runton, Cromer, Norfolk NR27 9QH
Tel: 01263 837339  Fax: 01263 837132
e-mail: bakewekk@norfolkshirehorse.fsnet.co.uk
website: www.norfolk-shirehorse-centre.co.uk

Shires, Suffolk Punches and Clydesdales are among the stars of the show at the **Norfolk Shire Horse Centre**, and visitors can meet these wonderful, gentle giants at close quarters in the front yard stables. Two large museum sheds contain a video room and an indoor

demonstration area, and also on show are carts, coaches, gypsy caravans and farm machinery of yesteryear. Next to the museum is a children's play area.

A short walk through a meadow brings visitors to the area where the

small animals are kept in their sheds and pens and aviaries. This really is a paradise for animal lovers: native pony mares with their foals, donkeys, Dexter cows, pigs, goats, lambs, guinea pigs, rabbits, chipmunks, chinchillas, cage birds. The ducks and geese have a great time in their own little pond. Twice a day the centre's proprietor, David Blakewell, accompanies demonstrations with a friendly, informative talk about the heavy horses; themes include harnessing and working the horses with the old machinery. Children can have a ride in a cart and join in the feeding of small animals. Numerous specials events are held throughout the summer, including foal days, blacksmiths days, sheepdog days, plough days and harvesting with the heavy horses. Dogs are welcome on leads; the site has a two-acre car park, a café and a gift shop.

Next to the centre, in the same ownership, West Runton Riding Stables offer instruction and accompanied rides for both novice and more experienced riders. The Stables are open throughout the year, the Shire Horse Centre from April to October. Follow the brown tourist signs off the A149 Cromer-Sheringham road or the A148 Cromer-Holt road.

as war-horses and draught animals. Several other heavy breeds, such as the Suffolk Punch, Clydesdale and Percheron, also have their home here, along with no fewer than nine different breeds of pony. The Centre also has a video room showing a 30-minute film, a small animals' enclosure and an adventure playground for children, a cafe and gift shop. A horse-drawn cart will transport you around the village and at the West Runton Riding School (on site) you can hire riding horses by the hour.

### AYLMERTON

**3 miles W of Cromer on minor road off the A148**

Aylmerton is home to one of Norfolk's grandest houses, **Felbrigg Hall** (National Trust - see panel opposite). Thomas Windham began rebuilding the old manor house at Felbrigg in the 1620s, erecting in its place a grand Jacobean mansion with huge mullioned windows, pillared porch, and at roof-level a dedication in openwork stone: *Gloria Deo in Excelsis*, 'Glory to God in the Highest'. Later that century, Thomas' grandson William Windham I married a wealthy heiress and added the beautifully proportioned Carolean West Wing, where visitors can

attraction is undoubtedly the **Norfolk Shire Horse Centre** (see panel above) where twice a day, during the season, these noble beasts are harnessed up and give a half-hour demonstration of the important role they played in agricultural life right up until the 1930s. They are the largest (19 hands/6 feet 4 inches high) and heaviest horses in the world, weighing more than a ton, and for generations were highly valued both see portraits of the happily married couple painted by Sir Peter Lely. Their son, William Windham II, returning from his four-year-long Grand Tour, filled the house with treasures he had collected - so many of them that he had to extend the Hall yet again. The Windham family's ownership of Felbrigg Hall came to a tragi-comic end in the 1860s when William Frederick Windham inherited the estate. William was one of the great English eccentrics. He loved uniforms. Accoutred in the Felbrigg blue and red livery, he would insist on serving at table; in guard's uniform he caused chaos on the local railway with his arbitrary whistle-blasts; dressed as a policeman, he sternly rounded up the ladies of easy virtue patrolling London's Haymarket. Inevitably, 'Mad' Windham fell prey to a pretty fortune-hunter and Felbrigg was only saved from complete bankruptcy by his death at the age of 26.

The Hall was acquired by the National Trust in 1969, complete with its 18th century furnishings, collection of paintings by artists such as Kneller and van der Velde, and a wonderful Gothic library. There are extensive grounds which include a Walled Garden containing an elegant octagonal dove-house, an Orangery of 1707 sheltering an outstanding collection of camellias, many woodland and lakeside walks, and a restaurant, tea room and shop.

## SHERINGHAM
**5 miles W of Cromer on the A149**

Sheringham has made the transition from fishing village to popular seaside resort with grace and style. There are plenty of activities on offer, yet Sheringham has managed to avoid the brasher excesses of many English seaside towns. The beach here is among the cleanest in England, and markedly

### FELBRIGG HALL

Garden and Park, Felbrigg, Norwich NR11 8PR
Tel: 01263 837444  Fax: 01263 837032

**Felbrigg** is one of the finest seventeenth century houses in England. The rooms are filled with furniture, pictures and books bought by generations of families who lived in the Hall. It is the completeness of the collections that makes Felbrigg an important country house today. The house is famous for its plasterwork and for the paintings collected by William Windham II on his 'Grand Tour' of the continent (1738-42). The restored domestic wing gives an insight to below stairs. The south front of the house was added to and

© NTPL

adapted over the years, most notably in the 1680s when the west wing was added, and in the 1750s when the interior was re-modelled and the new domestic quarters built to the east.

The early eighteenth century orangery in the West Garden is stocked with impressive camellias. From here, the ha-ha wall gives the impression that the garden and parkland are continuous. The path through the Victorian pleasure garden leads to an eighteenth century walled garden with a working octagonal dovecote. Originally used to grow vegetables for the Hall, the garden has old varieties of espalier fruit trees, herbs and the national collection of colchicum (autumn crocus).

© NTPL

## WESTCLIFFE GALLERY

2-8 Augusta Street, Sheringham, Norfolk NR26 8LA
Tel: 01263 824320  Fax: 01263 821731
e-mail: sparks@westcliffe.fsnet.co.uk

Opened in 1978 and run by Richard and Sheila Parks **Westcliffe Gallery** specialises in quality 19th century through to contempory works, by leading professional artists. The gallery also displays for sale, a selection of fine 18th and 19th century furniture. Occupying a large corner position fronting Augusta Street, the gallery fills three floors. The ground floor

and lower floor boasts an excellent selection of paintings together with antique furniture in a natural room setting. Portraits and landscapes, expertly executed and framed, line the walls, complemented by exquisite dining tables and chairs, chests of drawers and other finely crafted furnishings.

The tasteful lighting and relaxed ambience make searching for that unique work of art a very enjoyable experience. The first floor houses the framing and restoration workshops, where the highly skilled team replicate traditional frame making and gilding, alongside innovative new contemporary designs in framing. There is a full restoration service for oils, watercolours and prints. Valuations are undertaken, and advice on art purchasing and collecting is available. *Open:* Daily 10am - 1pm and 2pm - 5pm Open Sundays from July to September and Bank Holidays.

## CROWES

32 Station Road, Sheringham, Norfolk NR26 8RF
Tel: 01263 822891  Fax: 01263 823081

Originally a guesthouse built in 1897, **Crowes** was converted into a handsome shop some 60 years ago, with a further conversion in 1993 creating a total of seven retail spaces. Located just two minutes from Sheringham Station, this treasure trove of antiques and collectibles houses everything from tin toys to period lamps, together with a good selection of English and Chinese pottery, modern china, garden

accessories, bronze figurines (including pieces by noted sculptor Paul Jenkins), oil lamps, brass and copperware, reproduction swords and other military memorabilia, Art Nouveau and Art Deco figurines, and wooden sea trunks and other 'nautacalia', displayed over two floors of this spacious and attractive shop.

Owner Louise Punter, who took over from Mike Crowe who established the business in 1943, leads a knowledgeable and friendly staff who are happy to offer their advice and help.

different from the shingle beaches elsewhere on this part of the coast. Consisting mainly of gently sloping sand, it is excellent for bathing and the team of lifeguards makes it ideal for families with children. Rainfall at Sheringham is one of the lowest in the county, and the bracing air has also recommended the town to sufferers from rheumatism and respiratory problems.

*North Norfolk Railway*

A small fleet of fishing boats still operates from here, mostly concentrating on crabs and lobsters, but also bringing in catches of cod, skate, plaice, mackerel and herring. Several original fishermens' cottages remain, some with lofts where the nets were mended. Sheringham has never had a harbour, so boats are launched from the shore where stacks of creels stand as they have for generations. A 'golden lobster' in the town's coat of arms celebrates this traditional industry.

Like so many other former fishing villages in England, Sheringham owes its transformation into a resort to the arrival of the railway. During the Edwardian peak years of rail travel, some 64 trains a day steamed into the station but the line became yet another victim of the Beeching closures of the 1960s. Devotees of steam trains joined together and, by dint of great effort and enthusiasm, managed to re-open the line in 1975 as the **North Norfolk Railway**, better known as **The Poppy Line**.

The name refers to 'Poppyland", a term given to the area by the Victorian journalist Clement Scott who visited in pre-herbicide days when the summer fields were ablaze with poppies. In 1883, Scott travelled to Cromer on the newly-opened Great Eastern Railway's extension from Norwich. Walking out of the town, he was entranced by the tranquillity of the countryside. In his dispatch to the *Daily Telegraph* he wrote: 'It is difficult to convey an idea of the silence of the fields through which I passed, or the beauty of the prospect that surrounded me - a blue sky without a cloud across it, a sea sparkling under a haze of heat, wild flowers in profusion around me, poppies predominating everywhere ...' Spurred by Scott's enthusiasm, a succession of notable Victorians made their way here - painters, writers, actors, even a youthful Winston Churchill. Later, during the Second World War, Churchill returned to the area, staying at Pear Tree Cottage in Mundesley.

Although greatly diminished in number, plenty of brilliant poppies can still be seen as you travel the scenic five-mile journey from Sheringham to Holt. The railway operates up to eight trains daily in each direction during the season, March to October, and there are special Saturday evening and Sunday lunchtime services when you can dine in style in one of the Pullman coaches from the old 'Brighton Belle'.

## WEYBOURNE FOREST LODGES

Sandy Hill Lane, Weybourne, Holt,
Norfolk  NR25 7HW
Tel: 01263 588440  Fax: 01263 588588
website: www.weybourneforestlodges.co.uk

Open all year round, **Weybourne Forest Lodges** is a small
family-owned-and-run development of beautiful timber
lodges set in a unique position in an Area of Outstanding
Natural Beauty. Close to the coast at Weybourne and
midway between Holt and Sheringham, peace and quiet
await visitors here. Most of the seven lodges are Scandinavian style A-frames, the others being single-
storey timber properties. Charming and welcoming, the lodges sleep between two  and six people and
are set in a private pine forest amidst hundreds of acres of woodland and heath adjoining National
Trust property. An idyllic place perfect for walkers, birdwatchers and anyone who appreciates the joys
of nature, guests can walk the three miles into Sheringham without passing any houses, just fields,
woodland and coastal cliffs. The North Norfolk steam railway's 'Poppy Line' runs along the fields
below the forest, and Weybourne Station is just five minutes walk away. This is one of the loveliest
train journeys in the British Isles, and is often used in films and television programmes – most recently
in an ITV version of a P D James novel.

These picturesque and extremely comfortable lodges are equipped for holidays at any time of year.
Warm, cosy and welcoming, each one has its own balcony, and parking adjacent for two cars. All
bedding is provided. Some of the lodges are accessible to wheelchairs. All are tastefully furnished and
decorated to a high standard of comfort and quality. There is a laundry on site with a washing machine
and tumble dryer. Visitors may also obtain temporary membership at the nearby leisure centre, where
they can enjoy the 25-metre indoor heated swimming pool, children's pool, gym, spa bath, steam
room and sauna. On site there is also a small menagerie with pigs, sheep, ducks, rabbits, red squirrels,
a horse and a pony. Owners Chris and Sue live on the site and aim to provide all their guests with
happy and memorable holidays.

Just to the west of the town, at Upper Sheringham, footpaths lead to the lovely grounds of **Sheringham Park** (National Trust). The Park was landscaped by Humphrey Repton, who declared it to be his 'favourite and darling child in Norfolk'. There are grand views along the coast, dense growths of oak, beech and fir trees and banks of rhododendrons which are at their most dazzling in late May and June.

There's yet more grand scenery at the aptly-named **Pretty Corner**, just to the east of the A1082 at its junction with the A148. This is a particularly beautiful area of woodland and also offers superb views over the surrounding countryside.

## WEYBOURNE

**9 miles W of Cromer on the A149**

Here, the shingle beach known as **Weybourne Hope** (or Hoop) slopes so steeply that an invading fleet could bring its ships right up to the shore. Which is exactly what the Danes did many times during the 9th and 10th centuries. A local adage states that 'He who would Old England win, Must at Weybourne Hoop begin,' and over the centuries care has been taken to protect this stretch of the coast. A map dated 1st May 1588 clearly shows 'Waborne Fort', and Holt's Parish Register for that year of the Armada notes that 'in this yeare was the town of Waborne fortified with a continuall garrison of men bothe of horse and foote with sconces (earthworks) ordinaunce and all manner of appoyntment to defend the Spannyards landing theare.'

As it turned out, the 'Spannyards' never got close, but during both World Wars the same concern was shown for defending this vulnerable beach. The garrison then became the Anti-Aircraft Permanent Range and Radar Training

### BOLDING WAY HOLIDAY COTTAGES

'The Stables', Bolding Way, Weybourne, Holt, Norfolk NR25 7SW
Tel: 01263 588666
e-mail: holidays@boldingway.co.uk
website: www.boldingway.co.uk

Quiet and secluded, **Bolding Way Holiday Cottages** have been converted from two original properties – the barn and stables – in a tasteful renovation that ensures the highest standards of comfort and quality. The five period cottages date from as early as the 15th century and sleep between two and eight guests. Expertly converted in traditional manner, with pan-tiled roofs and flint and brickwork, the cottages are set in two acres of gardens amid five acres of rolling countryside. Home-cooked meals and buffets can be prepared

by the professional chef and served to guests in their cottage; specialist services include holistic therapies; family and holiday celebrations are happily arranged.

Handy for Weybourne, North Norfolk Railway, Mickleburgh Collection and the Cley Marshes, the cottages make an excellent base from which to explore the surrounding region and further afield throughout Norfolk. The ETC has granted the cottages Welcome Host, Welcome All and Food Hygiene awards, as well as a rating of 4 Stars.

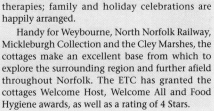

## THE MUCKLEBURGH COLLECTION

Weybourne Camp, Weybourne, Norfolk NR25 7EG
Tel: 01263 588210   Fax: 01263 588425

The Museum is now in its 16th season and was founded by the late C. Berry Savory in 1988. The collection has been expanding each year since its inception and now boasts a tank hall, built with a donation by Robert Curson, a former Desert Rat, and a display on St John Ambulance going back to the Middle Ages and incorporating a modern day display.

The collection features 16 working tanks and at least 3000 other exhibits, including model ships, anti-aircraft guns, uniforms and other items from the First and Second World Wars. The Norfolk and Suffolk Yeomanry through the ages, is also on exhibition here.

The North Norfolk Amateur Radio group have their radio sets on show in one of the old buildings and are available, at various times during the season, for you to try your hand at Morse code .

On any Sunday throughout the season, you can see the Panzer 68 put through its paces, and take a thrilling ride on the Gama Goat. This six-wheeled armoured personnel carrier takes you on a ride along the coastal path. Bumpy but fun!

Whatever your requirements, large groups can be accommodated at reduced prices, available on request. There is an excellent restaurant serving hot and cold meals and birthday parties can be catered for. The extensive gift shop caters for all ages and pockets.

## THE STABLES

Feathers Yard, Holt, Norfolk  NR25 6BW
Tel: 01263 712020

**The Stables** – which, as its name suggests, began life as the stabling area for the Feathers Hotel, located to the front of the shop – is a large and handsome boutique selling high-quality clothing for all ages. Everything from smart casual to formalwear can be found here, with wedding clothes from the likes of Presen and Rosie's, skirts, knitwear and jackets from Sweden, Spain and Ireland featuring brand

names such as Devernois, Chatham, Simorra, Avoca and Prêt à Porter, and evening wear from Michel Ambers.

The range of accessories includes shoes, boots, sandals, handbags, gloves, hats, scarves, belts and more, all expertly crafted and created from a variety of beautiful fabrics, from silks and woollens to leatherwork. Owner Ann Yarham is ably assisted by Jan, and has been in the fashion industry since the 1960s. Together with their experienced staff, they offer knowledgeable and friendly service to all their customers.

Wing, providing instruction for National Servicemen until the camp finally closed in 1959. It was reckoned that by then some 1,500,000 shells had been fired out to sea. The site has since been returned to agricultural use, but the original NAAFI building remains and now houses **The Muckleburgh Collection** (see panel opposite), a fascinating museum of military vehicles, weapons and equipment, most of which has seen action in battlefields all over the world. All of the tanks, armoured cars and amphibious vehicles on display can be inspected at close quarters, and there are regular tank demonstrations. Meals and snacks are available - served in a NAAFI-style canteen. Incidentally, despite Weybourne's exposed position, it has in fact only been attacked once, by the Luftwaffe on 11th July 1940. A stick of bombs landed in the main street and badly damaged two cottages.

## Bodham
**9 miles W of Cromer off the A148**

About midway between Bodham and Weybourne, in the grounds of the Kelling Park Hotel, is the **East Anglian Falconry Centre** which, in addition to having daily flying displays, is also the largest sanctuary in the country for injured owls and birds of prey. The centre keeps and cares for over 200 birds, among them kestrels and sparrowhawks, as well as a number of rarer birds such as goshawks, peregrine falcons, harriers and redtail hawks, eagles and snowy owls.

## Holt
**10 miles W of Cromer on the A148**

A perennial finalist in the Anglia in Bloom competition, Holt's town centre always looks a picture, with hanging baskets and flowers everywhere. Back in 1892, a guide-book to the county

## WOOD 'N' THINGS

15 Chapel Street, Holt, Norfolk  NR25 6BA
Tel: 01263 713720  Fax: 01263 710780
e-mail: hyattbruin@aol.com

**Wood 'n' Things** offers a distinctive mix of affordable antique furniture and fittings. Situated in a courtyard in the centre of Holt, and originally two cottages dating back to the 1700s, there are three display rooms (two on the ground floor) featuring a range of collectibles. There's Doulton china, clocks and kitchenware such as copper kettles, gramophones, glass lights from the 1930s to

1950s, Art Deco vases and jugs, mahogany and oak bureaux and writing desks, Victorian oil lamps, sports equipment from days gone by – leather footballs, cricket balls and rugby balls, boots, ice skates, tennis rackets, golf clubs with hickory shafts, including an original putter of the type used by W J Travis in 1904 when he won the US Open – and much more.

In a separate warehouse there are full bedroom suites, display cabinets and other specialist items. This excellent shop also offers a full restoration service, and can make furniture to order.

## ART-E-FAX

One Fish Hill, Holt, Norfolk  NR25 6BD
Tel: 01263 713136  Fax: 01263 710763
e-mail: sales@art-e-fax.com
website: www.art-e-fax.com

Fine art and design-led giftware can be found at **Art-e-fax**, a truly unique gallery that has, since it opened in April of 2002, built up a well-deserved reputation as North Norfolk's premier gallery. The handsome Georgian building in which it makes its home has been carefully renovated to retain all its original charm while providing the very best space in which to appreciate the artwork on display. Owner and manager Tom Leask – ably assisted by Harriet Calder and Kathy Burgoine – offer an innovative service and a relaxed ambience befitting a 21st century art venue.

The 1,000-square-foot gallery is accessible to people with disabilities. Spacious and attractive, it is the ideal setting for the gallery's innovative range of international artwork, which includes original paintings and limited edition prints by award-winning artists and fresh new talents. In addition to the extensive collection of contemporary images, the gallery stocks a selection of exclusive Scandinavian glassware from Kosta Boda and Orrefors, together with jewellery and objets d'art from Georg Jensen. Winner of the Fine Art Trade Guild New Business Award 2003, this superb gallery is well worth a visit. Open: Six days a week, 10 – 5.

## the passion of flowers

two chapel yard, holt, norfolk NR25 6HX

Tel/Fax: 01263 713933   website: www.thepassionofflowers.co.uk

Specialising in orchids and unusual blooms, **the passion of flowers** is a distinctive shop offering a range of exciting plants and floral arrangements. Proprietor Rita Levitt, a fully trained florist with many years experience, ran a shop in London before moving to Holt in 2003. She frequently travels abroad to buy unique pots that are displayed and sold in the shop. Located in the former fire station, the interior of this lovely shop has brightly coloured walls that make a charming background to the marvellous display of flowers. All staff are qualified in floristry, and are happy to offer their help and advice in choosing the perfect blooms for every occasion.

described Holt as 'A clean and very prettily situated market town, being planted in a well undulating and very woody neighbourhood.' More than a century later, one can't quarrel with that characterisation.

The worst day in the town's history was May 1st, 1708, when a raging fire consumed most of the town's ancient houses. The consequent rebuilding replaced them with some elegant Georgian houses, gracious buildings which played a large part in earning the town its designation as a Conservation Area.

The town's most famous building, **Gresham's School**, somehow escaped the disastrous conflagration of 1708. Founded in 1555 by Sir John Gresham, the school began as an altruistic educational establishment, its pupils accepted solely on the basis of their

## Doodle Pots

1A New Street, Holt, Norfolk NR25 6JJ

Tel: 01263 713135

e-mail: rachel@doodlepots.com

**Doodle Pots** is a great idea come to life: a 'ceramic café' where guests can create their own unique gifts: hand-painted plates, baby footprints on tiles, mugs, vases and more. Owner Rachel Parker attended Chelsea Art College; this marvellous shop is her hobby extended and developed into a thriving business. There are stencils and books to inspire you, while the helpful staff are always on hand to offer guidance and advice.

Fun for children and adults alike, painting pottery is relaxing and theraputic too with delicious cappuccino and hot cholcolate available. Finished pieces are glazed and fired and are available in three to four days, when they can be picked up or delivered. If you use the special acrylic paints, items can be taken away the same day. Ideal for parties, group bookings are available. Open Monday-Saturday 10-5, Sundays in summer, by arrangment at other times. Rachel takes commissions for wedding platters, christening plates and can work with you on a special design.

## MEADOW DAIRIES

37 Bull Street, Holt, Norfolk NR25 6HP
Tel/Fax: 01263 712229

Specialising in local produce – bread from local bakeries, home-made
cakes, freshly made sandwiches, meat pies, quiches, samosas and more,
together with an extensive range of cheeses, milk and yogurts from
local dairies – **Meadow Dairies** is the place to find fresh, delicious foods
and condiments. The range of produce here includes a selection of olives,
chutneys, Mediterranean foods, jams, natural and organic fruit juices,
sliced meats and more, all sold from this cosy and welcoming shop in
the centre of Holt.

academic promise. Since then, the school
has abandoned both its town centre
location and its founder's commitment
to educating, free, those bright children
who could not otherwise afford it.
Placing your child here, today, will
drain more than £15,000 each year
from your income.

Solace yourself with the thought that
among the school's many distinguished
alumni are the dour creator of the BBC,

Lord Reith, the poets W H Auden and
Stephen Spender, and the composer
Benjamin Britten.

Look out for one of Holt's most
unusual buildings, **Home Place**.
Designed and built in 1903-5 by E S
Prior, an architect follower of the Arts &
Crafts movement, the exterior of the
house is completely covered with an
ingeniously contrived cladding of
local pebbles.

## EMCY GARDEN & LEISURE

Weybourne Road, Holt, Norfolk NR25 7ER
Tel: 01263 711574  Fax: 01263 713126
e-mail: emcy@emcy.co.uk
website: www.emcy.co.uk

**Emcy Garden & Leisure** has grown during its 11-year
history at its present site near Holt into a large indoor
and outdoor centre, as designed and developed by
owners Mike and Caroline Crane. Everything required
to create the perfect garden is here, from

The site includes large outdoor areas with terracotta
pots, seasonal outdoor plants, shrubs, trees and herbs, and a plant tunnel with seasonal bedding and
indoor plants and vegetables, while the extensive indoor space boasts a wide range of garden tools,

plant care and maintenance products, pet and pond
products, garden furniture, decorative features, and
machinery, and water features. The range of plants, cut
flowers and fresh vegetables is superb. The friendly,
knowledgeable staff are happy to offer assistance and
advice. The entire site is accessible for customers in
wheelchairs, and there is a ride-on buggy for customers
who need assistance with mobility. Disabled parking is
also available in the large carpark. And after a leisurely
browse through the centre, the coffee shop is an excellent
place to refuel, with a selection of tempting home-baked
goods, snacks, hot and cold drinks and ices.

## CLEY-NEXT-THE-SEA

**12 miles W of Cromer on the A149**

Cley's name is no longer appropriate. Cley-a-mile-away-from-the-Sea would be more truthful. But in early medieval times, Cley (pronounced Cly, and meaning clay) was a more important port than King's Lynn, with a busy trade exporting wool to the Netherlands. In return, Cley imported a predilection for houses with curved gables, Flemish bricks and pantiles. The windmill overlooking the harbour adds to the sense that a little piece of Holland has strayed across the North Sea. This is the famous **Cley Mill**, the subject of thousands of paintings. Built in 1713 and in use until 1921, the Mill is open to visitors during the season (afternoons

*Cley Windmill*

only), and also offers bed and breakfast.

The village's prosperity in the past is reflected in the enormous scale of its 14th/15th century parish church, **St Mary's**, whose south porch is particularly notable for its fine stonework and 16 armorial crests. The gorgeous fan-vaulted roof is decorated with bosses carved with

### CLEY SMOKEHOUSE

High Street, Cley-next-the-Sea, Holt, Norfolk NR25 7RF
Tel/Fax: 01263 740282
e-mail: enquiries@cleysmokehouse.com
website: www.cleysmokehouse.com

An excellent range of fresh fish and seafood awaits you at **Cley Smokehouse**. Situated in the High Street, the building dates back to the late 1600s and was once part of the Customs bonded warehouse.

Owner Glen Weston is from a well-known fishing family locally, and still has his own fishing boat. He knows the freshest fish when he sees it, and chooses only the finest for smoking. Everything at

this fine shop is 'hand-crafted' by Glen and his team, as they do all the cutting, preparing and smoking on the premises, in two smokehouses situated behind the shop.

Kippers and eels are two specialities, but there are also delicious bloaters, mackerel, haddock, salmon, red herrings, cod roe and trout sold here. All are locally caught. Other tempting goods are pâtés and home-made taramasalata. The service is always friendly and helpful, and the shop also boasts an excellent mail-order service.

# *Blakeney*

**Distance:** 3.1 miles (4.83 kilometres)

**Typical time:** 90 mins

**Height gain:** 15 metres

**Map:** Explorer 24

**Walk:** www.walkingworld.com
ID:2103

**Contributor:** Joy & Charles Boldero

## Access Information:

Norfolk Bus routes: Freecall 0500 626116 9.00am to 5.00pm, Monday to Friday. There is a free car park half way down the main street where the walk begins.

## Description:

This is a very pleasurable walk with good paths and no stiles. There are fine views of the coastline. Blakeney is a very popular and pretty village on the North Norfolk coast. The River Glaven is tidal and fills the quayside channel at high tide. It is a place for sailing, safe for small children to bathe and fish and where the boats wait to take passengers out to Blakeney Point to see the seals. The outer route is along field edges and returns along the Norfolk Coastal Path which runs beside the marshes.

## Features:

River, Pub, Toilets, Church, National Trust/ NTS, Wildlife, Birds, lowers, Great Views, Butterflies, Food Shop

## Walk Directions:

**1** Turn left up the narrow street with its attractive flinted cottages. Just past the Methodist church and opposite Coronation Cottage turn right along Little Lane. At the T junction turn left along New Road, then right along a residential road.

**2** Turn right at a finger-post sign along a gravel track with pretty flinted cottages. It then becomes a rough path alongside a field.

**3** Turn left along the road and very soon turn right at a finger-post sign along a driveway. There are fine views here of the marshes. As the driveway goes right keep ahead to a house, and then go left at a yellow marker sign beside the field edge with a hedge on the right. The path winds and the hedge is then on the left with a thatched house on the hill ahead. Just before the gate the path goes left.

**4** Turn right along the road, then left at a finger-post sign ahead along a grass path leading downhill.

**5** At a T junction of paths turn right along the Norfolk Coastal Path which takes you into Blakeney. This path goes beside the marshes where sea lavender and wading birds can be seen.

**6** Turn left along the pavement and beside the Quay.

**7** Turn right up the narrow street with the White House Hotel ahead and back to the car park.

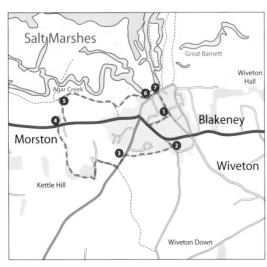

angels, flowers, and a lively scene of an old woman throwing her distaff at a fox running away with her chickens.

From Cley it's possible to walk along the shoreline to **Blakeney Point**, the most northerly extremity of East Anglia. This spit of land that stretches three miles out into the sea is a twitcher's paradise. Some 256 species of birds have been spotted here, and the variety of flora is scarcely less impressive: almost 200 flowering species have been recorded.

### BLAKENEY
#### 14 miles W of Cromer on the A149

One of the most enchanting of the North Norfolk coastal villages, Blakeney was a commercial port until the beginning of the 20th century, when silting up of the estuary prevented all but pleasure craft from gaining access. The silting has left a fascinating landscape of serpentine creeks and channels twisting their way through mud banks and sand hills. In a side street off the quay is the 14th century **Guildhall** (English

*Blakeney Harbour*

Heritage), which was probably a private house and contains an interesting undercroft, or cellar, which is notable as an early example of a brick-built vaulted ceiling.

The beautifully restored Church of St Nicholas, set on a hill overlooking village and marshland, offers the visitor a lovely Early English chancel, built in 1220, and the magnificent west tower, 100 feet high, a landmark for miles around. In a small turret on the northeast corner of the chancel a light would once burn as a beacon to guide ships safely into Blakeney Harbour.

### GLANDFORD
#### 12 miles W of Cromer off the B1156

Near this delightful village, the **Natural Surroundings Wild Flower Centre** is dedicated to gardening with a strong ecological emphasis. There are wild flower meadows and gardens, organic vegetable and herb gardens, nurseries, a nature trail alongside the unspoilt River Glaven, and the Centre also organises a wide range of events with a conservation theme. A short walk down the valley from the Centre is the **Glandford Shell Museum**, a lovely Dutch-style building which houses the private collection of Sir Alfred Jodrell, a unique accumulation of sea shells gathered from beaches all around the world, together with a fascinating variety of artefacts made from them.

A couple of miles south of Glandford you'll find a building of 1802 which, year after year, has been awarded the title of 'Top Tourist Attraction in North Norfolk'. **Letheringsett Watermill** stands on the site of an earlier mill recorded in the *Doomsday Book*, and was rescued

*Letheringsett Watermill*

from near-dereliction in the 1980s. This fully functional, water-powered mill produces 100% wholewheat flour from locally grown wheat; there are regular demonstrations of the milling process, with a running commentary from the miller; and the end product can be purchased in the gift shop.

## LANGHAM

### 14 miles W of Cromer off the A149/A148

The minor road leading south from Morston will bring you, after a mile or so, to **Langham Glass & Rural Crafts** where, in a wonderful collection of restored 18th century barn workshops, you watch a variety of craftspeople exercising their traditional skills. In addition to the now famous Langham Glass works where a master glass-maker will give a running commentary, there's a pyrographer, wood-turner, stained glass maker, and glass engraver. The Factory Gift Shop is well stocked with their creations, the Antiques & Collectibles

Shop offers a wide variety of items from Victorian china to Lalique, and there's also a walled garden, seven-acre maize maze, adventure playground and restaurant.

## MORSTON

### 13 miles W of Cromer on the A149

Great stretches of salt marshes and mud flats lie between this pleasant village and the sea, which is reached by way of a tidal creek that almost disappears at low tide. Morston is a particularly pleasing village with quiet lanes and clusters of cottages built from local flint cobbles. If the church tower looks rather patched-up, that's because it was struck by lightning in 1743. It's said that local people took this as a sign that the Second Coming of Christ was imminent, and that repairing their church was therefore pointless. It was many years before restoration work was finally undertaken, by which time the fabric of the tower had deteriorated even further.

## STIFFKEY

### 16 miles W of Cromer on the A149

Regarded as one of the prettiest villages in the county, Stiffkey lies beside the little river of the same name. Pronounced 'Stewkey', the name means 'island of tree stumps' and is most likely derived from the marshy river valley of reed beds and fallen trees, which indeed gives the village the appearance of an island. At the east end of the village is the church of St John the Baptist; from the churchyard there are fine views of the river and of Stiffkey Hall to the south. All that now remains of this once-impressive building, built by the Bacon

**STIFFKEY ANTIQUES**

The Old Chapel, Wells Road, Stiffkey, Wells-next-the-Sea,
Norfolk NR23 1AJ
Tel: 01328 830690  Fax: 01328 830005
Mobile: 07855 371779

Set in a former Methodist chapel built in 1900, **Stiffkey Antiques** is a charming and bright antiques emporium with excellent displays of the many wonderful pieces sold here. The shop specialises in restored genuine antique door furniture and window fittings, and include locks, door knobs, hooks, door plates and handles, bell-pushes, letter plates, knockers, escutcheons and more, together with antique lamps, fenders, fire accessories and home decoration.

family in 1578, are the towers, one wing of the house, and the 17th century gatehouse. The stately ruins of the great hall have been transformed into a rose terrace and sunken garden and are open to the public.

The former Rectory is a grand Georgian building, famous as the residence of the Revd Harold Davidson, Rector of Stiffkey during the 1920s and 1930s. Rather like the central character in Michael Palin's film *The Missionary*, Harold launched a personal crusade to save the fallen women of London, and caused much gossip and scandal by doing so. Despite the fact that his notoriety regularly filled the church to capacity, he constantly fell foul of the ecclesiastical authorities and eventually lost his living. There is a rather bizarre ending to his story. After handing over the keys of Stiffkey Rectory, Harold joined a travelling show and was later killed by a lion whose cage he was sharing.

To the north of the village are the **Stiffkey Salt Marshes**, a National Trust nature reserve which turns a delicate shade of purple in July when the sea lavender is in bloom. Here on the sandflats can be found the famous 'Stewkey blues' - cockles which are highly regarded as a delicacy by connoisseurs of succulent bivalve molluscs.

A couple of miles south of Stiffkey

stand the picturesque ruins of **Binham Priory** (English Heritage), its magnificent nave still serving as the parish church. This represents only about one-sixth of the original Priory, founded in 1091 by a nephew of William the Conqueror. The church is well worth a visit to see its unusually lofty interior with a Monk's Walk at roof level, its Seven Sacraments font, and noble west front.

# HUNSTANTON

The busy seaside resort of Hunstanton can boast two unique features: one, it has the only cliffs in England made up of colourful levels of red, white and brown strata, and two, it is the only east coast resort that faces west, looking across The Wash to the Lincolnshire coast and the unmistakeable tower of the 272-foot high Boston Stump (more properly described as the Church of St Botolph).

Hunstanton town is a comparative newcomer, developed in the 1860s by Mr Hamon L'Estrange of nearby Hunstanton Hall to take advantage of the arrival of the railway here, and to exploit the natural appeal of its broad, sandy beaches. The centre is well-planned with mock-Tudor houses grouped around a green that falls away to the shore.

Hunstanton's social standing was

assured after the Prince of Wales, later Edward VII, came here to recover from typhoid fever. He stayed at the Sandringham Hotel which, sadly, has since been demolished, along with the grand Victorian pier and the railway. But Hunston, as locals call the town, still has a distinct 19th century charm about it and plenty to entertain visitors.

The huge stretches of sandy beach, framed by those multi-coloured cliffs, are just heaven for children who will also be fascinated by the **Sea Life Sanctuary**, on Southern Promenade, where an underwater glass tunnel provides a wonderful opportunity to watch the varied and often weird forms of marine life that inhabit Britain's waters. A popular excursion from Hunstanton is the boat trip to Seal Island, a sandbank in The Wash where seals can indeed often be seen sunbathing at low tide.

# AROUND HUNSTANTON

### WELLS-NEXT-THE-SEA

**17 miles E of Hunstanton on the A149**

There's no doubt about the appeal of Wells' picturesque quayside, narrow streets and ancient houses. Wells has been a working port since at least the 13th century, but over the years the town's full name of Wells-next-the-Sea

has become increasingly inapt - its harbour now stands more than a mile from the sea. In 1859, to prevent the harbour silting up altogether, Lord Leicester of Holkham Hall built an Embankment cutting off some 600 acres of marshland. This now provides a pleasant walk down to the sea.

The Embankment gave no protection, however, against the great floods of 1953 and 1978. On the 11th January 1978 the sea rose 16 feet 1 inch above high tide, a few inches less than the 16 feet 10 inches recorded on the 31st January 1953 when the flood-waters lifted a ship on to the quay. A silo on the harbour is marked with these abnormal levels.

Running alongside the Embankment is the **Harbour Railway**, which trundles from the small museum on the quay to the lifeboat station by the beach. This narrow-gauge railway is operated by the same company as the **Wells—Walsingham Light Railway** which carries passengers on a particularly lovely ride along the route of the former Great Eastern Railway to Little Walsingham. The four-mile journey takes about 20 minutes with stops at Warham St Mary and Wighton. Both the WWR and the Harbour Railway services are seasonal. In a curious change of function, the former GER station at Wells is now home to the well-known Burnham Pottery, the former signal box is now the station, while the

old station at Walsingham is now a church!

In addition to being the largest of North Norfolk's ports, Wells is also a popular resort with one of the best beaches in England, bordered by the curiously named **Holkham Meals**, a plantation of pines established here in the 1860s to stabilise the dunes.

*Holkham Hall*

## HOLKHAM
**16 miles E of Hunstanton on the A149**

If the concept of the Grand Tour ever needed any justification, **Holkham Hall** (see panel on page 64) amply provides it. For six years, from 1712 to 1718, young Thomas Coke (pronounced Cook) travelled extensively in Italy, France and Germany, studying and absorbing at first hand the glories of European civilisation. And, wherever possible, buying them. When he returned to England, Coke realised that his family's modest Elizabethan manor could not possibly house the collection of treasures he had amassed. The manor would have to be demolished and a more worthy building erected in its place.

During his travels in Italy, Coke had been deeply impressed by the cool, classical lines favoured by the Renaissance architect Andrea Palladio. Working with his friend Lord Burlington - another fervent admirer of Palladio - and the architect William Kent, Coke's monumental project slowly took shape. Building began in 1734 but was not completed until 1762, three years after Coke's death.

The completed building, its classical balance and restraint emphasised by the pale honey local brick used throughout, has been described as 'the ultimate achievement of the English Palladian movement'. As you step into the stunning entrance hall, the tone is set for the rest of the house. Modelled on a Roman Temple of Justice, the lofty coved ceiling is supported by 18 huge fluted columns of pink Derbyshire alabaster, transported to nearby Wells by river and sea.

Historically the most important room at Holkham is the Statue Gallery, which contains one of the finest collections of classical sculpture still in private ownership. In this sparsely furnished room there is nothing to distract one's attention from the sublime statuary that has survived for millennia, among it a bust of Thucydides (one of the earliest portrayals of man) and a statue of Diana, both of which have been dated to 4BC.

Each room reveals new treasures: Rubens and Van Dyck in the Saloon , the Landscape Room with its incomparable collection of paintings by Lorrain, Poussin and other masters, the Brussels tapestries in the State Sitting Room and, on a more domestic note, the vast, high-ceilinged kitchen which remained in use until 1939 and still displays the original pots and pans.

Astonishingly, the interior of the

## HOLKHAM HALL & BYGONES MUSEUM

Wells-next-the-Sea, Norfolk NR23 1AB
Tel: 01328 710227  Fax: 01328 711707
e-mail: enquiries@holkham.co.uk
website: www.holkham.co.uk

Holkham Hall has been the home of the Coke family and the Earls of Leicester for almost 250 years. Built between 1734 and 1764 by Thomas Coke, 1st Earl of Leicester, and based on a design by William Kent, this fine example of an 18th century Palladian-style mansion reflects Thomas Coke's natural appreciation of classical art developed during his Grand Tour. The house is constructed of local yellow brick with a magnificent entrance hall of English alabaster.

The State Rooms occupy the first floor and contain Roman statuary, paintings by Rubens, Van Dyck, Claude, Poussin and Gainsborough, and original furniture.

On leaving the house, visitors pass Holkham Pottery and its adjacent shop, both under the supervision of the Countess of Leicester. Fine examples of local craftsmanship are for sale, including the Holkham Florist Ware.

Beyond are the 19th century stables, now housing the **Holkham Bygones Collection**: some 4,000 items ranging from working steam engines, vintage cars and tractors to craft tools and kitchenware. A History of Farming exhibition is adjacent to the Museum.

The house is set in a 3,000-acre park with a herd of 800 fallow deer. On the one-mile-long lake are many species of wildfowl. Two walks encircle either the lake or agricultural buildings.

Holkham Nursery Gardens occupy the 18th century walled Kitchen Garden; a large range of stock is on sale to the public. The estate also owns the internationally-renowned Victoria Hotel, which is just opposite the entrance to Holkham Beach, where visitors can stroll for miles on golden sands.

The Hall is open to visitors seasonally, usually from the end of May until the end of September, Thursday to Monday from 1 p.m. to 5 p.m. (last admissions 4.30 p.m.).

During the month of May there is an audio tour of the Hall offered on a 'turn up and join in' basis at 3 p.m. Thursday to Monday. The Hall regrets that late-comers will not be admitted, and that there is a limit of 40 people per tour.

The Hall is also open on all Bank Holidays from 11.30 a.m. until 5 p.m. (last admissions 4.30 p.m.). The Bygones Museum is open Easter Bank Holiday and then from May until September, Thursday to Monday from 12 noon. to 5 p.m.

The Stables Café and the Pottery Shop are open Easter Bank Holiday and then May – October Thursday to Tuesday 10 – 5.30.

Private guided tours are available out of season by arrangement.

house remains almost exactly as Thomas Coke planned it, his descendants having respected the integrity of his vision. They concentrated their reforming zeal on improving the enormous estate. It was Coke's great-nephew, Thomas William Coke (1754-1842), in particular who was responsible for the elegant layout of the 3,000-acre park visitors see today. Universally known as 'Coke of Norfolk', Thomas was a pioneer of the Agricultural Revolution, best known for introducing the idea of a four-crop rotation. He was also a generous patron of agricultural innovations, and the 'Sheep Shearings' he inaugurated - gatherings to which several hundred people came to exchange ideas on all aspects of agriculture, were the direct forerunners of the modern agricultural show.

The Thomas Coke who had built the house had been created Earl of Leicester in 1744, but as his only son died before him, the title lapsed. However, when his grand-nephew, 'Coke of Norfolk' was elevated to the peerage by Queen Victoria in 1837, he adopted the same title. The present Earl, the 7th, lives at Holkham in the private apartments known as the Family Wing, but still uses the State Rooms when entertaining guests. The Earl continues in the tradition of 'Coke of Norfolk' by overseeing the vast estate with its 30 tenant farmers and more than 300 houses: the Countess has established a new tradition by setting up the Holkham Pottery in the former brickworks.

## BURNHAM THORPE
**11 miles E of Hunstanton off the B1355**

From the tower of All Saints' Church, the White Ensign flaps in the breeze; the only pub in the village is the *Lord Nelson*; and the shop next door to it is called the Trafalgar Stores. No prizes for deducing

## WHITEHALL FARM

Walsingham Road, Burnham Thorpe,
Norfolk PE31 8HN
Tel: 01328 738416  Fax: 01328 730937
Mobile: 07050 247390
e-mail: barrysoutherland@aol.com
website: www.whitehallfarm-accommodation.com

On the outskirts of Burnham Thorpe, just two miles from the North Norfolk Coast, **Whitehall Farm** is a working arable farm. The farmhouse is charming and gracious – mainly 17th century but dating back in parts to 1100 – that offers high-quality accommodation and makes an ideal touring base. Owners Barry and Valerie Southerland have lived and farmed here for many years – Barry was born in the farmhouse – and Valerie started offering B&B accommodation in 1996.

There are three comfortable and handsomely decorated and furnished guest bedrooms (a double, twin and family room), all with every amenity and facility guests could expect. The farm can also provide stabling and a post and rail paddock – and there are ample lanes and bridleways, and miles of flat sands at Holkham beach nearby – and there is also a well-kept, quiet caravan site with electric hook-up, shower and washroom facilities on the farm. Open all year round. 4 Diamonds ETC and AA.

## HOUSE BAIT II

Garage Forecourt, Creake Road,
Burnham Market, Norfolk PE31 8HF
Tel: 01328 730583  Fax: 01328 730583
e-mail: miv.watts@virgin.net
website: www.housebait.co.uk

Miv Watts and Zara Bolingbroke-Kent offer all their customers a complete interior design service and a select range of giftware at **House Bait II**, a showroom for furniture and decorating inspiration. Everything needed to make your decorative dreams come true can be found here, where an eclectic mix of French and Far Eastern furniture and artefacts, modern and traditional fabrics from names such as Claremont, Jason D'Souza, Kathryn Ireland, Celia Birtwell, V V Rouleaux and Roger Gates, ceramics, antiques, decorative lighting and linens are brought together under one

roof. Zara has worked for Lady Victoria Weymouth, Mohammed al Fayed and Arcadia, designing office and retail space, while Miv trained at Burberry's, Haymarket as a display artist.

After working for many years as a set- and costume-designer for films in the UK, Miv and her family (including daughter Naomi Watts, the acclaimed actress) emigrated to Australia where Miv continued her design work for television, returning to England and moving to Norfolk where she decided to diversify into the interior design business. Clients such as Omar Sharif, Lee Remick, David Essex, the Marquis of Chomondeley, Viscount Coke at Holkham, the Everyman theatre in Hampstead and

hotels such as The Victoria in Holkham – a refurbishment that helped the hotel earn a place in *Tatler's* list of the top 100 hotels in the world – can attest to her skills in refurbishment and design. Her eye is unfailing and her enthusiasm positively infectious. She first opened House Bait – selling ready-made soft furnishings, nightwear, Cote Bastide bath products and candles, Madeleine Spencer jewellery and an select range of giftware - then added House Bait II to offer customers a range of unusual but always tasteful and expertly crafted antiques and decorative items for the home.

The motto for the shops – 'House Bait – Beautiful reasons for staying at home' takes as its inspiration William Morris's famous epithet 'Have nothing in your house that you do not know to be useful or believe to be beautiful.' These are words to live by, brought to life in this exquisite shop. Friendly, casual and professional, Zara and Miv have created a shop where ideas and inspiration for making each room of your house a true expression of the comfort, relaxation, warmth and fun that the word 'home' evokes.

## THE LORD NELSON

Walsingham Road, Burnham Thorpe,
Norfolk PE31 8HL
Tel/Fax: 01328 738241
e-mail: enquiries@nelsonslocal.co.uk
website: www.nelsonslocal.co.uk

The Lord Nelson is a marvellous 17ᵗʰ-century traditional inn offering the very best in food, drink and hospitality. Original features such as the flagstone floors, wooden settles and open fires guarantee this distinguished pub's ambience. Guests are invited to try the famous (or infamous!) 'Nelson's Blood', a secret recipe of rum and mixed spices made and sold only on the premises, or can of course partake in any of the excellent range of Real Ales -straight from the barrel, wines and spirits sold here.

The food has been awarded the AA rosette, with a menu of delicious and hearty traditional favourites and more innovative dishes expertly prepared, including fresh local seafood. Booking advised at lunch (12 – 2) and dinner (7 – 9). Lord Nelson himself used to visit what is now the bar, while in the no-smoking dining area the walls are adorned with original paintings and prints depicting Nelson and his seafaring exploits. There is also a self-contained dining room that seats up to 45 and can be used for private functions and meetings, and a spacious garden area complete with children's play equipment.

that Burnham Thorpe was the birthplace of Horatio Nelson. His father, the Revd Edmund Nelson, was the Rector here for 46 years; Horatio was the sixth of his eleven children.

Parsonage House, where Horatio was born seven weeks' premature in 1758, was demolished during his lifetime, but the pub (one of more than 200 hostelries across the country bearing the hero's name) has become a kind of shrine to Nelson's memory, its walls covered with portraits, battle scenes and other marine paintings.

There's more Nelson memorabilia in the church, among it a crucifix and lectern made with wood from *HMS Victory*, a great chest from the pulpit used by the Revd Nelson, and two flags from *HMS Nelson*. Every year on Trafalgar Day, October 21st, members of the Nelson Society gather at this riverside church for a service in commemoration of the man

who had specified in his will that he wanted to be buried in its country graveyard 'unless the King decrees otherwise'. George III did indeed decree otherwise, and the great hero was interred in St Paul's Cathedral.

A little over a mile to the south of Burnham Thorpe stand the picturesque ruins of **Creake Abbey** (English Heritage, free), an Augustinian monastery founded in 1206. The Abbey's working life came to an abrupt end in 1504 when, within a single week, every one of the monks died of the plague.

## BURNHAM MARKET

### 9 miles E of Hunstanton on the B1155

There are seven Burnhams in all, strung along the valley of the little River Burn. Burnham Market is the largest of them, its past importance reflected in the wealth of Georgian buildings surrounding the green and the two

churches that lie at each
end of its broad main
street, just 600 yards
apart. In the opinion of
many, Burnham Market
has the best collection of
small Georgian houses in
Norfolk, and it's a delight
to wander through the
yards and alleys that link
the town's three east—
west streets.

Burnham Overy

Burnham Market also
boasts two excellent
bookshops and probably
the best hat shop in the
county. Auctions are held
on the village green every other Monday
in summer.

## BRANCASTER STAITHE

**9 miles NE of Hunstanton on the A149**

In Roman times a castle was built near
Brancaster to try and control the Iceni,
Boudicca's turbulent tribe. Nothing of it
remains, although a Romano-British
cemetery was discovered nearby in 1960.
In the 18th century, this delightful
village was a port of some standing,
hence the 'Staithe', or quay, in its name.
The waterborne traffic in the harbour is
now almost exclusively pleasure craft,
although whelks are still dredged from
the sea bed, 15 miles out, and mussels are

farmed in the harbour itself.

From the harbour a short boat trip will
take you to Scolt Head Island (National
Trust), a three-and-a-half mile sand and
shingle bar separated from the mainland
by a narrow tidal creek. It was originally
much smaller, but over the centuries
deposits of silt and sand have steadily
increased its size, and continue to do so.
Scolt Head is home to England's largest
colony of Sandwich terns, who flock
here to breed during May, June and July.
A Nature Trail leads past the ternery
(closed during the breeding season) and
on to a fascinating area where a rich
variety of plantlife and wildlife abounds.
During the summer the sea asters, sea

## STAITHE ANTIQUES

Main Road, Brancaster Staithe, Norfolk  PE31 8BJ
Tel: 01485 210600

Step back in time at **Staithe Antiques** where Georgian,
Regency and Victorian mahogany, walnut and oak
furniture are the speciality. The selection is ever changing
and is complemented by an interesting selection of clocks,
paintings, prints, porcelain, pottery and glassware. Walk
through the dining room which houses antique pine
furniture, treen, bygones and collectables, and carry on
into the garden area for a range of garden statuary,
benches, tables, urns and pots. Open 7 days a week.

## THE TITCHWELL MANOR HOTEL

Titchwell, Brancaster, King's Lynn, Norfolk PE31 8BB
Tel: 01485 210221 Fax: 01485 210104
e-mail: margaret@titchwellmanor.co.uk
website: www.titchwellmanor.com

On the main coast road (A19) between Hunstanton and
Brancaster, **The Titchwell Manor Hotel** combines the best
of traditional elegance and modern style. The 15 guest
bedrooms are charming and gracious, with all home comforts
and luxury touches that will delight every guest. Seven rooms
are on the ground floor; some offer superb views across the marshes to the sea. The guests' lounge and
bar are perfect for relaxing; the manor is renowned for its excellent food which makes use of the very
best local produce including fresh fish and seafood.

lavender and sea pinks put on a colourful display, attracting many different types of moths and butterflies.

## TITCHWELL

**7 miles E of Hunstanton on the A149**

Perhaps in keeping with the village's name, the church of **St Mary** at Titchwell is quite tiny - and very pretty indeed. Its circular, probably Norman tower is topped by a little 'whisker' of a spire, and inside is some fine late 19th century glass.

Just to the west of the village is a path leading to **Titchwell Marsh**, a nationally important RSPB reserve comprising some 420 acres of shingle beach, reed beds, freshwater and salt-marsh. These different habitats encourage a wide variety of birds to visit the area throughout the year, and many of them breed on or around the reserve. Brent geese, ringed plovers, marsh harriers, terns, waders and shore larks may all be seen, and two of the three hides available are accessible to wheelchairs.

## DOCKING

**9 miles SE of Hunstanton on the B1454 & B1153**

One of the larger inland villages, Docking was at one time called Dry Docking because, perched on a hilltop 300 feet above sea level, it had no water supply of its own. The nearest permanent stream was at Fring, almost three miles away, so in 1760 the villagers began boring for a well. They had to dig some 230 feet down before they finally struck water, which was then sold at a farthing

## NORFOLK BARN

Brancaster Road, Docking, Norfolk PE31 8NB
Tel: 01485 518846 Fax: 01485 518851 website:
www.norfolkbarn.co.uk

The **Norfolk Barn** is a very interesting reclamation yard and
antiques centre featuring an extensive and varied range of
reclaimed materials including bricks, tiles, slates, pamments,
oak beams, sleepers, yorkstone and more, with constantly
changing stock. For the garden, there is a selection of pots,
urns, statuary, chimney pots, tables and benches. In the
showroom are stripped pine doors, fireplaces and bathroom
fittings plus a range of traditionally crafted ironmongery. Furniture is predominantly antique pine
and includes tables, chairs, dressers, chests of drawers, wardrobes, desks etc. with paintings, prints,
bygones and collectables to brighten your home. Open 7 days a week.

## PILGRIMS REACH RESTAURANT AND FREEHOUSE

High Street, Docking, Norfolk  PE31 8NH
Tel: 01485 518383

**Pilgrims Reach Restaurant and Freehouse** on the edge of the
village of Docking is certainly worth making a pilgrimage to
for its excellent food and drink, attentive service and hospitality.
There's a relaxed and welcoming atmosphere at this jolly inn,
owned and run by James Lee. Together with his friendly, helpful
staff, he offers the very best in hospitality to all his guests.

The restaurant is housed in a traditional Norfolk building
of brick, chalk and flint, parts of which are believed to date
back to the 16th century. The interior is adorned with some
fascinating local memorabilia: old hand tools, eel picks, the tools of the shepherd's trade, old implements
used by marshmen and thatchers – all relating to a bygone Norfolk when life was lived at a gentler pace.
A collection of old photographs of wherries and punts on the Norfolk Broads, and sailing vessels and
lifeboats on the Norfolk coast, enhance the strong 'local flavour' of the place.

Flavours of an altogether more fulsome kind are in evidence on the quite outstanding menu, in
which fish dishes have pride of place – Narborough trout with a Sauternes and dill butter sauce, for
example, or baked fillet of cod stuffed with asparagus and prawns. If mussels are on the menu, only a
couple of hours may have elapsed between their being harvested and served up on your plate. There's a
special mussel menu in winter, a crab menu in summer. For guests who'd prefer to have meat, poultry or
vegetarian dishes, the menu can oblige with organically-reared Norfolk Red Poll beef, Norfolk venison
and game. Delicious poultry and vegetarian dishes are also available. All make use of top-quality
ingredients, meticulously prepared.

A great deal of expert knowledge has also shaped the wine list, and the Woodfordes Brewery supplies
a range of real ales. Other potables include a selection of lagers, spirits and soft drinks.

Pilgrims Reach is open Monday and Wednesday to Saturday 7 – 11 p.m.; Sundays 12.00 – 2.30 and
7 – 10.30 p.m. Closed Tuesdays.

## HOLLAND HOUSE

Chequers Street, Docking, Norfolk PE31 8LH
Tel: 01485 518335
e-mail: HHouseDocking@aol.com

Built between 1720 and 1750, **Holland House** has during its long and distinguished lifetime been the village meeting house, a dowager house and a family home. Today it is a gracious and charming place to choose for accommodation, with three guest bedrooms (two doubles and a family suite), a private guests' lounge and lovely dining room. One of the double rooms boasts a four-poster bed, all have private amenities, and all are sumptuously and comfortably decorated and furnished. Located near the village church, there is ample off-road parking and a splendid walled garden where guests are welcome to roam to their hearts' content.

This lovely old rambling house, though large, retains the feeling of a cosy family home. The interior has been lovingly restored by owners Karen and Mitch, who together offer all guests a warm welcome and genuine hospitality. In the guests' lounge there are framed specimens of wallpaper uncovered during restoration work that date from 1785 and 1840. The lamps outside the main door are original from London Bridge; other 'finds' include the copper boiler set in a brick surround dating from 1800 – all of these features add to the charm and cosiness of this superior establishment.

(0.1p) per bucket. A pump was installed in 1928, but a mains supply didn't reach Docking until the 1930s.

## HOLME-NEXT-THE-SEA

**3 miles NE of Hunstanton off the A149**

This village is notable chiefly as the northern end of the **Peddar's Way**, the 50-mile pedestrian trail that starts at the Suffolk border near Thetford and, almost arrow-straight for much of its length, slices across northwest Norfolk to Holme, with only an occasional deviation to negotiate a necessary ford or bridge. This determinedly straight route was already long-trodden for centuries before the Romans arrived, but they incorporated long stretches of it into their own network of roads. It was from the Latin word *pedester* that the route takes its name. With few gradients of any consequence to negotiate, the Peddar's Way is ideal for the casual walker. At

Holme, the Peddar's Way meets with the Norfolk Coastal Footpath, a much more recent creation. Starting at Hunstanton, it closely follows the coastline all the way to Cromer.

Holme-next-the-Sea is of course famous in part as the site of 'Sea Henge', a 4,500-year-old Bronze Age tree circle discovered on Holme Beach. This early religious monument was removed by English Heritage for study and preservation to Flag Fen, Peterborough, though after its restoration it is hoped that it will be returned to Holme.

## RINGSTEAD

**3 miles E of Hunstanton off the A149**

Another appealing village, with pink and white-washed cottages built in wonderfully decorative Norfolk carrstone. A rare Norman round tower, all that survives of St Peter's church, stands in the grounds of the former

## THE GIN TRAP INN

6 High Street, Ringstead, Hunstanton,
Norfolk  NPE36 5JU
Tel: 01485 525624  Fax: 01485 525321
e-mail: info@gintrap.co.uk
website: www.gintrap.co.uk

The delightfully-named **Gin Trap Inn** is a haven of rural peace and tranquillity. This lovely country inn with rooms and self-catering cottages dates back to the 17th century, when it began life as a coaching inn for weary travellers making their way through rural Norfolk, and is located in a quiet village on the Peddar's Way and near the scenic Northwest Norfolk coast.

The bar area of the inn is warm and welcoming, with an open stove and pew bench seating. The ceilings are beamed, and adorned with traditional farming implements. Half of the bar area is no-smoking. This Free House serves a range of Woodfords cask ales and Adnams ales, as well as 'own label' Gin Trap bitter. There is also an extensive wine list. In the restaurant, locally-sourced organic meats – lamb, pork and beef – are used whenever possible and the menus are changed weekly. They always feature a selection of delicious, freshly prepared home-cooked meals.

Accommodation at this superb inn comprises three spacious en suite double guest bedrooms within the inn itself, and two charming self-catering cottages that sleep up to six. The guest bedrooms are handsomely appointed and tastefully and comfortably decorated and furnished. The cottages have been carefully converted from old farm buildings and are surrounded by beautiful countryside. They boast lovely interiors, decorated and furnished in traditional country house style with supremely comfortable beds, sofas and armchairs, attractive prints, curtains, lamps and everything that will enhance visitors' comfort and enjoyment while staying in this cosy and homely environment. Both have garden furniture and access to nearly an acre of garden.

The inn makes a perfect base from which to explore the many sights and attractions of the region, being within easy distance of the coast, attractive villages, good walking and centres such as King's Lynn. The owners also run The Ringstead Gallery close by.

## RINGSTEAD GALLERY

Ringstead, Hunstanton,
Norfolk PE36 5JZ
Tel: 01485 525316
Fax: 01485 525321
e-mail: ringstead.gallery@btinternet.com
website: www.ringsteadgallery.com

Adjacent to The Gin Trap Inn, **The Ringstead Gallery** is housed in a lovely old whitewashed former stables. With an upstairs gallery and display areas downstairs, this is a showcase for an excellent selection of the work of contemporary artists working in media including oils, watercolours and pastels, bronzes and turned wood. The work in oils and watercolours of renowned artists such as Lawrie

Williamson, Jeremy Barlow, David Greenall, Philip Gardner, Neil Cox and Peter Barker are proudly displayed at this fine gallery, together with sculpture by the likes of Sue Riley and Rosemary Cook, and wood-turned pieces by Richard Chapman. Many of the works capture the beguiling Norfolk landscape.

Owners Don and Margaret Greer are knowledgeable and very helpful with all their visitors. They established this gallery in 1974, at which time the building was derelict. They carefully and tastefully renovated it to provide the perfect setting in which to showcase works of art. The beamed ceilings and excellent lighting enhance the very pleasant experience of wandering through the gallery to admire the many different pieces on display. A wooden staircase leads to the upper floor gallery, which contains a delightful, eclectic range of paintings and sculpture.

From the fine turned wood and oak furniture to the bronzes, sculpture, paintings and limited editions, all the work exhibited bears testimony to a high standard of artistry and craftsmanship. The gallery holds between six and eight one-artist exhibitions throughout the year, as well as ongoing shows featuring the work of several artists. Please telephone for details of opening times.

Rectory and adds to the visual charm.

In a region well-provided with excellent nature reserves, the one on **Ringstead Downs** is particularly attractive, and popular with picnickers. The chalky soil of the valley provides a perfect habitat for the plants that thrive here and for the exquisitely marked butterflies they attract.

### OLD HUNSTANTON

**1 mile N of Hunstanton off the A149**

With its mellow old houses and narrow winding lanes, Old Hunstanton is utterly charming. The sand dunes and creeks provide a perfect habitat for interesting varieties of colourful flora - sea poppies, samphire, marram and sea lavender and more. The glorious sands continue here, and the **Norfolk Coastal Footpath** leads eastwards all the way to Cromer, some 36 miles distant.

### GREAT BIRCHAM

**7 miles SE of Hunstanton off the B1153**

A couple of miles south of Docking stands the five-storey **Great Bircham Windmill**, one of the few in Norfolk to have found a hill to perch on, and it's still working. If you arrive on a day when there's a stiff breeze blowing, the windmill's great arms will be groaning around; on calm days, content yourself with tea and home-made cakes in the tearoom, and take home some bread baked at the Mill's own bakery.

### HEACHAM

**3 miles S of Hunstanton off the A149**

**Heacham Park Fishery** on Pocahontas Lake is set within the original boundary of Heacham Hall. This three-and-a-half acre freshwater late was re-established in 1996. Spring 1997 saw the introduction to the lake of specimen carp, to be followed in 1998 by rudd, bream, perch and roach. The lake takes its name from the renowned Native American princess, who married into the Rolfe family, owners of Heacham Hall, and lived here in the 1600s.

Just outside this charming village is the famous **Norfolk Lavender**, the largest lavender-growing and distilling operation in the country. Established in 1932, it is also the oldest. The information point at the western entrance is sited in an attractive listed building which has become something of a Norfolk landmark. On entering the site, visitors instinctively breathe in, savouring the unmistakable aroma that fills the air. Guided tours of the grounds run throughout the day from the Spring Bank Holiday until the end of September, and during the lavender harvest, visitors can tour the distillery and see how the wonderful fragrance is made.

As well as being a working farm, this is also

*Harvesting Lavender*

the home of the National Collection of Lavenders, a living botanical dictionary which displays the many different colours, sizes and smells of this lovely plant. Amongst other attractions at Norfolk Lavender are a Fragrant Meadow Garden, Fragrant Plant Centre, Herb Garden, a gift shop selling a wide variety of products, and a tearoom serving cream teas and even lavender-and-lemon scones!

## SNETTISHAM
**5 miles S of Hunstanton off the A149**

Snettisham is best known nowadays for its spacious, sandy beaches and the **RSPB Bird Sanctuary**, both about two miles west of the village itself. But for centuries Snettisham was much more famous as a prime quarry for carrstone, an attractive soft-red building-block that provided the 'light relief' for the walls of thousands of Georgian houses around the country, and for nearby Sandringham House. The carrstone quarry is still working, its product now destined mainly for 'goldfish ponds and the entrance-banks of the more pretentious types of bungalow. Unfortunately, one has to go to the British Museum in London to see

Snettisham's greatest gift to the national heritage: an opulent collection of gold and silver ornaments from the 1st century AD, the largest hoard of treasure trove ever found in Britain, discovered here in 1991.

## DERSINGHAM
**7 miles S of Hunstanton off the A149**

This large village just north of Sandringham was actually the source of the latter's name: in the *Domesday Book*, the manor was inscribed as 'Sant-Dersingham'. Norfolk tongues found 'Sandringham' much easier to get around. Dersingham village has expanded greatly in recent years and modern housing has claimed much of Dersingham Common, although there are still many pleasant walks here through **Dersingham Wood** and the adjoining Sandringham Country Park.

## SANDRINGHAM
**8 miles S of Hunstanton off the A149/B1140**

A couple of miles north of Castle Rising is the entrance to **Sandringham Country Park** and **Sandringham House**, the royal family's country retreat. Unlike the State Rooms at Windsor Castle and Buckingham Palace, where visitors marvel at the awesome trappings of majesty, at Sandringham they can savour the atmosphere of a family home. The rooms the visitor sees at Sandringham are those used by the royal family when in residence, complete with family portraits and photographs, and comfy armchairs. Successive royal owners have

*Sandringham House*

## SANDRINGHAM HOUSE

Sandringham, Norfolk PE35 6EN
Tel: 01553 772675  Fax: 01553 541571
e-mail: enquiries@sandringhamestate.co.uk

**Sandringham House** is the charming country retreat of Her Majesty The Queen hidden in the heart of 60 acres of beautiful wooded gardens. Still maintained in the style of Edward and Alexandra, Prince and Princess of Wales (later King Edward VII and Queen Alexandra), all the main ground-floor rooms used by the Royal Family, full of their treasured ornaments, portraits and furniture, are open to the public. More family possessions are displayed in the Museum housed in the old stable and coach houses; these include vehicles ranging in date from the first car owned by a British monarch, a 1900 Daimler, to a half-scale Aston Martin used by Princes William and Harry. A new display tells the mysterious tale of the Sandringham Company, who fought and died at Gallipoli in 1915, recently the subject of a television film *All the King's Men*. A free Land Train from within the entrance will carry passengers less able to walk through the grounds to the House and back.

leather-covered seat, apparently a common amenity in great houses of the 19th century. In the same room, with its attractively carved Minstrels' Gallery, hangs a fine family portrait by one of Queen Victoria's favourite artists, Heinrich von Angeli. It shows the Prince of Wales (later Edward VII), his wife Alexandra and two of their children, with Sandringham in the background.

The Prince first saw Sandringham on 4th February 1862. At Victoria's instigation, the 20-year-old heir to the throne had been searching for some time for a country property, a refuge of the kind his parents already enjoyed at Balmoral and Osborne. A courtier accompanying the Prince reported back that although the outside of the house was ugly, it was pleasant and convenient within, and set in pretty grounds. The surrounding countryside was plain, he went on, but the property was in excellent order and the opportunity of securing it should not be missed. Within days, the purchase

furnished the house with an intriguing medley of the grand, the domestic and the unusual. Entering the principal reception room, The Saloon, for example, you pass a weighing-machine with a

was completed.

Most of the 'ugly' house disappeared a few years later when the Prince rebuilt the main residence; the 'pretty grounds' have matured into one of the most beautiful landscaped areas in the country. And the 'plain' countryside around - open heath and grassland overrun by rabbits - has been transformed into a wooded country park, part of the coastal Area of Outstanding Natural Beauty.

One of the additions the Prince made to the house in 1883 was a Ballroom, much to the relief of Princess Alexandra. 'It is beautiful I think & a great success.' she wrote, '& avoids pulling the hall to pieces each time there is a ball or anything'. This attractive room is now used for cinema shows and the estate workers' Christmas party. Displayed on the walls is a remarkable collection of Indian weapons, presented to the Prince during his state visit in 1875-6; hidden away in a recess are the two flags planted at the South Pole by the Shackleton expedition.

Just across from the house, the old coach-houses and stables have been converted into a fascinating museum. There are some truly splendid royal vehicles here, including the first car bought by a member of the royal family - a 1900 Daimler - and an evocative series of old photographs depicting the life of the royal family at Sandringham from 1862 until Christmas 1951. Other attractions at Sandringham include a visitors centre, adventure playground, nature walks, souvenir shop, restaurant and tearoom.

# LOCATOR MAP

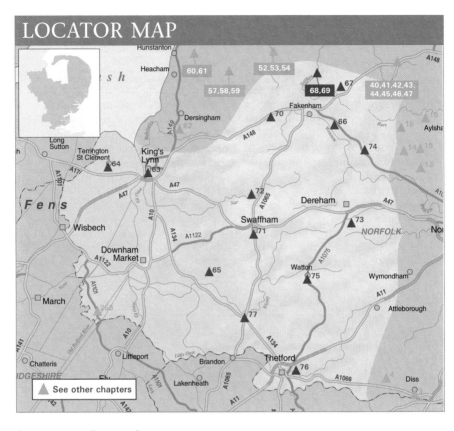

▲ See other chapters

Advertisers and Places of Interest

63  Doric Arts Gallery & Framing Workshop,
     King's Lynn                                    Page 80
64  Japanese Garden, Terrington St Clement,
     King's Lynn                                    Page 83
65  Oxburgh Hall, Oxburgh,
     King's Lynn                                    Page 87
66  Pensthorpe Waterfowl Park & Nature Reserve,
     Pensthorpe, Fakenham                           Page 88
67  The Thursford Collection, Thursford,
     Fakenham                                       Page 89
68  The Wells Deli Company,
     Little Walsingham                              Page 90
69  Walsingham Shirehall Museum
     & Abbey Grounds,
     Little Walsingham                              Page 91

70  Daphne Cooper at Millstone,
     East Rudham                                    Page 93
71  Swaffham Museum, Swaffham                       Page 95
72  The Post House, Stocks Green,
     Castle Acre                                    Page 97
73  Clinton House & Cottage, Yaxham,
     Dereham                                        Page 98
74  Moor Farm Stable Cottages, Foxley,
     Dereham                                        Page 100
75  Peter Conoley & Son, Watton,
     Thetford                                       Page 101
76  Thetford Garden Centre, Kilverstone,
     Thetford                                       Page 103
77  Lynford Hall Country House Hotel,
     Mundford, Thetford                             Page 104

# KING'S LYNN AND WEST NORFOLK   3

It may surprise readers to learn that King's Lynn, on the Great Ouse three miles inland from The Wash, was one of England's most important ports in medieval times, sitting at the southern end of an underwater maze of sandbanks. Keels were shallower then, of course, but without such modern aids as echo-sounders it must still have taken sailing skills of a high order to navigate one's way into the safety of King's Lynn harbour. Along most of The Wash's 50-mile shoreline there is no human habitation: good news for the more than 160,000 wading birds and 51,000 wild ducks who have claimed the coast for themselves. To the northeast of King's Lynn is the prosperous market town of Fakenham, around which lie a remarkable variety of places of interest. To the north, in the valley of the River Stiffkey, the Shrine of Our Lady of Walsingham was in medieval times second only to that of Thomas à Becket at Canterbury as a pilgrim destination. To the northeast, the Thursford Collection is home to an astonishing gathering of steam-powered engines of every description, including a monumental Wurlitzer organ. On the eastern outskirts of the town you can visit the premier collection of endangered and exotic waterbirds to be found in Europe, and over to the west stands the Marquess of Cholmondely's majestic home, Houghton Hall.

*Drainage Windmill, Norfolk*

South of King's Lynn, the countryside never quite decides whether it belongs to the Cambridgeshire fenland, with its bread-board level contours and over-arching skyscapes, or to the subtly-rounded undulations of central Norfolk where each twist of the road reveals yet another unblemished rural scene.

Breckland, which extends for more than 360 square miles in southwest Norfolk and northwest Suffolk, is underlain by chalk with only a light covering of soil. The name 'Breckland' comes from the dialect word *breck*, meaning an area of land which has been cultivated for a while and then allowed to revert to heath after the soil has become exhausted. This quiet corner of the county is bounded by the Rivers Little Ouse and Waveney, which separate Norfolk from Suffolk.

# KING'S LYNN

In the opinion of James Lee-Milne, the National Trust's architectural authority, 'The finest old streets anywhere in England' are to be found at King's Lynn. Tudor, Jacobean and Flemish houses mingle harmoniously with grand medieval churches and stately civic buildings. It's not surprising that the BBC chose the town to represent early 19th century London in their production of *Martin Chuzzlewit*. It seems, though, that word of this ancient sea-port's many treasures has not yet been widely broadcast, so most visitors to the area tend to stay on the King's Lynn bypass while making their way to the better-known attractions of the north Norfolk coast. They are missing a lot.

The best place to start an exploration of the town is at the beautiful church of **St Margaret**, founded in 1101 and with a remarkable leaning arch of that original building still intact. The architecture is impressive, but the church is especially famous for its two outstanding 14th century brasses, generally reckoned to be the two largest and most monumental in the kingdom. Richly engraved, one shows workers in a vineyard, the other, commemorating Robert Braunche, represents the great feast which Robert hosted at King's Lynn for Edward III in 1364.

Marks on the tower doorway indicate the church's, and the town's, vulnerability to the waters of the Wash and the River Great Ouse. They show the high-water levels reached during the great floods of 11 March 1883 (the lowest), 31 January 1953 and 11 January, 1978.

The organist at St Margaret's in the mid 18th century was the celebrated writer on music, Dr Charles Burney, but

## DORIC ARTS GALLERY AND FRAMING WORKSHOP

5 King Street, King's Lynn, Norfolk  PE30 1ET
Tel/Fax: 01553 777960
e-mail: rbatdoricarts@aol.com

Just a few yards from the Custom House Tourist Information Centre and a short walk from the historic wharf area and Green Quay Museum, **Doric Arts Gallery and Framing Workshop** is well worth a visit.

For owner Russell Boulter, a lifelong interest in art and photography has found its fulfilment in this gallery. Together with business partner Clare Walker, who has 20 years' experience in gallery work and expertise in fine art framing, they have made this a success. The gallery specialises in contemporary and 20th century art, including original prints, etchings, ceramics and sculpture. The collection also include large outdoor pieces

in various media – stone, steel, bronze and wood.

The gallery hosts regularly changing exhibitions of themed group and solo shows throughout the year. The gallery also supports major art festivals in the area including the King's Lynn Festival.

The framing workshop offers a very special bespoke service, the opportunity for clients to work closely with the gallery to form a creative partnership. Choosing from a vast range of frames from contemporary to classical mouldings, customers are sure to find a style and design that suits their taste and budget.

*Kings Lynn Tuesday Market*

his daughter Fanny was perhaps even more interesting. She wrote a best-selling novel, *Evelina*, at the age of 25, became a leading light of London society, a close friend of Dr Johnson and Sir Joshua Reynolds, and at the age of 59 underwent an operation for breast cancer without anaesthetic. She only fainted once during the 20-minute operation, and went on to continue her active social life until her death at the ripe old age of 87.

Alongside the north wall of St Margaret's is the **Saturday Market Place**, one of the town's two market places, where visitors can explore The Old Gaol House, an experience complete with the sights and sounds of the ancient cells. A few steps further is one of the most striking sights in the town, the **Guildhall of the Holy Trinity** with its distinctive chequerboard design of black flint and white stone. The Guildhall was built in 1421, extended in Elizabethan times, and its Great Hall is still used today for wedding ceremonies and various civic events.

Next door to the Guildhall is the Town Hall of 1895, which in a good-neighbourly way is constructed in the same flint-and-stone pattern. The Town Hall also houses the **Museum of Lynn Life** where, along with displays telling the story of the town's 900 years, you can also admire the municipal regalia. The greatest treasure in this collection is King John's Cup, a dazzling piece of medieval workmanship with coloured enamel scenes set in gold. The Cup was supposed to be part of King John's treasure which had been lost in 1215 when his overburdened baggage train was crossing the Nene Estuary and sank into the treacherous quicksands. This venerable legend is sadly undermined by the fact that the Cup was not made until 1340, more than a century after John's death.

A short distance from the Town Hall, standing proudly by itself on the banks of the River Purfleet, is the handsome **Custom House** of 1683, designed by the celebrated local architect Henry Bell.

There's not enough space here to list all of the town's many other important buildings, but mention must be made of the **Hanseatic Warehouse** (1428), the **South Gate** (1440), the **Greenland Fishery Building** (1605), and the **Guildhall of St George**, built around 1406 and reputedly the oldest civic hall in England. The Hall was from time to time also used as a theatre; it's known that Shakespeare's travelling company played here, and is considered highly likely that the Bard himself trod the boards. If true, his appearance would be very appropriate, since the Guildhall is now home to the **King's Lynn Arts**

**Centre**, active all year round with events and exhibitions and since 1951 the force behind an annual Arts Festival in July with concerts, theatre and a composer in residence. Some of the concerts are held in St Nicholas' Chapel, a medieval building whose acoustics outmatch those of many a modern concert hall.

At **Caithness Crystal** Visitor Centre, you can watch craftsmen at close quarters as they shape and manipulate glass into beautiful objets d'art.

## AROUND KING'S LYNN

### Castle Rising
**5 miles NE of King's Lynn off the A148/A149**

As the bells ring for Sunday morning service at Castle Rising, a group of elderly ladies leave the mellow redbrick Bede House and walk in procession to the church. They are all dressed in long scarlet cloaks, emblazoned on the left breast with a badge of the Howard family arms. Once a year, on Founder's Day, they add to their regular Sunday costume a tall-crowned hat typical of the Jacobean period, just like those worn in stereotypical pictures of broomstick-flying witches.

These ladies are the residents of the almshouses founded by Henry Howard, Earl of Northampton in 1614, and their regular Sunday attendance at church was one of the conditions he imposed on the original 11 needy spinsters who were to enjoy his beneficence. Howard also required that each inmate of his 'Hospital of the Holy and Undivided Trinity' must also 'be able to read, if such a one may be had, single, 56 at least, no common beggar, harlot, scold, drunkard, haunter of taverns, inns or alehouses'.

The weekly *tableau vivant* of this procession to the church seems

*The Castle, Castle Rising*

completely in keeping with this picturesque village, which rates high on any 'not to be missed' list of places to visit in Norfolk. The church to which the women make their way, St Lawrence's, is an outstanding example of Norman and Early English work, even though much of it has been reconstructed. But overshadowing everything else in this pretty village is the massive **Castle Keep** (English Heritage), its well-preserved walls rising 50 feet high, and pierced by a single entrance. The Keep's towering presence is made even more formidable by the huge earthworks on which it stands. The Castle was built in 1150, guarding what was then the sea approach to the River Ouse. (The marshy shore is now some three miles distant and still retreating.)

Despite its fortress-like appearance, Castle Rising was much more of a residential building than a defensive one. In 1331, when Edward III found it necessary to banish his ferocious French-born mother, Isabella, to some reasonably comfortable place of safety, he chose this far-from-London castle. She was to spend some 27 years here before her death in 1358, never seeing her son again during that time. How could Edward treat his own mother in such a way? Her crime, in his view, was that the 'She-Wolf of France', as all her enemies and many of her friends called Isabella, had joined forces with her lover Mortimer against her homosexual husband Edward II (young Edward's father) and later colluded in the king's grisly murder at Berkeley Castle. A red-hot poker, inserted anally, was the instrument of his death. For three years after that loathsome assassination,

Isabella and Mortimer ruled England as Regents. The moment Edward III achieved his majority, he had Mortimer hung, drawn and quartered. His mother he despatched to a lonely retirement at Castle Rising.

Six and a half centuries later, the spacious grounds around the castle provide an appropriate backdrop for an annual display by members of the White Society. Caparisoned in colourful medieval garments and armed with more-or-less authentic replicas of swords and halberds, these modern White Knights stage a battle for control of the castle.

## TERRINGTON ST CLEMENT

**6 miles W of King's Lynn off the A17**

Terrington St Clement is a sizable village notable for the '**Cathedral of the Marshland**', a 14th century Gothic masterwork more properly known as St Clement's church, and for the **African**

## JAPANESE GARDEN

22 Chapel Road, Terrington St Clement, King's Lynn, Norfolk PE34 4ND
Tel/Fax: 01553 828874
website: www.rhs.org.uk

For a truly comprehensive range of rare and unusual Japanese plants, the **Japanese Garden** at Ornamental Conifers Specialist Nursery is the place to go. Here visitors have the chance to see a one-acre Japanese garden in all its glory, to glean planting ideas and advice from the knowledgeable, helpful staff, and to buy from the wide range of plants in stock. These include slow-growing Hinoki cypresses in containers, Japanese acers, bamboo, bonsai and more, including Japanese garden ornaments.

Advice on maintenance and cultivation is available, and the

specialist bed-/garden-planning service will help you design your bed or garden before you buy the plants to turn it into a reality. The nursery's one-acre site offers probably the largest selection of container-grown evergreen plants in Norfolk, with over 300 varieties available throughout the year. Entry to the garden is free, and it is open 6 days per week (closed Wednesdays) from 9.30 – 5 (closed 21st December to 1st February).

# Shouldham Warren

| | |
|---|---|
| **Distance:** | 3.1 miles (4.83 kilometres) |
| **Typical time:** | 90 mins |
| **Height gain:** | 10 metres |
| **Map:** | Explorer 236 |
| **Walk:** | www.walkingworld.com ID:2108 |
| **Contributor:** | Joy & Charles Boldero |

## Access Information:

Norfolk Bus routes: Freecall 0500 626116 9a.m. to 5p.m. Monday to Friday to the village of Shouldham. You can start the walk from Point 6 at *. However the walk starts at the free Forestry car park at Shouldham Warren. The village of Shouldham is situated 2 miles north of the A1122 at Fincham which is 8 miles west of Swaffham. To reach the Warren go north up Eastgate Street out of the village and keep ahead along rough track where road goes right.

## Description:

The outward route is through woodland to Shouldham village and back by country lanes through the village. There is an excellent pub, the King's Arms, which has an extensive menu

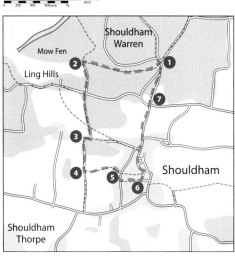

and is open every day. The famous October conker championships used to take place at the King's Arms. Many centuries ago Shouldham, was famous for the healing waters of the Chalybeate spring, a natural mineral water which was impregnated with iron salts. Shouldham was also a popular place centuries ago for its market and fair held each autumn time.

## Features:

Pub, Toilets, Church, Wildlife, Birds, Flowers, Great Views, Butterflies, Food Shop

## Walk Directions:

**1** From the Forestry notice board go back along the track for a very short distance. Turn right immediately after the flat concrete with these markings on it. SU-WO-24 &6. Keep the deep ditch on the left. It is advisable in hot weather to keep dogs to the main path as adders could be in the bracken beside the path. The smell of the fox is quite strong along here!

**2** Go round the barrier and turn left over the wide earth bridge. Go along a tree-lined path, take either path at the fork. Cross the track and continue along the track opposite.

**3** At a T junction of tracks turn right with a farm house ahead. After about 70 paces turn left along another track.

**4** At the finger post sign turn left along a wide grass path between fields with houses ahead. Go through a gate, continue along a narrower path, then driveway, then track.

**5** Turn right along the village street. Opposite 'The Cottage' at the finger post sign turn left along a tarmac lane.

**6** At the T junction turn right along a lane. Turn left opposite the King's Arms in Shouldham beside the Green with an old village pump on it (* You could start the walk from here). Turn left along Eastgate Street, continue along New Road and Warren Road.

**7** At the righthand bend - Spring Lane, keep straight ahead along a wide track to the start of the walk.

Violet Centre, where some quarter of a million violets are grown each year, in a wide range of colour and species.

## DOWNHAM MARKET

### 10 miles S of King's Lynn off the A10/A1122

Once the site for a major horse fair, this compact little market town stands at the very edge of the Fens, with the River Great Ouse and the New Bedford Drain running side by side at its western edge. Many of its houses are built in the distinctive brick and carrstone style of the area. One of the finest examples of this traditional use of local materials can be seen at Dial House in Railway Road, built in the late 1600s.

The parish church has managed to find a small hill on which to perch. It's an unassuming building with a rather incongruously splendid glass chandelier from the 1730s. Another feature of the town, much loved by postcard manufacturers, is the elegant, riotously decorated cast-iron **Clock Tower** in the market place. This was erected in 1878 at a cost of £450. The tower's backdrop of attractive cottages provides a charming setting for a holiday snap.

Two great names are associated with this small town: Charles I, disguised as a clergyman, stayed at Downham Market for a night during his flight after the Battle of Naseby, and Horatio (later Lord) Nelson, son of the parson of Burnham Thorpe, was sent to the little school here.

Near Downham Bridge on the A1122 you will find **Collectors World** and the **Magical Dickens World**. The first boasts a plethora of farming and household memorabilia, carts, carriages, radios, cameras, antique and collectible dolls, Armstrong Siddeley cars and much more, with rooms dedicated to Barbara Cartland, Horatio Nelson, the 1960s and more. Dickens World offers visitors a chance to step back in time into a maze of late 19th century streets, shops, sights and sounds.

## STOW BARDOLPH

### 8 miles S of King's Lynn off the A10

**Holy Trinity** church at Stow Bardolph houses one of the oddest memorials in the country. Before her death in 1744, Sarah Hare, youngest daughter of the Lord of the Manor, Sir Thomas Hare, arranged for a life-sized effigy of herself to be made in wax. It was said to be an exceptionally good likeness: if so, Sarah appears to have been a rather uncomely maiden, and afflicted with boils to boot. Her death was attributed to blood poisoning after she had pricked her finger with a needle, an act of Divine retribution, apparently, for her sin of sewing on a Sunday. Sarah was then attired in a dress she had chosen herself, placed in a windowed mahogany cabinet, and the monument set up in the Hare family's chapel, a grandiose structure which is larger than the chancel of the church itself.

## DENVER

### 2 miles S of Downham Market off the A10/A1122

**Denver Sluice** was originally built in 1651 by the Dutch engineer, Cornelius Vermuyden, as part of a scheme to drain 20,000 acres of land owned by the Duke of Bedford. Various modifications were made to the system over the years, but the principle remains the same, and the oldest surviving sluice, built in 1834, is still in use today. Running parallel with it is the modern **Great Denver Sluice**, opened in 1964; together these two sluices control the flow of a large complex of rivers and drainage channels, and are able to divert floodwaters into the Flood Relief Channel that runs alongside the Great Ouse.

The two great drainage cuts constructed by Vermuyden are known as the Old and New Bedford rivers, and the strip of land between them, never more than 1,000 yards wide, is called the Ouse Washes. This is deliberately allowed to flood during the winter months so that the fields on either side remain dry. The drains run side by side for more than 13 miles, to Earith in Cambridgeshire, and this has become a favourite route for walkers, with a rich variety of bird, animal and insect life to be seen along the way.

**Denver Windmill**, built in 1835 but put out of commission in 1941, when the sails were struck by lightning, re-opened in 2000. This wonderful working mill set on the edge of the Fens has been carefully restored. On-site attractions include a visitor centre, craft workshops,

*Denver Windmill*

bakery and tea shop. Holiday accommodation is also available.

### HILGAY
**3 miles S of Downham Market off the A10**

When the *Domesday Book* was written, Hilgay was recorded as one of only two settlements in the Norfolk fens. It was then an island, its few houses planted on a low hill rising from the surrounding marshland. The village is scarcely any larger today, and collectors of unusual gravestones make their way to its churchyard seeking the last resting place of George William Manby. During the Napoleonic wars, Manby invented a rocket-powered life-line that could be fired to ships in distress. His gravestone is carved with a ship, an anchor, a depiction of his rocket device and an inscription that ends with the reproachful words, 'The public should have paid this tribute.'

### OXBOROUGH
**10 miles SE of Downham Market off the A134**

How many hamlets in the country, one wonders, can boast two such different buildings of note as those to be seen at Oxborough? First there's the church of **St John the Evangelist**, remarkable for its rare brass eagle lectern of 1498 and its glorious Bedingfeld Chapel of 1525, sheltering twin monuments to Sir Edmund Bedingfeld and his wife fashioned in the then-newly popular material of terracotta.

It was Sir Edmund who built **Oxburgh Hall** (National Trust), a breathtakingly lovely moated house built of pale-rose brick and white stone. Sir Edmund's descendants still live in what a later architect, Pugin, described as 'one of the noblest specimens of domestic architecture of the 15th century.' Henry VII and his Queen, Elizabeth of York, visited in 1487 and lodged in the splendid State Apartments which form a bridge between the lofty gatehouse towers, and ever since have been known as the King's Room and the Queen's Room. On display here is the original Charter of 1482, affixed with Edward IV's Great Seal of England, granting Sir Edmund permission to build with 'stone, lime and sand', and to fortify the building with battlements. These rooms also house some magnificent period furniture, a collection of royal letters to the Bedingfelds, and the huge Sheldon Tapestry Map of 1647 showing Oxfordshire and Berkshire.

Another more poignant tapestry, known as the Marian Needlework, was the joint handiwork of Elizabeth, Countess of Shrewsbury, and Mary, Queen of Scots, during the latter's captivity here in 1570. The Bedingfelds seemed always to draw the short straw when the Tudors needed someone to discharge an unpleasant or difficult task. It was an earlier Sir Edmund who was charged with the care of Henry VIII's discarded wife, Catherine of Aragon; Edmund's son, Sir Henry, was given the even more onerous task of looking after the King's official bastard, the Princess Elizabeth. After Elizabeth's accession as Queen, Sir Henry presented himself at Court, no doubt with some misgivings. Elizabeth received him civilly but, as he was leaving, tartly observed that 'if we have any prisoner whom we would have hardlie and strictly kept, we will send him to you.'

## OXBURGH HALL

Garden and Estate, Oxborough, King's Lynn PE33 9PS
Tel: 01366 328258  Fax: 01366 328066

**Oxburgh Hall** is a lovely moated house built in 1482 at the end of the War of the Roses by the Bedingfeld family who still live here and given to the National Trust in 1952. The Bedingfelds moved in the dangerous world of Tudor high politics and the second Sir Edmund guarded Henry VIII's first queen, Catherine of Aragon. In later times, the family were fined for their Catholic faith and allegiance to King Charles.

The tranquil moat and well kept gardens make an unforgettable first impression. The gardens' most striking feature is a French parterre laid out by the 6th

© NTPL

Baronet and his wife c 1845. The Hall has a magnificent Gatehouse, a masterpiece of late medieval brickwork. Despite the moat and battlements, Sir Edmund Bedingfeld built it to impress rather than to exclude. From the battlements you can take in the Norfolk landscape. Henry VII and his Queen, Elizabeth of York, stayed here in 1487.

Inside, there are many rooms and items of note. The south passage reflects the 6th Baronet's fascination in heraldry and much of the furniture is dark and carved, emphasising the medieval origins of Oxburgh. An interesting architectural feature is a circular brick staircase and you can also see a priest's hole, where Sir Henry hid his fellow Catholics suffering persecution under Elizabeth I. Needlework panels, arriving at Oxburgh as part of a dowry, were worked by Mary Queen of Scots and Bess of Hardwick. The library still has its original 1850s decoration and fittings including the flock-on-gilt wallpaper.

© NTPL

As staunch Catholics, the Bedingfelds were, for the next two and a half centuries, consigned to the margins of English political life. Their estates dwindled as portions were sold to meet the punitive taxes imposed on adherents of the Old Faith. By the middle of the 20th century, the Bedingfelds long tenure of Oxburgh was drawing to a close. In 1951 the 9th Baronet, another Sir Edmund, sold Oxburgh to a builder, who promptly announced his intention of demolishing the house. Sir Edmund's mother, the Dowager Lady Sybil, was shocked by such vandalism and used her considerable powers of persuasion to raise sufficient funds to buy back the house. She then conveyed it into the safe keeping of the National Trust.

The grounds at Oxburgh provide the perfect foil for the mellow old building, reflected in its broad moat. There's a wonderfully formal and colourful French garden, a walled kitchen garden, and woodland walks.

## FAKENHAM

Fakenham is a busy and prosperous-looking market town, famous for its National Hunt Racecourse, antique & bric-a-brac markets and auctions, and as a major agricultural centre for the region. Straddling the River Wensum, this attractive country town has a

### PENSTHORPE WATERFOWL PARK & NATURE RESERVE

Pensthorpe, Fakenham, Norfolk NR21 0LN
Tel: 01328 851465  Fax: 01328 855905

Southeast of Fakenham, off the A1067, the **Pensthorpe Waterfowl Park & Nature Reserve** is a 200-acre site with a world-renowned collection of waterfowl. As well as familiar native breeds, birds from all over the world are represented, including king eiders and harlequins from the Arctic; diminutive pygmy geese from tropical Africa; the Javan tree duck; and the sacred, glossy and scarlet ibises. The flock of endangered red-breasted geese, native to northern Siberia, is a special attraction, as is the unusual oldsquaw (long-tailed duck) that is the symbol of the Pensthorpe Waterfowl Trust. Walk-through aviaries, bird hides and strategically sited feeding stations around the lakes allow close contact with the birds, and access to all areas is easy thanks to specially built colour-coded paths. Animal life as well as bird life abounds here, including otters, voles, red squirrels and the secretive, humble slow worm, and there is also a wide range of insect and plant life to be discovered. Among other attractions within the site are a children's adventure playground, exhibition centre, wildlife gift shop and licensed restaurant.

Pensthorpe Waterfowl Trust is a charitable trust whose aims are to protect waterfowl and wetland habitats; to encourage public appreciation of the importance of wetlands for wildlife; to work with young people and schools to develop a sense of enjoyment of the natural world and an appreciation of the need for wildlife conservation; and to provide facilities to promote the enjoyment of waterfowl and other wildlife on the Pensthorpe Reserve.

number of fine late18th and early 19th century brick buildings in and around the Market Place. And it must surely be one of the few towns in England where the former gasworks (still intact) have been turned into a **Museum of Gas & Local History**, housing an impressive historical display of domestic gas appliances of every kind. Fakenham Church also has an unusual feature, a powder room - a room over the large porch, built in 1497, used for storing gunpowder. Even older than the church is the 700-year-old hunting lodge, built for the Duchy of Lancaster, which is now part of the Crown Hotel. As an antidote to the idea that Norfolk is unremittingly flat, take the B1105 north out of Fakenham and after about half a mile take the first minor road to the left. This quiet road loops over and around the rolling hills, a 10-mile drive of wonderfully soothing countryside that ends at Wells-next-the-Sea.

# AROUND FAKENHAM

Southeast of Fakenham, off the A1067, **Pensthorpe Waterfowl Park** (see panel opposite) is home to Europe's best collection of endangered and exotic waterbirds. Over 120 species of waterfowl can be seen here in their natural surroundings, a wonderful avian refuge where you may come across anything from a scarlet ibis to the more familiar oystercatcher, along with avocets and ruff. The spacious walk-through enclosures offer close contact with shy wading birds, and in the Dulverton Aviary elegant spoonbills and bearded tits vie for your attention. There are good facilities for children and visitors with disabilities, a Wildlife Brass Rubbing Centre, nature trails through 200 acres of the Wensum Valley countryside, and a restaurant and a shop.

## THURSFORD GREEN
**4 miles NE of Fakenham off the A148**

About two minutes walk from Thursford Green stands what is perhaps the most unusual museum in Norfolk, **The Thursford Collection Sight and Sound Spectacular** (see panel below). George Cushing began this extraordinary collection of steam-powered traction engines, fairground organs and carousels back in 1946 when 'one ton of tractor cost £1'. Perhaps the most astonishing exhibit is a 1931 Wurlitzer organ whose 1,339 pipes can produce an amazing

## THE THURSFORD COLLECTION

Thursford Green, Thursford, Fakenham, Norfolk NR21 0AS
Tel: 01328 878477   Fax: 01328 878415

The Thursford Collection is like no museum you have ever seen or will find anywhere else in the world. Walk into a glittering Aladdin's cave of majestic old road engines and mechanical organs of magical variety, gleaming with colour. There is a live show featuring the mighty Wurlitzer and a programme of music from the nine very different mechanical pipe organs.

Old farm buildings, transformed into a small village, with a touch of Charles Dickens' England, house the Thursford shops. The Pantry/Sweet shop has a large selection of preserves, pickles, wines and other perishable goods, many of them made locally, including fudge made on the premises. The Stable shop has gifts for all ages including cassettes, CD's and videos of the Thursford music, plus a picture gallery. The Corner shop has a vast range of collectable gifts of all prices for all ages and tastes.

## THE WELLS DELI COMPANY

2 Wells Road, Little Walsingham, Norfolk  NR22 6DJ
Tel: 01328 821578
e-mail: bob@wellsdeli.co.uk
website: www.wellsdeli.co.uk

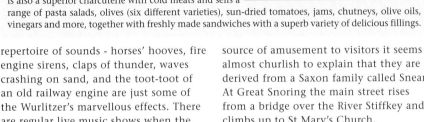

Just two minutes from the centre of town, **The Wells Deli Company** is a clean and well-lit shop with an amazing array of delicious goods for sale. Specialising in cheeses, with 40-50 English and French varieties in stock, the shop is also a superior charcuterie with cold meats and sells a range of pasta salads, olives (six different varieties), sun-dried tomatoes, jams, chutneys, olive oils, vinegars and more, together with freshly made sandwiches with a superb variety of delicious fillings.

repertoire of sounds - horses' hooves, fire engine sirens, claps of thunder, waves crashing on sand, and the toot-toot of an old railway engine are just some of the Wurlitzer's marvellous effects. There are regular live music shows when the Wurlitzer displays its virtuosity. Other attractions include a steam-powered Venetian Gondola ride, shops selling a wide variety of goods, many of them locally made, and a tearoom.

A mile or so north of the Thursford museum, in the village of Hindringham, Mill Farm Rare Breeds is home to dozens of cattle, sheep, pigs, goats, ponies, poultry and waterfowl which were once commonplace but are now very rare. These intriguing creatures have some 30 acres of lovely countryside to roam around. Children are encouraged to feed the animals and there's also an adventure playground, crazy golf course, craft & gift shop, picnic area and tearoom.

### GREAT SNORING

**5 miles NE of Fakenham off the A148**

The names of the twin villages, Great and Little Snoring, are such a perennial

source of amusement to visitors it seems almost churlish to explain that they are derived from a Saxon family called Snear. At Great Snoring the main street rises from a bridge over the River Stiffkey and climbs up to St Mary's Church.

### LITTLE WALSINGHAM

**5 miles N of Fakenham on the B1105**

Every year, some half a million pilgrims make their way to this little village of just over 500 souls, noted for its

*Little Walsingham*

impressive timber-framed buildings and fine Georgian façades, to worship at the **Shrine of Our Lady of Walsingham**. In 1061 the Lady of the Manor of Walsingham, Lady Richeldis de Faverches, had a vision of the Holy Virgin in which she was instructed to build a replica of the Holy House in Nazareth, the house in which the Archangel Gabriel had told Mary that she would be the mother of Christ. Archaeologists have located the original house erected by Lady Richeldis. It was just 13 feet by 23 feet and made of wood, later to be enclosed in stone.

These were the years of the Crusades, and the **Holy House** at Walsingham soon became a major centre of pilgrimage, because it was regarded by the pious as an authentic piece of the Holy Land. Around 1153, an **Augustinian Priory** was established to protect the shrine, now encrusted with jewels, gold and silver, and to provide accommodation for the pilgrims. The Priory is in ruins now but the largest surviving part, a stately Gatehouse on the east side of the High Street is very impressive.

For almost 500 years, Walsingham prospered. Erasmus of Rotterdam visited in 1511 and was critical of the rampant commercialisation of the Shrine with its plethora of bogus relics and religious souvenirs for sale. He was shown a gigantic bone, 'the finger-joint of St Peter' no less, and in return for a small piece of translation was presented with a highly aromatic fragment of wood - a sliver of a bench on which the Virgin had once seated herself.

In the same year that Erasmus visited, Henry VIII also made the pilgrimage that all his royal predecessors since Richard I had undertaken. He stayed overnight at the enchanting early-Tudor mansion, **East Barsham Hall**, a glorious medley of mullioned windows, towers, turrets, and a group of 10 chimneys, each one individually carved with an amazing variety of styles. Since the King's visit the Hall has had a succession of owners over the years, among them a Hapsburg Duke who entertained his neighbours in truly Imperial style before disappearing, leaving behind some truly imperial debts, and the brothers Gibb of the pop

### WALSINGHAM SHIREHALL MUSEUM & ABBEY GROUNDS

Common Place, Little Walsingham, Norfolk NR22 6BP
Tel: 01328 820510/820259  Fax: 01328 820098
e-mail: walsingham.museum@farmline.com

Set in the picturesque village of Little Walsingham, the early 16th century building that now houses the **Walsingham Shirehall Museum** was used as a hostel for important visitors as it was only 80 feet away from the Priory Church. In the 1770s it was converted into the shirehall for the quarter sessions, which were held here until 1861; the petty sessions continued until 1971.

The courtroom has survived unaltered since it was last used and is now part of the 'hands-on' museum, which includes a comprehensive display on Walsingham as a place of pilgrimage since 1061, as well as local artefacts and photographs. The building also houses local tourist information and a well-stocked gift shop, and is the entrance to the historic Abbey grounds, which contain the remains of the Augustinian Priory and the site of the original shrine and holy house.

group the Bee Gees. The Hall is today owned by a London businessman and is not open to the public, but it stands for all to see as they enter the village.

After his overnight stay at East Barsham Hall, Henry VIII, like most other pilgrims, went first to the **Slipper Chapel**, a beautiful 14th century building about a mile away in Houghton St Giles. Here he removed his shoes and completed the last stretch on foot. Despite this show of piety, some 25 years later Henry had no hesitation in closing the Priory along with all the other monastic institutions in his realm, seizing its treasures and endowments, and having its image of the Virgin publicly burnt at Chelsea.

Little Walsingham itself is an exceptionally attractive village, set in the midst of parks and woodlands, with the interesting 16th century octagonal **Clink in Common Place**, used in medieval times as a lock-up for petty offenders, the scanty ruins of Walsingham's **Franciscan Friary** of 1347, and the former **Shire Hall**, which is now a museum and tourist information centre.

## GREAT WALSINGHAM
### 5 miles N of Fakenham on the B1388

English place names observe a logic of their own, so Great Walsingham is of course smaller than Little Walsingham. The two villages are very different in atmosphere and appearance, Great Walsingham displaying the typical layout of a rural Norfolk settlement, with attractive cottages set around a green watered by the River Stiffkey, and dominated by a fine 14th century church, **St Peter's**, noted for its superb window tracery, wondrously carved Norman font, and perfectly preserved 15th century carved benches.

## WIGHTON
### 7 miles N of Fakenham on the B1105

Wighton Post Office must be one of very few in the country where you can buy a postal order and a pint at the same time. This happy state of affairs has come about because the post office desk is located in the bar of the village pub, The Carpenters Arms. The desk is open two days a week and provides all the normal post office services apart from passports and Road Tax licences. This unusual arrangement has been featured on the TV programme *Country File*.

Just outside the village, the Wells—Walsingham Light Railway trundles its way between Little Walsingham and Wells-next-the-Sea. The longest 10¼-inch narrow-gauge steam railway in the world, it runs throughout the summer along a 20-minute scenic journey through the North Norfolk countryside.

## TATTERFORD
### 5 miles SW of Fakenham off the A148 or A1065

This tiny village is well known to botanists for **Tatterford Common**, an unspoilt tract of rough heathland with tiny ponds, some wild apple trees and the River Tat running through it to join the River Wensum about a mile away.

About four miles west of Tatterford stands **Houghton Hall**, home of the Marquess of Cholmondely and one of Norfolk's most magnificent buildings. This glorious demi-palace was built in the Palladian style during the 1720s by Sir Robert Walpole, England's first Prime Minister. The Walpoles had been gentlemen of substance here since the 14th century. With his family revenues augmented by the considerable profits Sir Robert extracted from his political office, he was in a position to spend lavishly and ostentatiously on his new house. The first step was to destroy completely the village of Houghton (it spoilt the view), and re-house the villagers a mile away at New Houghton.

Although Sir Robert deliberately cultivated the manner of a bluff, down-to-earth Norfolk squire, the personal decisions he made regarding the design and furnishings of the house reveal a man of deep culture and refined tastes. It was he who insisted that the Hall could not be built in homely Norfolk brick, and took the expensive decision to use the exceptionally durable stone quarried at Aislaby in North Yorkshire and transport it by sea from Whitby to King's Lynn. More than two and a half centuries later, the Aislaby stone is still flawless, the only sign of its age a slight weathering that has softened its colour to a creamy gold.

To decorate the interior and design the furniture, Sir Robert commissioned the versatile William Kent. Kent was at the peak of his powers - just look at the decoration in the Stone Hall, the exquisite canopied bed in the Green Velvet Bedchamber, and the finely-carved woodwork throughout which made impressive use of the newly-discovered hardwood called mahogany. And then there were the paintings, an incomparable collection of Old Masters personally selected by Sir Robert. Sadly, many of them are now in the Hermitage Museum in St Petersburg, sold by his wastrel grandson to the Empress Catherine of Russia.

This grandson, George, 3rd Earl of Orford, succeeded to the title at the age of 21 and spent the next 40 years dissipating his enormous inheritance. When his uncle Horace (the 4th Earl, better known as Horace Walpole, novelist, MP and inveterate gossip)

succeeded to the title he found 'Houghton half a ruin ... the two great staircases exposed to all weathers; every room in the wings rotting with wet; the park half-covered with nettles and weeds; mortgages swallowing the estate, and a debt of above £40,000.'

Houghton's decline was arrested when the Hall passed by marriage to the Marquess of Cholmondely, Lord Great Chamberlain, in 1797. But it wasn't until 1913, when George, later the 5th Marquess, moved into the house with his new wife, Sybil Sassoon, that Houghton was fully restored to its former state of grace. The depleted collection of paintings was augmented with fine works by Sir Joshua Reynolds and others from Cholmondely Castle in Cheshire, and the Marchioness introduced new collections of exquisite French furniture and porcelain.

One of the 6th Marquess' interests was military history, and in 1928 he began the astonishing Model Soldiers Collection now on display at Houghton. More than 20,000 perfectly preserved models are deployed in meticulous reconstructions of battles such as Culloden and Waterloo, and in one exhibit, recreating the Grand Review of the British Army in 1895, no fewer than 3,000 figures are on parade.

### East Raynham

**3 miles SW of Fakenham on the A1065**

**Raynham Hall** is another superb Palladian mansion, designed by Inigo Jones and with magnificent rooms created a century later by William Kent. The house is only open to the public by appointment since it is the private residence of the 7th Marquess of Townshend. It was his 18th century ancestor, the 2nd Viscount (better known as 'Turnip' Townshend), who revolutionised English agriculture by promoting the humble turnip as an effective means of reclaiming untended land for feeding cattle in winter, and along with wheat, barley and clover, as part of the four-year rotation of crops that provided a cycle of essential nutrients for the soil. The Townshend family have owned extensive estates in this area for centuries, and in St Mary's Church there are some fine monuments to their ancestors, the oldest and most sumptuous of which commemorates Sir Roger, who died in 1493.

## SWAFFHAM

Swaffham's one-time claim to be the 'Montpellier of England' was justified by the abundance of handsome Georgian houses that used to surround the large, wedge-shaped market place. A good number still survive, along with the **Assembly Room** of 1817 where the quality would foregather for concerts, balls and soirees. The central focus of the market square is the elegant **Butter Cross**, presented to the town by the Earl of Orford in 1783. It's not a cross at all, but a classical lead-covered dome standing on eight columns and surmounted by a life-size statue of Ceres, the Roman goddess of agriculture - an appropriate symbol for this busy market town, from which ten roads radiate out across the county.

From the market place an avenue of limes leads to the quite outstanding Church of **St Peter & St Paul**, a 15th century masterpiece with one of the very best double hammerbeam roofs in the county, strikingly embellished with a host of angels, their wings widespread. The unknown mason who devised the church's harmonious proportions made it 51 feet wide, 51 feet high and 102 feet long. Carved on a bench-end here is a man in medieval dress accompanied by a dog on a chain. The same two figures are incorporated in the town's coat of arms, and also appear in the elegantly designed town sign just beyond the market place. The man is 'The Pedlar of Swaffham', a certain John Chapman who, according to legend, dreamed that if he made his way to London Bridge he would meet a stranger who would make him rich. The pedlar and his dog set off for London, and on the bridge he was eventually accosted by a stranger who asked him what he was doing there. John recounted his dream. Scoffingly, the stranger said 'If I were a dreamer, I should go to Swaffham. Recently I dreamt that in Swaffham lived a man named Chapman, and in his garden, buried under a tree, lay a treasure.' John hastily returned home, uprooted the only tree in his garden, and unearthed two jugs full of gold coins.

There was indeed a John Chapman who contributed generously to the building of the parish church in the late 1400s. Cynics claim that he was a wealthy merchant, and that similar tales occur in the folklore of most European countries. Whatever the truth, there's no doubt that the people of Swaffham took the story to their hearts.

John Chapman may be Swaffham's best-known character locally, but internationally the name of Howard

## SWAFFHAM MUSEUM

Town Hall, 4 London Street, Swaffham,
Norfolk PE37 7DQ
Tel: 01760 721230  Fax: 01760 720469
e-mail: swaffhammuseum@ic24.net
website: www.aboutswaffham.co.uk

Swaffham's Town Hall, a handsome redbrick building in the heart of the market place, is the setting for the excellent **Swaffham Museum**. The building itself has an interesting history: originally the home of 18th century brewer John Morse, it became the home of Swaffham Urban District Council in 1955; the Museum has been here since it opened in 1986. The Museum focuses on the social history of the town and the surrounding villages, and the collections cover many aspects of life including trade, industry and domestic life from prehistoric times to the present. This 'house of mystery and discovery' has many individual attractions. One of the highlights is the DM Symonds Collection of handmade figurines, donated by Mrs Ann Peal in memory of her father Derrick Maurice Symonds (1922-1993), author, teacher, artist and craftsman. The collection consists of 66 hand-crafted figures or groups based on characters taken from the works of Tolkien, Dickens, Shakespeare and the Commedia dell'Arte. All the costumes were designed and made by Mr Symonds over a period of years.

One of the town's best-known stories, illustrated in the Museum, concerns John Chapman, 'ye pedlar of Swaffham who did by a dream find a great treasure' (see text above). John Chapman is perhaps a figure of legend, but two who were very much real-life sons of Swaffham were Captain William Earl Johns, author of the Biggles stories, and Howard Carter, the Egyptologist who discovered the tomb of Tutankhamun in the Valley of the Kings at Luxor in 1922. His mummy was a Swaffham girl, the daughter of a builder, while his father was a fairly successful artist. The fascinating stories of Captain Johns and Howard Carter are told in the Museum, and one of the other major attractions is the splendid Sporle Collection of locally-found artefacts.

Swaffham Museum offers excellent research and education facilities through a library of pictures, photographs, press cuttings and other documents, and staff are on hand to help with family trees or identifying objects found by visitors. The Museum and its souvenir shop are open Tuesday to Sunday from April to October.

Carter, the discoverer of Tutankhamen's tomb, is much better known. Carter was born at Swaffham in 1874; his death in 1939 was attributed by the popular press to 'the Curse of Tutankhamen'. If so, it must have been an extremely sluggish curse. Some 17 years had elapsed since Carter had knelt by a dark, underground opening, swivelled his torch and found himself the first human being in centuries to gaze upon the astonishing treasures buried in the tomb of the teenage Pharaoh.

**Swaffham Museum** in the Town Hall is the setting for the story of the town's past. Visitors can follow Howard Carter's road to the Valley of the Kings, see the Symonds Collection of handmade figurines, and admire the Sporle collection of locally-found artefacts.

Move on some 1,400 years from the death of Tutankhamen to Norfolk in the 1st century AD. Before a battle, members of the Iceni tribe, led by Boudicca, would squeeze the blue sap of the woad plant onto their faces in the hope of frightening the Roman invaders (or any other of their many enemies). At **Cockley Cley Iceni Village and Museums**, three miles southwest of Swaffham off the A1065, archaeologists have reconstructed a village of Boudicca's time, complete with wooden huts, moat, drawbridge and palisades. Reconstruction though it is, the village is remarkably effective in evoking a sense of what daily life entailed more than 1,900 years ago.

A more recent addition to Swaffham's attractions is the **EcoTech Discovery Centre**, opened in 1998. Through intriguing interactive displays and hands-on demonstrations, visitors can

discover what startling innovations current, and possible, technology may have in store for us during the next millennium.

# AROUND SWAFFHAM

## CASTLE ACRE

**4 miles N of Swaffham off the A1065**

Set on a hill surrounded by water meadows, Castle Acre seems still to linger in the Middle Ages. William de Warenne, William the Conqueror's son-in-law, came here very soon after the Conquest and built a Castle that was one of the first, and largest, in the country to be built by the Normans. Of that vast fortress, little remains apart from the gargantuan earthworks and a squat 13th century, gateway.

Much more has survived of **Castle Acre Priory**, founded in 1090 and set in fields beside the River Nar. Its glorious West Front gives a powerful indication of how majestic a triumph of late Norman architecture the complete Priory must have been. With five apses and twin towers, the ground plan was modelled on the Cluniac mother church in

*Castle Acre Priory*

## THE POST HOUSE

Stocks Green, Castle Acre, Norfolk PE32 2AE
Tel/Fax: 01760 755174
e-mail: clash52@btopenworld.com
website: www.posthousecrafts.co.uk

Lee and Carolyn Ash take justified pride in **The Post House**, a handsome and distinctive craft shop selling an impressive range of gifts and cards. Here in this emporium extraordinary pieces include local handmade pottery, candles, wooden bowls, jewellery and textiles. Treasures also include medieval style artifacts and fossils. Amongst these precious stones, gargoyles, local maps and books Carolyn has her workshop. A renowned designer with her own range of handpainted ceramic tiles fired in her kiln, she loves working to commission for bathrooms, kitchen and wall panels, she also has a unique range of cards, wrapping paper and tiled mirrors. Lee is an accomplished furniture designer and maker of beautiful bespoke pieces for the home including freestanding butler sink stands, cabinets and shelves in traditional woods, working to private commission. With a wealth of knowledge and design skills at their disposal they can help customers choose something to suit their taste and budget or to make the perfect gift.

Burgundy, where William de Warenne had stayed while making a pilgrimage to Rome. Despite the Priory's great size, it appears that perhaps as few as 25 monks lived here during the Middle Ages - and in some comfort, judging by the well-preserved Prior's House, which has its own bath and built-in wash-basin. The Priory lay on the main route to the famous Shrine at Walsingham, with which it tried to compete by offering pilgrims a rival attraction in the form of an arm of St Philip.

Today the noble ruins of the Priory are powerfully atmospheric, a brooding scene skilfully exploited by Roger Corman when he filmed here for his screen version of Edgar Allan Poe's ghostly story, *The Tomb of Ligeia*.

Castle Acre village is extremely picturesque, the first place in Norfolk to be designated a Conservation Area, in 1971. Most of the village, including the

15th century parish church, is built in traditional flint, with a few later houses of brick blending in remarkably happily.

### LITCHAM
**11 miles NE of Swaffham on the B1145**

Small though it is, this village strung alongside the infant River Nar can boast an intriguing **Village Museum**, with displays of local artefacts from Roman times to the present, an extensive collection of photographs, some of which date back to 1865, and an underground lime kiln.

### DEREHAM
**16 miles W of Norwich on the A147**

One of the most ancient towns in the county, Dereham has a recorded history stretching back to AD654 when St Withburga founded a Nunnery here. Her name lives on at St Withburga's Well, just to the west of the church. This is where she was laid to rest but, some 300 years later, the Abbot and monks of Ely robbed her grave and ensconced the precious, fundraising relic in their own Cathedral. In the saint's desecrated grave a spring suddenly bubbled forth, its waters possessed of miraculous healing properties, and St Withburga's shrine attracted even more pilgrims than before. Some still come.

In the church of St Nicholas, the second largest in Norfolk, there are features from every century from the 12th to the 16th: a magnificent lantern tower, a lofty Bell Tower, painted roofs, and a Seven Sacrament Font. This is the largest of these notable fonts, of which only 30 have survived - 28 of them in Norfolk and Suffolk.

In the northeast transept is buried a poet, some of whose lines have become embedded in the language:

*'Variety's the very spice of life, the monarch of all I survey*
*God made the country and man made the town.'.*

They all came from the pen of William Cowper who, despite being the author of such cheery poems as 'John Gilpin', suffered grievously from depression, a condition not improved by his association with John Newton, a former slave-trader who had repented and become 'a man of gloomy piety'. The two men collaborated on a book of hymns that included such perennial favourites as 'Oh! for a closer walk with God', 'Hark, my soul, it is the Lord' and 'God moves in a mysterious way'. Cowper spent the last four years of his life at Dereham, veering in and out of madness. In a late-flowering romance he had married the widow Mary Unwin, but the strain of caring for the deranged poet

## CLINTON HOUSE AND COTTAGE

Well Hill, Clint Green, Yaxham, Dereham,
Norfolk NR19 1RX
Tel/Fax: 01362 692079
e-mail: clintonholidays@tesco.net
website: www.norfolkcountrycottage.co.uk

A charming Country House set in the peaceful hamlet of Clint Green. The house sleeps nine plus two cots. The spacious hall leads to a large conservatory overlooking the patio and mature gardens which include a tennis court/croquet lawn. The lovely old beamed lounge features an inglenook fireplace with woodburner. A large dining room seating 8-12 is next to the well fitted oak kitchen, which is fully equipped. There are four tastefully decorated and comfortable bedrooms.

The cosy Cottage is equally charming and comfortable sleeping two/four. It is set in the grounds of the House having its own well-fenced and private garden and patio. Two public houses with restaurant are within five minutes walk and there is trout fishing, swimming and golf nearby. Located two miles south of East Dereham the accommodation makes an excellent base for exploring the region: Norwich, King's Lynn, The Broads, Norfolk coast, Thetford and Sandringham are all within easy reach. 4 Stars ETB.

drove her in turn to insanity and death. She, too, is buried in the church.

William Cowper died four years after Mary, in 1800. Three years later, another celebrated writer was born at the quaintly named hamlet of **Dumpling Green** on the edge of the town. George Borrow was to become one of the great English travel writers, producing books full of character and colour such as *Wild Wales* and *The Bible in Spain*. In his autobiographical novel *Lavengro* he begins with a warm recollection of the town where he was born: 'I love to think on thee, pretty, quiet D[ereham], thou pattern of an English market town, with thy clean but narrow streets branching out from thy modest market place, with thine old-fashioned houses, with here and there a roof of venerable thatch.' The house in which George Borrow was born, Borrow's Hall, still stands in Dumpling Green.

A much less attractive character connected with Dereham is Bishop Bonner, the enthusiastic arsonist of Protestant 'heretics' during the unhappy reign of Mary Tudor. He was rector of the town before being appointed Bishop of London, and he lived in the exquisite thatched terrace now called **Bishop Bonner's Cottages**. The exterior is ornamented with delightful pargetting, a frieze of flower and fruit designs below the eaves, a form of decoration which is very unusual in Norfolk. The cottages now house a small museum.

## GRESSENHALL
### 3 miles NW of Dereham off the B1146

The **Roots of Norfolk at Gressenhall** collection is housed in an impressive late 18th century former workhouse built in rose-red brick. Gressenhall Workhouse was designed to accommodate some 700 unfortunates, so it was built on a very grand scale indeed. Now one of the UK's

leading rural life museums and among Norfolk's top family attractions, there's ample room for the many exhibits illuminating the working and domestic life of Norfolk people over the last 150 years. Farming the old-fashioned way is there to be discovered on Union Farm, where heavy animals still work the fields. A stroll along the 1930s village high street takes in the grocer's, post office and schoolroom. The surrounding 50 acres of unspoilt countryside are perfect for walking. The site hosts numerous special events during the season, ranging from Steam Days to an international folk dance festival with more than 200 dancers taking part.

A mile or so south of Gressenhall, the tiny community of **Dillington** has great difficulty in getting itself noticed on even the most large-scale of maps. This very Hidden Place is worth seeking out for **Norfolk Herbs at Blackberry Farm**, a specialist herb farm located in a beautiful wooded valley. Visitors are invited to browse through a vast collection of aromatic, culinary and medicinal herb plants, and to learn all about growing and using herbs.

## BRISLEY
### 7 miles N of Dereham on the B1145

Brisley village is well known to local historians and naturalists for its huge expanse of heathland, some 170 acres of it. It's reckoned to be the best example of unspoilt common in Norfolk, and at its centre are scores of pits that were dug out in medieval times to provide clay for the wattle-and-daub houses of the period. Another feature of interest in the village is Gately Manor (private), an Elizabethan manor house standing within the remains of a medieval moat, and yet another moated house at Old Hall Farm in the southwest corner of the green.

## MOOR FARM STABLE COTTAGES

Moor Farm, Foxley, Dereham, Norfolk NR20 4QP
Tel/Fax: 01362 688523
e-mail: moorfarm@aol.com
website: www.moorfarmstablecottages.co.uk

With 12 attractive and welcoming self-catering cottages, and two more due for completion by the summer of 2004, **Moor Farm Stable Cottages** offer excellent accommodation. The farm buildings have been tastefully and sensitively converted and refurbished to provide a high standard of comfort and quality. Sleeping between four and seven people, each one is individual in character – some are modern, some date back centuries – and offer fully equipped kitchens and every facility and comfort guests can expect. All but one offer ground-floor accommodation, and two have been specially designed for people with disabilities.

Located in Foxley, just 7 miles northeast of Dereham, the cottages are within easy reach of many sights and attractions including Norwich, the north coast and King's Lynn. Guests can enjoy full use of the extensive grounds, which include a well-stocked fishing lake managed by the local fishing club and stocked mainly with mirror carp. Moor Farm also possesses fishing rights to the River Wensum, nearby. The farm also welcomes guests keen on metal-detecting, giving them access to the surrounding 260 acres of farmland and fields. There is dedicated space for children with a play and activity area.

## NORTH ELMHAM
### 6 miles N of Dereham off the B1110

Near the village of North Elmham stand the sparse remains of a Saxon Cathedral. North Elmham was the seat of the Bishops of East Anglia until 1071, when they removed to Thetford (and then, 20 years later, to Norwich). Although there had been a cathedral here since the late 7th century, what has survived is mostly from the 11th century. Despite its grand title, the T-shaped ground plan reveals that the cathedral was no larger than a small parish church.

## WATTON
### 10 miles SW of Dereham on the A1075

Watton's striking town sign depicts the 'Babes in the Wood' of the famous nursery story. The story, which was already current hereabouts in the 1500s, relates that as Arthur Truelove lay dying he decided that the only hope for his two

children was to leave them in the care of their uncle. Unfortunately, the uncle decided to help himself to their inheritance and paid two men to take the children into nearby **Wayland Wood** and kill them. In a moment of unexpected compassion, one of the men decided that he could not commit the dastardly act. He disposed of his accomplice instead, and abandoned the children in the wood to suffer whatever fate might befall them. Sadly, unlike the nursery tale in which the children find their way back home and live happily ever after, this unfortunate brother and sister perished. Their ghosts are said to wander hand in hand through the woods to this day.

Wayland Wood is now owned by the Norfolk Naturalist Trust, and is believed to be one of the oldest in England; **Griston Hall** (private), half a mile south of the wood, is a Grade II listed building, reputedly once the home of the 'Wicked

## PETER CONOLEY & SON

Watton Goldsmiths & Jewellers,
54A High Street, Watton, Thetford,
Norfolk IP25 6AE
Tel: 01953 882981

A family-run business, **Peter Conoley & Son** is a
superior jeweller's and goldsmith's owned and

managed by Peter,
his wife Margaret
and their son
Mark. Peter trained
as a goldsmith at
Hatton Garden,
London, and handed down the family knowledge of fine jewellery to
his son. Trading for over 20 years here in Watton and also in another
shop in Market Place, Norwich, run by their daughter Clare and
her husband Robert, Peter's long experience shows in the excellent
pieces for sale.

Specialising in beautiful gold chains, bracelets, pendants and rings,
all pieces are handmade on site in the well-equipped workshop by
Peter and Mark. Items can also be made to customers' unique
specifications, designs and styles. In addition to the handmade pieces
created and crafted here, other items are for sale including platinum
chains, bracelets and lockets, diamonds, gemstones and a large
selection of leather and metal watch straps.

Uncle' in the real-life *Babes in the
Wood* story.

Watton itself boasts an unusual **Clock
Tower**, dated 1679, standing at the
centre of its long main street.

### THOMPSON

**12 miles SW of Dereham on minor road off the
A1075**

This is a quiet village with a marshy
man-made lake, **Thompson Water**, and a
wild common. **The Peddars Way** long-
distance footpath passes about a mile to
the west and, about the same distance to
the northeast, the Church is a splendid
early 14th century building notable for its
fine carved screen and choice 17th
century fittings.

### ATTLEBOROUGH

**12 miles S of Dereham off the A11**

The greatest glory of this pleasant market
town is to be found in its church of **St**

**Mary**. Here, a remarkable 15th century
chancel screen stretches the width of the
church and is beautifully embellished
with the arms of the 24 bishoprics into
which England was divided at that time.
The screen is generally reckoned to be
one of the most outstanding in the
country, a remarkable survivor of the
Reformation purging of such beautiful
creations from churches across the land.

Collectors of curiosities will be
interested in a strange memorial in the
churchyard. It takes the form of a
pyramid, about 6 feet high, and was
erected in 1929 to mark the grave of a
local solicitor with the rather splendid
name of Melancthon William Henry
Brooke, or 'Lawyer' Brooke as he was
more familiarly known. Melancthon was
an amateur Egyptologist who became
convinced by his studies of the Pharoahs'
tombs that the only way to ensure an
agreeable after-life was to be buried

beneath a pyramid, precisely placed and of the correct physical dimensions. Several years before his death, he gave the most punctilious instructions as to how this assurance of his immortal existence should be constructed and located.

A couple of miles west of Attleborough, the **Tropical Butterfly Gardens and Bird Park** is set in 2,400 square feet of landscaped tropical gardens and provides a congenial home for hundreds of exotic tropical butterflies. There's also a Falconry Centre, waterside walk, garden centre, gift shop, coffee shop and tea gardens.

# THETFORD

Some 2,000 years ago, Thetford may well have been the site of **Boudicca's Palace**. In the 1980s, excavations for building development at Gallows Hill, north of the town, revealed an Iron Age enclosure. It is so extensive it may well have been the capital of the Iceni tribe which gave the Romans so much trouble. Certainly, the town's strategic location at the meeting of the Rivers Thet and Little Ouse made it an important settlement for centuries. At the time of the *Domesday Book*, 1086, Thetford was the sixth-largest town in the country and the seat of the Bishop of East Anglia, with its own castle, mint and pottery.

Of the **Castle**, only the 80-foot motte remains, but it's worth climbing to the top of this mighty mound for the views across the town. An early Victorian traveller described Thetford as 'An ancient and princely little town ... one of the most charming country towns in England.' Despite major development all around, the heart of the town still fits that description, with a goodly number of medieval and Georgian houses

presenting an attractive medley of flint and half-timbered buildings. Perhaps the most striking is the **Ancient House Museum** in White Hart Street, a magnificent $15^{th}$ century timber-framed house with superb carved oak ceilings. It houses the Tourist Information Centre and a museum where some of the most interesting exhibits are replicas of the Thetford Treasure, a $4^{th}$ century hoard of gold and silver jewellery discovered as recently as 1979 by an amateur archaeologist with a metal detector. The originals of these sumptuous artefacts are housed in the British Museum in London.

Even older than the Ancient House is the $12^{th}$ century **Cluniac Priory** (English Heritage), now mostly in ruins but with an impressive $14^{th}$ century gatehouse still standing. During the Middle Ages, Thetford could boast 24 churches; today, only three remain.

Thetford's industrial heritage is vividly displayed in the **Burrell Steam Museum**, in Minstergate, which has full-size steam engines regularly 'in steam', re-created workshops and many examples of vintage agricultural machinery. The Museum tells the story of the Burrell Steam Company, which formed the backbone of the town's industry from the late 18th to the early 20th centuries, their sturdy machines famous around the world.

In King Street, the Thomas Paine Statue commemorates the town's most famous son, born here in 1737. The revolutionary philosopher, and author of *The Rights of Man* emigrated to America in 1774, where he helped formulate the American Bill of Rights. Paine's democratic views were so detested in England that even ten years after his death in New York, the authorities refused permission for his admirer, William Cobbett, to have the remains

## THETFORD GARDEN CENTRE

Kilverstone, Thetford, Norfolk IP24 2RL
Tel: 01842 763267 Fax: 01842 751109

**Thetford Garden Centre** is set in eight acres of Norfolk parkland, and features a comprehensive range of everything needed for the garden together with gifts and furniture for the home, clothing, and a coffee shop. The plant area has earned a growing reputation for outstanding quality, with plants sourced direct from the best growers in the country and throughout Europe.

The garden equipment and machinery sold here includes most major brands of hovers, mowers and ride-ons – and a garden machinery servicing department – landscaping fencing, stoneware, hardwood, metal, resin and cane furniture, also garden sundries such as pots and tubs, bird care, garden clothing, hanging baskets, seeds and propagation accessories, and more. The gift shop offers a wide range of products to suit all tastes, including pottery, glassware, soft toys, collectibles, pictures and cards, silk flowers, scented gifts and speciality foods. Each department is staffed by friendly and knowledgeable assistants who are pleased to help. And after a leisurely browse through all these wares, what better than a relaxing hot or cold drink and light meal or sweet or savoury snack in the coffee shop?

buried in his home country. And it wasn't until the 1950s that Thetford finally got around to erecting a statue in his honour. Ironically for such a robust democrat, his statue stands in King Street and opposite **The King's House**, named after James I, who was a frequent visitor here between 1608 and 1618. At the Thomas Paine Hotel in White Hart Street, the room in which it is believed that Paine was born is now the Honeymoon Suite, complete with four-poster bed.

To the west of the town stretch the 90 square miles of **Thetford Forest**, the most extensive lowland forest in Britain. The Forestry Commission began planting in 1922, and although the woodland is largely given over to conifers, with Scots and Corsican Pine and Douglas Fir predominating, oak, sycamore and beech can also be seen throughout. There is a particularly varied trail leading from the

Forestry Commission Information Centre which has detailed information about this and other walks through the area.

On the edge of the forest, about two miles west of Thetford, are the ruins of **Thetford Warren Lodge**, built around 1400. At that time a huge area here was preserved for farming rabbits, a major element of the medieval diet. The vast warren was owned by the Abbot of Thetford Priory, and it was he who built the Lodge for his gamekeeper.

Still in the forest, reached by a footpath from the village of Santon Downham, are **Grimes Graves** (English Heritage), the earliest major industrial site to be discovered in Europe. At these unique Neolithic flint mines, Stone Age labourers extracted the materials for their sharp-edged axes and knives. It's a strange experience entering these 4,000 year old shafts which descend some 30 feet to an underground chamber. (The

## LYNFORD HALL COUNTRY HOUSE HOTEL

Lynford Hall, Mundford, nr Thetford,
Norfolk IP26 5HW
Tel: 01842 878351  Fax: 01842 878252
e-mail: enquiries@lynfordhallhotel.co.uk
website: www.lynfordhallhotel.co.uk

Lynford Hall is a splendid Grade II Listed mansion, built in the Jacobean style between 1857 and 1862 by William Burn. There have been many royal visitors

including Edward VII, George V and Queen Mary. During the 1930's, ambassador Joseph Kennedy and his son John F Kennedy were also guests at the Hall.

Now it is owned by the Organic Group, it has undergone an on going programme of restoration and renovation. Today, **Lynford Hall Country House Hotel** comprises of 21 bedrooms, all individually furnished in keeping with the style of an English country house.

The Duvernay Restaurant is an elegant room with ornate ceilings and fine views over the formal gardens and lake. It is renowned for it's organic produce with vegetables handpicked from the gardens. The dishes offer imaginative but traditional English dishes. The Wellingtonia Public bar offers a cosy warm and friendly atmosphere to have a drink while sitting next to a roaring log fire.

Lynford Hall is one of East Anglia's premier hotel, conference and wedding venues. At less than one hour away from all cities and towns in the county, it is conveniently located. The Hall is surrounded by 27 acres of mature gardens and grounds set within Thetford Forest Park. It has an idyllic setting for a relaxing weekend and an opportunity to go exploring. Leisure pursuits such as walking, cycling, horse riding, golfing and fishing are easily accessible.

experience is even better if you bring your own high-powered torch.)

# AROUND THETFORD

## MUNDFORD

**8 miles NW of Thetford on the A1065/A134**

Mundford is a large Breckland village of flint-built cottages, set on the northern edge of Thetford Forest and with the River Wissey running by. If you ever watch television, you've almost certainly seen Lynford Hall, a mile or so northwest of Mundford. It has provided an impressive location for scenes in *Dad's Army, Allo, Allo, You Rang My Lord?* and *Love on a Branch Line*, as well as featuring in numerous television commercials. The Hall is a superb Grade II listed mansion, built for the Lyne-Stevens family in 1885 (as a hunting-lodge, incredibly) and designed in the Jacobean Renaissance style by William Burn.

## EAST HARLING

**8 miles E of Thetford on the B1111**

This attractive little town boasts a beautiful 15th century church in a pastoral location beside the River Thet. Inside, a magnificent hammerbeam roof crowns the lofty nave, there's some outstanding 15th century glass and, in the Harling Chapel, the fine marble **Tomb of Robert Harling**. Harling was one of Henry V's knights, who met his death at the siege of Paris in 1435. Since this was long before the days of refrigeration, the knight's body was instead stewed, then stuffed into a barrel and brought back to East Harling for a ceremonious burial.

The church houses another equally sumptuous memorial, the **Tomb of Sir Thomas Lovell**. Sculpted in alabaster, Sir Thomas is an imposing figure, clad in armour with a long sword, his head resting on a helmet, his feet on a spray of peacock's feathers. He and his wife lie beneath a wondrously ornamented canopy, decorated with multi-coloured shields and pinnacles.

## BANHAM

**12 miles E of Thetford on the B1114**

**Banham Zoo** provides the opportunity to come face to face with some of the world's rarest wildlife - many of the animals who find a home here otherwise face extinction. The Zoo is particularly concerned with monkeys and apes, but in the 25 acres of landscaped gardens you'll also come across tigers, cheetahs, lemurs, penguins and many other species. There are educational talks and displays, a children's play area, Shire Horse dray rides, and a restaurant.

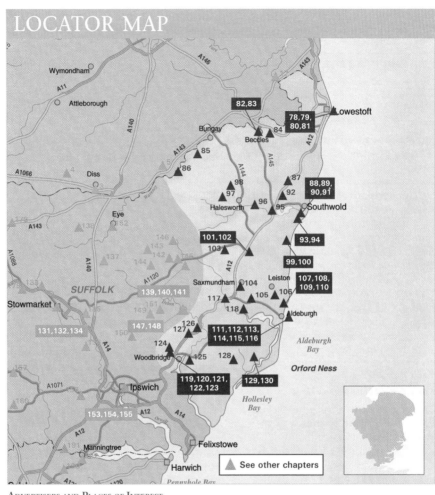

# LOCATOR MAP

Wymondham

Attleborough

A146

A11

A140

A143

A1066

Diss

Bungay

Beccles

Lowestoft

82,83

78,79, 80,81

84

85

86

98

97

Halesworth

96

87

92

88,89, 90,91

95

Southwold

Eye

A143

A1088

A140

SUFFOLK

Stowmarket

101,102

103

A12

Saxmundham

104

139,140,141

117

118

105

Leiston

106

93,94

99,100

107,108, 109,110

Aldeburgh

131,132,134

147,148

126

127

124

125

A14

Woodbridge

111,112,113, 114,115,116

128

Aldeburgh Bay

A1071

Ipswich

119,120,121, 122,123

129,130

Orford Ness

Hollesley Bay

153,154,155

A12

A14

Manningtree

Felixstowe

Harwich

▲ See other chapters

ADVERTISERS AND PLACES OF INTEREST

78  Lowestoft Maritime Museum,
    Lowestoft                          Page 108
79  Pyramid Egyptian Arts & Crafts,
    Lowestoft                          Page 109
80  Crystal Waters Traditional Smokehouse,
    Lowestoft                          Page 110
81  Somerleyton Hall & Gardens,
    Lowestoft                          Page 112
82  The Needlecraft Shop, Beccles      Page 113
83  The Parish Lantern, Beccles        Page 113
84  The Swan Inn, Barnby, Beccles      Page 115
85  Norfolk & Suffolk Aviation Musuem, Flixton,
    Bungay                             Page 116
86  Weston House Farm, Mendham,
    Harleston                          Page 117

87  Poplar Hall, Frostenden,
    Southwold                          Page 118
88  The Cotton Tree, Southwold         Page 119
89  The Amber Shop & Museum,
    Southwold                          Page 120
90  The Residence at Sutherland House Restau-
    rant, Southwold                    Page 120
91  Southwold Pier, Southwold          Page 121
92  The Angel Inn, Wangford,
    Southwold                          Page 122
93  The Parish Lantern, Walberswick,
    Southwold                          Page 123
94  The Bell Inn, Walberswick,
    Southwold                          Page 123

# THE SUFFOLK COAST 4

Suffolk is of course very much a maritime county, with over 50 miles of coastline. The whole coast is a conservation area, which the 50-mile Suffolk Coastal Path makes walkable throughout. With all the miles of meandering rivers and superb stretches of coastline, it is only natural that watery pursuits are a popular pastime, and everything from sailing to scuba diving, angling to powerboat racing, is available. Many of the local museums also have a nautical theme, and the Suffolk coast has been a source of inspiration for many of the nation's most distinguished artists, writers and composers.

The sea brings its own dangers, even in human form, and it was against the threat of a Napoleonic invasion that Martello Towers were built in southeastern Suffolk, in the tradition of Saxon and Tudor forts and the precursors of concrete pillboxes. Starting just before the end of the 18th century, over 100 of these sturdy circular fortified towers were built along the coast from Suffolk to Sussex. Aldeburgh's at Slaughden is the most northerly (and the largest), while the tower at Shoreham in Sussex the southernmost.

ADVERTISERS AND PLACES OF INTEREST

| | | |
|---|---|---|
| 95 Sole Bay Pine Company, Blythburgh | Page 125 | |
| 96 The Old Vicarage, Wenhaston, Halesworth | Page 125 | |
| 97 Chediston Pottery, Chediston, Halesworth | Page 126 | |
| 98 P & R Antiques Ltd, Spexhall, Halesworth | Page 126 | |
| 99 Bridge Nurseries, Dunwich, Saxmundham | Page 127 | |
| 100 The Ship Inn Dunwich, Dunwich, Saxmundham | Page 128 | |
| 101 Suffolk House Antiques, Yoxford | Page 129 | |
| 102 The Griffin Inn, Yoxford | Page 130 | |
| 103 Park Farm B&B and Cottages, Sibton, Saxmundham | Page 130 | |
| 104 Palmer & Burnett, Saxmundham | Page 131 | |
| 105 The Old Chequers Restaurant, Friston, Aldeburgh | Page 132 | |
| 106 Aldringham Arts & Crafts Market, Aldringham, Leiston | Page 132 | |
| 107 The Meare Shop & Tearoom, Thorpeness, Aldeburgh | Page 133 | |
| 108 Thorpeness Country Club & Dolphin Inn, Thorpeness, Aldeburgh | Page 134 | |
| 109 The Thorpeness Hotel & Golf Club, Thorpeness, Aldeburgh | Page 134 | |
| 110 Saseenos Holiday Cottage, Thorpeness | Page 135 | |
| 111 The Brudenell Hotel, Aldeburgh | Page 136 | |
| 112 Ocean House, Aldeburgh | Page 136 | |
| 113 152 Aldeburgh, Aldeburgh | Page 137 | |
| 114 The White Lion Hotel, Aldeburgh | Page 138 | |
| 115 Orlando's of Aldeburgh, Aldeburgh | Page 138 | |
| 116 Wentworth Hotel & Restaurant, Aldeburgh | Page 139 | |
| 117 Snape Maltings, Snape, Aldeburgh | Page 142 | |
| 118 Friday Street Farm Shop & Tea Room, Farnham, Saxmundham | Page 144 | |
| 119 Aspens Jewellers, Woodbridge | Page 144 | |
| 120 Ye Olde Bell & Steelyard, Woodbridge | Page 145 | |
| 121 Spice Bar, Restaurant & Café, Woodbridge | Page 145 | |
| 122 The Cotton Tree, Woodbridge | Page 146 | |
| 123 Melton Hall, Woodbridge | Page 146 | |
| 124 The Turks Head, Haskerton, Woodbridge | Page 147 | |
| 125 Sutton Hoo, Sutton Hoo, Woodbridge | Page 148 | |
| 126 The Greyhound Inn, Pettistree, Wickham Market | Page 148 | |
| 127 Kitty's Homestore, Wickham Market, Woodbridge | Page 149 | |
| 128 Butley Pottery, Gallery & Barn Café, Butley, Woodbridge | Page 150 | |
| 129 Richardson's Smokehouse, Orford | Page 152 | |
| 130 Holiday Cottage, Orford | Page 153 | |

The marshes by the coast have traditionally been a source of reeds, the raw material for the thatch that is such a pretty sight on so many Suffolk buildings. Reed-cutting happens between December and February, the beds being drained in preparation and reflooded after the crop has been gathered. Thatching itself is a highly skilled craft, but 10 weeks of work can give a thatched roof 50 years of life. Organised walks of the reed beds take place from time to time – wellies essential.

## LOWESTOFT

The most easterly town in Britain had its heyday as a major fishing port during the late 19th and early 20th centuries, when it was a mighty rival to Great Yarmouth in the herring industry. That industry has been in major decline since the First World War, but Lowestoft is still a fishing port and the trawlers still chug into the harbour in the early morning with the catches of the night. Guided tours of the fish market and the harbour are available.

Lowestoft is also a popular holiday resort, the star attraction being the lovely South Beach with its golden sands, safe swimming, two piers and all the

### LOWESTOFT MARITIME MUSEUM

Sparrows Nest Park, Whapload Road, Lowestoft, Suffolk NR32 1XG
Tel: 01502 561963

Anyone with an interest in the sea and ships should steer a steady course for Britain's most easterly museum under the lighthouse on Whapload Road. Open daily from May to September, **Lowestoft Maritime Museum** specialises in the history of the Lowestoft fishing fleet, from early sail to steam and through to the modern

diesel-powered vessels. Methods of fishing are recorded, including trawling and the no longer practised driftnet fishing for herring, and other displays depict the evolution of lifeboats and the town's association with the Royal Navy. A replica of the aft cabin of a steam drifter and a fine picture gallery are other attractions of this fascinating museum, where the attendants are ex-seamen and others interested in the port of Lowestoft. They are all delighted to answer any questions visitors have about the Museum and its exhibits. School

parties are particularly welcome, with takeaway educational packs available, and out-of-season parties can be catered for with notice. The Museum, which is maintained by members of the Lowestoft and East Suffolk Maritime Society, was established in 1968 and extended in 1978, when the Duke of Edinburgh was guest of honour. The objects of the Society are to educate the public in shipping, old and modern, in Lowestoft and the County of Suffolk, and in trades and crafts associated with shipping lore in general and in particular to maintain the Museum.

expected seaside amusements and entertainments. **Claremont Pier**, over 600 feet in length, was built in 1902, ready to receive day-trippers on the famous Belle steamers. The buildings in this part of town were developed in mid-Victorian times by the company of Sir Samuel Morton Peto, also responsible for Nelson's Column, the statues in the Houses of Parliament, the Reform Club and Somerleyton Hall.

At the heart of the town is the old harbour, home to the **Royal Norfolk & Suffolk Yacht Club** and the **Lifeboat Station**. Further upriver is the commercial part of the port, used chiefly by ships carrying grain and timber. The history of Lowestoft is naturally tied up with the sea, and much of that history is recorded in fascinating detail in the **Lowestoft & East Suffolk Maritime Museum** (see panel opposite) with model boats, fishing gear, a lifeboat cockpit,

paintings and shipwrights' tools. The setting is a flint-built fisherman's cottage in Sparrow's Nest Gardens. The **Royal Naval Patrol Museum** nearby remembers the minesweeping service in models, photographs, documents and uniforms.

Lowestoft had England's first lighthouse, installed in 1609. The present one dates from 1874. Also in Sparrow's Nest Gardens is the **War Memorial Museum**, dedicated to those who served during the Second World War. There's a photographic collection chronicling the bombing of the town, aircraft models and a chapel of remembrance.

St Margaret's Church, notable for its decorated ceiling and copper-covered spire, is a memorial to seafarers, and the north aisle has panels recording the names of fishermen lost at sea from 1865 to 1923.

---

## PYRAMID EGYPTIAN ARTS & CRAFTS

149 High Street, Lowestoft, Suffolk  NR32 1HR
Tel: 01502 581154  Fax: 01502 581157
e-mail: info@pyramidtrading.co.uk
website: www.pyramidtrading.co.uk

Unrivalled in the UK, **Pyramid** specialises in Egyptian arts and crafts. Founded in 2000, this family-run shop occupies one of the oldest buildings in Lowestoft's High Street. Many of the pieces are unique to the country, as they are imported directly from Egypt. The extensive showrooms boast a fabulous range of clothing - including belly dancing costumes and accessories - together with beautiful jewellery, linens, hand-painted papyrus pictures, cards and scrolls, carpets, brass and copperware, and a stunning range of Egyptian glassware.

Owners Pat and Jim Hughes make two trips to Egypt a year, to source the best wares to sell here. Jim's mother was born in Egypt, while Pat worked in Cairo for the British Council – thus was born their love of the traditional arts and crafts of Egypt. This fine shop also boasts a superior range of unusual gifts from the UK: it is one of the largest stockists in East Anglia for the famous Simon Drew cards, pictures, mugs, T-shirts, tea towels, aprons and more.

## CRYSTAL WATERS TRADITIONAL SMOKEHOUSE

6 Cooke Road, South Lowestoft Industrial Estate, Lowestoft, Suffolk NR33 7NA
Tel: 01502 586866  Fax: 01502 586966

Specialist in quality English and Continental seafoods, **Crystal Waters Ltd** boasts five smokehouses on site, preparing a range of delicious fish and seafood including kippers, haddock, hot roast salmon, monkfish and smoked prawns. World of Fish, part of this superb complex, boasts what is probably the largest selection of wet and exotic fish in the area: Cromer crabs, lobster, tiger prawns, Red Snapper, Red Mullet, tuna, swordfish, parrot fish, Grouper, shark, sardines, squid and king scallops, frozen or smoked.

Well-known stockists for 11 market stalls a week throughout Suffolk and Essex, this family-run business is a partnership between mother-and-sons Lynda, Daniel, Alan and Bryan Eastwood, all experienced fishmongers. Top restaurateurs and cookery schools also turn to the Eastwoods for fish and seafood, not least because their traditional smoking methods bring out the very best flavours of their wares. Their take-home service provides customers with leak-proof, insulated cool-boxes packed with ice. *Open:* Tuesday to Friday 8 – 5; Saturdays 8 – 3.

Lowestoft also has some interesting literary and musical connections. The Elizabethan playwright, poet and pamphleteer Thomas Nash was born here in 1567. His last work, *Lenten Stuffe*, was a eulogy to the herring trade and specifically to Great Yarmouth. Joseph Conrad (Jozef Teodor Konrad Korzeniowski), working as a deckhand on a British freighter bound for Constantinople, jumped ship here in 1878, speaking only a few words of the language in which he was to become one of the modern masters. Benjamin Britten, the greatest English composer of the 20th century, is associated with several places in Suffolk, but Lowestoft has the earliest claim, for it is here that he was born in 1913.

Just north of town, with access from the B1385, **Pleasurewood Hill** is the largest theme park in East Anglia.

**Oulton Broad**, on the western edge of Lowestoft, is a major centre of amusements afloat, with boats for hire and cruises on the Waveney. It also attracts

*Lowestoft Harbour*

visitors to Nicholas Everitt Park to look around **Lowestoft Museum**, housed in historic Broad House. Opened by the Queen and Prince Philip in 1985, the museum displays archaeological finds from local sites, some now lost to the sea, costumes, toys, domestic bygones and a fine collection of Lowestoft porcelain. (The porcelain industry lasted from about 1760 to 1800, using clay from the nearby Gunton Hall Estate. The soft-paste ware, resembling Bow porcelain, was usually decorated in white and blue.)

Lowestoft's **ISCA Maritime Museum** has a unique collection of ethnic working boats, including coracles, gondolas, junks, dhows, sampans and proas.

## AROUND LOWESTOFT

### BLUNDESTON
**4 miles N of Lowestoft off the A12**

Known chiefly as the village used by Charles Dickens as the birthplace of that writer's 'favourite child', David Copperfield, the morning light shining on the sundial of Blundeston's church – which has the tallest, narrowest Saxon round tower of any in East Anglia – greeted young David as he looked out of his bedroom window in the nearby Rookery. He said of the churchyard: 'There is nothing half so green that I know anywhere, as the grass of that churchyard, nothing half so shady as its trees; nothing half so quiet as its tombstones.'

Blundeston has another notable literary connection: Blundeston Lodge was once the home of Norton Nichols, whose friend the poet Gray is reputed to have taken his inspiration for *An Elegy Written in a Country Church Yard* while staying there.

### LOUND
**5 miles N of Lowestoft off the A12**

Lound's parish church of **St John the Baptist**, in the very north of the county, is sometimes known as the 'golden church'. This epithet is the result of the handiwork of designer/architect Sir Ninian Comper, seen most memorably in the gilded organ-case with two trumpeting angels, the font cover and the rood screen. The last is a very elaborate affair, with several heraldic arms displayed. The surprise package here is the modern St Christopher mural on the north wall. It includes Sir Ninian at the wheel of his Rolls Royce – and in 1976 an aeroplane was added to the scene!

### SOMERLEYTON
**5 miles NW of Lowestoft on the B1074**

**Somerleyton Hall** (see panel on page 112), one of the grandest and most distinctive of stately homes, is a splendid Victorian mansion built in Anglo-Italian style by Samuel Morton Peto. Its lavish architectural features are complemented by fine state rooms, magnificent wood carvings (some by Grinling Gibbons) and notable paintings. The grounds include a renowned yew-hedge maze, where people have been going round in circles since 1846, walled and sunken gardens, and a 300-foot pergola. There's also a sweet little miniature railway, and **Fritton Lake Countryworld**, part of the Somerleyton Estate, is a 10-minute drive away. The Hall is open to the public on most days in summer.

Samuel Morton Peto learned his skills as a civil engineer and businessman from his uncle, and was still a young man when he put the Reform Club and Nelson's Column into his CV. The Somerleyton Hall he bought in 1843 was a Tudor and Jacobean mansion. He and

## SOMERLEYTON HALL & GARDENS

Lowestoft, Suffolk NR32 5QQ
Tel: 01502 730224  Fax: 01502 732143
website: www.somerleyton.co.uk

The stately home of Lord and Lady Somerleyton is a splendid early Victorian mansion virtually rebuilt from the Tudor and Jacobean house that stood on the site. The Victorian building was designed by Sir Morton Peto and his architect John Thomas in elaborate Anglo-Italian style, and the façade has many lavish features and magnificent carved stonework. The house was bought from Sir Morton in 1863 by the carpet manufacturer Sir Francis Crossley, whose descendants have occupied it ever since; the present Lord Somerleyton is the great-grandson of Sir Francis.

The Oak Room, with 17th century panelling from the original Jacobean house, some outstanding wood carvings and an exquisite silver and gilt mirror made for the Doge's Palace in Venice, is one of

several superb rooms in this grandest of houses; others include the elegant Library, its walls lined with over 3,500 books; the Dining Room, adorned by some of the Hall's best paintings and some unusual pieces of silver; and the sumptuous ballroom. The splendour of the house is matched by the magnificent gardens, which contain a wide variety of beautiful trees, plants and borders, along with attractive displays of flowers provided by the Victorian glasshouses, which were designed by Sir Joseph Paxton, creator of the Crystal Palace. One of the highlights of the garden is the yew hedge maze, the work of the celebrated landscape gardener William Nesfield. It was planted in 1846, and has had visitors going round in circles ever since. Other features include some interesting statuary, the walled and sunken gardens and a 70' pergola with an unusual iron framework. A more recent attraction that appeals to all ages is a miniature railway offering fine views of the Hall and surrounding parkland.

his architect virtually rebuilt the place, and also built Somerleyton village, a cluster of thatched redbrick cottages. Nor was this the limit of Peto's achievements, for he ran a company which laid railways all over the world and was a Liberal MP, first for Norwich, then for Finsbury and finally for Bristol. His company foundered in 1863 and Somerleyton Hall was sold to Sir Francis Crossley, one of three brothers who made a fortune in mass-producing carpets. Crossley's son became Baron Somerleyton in 1916, and the Baron's

grandson is the present Lord Somerleyton.

### HERRINGFLEET

**5 miles NW of Lowestoft on the B1074**

Standing above the River Waveney, the parish church of St Margaret is a charming sight with its Saxon round tower, thatched roof and lovely glass. **Herringfleet Windmill** is a beautiful black-tarred smock mill in working order, the last survivor of the Broadland wind pump, whose job was to assist in draining the marshes. This example was built in 1820 and worked regularly until the 1950s. It contains a fireplace and a wooden bench, providing a modicum of comfort for a millman on a cold night shift. To arrange a visit call 01473 583352.

## BECCLES

**9 miles W of Lowestoft on the A146**

The largest town in the Waveney district at the southernmost point of the Broads, Beccles has in its time been home to Saxons and Vikings, and at one time the market here was a major supplier of herring (up to 60,000 a year) to the Abbey at Bury St Edmunds. At the height of its trading importance Beccles must have painted a splendidly animated picture, with wherries constantly on the move

*Beccles Marina*

transporting goods from seaports to inland towns. The same stretch of river is still alive, but now with the yachts and pleasure boats of the holidaymakers and weekenders who fill the town in summer. The regatta in July and August is a particularly busy time.

## THE NEEDLECRAFT SHOP

2 Station Road, Beccles, Suffolk NR34 9QQ
Tel: 01502 713543

Featuring the finest wools from suppliers such as Jaegar, Rowan, Sirdar, Appleton and Wendy, together with cross-stitch patterns, tapestry tools and much more, **The Needlecraft Shop** stocks everything you need to create excellent knitwear and decorative needlework. With over 30 years' experience, owners Janet and Joan can offer knowledgeable advice and expert service. This fine shop also boasts a range of haberdashery and craft accessories, and over 500 ready-made needlework kits, some featuring Skipper designs of Norfolk and Suffolk scenes.

## THE PARISH LANTERN

Exchange Square, Beccles, Suffolk NR34 9HH
Tel/Fax: 01502 711700

**The Parish Lantern** is a treasure trove of gifts, clothes, books (including volumes on topics of local interest and children's stories), candles, jewellery, toiletries and toys. The toys range from traditional wooden playthings to soft toys and games. This attractive and welcoming shop, set in an historic building dating back to the early 17th century, also features artwork by local artists. Upstairs there is a range of soft furnishings including cushions, curtains, drapes and fabrics.

## North Cove

| | |
|---|---|
| **Distance:** | 5.0 miles (8.0 kilometres) |
| **Typical time:** | 180 mins |
| **Height gain:** | 10 metres |
| **Map:** | Outdoor Leisure 40 |
| **Walk:** | www.walkingworld.com ID:2016 |
| **Contributor:** | Joy & Charles Boldero |

### Access Information:

Buses: TravelLine 0545 583358 Trains: Anglia Railways: 08457 484950. A 24 hour service. There is parking along the 'No Thro Road' in North Cove which is situated off the A146. At the roundabout A146/B1127 east of Beccles keep ahead along the A146 signed Lowestoft. After a very short distance, just before the North Cove sign, turn left, then right, with the pub on left, go under barrier and park.

### Description:

This is a pleasant walk along country lanes, tracks and beside the River Waveney, that path being part of the long distance one, Angles Way. The route takes you through the Castle Marsh Nature reserve where many birds

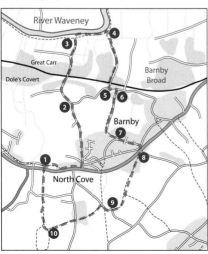

winter, flying over from Iceland and northern Europe. In summer other birds can be seen, also many butterflies and dragonflies. The Three Horse Shoes Inn is a very popular venue for food and the thatched church has 13th century wall paintings.

### Features:

River, Pub, Toilets, Church, Wildlife, Birds, Flowers, Great Views, Butterflies, Food Shop

### Walk Directions:

**1** Walk eastwards along the 'old' pavement with the church on the left. Turn left along Marsh Lane and keep left along it at the right hand bend. (New road to new housing estate, keep along the old one of Marsh Lane.)

**2** Turn left at 'No Thro Road' sign. It ends at the railway crossing. Cross the railway and continue along a tree-lined track opposite to the end. Climb the bank.

**3** Turn right along the riverside bank with the River Waveney on the left.

**4** Turn right down the bank to a stile and the notice board of Castle Marshes Reserve. Climb the stile and keep to the right of the meadow and the 'high' bank path. Follow this around to the next stile. Continue along a grassy path, cross the railway line and continue along a path.

**5** Turn left along a country lane. At the left hand bend turn right along a track.

**6** At the lefthand bend of the track keep straight ahead along the field edge. It becomes a tree-lined path.

**7** Turn left along School Meadow road. Turn right along the pavement to a garden centre.

**8** Turn left, signed 'Cycle and people' by the garden centre along a path. Cross the main road, turn right and cross the minor road. Go up a track by the caravan notice.

**9** Turn right along a country lane. At the right hand bend turn left along a track, signed 'By-way'. Cross the minor road and continue along a track opposite.

**10** At the lefthand bend turn right along a path between the crops. Continue across a field at the sign and the next two fields, with a church in view ahead. Cross the main road and go along a short path to the start of the walk.

Fire, sadly such a common part of small-town history, ravaged Beccles at various times in the 16th and 17th centuries, destroying much of the old town. For that reason the dwellings extant today are largely Georgian in origin, with handsome redbrick façades. One that is not is **Roos Hall**, a gabled building dating from 1583. Just outside the town, far enough away to escape the great fire of 1586, it was built to a Dutch design, underlining the links between East Anglia and the Low Countries forged by the wool and weaving trades. Elizabeth I stayed at the Hall just after it was completed, when she visited Beccles to present the town's charter; the occasion is depicted in the town sign. One of the hall's owners was Sir John Suckling (later to become Controller of the Household to James I), one of whose descendants was Lord Nelson. Any old hall worth its salt has a ghost, and the Roos representative is a headless coachman who is said to appear on Christmas Eve.

The parish church of **St Michael** was built in the second half of the 14th century by the Abbot of Bury. Its tower stands separate, built in the 16th century, rising almost 100 feet and containing a peal of bells. An unusual feature at the north façade is an outside pulpit taking the form of a small balcony. The priest could enter the pulpit from inside the church and preach to lepers, who were not allowed inside. Nelson's parents, the Reverend Edmund Nelson and Catherine Suckling, were married in St Michael's, as was the great Suffolk poet George Crabbe.

Another building with Dutch-style gables houses the **Beccles and District Museum**, whose contents include 19th century toys and costume, farm implements, items from the old town gaol and memorabilia from the sailing wherries, including a wealth of old photographs. Beccles, like Bungay, is an old printing town, and has the **William Clowes Museum of Print** on the site of the Newgate works of the famed printer. Here the visitor will learn about the history of printing since the 1800s, with woodcuts, books and machinery; tours of the factory are also available.

## BUNGAY

**9 miles N of Halesworth on the A144**

An ancient fortress town on the River Waveney, the river played an important part in Bungay's fortunes until well into the 18th century, with barges laden with coal, corn, malt and timber plying the route to the coast. The river is no longer navigable above Geldeston, but is a great attraction for anglers and yachtsmen.

Bungay is best known for its **Castle**, built in its original form by Hugh Bigod,

## THE SWAN INN

Swan Lane, Barnby, Beccles, Suffolk NR34 7QE
Tel: 01502 476646  Fax: 01502 711698

**The Swan Inn** has a fine and well-deserved reputation for excellent food, drink, service and hospitality. Specialising in fresh fish and seafood, meat-lovers and vegetarians will also find dishes to tempt them on the menu. Booking is advised at both lunch and dinner. The range of drinks includes wines direct from the growers in Italy and Portugal, and a selection of Cask Marque fine ales. The ambience at this excellent inn – which was shortlisted for Seafood Restaurant of the Year 2003 - is always relaxed; the staff always helpful and friendly. Holiday accommodation can be had here, too, in a welcoming self-contained three-bedroom apartment above the inn.

1st Earl of Norfolk, as a rival to Henry II's castle at Orford. In 1173 Hugh took the side of the rebellious sons of Henry, but this insurrection ended with the surrender of the castle to the King. Hugh was killed not long after this episode while on the Third Crusade; his son Roger inherited the title and the castle, but it was another Roger Bigod who came to Bungay in 1294 and built the round tower and mighty outer walls that stand today.

To the north of the castle are Bungay's two surviving churches of note (the *Domesday Book* records five). The Saxon round tower of **Holy Trinity** Church is the oldest complete structure in the town, and a brass plate on the door commemorates the church's narrow escape from the fire of 1688 that destroyed much of the town (similar disasters overtook many other towns with close-set timber-and-thatch buildings). The church of **St Mary** - now deconsecrated - was not so lucky, being more or less completely gutted. The

tower survives to dominate the townscape, and points of interest in the church itself include a woodcarving of the Resurrection presented by Rider Haggard, and a monument to General Robert Kelso, who fought in the American War of Independence.

A century before the fire, the church received a visit, during a storm, from the devilish Black Shuck, a retriever-like hound who, hot from causing severe damage at Blythburgh, raced down the nave and killed two worshippers. A weather vane in the market place puts the legend into verse:

*All down the church in midst of fire*
*The Hellish Monster Flew*
*And Passing onwards to the Quire*
*He many people slew.*

Nearby is the famous octagonal **Butter Cross**, rebuilt after the great fire of 1688 and topped by Justice with her scales and sword. This building was once used as a prison, with a dungeon below.

## NORFOLK & SUFFOLK AVIATION MUSEUM

The Street, Flixton, Nr. Bungay, Suffolk NR35 1NZ
Tel: 01986 896644
e-mail: nsam.flixton@virgin.net
website: www.aviationmuseum.net

Founded in 1972, the **Norfolk & Suffolk Aviation Museum** was officially opened to the public in 1976. Set in the picturesque Waveney Valley, the complex covers 7½ acres, with unique undercover exhibitions, military and civil, from the pioneer days through World War, the inter-war years, World War II right up to the present day.

The Museum incorporates the Museums of the 446th Bomber Group, Royal Observer Corps, RAF Bomber Command, Air-Sea Rescue and Coastal Command. More than 25 historic aircraft are on display, along with engines, missiles, guns, bombs and ejector seats. Throughout the Museum there are examples of aviation art, together with themed displays, including WWII decoy sites, Civil Defence, telephones, compasses, models and (perhaps the most fascinating of all) wreckology - the digging for the remains of aircraft in areas where they are known to have crashed.

Among the aircraft on display are an Avro Anson C19, the first aircraft acquired by the Museum; a Dassault Mystère IVA, a Vampire, a Meteor, a Javelin and two Westland helicopters. The Museum, officially recognised as East Anglia's Aviation Heritage Centre, is located on the B1062 off the A143 a mile west of Bungay. Admission is free, the Museum relying on money put in the donation boxes or spent in the shop or NAAFI.

Bungay Museum, housed in the Council offices in Broad Street, is home to an exhibition of local history including pictures, coins and photographs.

## EARSHAM

### 1 mile SW of Bungay off the A143

All Saints Church and Earsham Hall are well worth a visit, but what brings most people here is the Otter Trust, on the banks of the Waveney, where the largest collection of otters in natural enclosures are bred for re-introduction into the wild. Waterfowl, herons and deer are also kept here, and there are some lovely walks by the lakes and river.

## FLIXTON

### 2 miles SW of Bungay on the B1062

Javelin, Meteor, Sea Vixen, Westland Whirlwind: names that evoke earlier days of flying, and just four of the 20 aircraft on show at The Norfolk and Suffolk Aviation Museum (see panel opposite), on the site of a USAAF Liberator base during the Second World War. There's a lot of associated material, both civil and military, covering the period from the First World War to the present day. The museum incorporates the Royal Observer Corps Museum, RAF Bomber Command Museum, and the Museum and Memorial of the 446th Bomb Group - the Bungay Buckeroos.

Flixton is named after St Flik, the first Bishop of East Anglia, and he is depicted in the village sign.

## MENDHAM

### 6 miles SW of Bungay off the A143

This pretty little village on the Waveney was the birthplace of Sir Alfred Munnings RA, who was born at Mendham Mill, where his father was the miller. Sir Alfred's painting *Charlotte and her Pony* was the inspiration for the

## WESTON HOUSE FARM

Mendham, Harleston, Norfolk IP20 0PB
Tel: 01986 782206  Fax: 01986 783986
e-mail: holden@farmline.com

Set in an acre of garden, Weston House Farm is a 17th century Grade II listed farmhouse overlooking 600 acres of mixed farmland and offering excellent accommodation. This long, two-storey building has an attractive gabled-roof and is painted a pristine white – at one end there is a conservatory addition.

Featured in the *Which? B & B Guide*, the farmhouse has three guest bedrooms – a large double and twin overlooking the garden and surrounding countryside, and a ground-floor double – all decorated and furnished to the highest standards of taste and comfort.

Extremely comfortable and tastefully decorated throughout, the guests' lounge is spacious, with four lounge chairs and a large settee. There's an upright piano which guests are welcome to play along with a TV, books and other diversions. The room overlooks the handsome garden.

A delicious traditional breakfast is served in the gracious dining room. Quiet and secluded, this fine establishment on the Norfolk/Suffolk border makes a wonderful base for exploring the Suffolk Heritage Coast, the Norfolk Broads and the many sights and attractions of the region. Children and pets welcome. No smoking. 4 Diamonds ETB and AA.

village sign, which was unveiled by his niece Kathleen Hadingham.

### CARLTON COLVILLE

**3 miles SW of Lowestoft on the B1384**

Many a transport enthusiast has enjoyed a grand day out at the **East Anglia Transport Museum**, where children young and old (and very old) can climb aboard to enjoy rides on buses, trams and trolleybuses (one of the resident trolleybuses was built at the Garrett works in Leiston). The East Suffolk narrow-gauge railway winds its way around the site, and there's a 1930s street with all the authentic accessories, plus lorries, vans and steamrollers.

Also in Carlton Colville is the 15th century church of St Peter, which incorporated parts of other buildings when restored in the 19th century.

Carlton Marshes is Oulton Broad's nature reserve, with grazing marsh and fen, reached by the Waveney Way footpath.

### KESSINGLAND

**3 miles S of Lowestoft off the A12**

A small resort with a big history, Palaeolithic and Neolithic remains have come to light in Kessingland, and traces of an ancient forest have been unearthed on the sea bed. At the time of William the Conqueror, Kessingland prospered

with its herring industry and was a major fishing port rivalled only by Dunwich. The estuary gradually silted up, sealing off the river with a shingle bank and cutting off the village's major source of wealth. The tower of the church of St Edmund reaches up almost 100 feet – not unusual on the coast - where it provides a conspicuous landmark for sailors and fishermen.

Most of Kessingland's maritime trappings have now disappeared: the lighthouse on the cliffs was scrapped 100 years ago, the lifeboat lasted until 1936 (having saved 144 lives), and one of the several former coastguard stations was purchased by the writer Rider Haggard as a holiday home.

The village's major tourist attraction is the **Suffolk Wildlife Park**, 100 acres of coastal parkland that are home to a wide range of wild animals, from aardvarks to zebras by way of bats, flamingos, giraffes, meerkats and sitatunga. The flamingos have their own enclosure. Burmese pythons are used for snake-handling sessions – an experience that's definitely not for everyone!

### COVEHITHE

**7 miles S of Lowestoft off the A12**

Leave the A12 at Wrentham and head for the tiny coastal village of Covehithe, remarkable for its 'church within a

### POPLAR HALL

Frostenden Corner, Frostenden, nr Southwold, Suffolk NR34 7JA Tel: 01502 578549
website: www.southwold.ws/poplar-hall

Excellent self-catering accommodation is on hand in the grounds of 16th century thatched **Poplar Hall**, surrounded by quiet lanes, woods, meadows and secluded beaches. The Cottage (with double bedroom) and Lofthouse (with a double and twin) are characterful and welcoming, fully equipped and tastefully and comfortably decorated. Both have private gardens/patio areas. In the main house – beautifully furnished with many original features like the inglenook fires and exposed beamwork - there's B&B accommodation in three guest bedrooms (two doubles, one single).

church'. The massive church of **St Andrew**, partly funded by the Benedictine monks at Cluniac, was left to decline after being laid waste by Dowsing's men. The villagers could not afford a replacement on the same grand scale, so in 1672 it was decided to remove the roof and sell off some of the material. From what was left a small new church was built within the old walls. The original tower still stands, spared by Cromwell for use as a landmark for sailors.

# SOUTHWOLD

A town full of character and interest for the holidaymaker and for the historian. Though one of the most popular resorts on the east coast, Southwold has very little of the kiss-me-quick commercialism that spoils so many seaside towns. It's practically an island, bounded by creeks and marshes, the River Blyth and the North Sea, and has managed to retain the genteel atmosphere of the 19th century. There are some attractive buildings, from pink-washed cottages to elegant Georgian town houses, many of them ranged around a series of greens which were left undeveloped to act as firebreaks after much of the town was lost in the great fire of 1659.

In a seaside town whose buildings present a wide variety of styles, shapes and sizes, William Denny's **Buckenham House** is among the most elegant and interesting. On the face of it a classic Georgian town house, it's actually much older, dating probably from the middle of the 16th century. Richard Buckenham, a wealthy Tudor merchant, was the man who had it built and it was truly impressive in size, as can be deduced from the dimensions of the cellar (now

## THE COTTON TREE

Lifestyle Store, Cotton Tree House, 70 High Street, Southwold, Suffolk IP28 6DN
Tel: 01502 725 353  Fax: 01502 723 776
e-mail: info@thecottontree.co.uk
website:www.thecottontree.co.uk

There is something for everyone to enjoy at The Cotton Tree's flagship store in Southwold. Well known for her interior design expertise, Jules O'Dowd has created a very special space for clients and those interested in the colours and

textures of fine design. There's an impressive selection of  both traditional and contemporary furniture, stunning lamps and lighting in addition to fabrics and papers from your favourite houses such as Colefax, Liberty, Sanderson, Brunschwig & Fils, Osborne & Little, Colony and Ralph Lauren to name but a few.  Now stocking Farrow & Ball paint.

For more information on what The Cotton Tree could do for you or to find out more about our range of products, do pop into any of our stores across East Anglia.

## THE AMBER SHOP AND MUSEUM

Market Place, Southwold, Suffolk  IP18 6AE
Tel: 01502 723394

**The Amber Shop and Museum** are privately owned by Astrid and Robin Fournel, who also own Stephensons, the jewellers in Aldburgh. Robin, who has been in the jewellery trade for over 35 years, is one of the UK's leading authorities on amber, hence his involvement in creating a museum recognised as one of the leading amber museums in Europe.

The Amber Shop is the oldest and largest amber specialist in the UK, together with the museum, making it a most interesting place to visit. Admission is free. Over the years Robin has given talks to interested groups which have featured on radio, television, and in the national and local press.

The museum traces the history of amber, dating back millions of years, following a natural progression of what amber is, where it is found, its historical and modern usage, the age of the insects trapped in the resin and how they got there. Many of the superb amber carvings are regularly replaced with pieces loaned from European museums, nothing remains static, encouraging visitors to call in time and time again.

Knowledgeable friendly staff are on duty to answer any questions. The displays are outstanding and the shop itself is well stocked with amber jewellery. No visit to East Anglia is complete without a visit to the Amber Shop and Museum, especially to view the piece of amber recently trawled out of the sea just one mile north of Southwold. It weighs 2.2 kilograms. When visiting, produce this book to the sales assistant and you will be given a 10% discount on your purchases.

## THE RESIDENCE AT SUTHERLAND HOUSE RESTAURANT

56 High Street, Southwold, Suffolk  IP18 6DN
Tel: 01502 722260
e-mail: chefs@sutherlandhouse.co.uk  website: www.sutherland.co.uk

Sutherland House Restaurant is one of the oldest buildings in Southwold, dating back to the early 1600's. The Duke of York, (later King James), slept at Sutherland House prior to the Battle of Sole Bay in 1678. The Earl of Sandwich also stayed here, overslept following a tryst with a servant girl, and nearly missed his ship. Sadly he was killed in the battle and it is rumoured that on the anniversary of the battle, the servant girl appears, waiting for his return.

The Residence comprises a luxury suite and three beautifully furnished bedrooms. All rooms are equipped with the latest technology, TV, radio, DVD and video player and ISDN point. The attention to detail is superb and guests are pampered by the owners, Linda and Stephan Cornell, with touches such as high quality pure white towelling and bathrobes. The rooms were designed by a well known interior designer.

Breakfasts are legendary at Sutherland House, scrambled eggs with locally smoked salmon, freshly caught haddock accompanied by poached eggs, cooked to perfection, and so much more. At lunchtime the restaurant offers a bistro style menu and ambiance, in the evening a more formal approach is provided. Head chef, Nick Gardener, uses, where possible, locally grown products. He and his team are renowned for their fish dishes. The residence is the place to stay when in Southwold and Sutherland House Restaurant is most certainly the place to enjoy fine cuisine and an excellent selection of wines.

the Coffee House). Many fine features survive, including moulded cornices, carefully restored sash windows, Tudor brickwork and heavy timbers in the ceilings.

The town, which was granted its charter by Henry VII in 1489, once prospered, like many of its neighbours, through herring fishing, and the few remaining fishermen share the harbour on the River Blyth with pleasure craft. Also adding to the period atmosphere is the pier, though as a result of storm damage this is much shorter than in the days when steamers from London called in on their way up the east coast.

There are also bathing huts, and a brilliant white lighthouse that's over 100 years old. It stands 100 feet tall and its light can be seen 17 miles out to sea. Beneath the lighthouse stands a little Victorian pub, the **Sole Bay Inn**, whose name recalls a battle fought off

*Sole Bay Inn*

## SOUTHWOLD PIER

North Parade, Southwold, Suffolk IP18 6BN
Tel: 01502 722105
e-mail: admin@southwoldpier.demon.co.uk
website: www.southwoldpier.demon.co.uk

Voted Britain's Pier of the Year in 2002, **Southwold Pier** is the realisation of Chris and Helen Iredale's vision – a local project that boasts dining, shops, unique hand made amusements and many other sights and attractions at the pier pavilion and on the pier deck. Just 400 yards north of the town along the beach and promenade, the pier dates back to 1900, was rebuilt in 1999 and saw its grand opening in 2001.

The Pier Bar/Restaurant is the place to go for Adnams ales, lager, cider, spirits and soft drinks, together with bar snacks or hearty and delicious meals at lunch and dinner; Flippers Café serves breakfast, lunch and sweet and savoury snacks from a wonderful seafront

setting; the Hook, Line and Sinker Tea Room offers up a range of tempting cakes and pastries. In addition the pier boasts two function rooms, a gift emporium, 20 x 50 viewing telescope and impressive water clock. Day fishing permits are available.

*Southwold Seafront*

One of the best known is the Lord Nelson, where traces can be seen of a smugglers' passageway leading to the cliffs. Where there were smugglers, there are usually ghosts, and here it's a man in a frock coat who disappears into the cliff face. Adnams still use horse-drawn drays for local beer deliveries.

Southwold's maritime past is recorded in the **Museum** set in a Dutch-style cottage in Victoria Street. Open daily in the summer months, it records the famous battle and also features exhibits on local archaeology, geology and natural history, and the history of the Southwold railway. The **Southwold Sailors' Reading Room** contains pictures, ship models and other items, and at Gun Hill the **Southwold Lifeboat Museum** has a small collection of RNLI-related material with particular reference to Southwold. The main attraction at Gun Hill is a set of six 18-pounder guns, captured in 1746 at the Battle of Culloden and presented to the town (hitherto more or less undefended) by the Duke of Cumberland.

No visitor to Southwold should leave without spending some time in the

Southwold in 1672 between the British and French fleets and the Dutch. This was an episode in the Third Anglo-Dutch War, when the Duke of York, Lord High Admiral of England and later to be crowned James II, used Sutherland House in Southwold as his headquarters and launched his fleet (along with that of the French) from here. One distinguished victim of this battle was Edward Montagu, 1st Earl of Sandwich, great-grandfather of the man whose gambling mania did not allow him time for a formal meal. By inserting slices of meat between slices of bread, the 4th Earl ensured that his name would live on.

The Sole Bay Inn is one of several owned by the local brewery Adnams.

## THE ANGEL INN

High Street, Wangford, nr Southwold, Suffolk  NR34 8RL
Tel: 01502 578636  Fax: 01502 578535
website: www.angel-wangford.co.uk

A traditional village inn once on the main coaching route and dating back to the 16th century, **The Angel Inn** boasts many original features and a warm and welcoming ambience. Justly renowned for its excellent food, English fare on the menu includes an impressive range of starters and main courses, from local meats and seafood to vegetarian dishes. To accompany your meal is a selection of real ales, a good wine list, cider, stout, spirits and soft drinks. There are seven charming and comfortable en suite guest bedrooms for anyone seeking accommodation close to the local sights and attractions.

splendid church of **St Edmund King and Martyr**, which emerged relatively unscathed from the ravages of the Commonwealth. The lovely painted roof and wide screen are the chief glories, but the slim-stemmed 15th century pulpit and the Elizabethan Holy Table must also be seen. Inside the church there's also a splendid 'Jack o' the Clock' – a little wooden man in War of the Roses armour, holding a bell. A rope is pulled to sound the bell to mark the start of church services.

There's some great walking in the country around Southwold, both along the coast and inland. At **Wangford**, a mile or so inland, is the Perpendicular church of St Peter and St Paul, built on the site of a Benedictine priory. Even closer to Southwold is Reydon Wood Nature Reserve.

# SOUTHWOLD TO WOODBRIDGE

## WALBERSWICK
### 1 miles S of Southwold on the B1387

The story is familiar: flourishing fishing port; grand church; changing of the coastline due to erosion and silting; decline of fishing and trading; no money to maintain the church; church falls into disrepair. Towards the end of the 16th century, a smaller church was built within the original St Andrew's, by then in ruins through neglect. The situation in Walberswick had also been exacerbated by the seizing of church lands and revenues by the King, and by a severe fire.

Fishing hardly exists today, and boating in Walberswick is almost entirely

### THE PARISH LANTERN LTD

The Village Green, Walberswick, Southwold, Suffolk IP18 6TT
Tel: 01502 723173   Fax: 01502 725474

**The Parish Lantern** is set on two floors of a handsome Georgian building right on the village green in Walberswick. Here visitors will find a wealth of innovative crafts, gifts, pottery, toys, and paintings by local artists. This charming shop is well known for its tea room, where a range of freshly made cakes and light lunches can be enjoyed.

### THE BELL INN

Ferry Road, Walberswick, Southwold, Suffolk IP18 6TN
Tel: 01502 723109  Fax: 01502 722728
e-mail: bellinn@btinternet.com
website: www.blythweb.co.uk/bellinn

Just 400 yards from the sea, The lovely **Bell Inn** is a distinguished and distinctive 600-year-old inn with many traditional features and the best in hospitality. Original features such as the flagstone floors, low beamed ceilings and open fires enhance the inn's cosiness and appeal. The atmosphere is always friendly and relaxed. Renowned for its food, this award-winning inn (winner of the AA/Sea Food Industries 'Sea Food Award' for five years consecutively, and finalist in Suffolk Pub of the Year 2002) also boasts six comfortable en suite guest bedrooms.

*River Blyth, Walberswick*

a weekend and holiday activity. The tiny 'church within a church' is still in use, its churchyard a nature reserve. South of the village is the bird sanctuary of **Walberswick & Westleton Heaths**.

For more than two centuries, Walberswick has been a magnet for painters, with the religious ruins, the beach and the sea being favourite subjects for visiting artists. The tradition continues unabated, and many academics have also made their homes here.

## BLYTHBURGH

### 3 miles SW of Southwold, A1095 then A12

Blythburgh's church of **Holy Trinity** is one of the wonders of Suffolk, a stirring sight as it rises from the reed beds, visible for miles around and floodlit at night to spectacular effect. This 'Cathedral of the Marshes' reflects the days when Blythburgh was a prosperous port with a bustling quayside wool trade. With the silting up of the river, trade rapidly fell

off and the church fell into decay. In 1577 the steeple of the 14th century tower was struck by lightning in a severe storm; it fell into the nave, shattering the font and taking two lives. The scorch marks visible to this day on the north door are said to be the claw marks of the Devil in the guise of hellhound Black Shuck, left as he sped towards Bungay to terrify the congregation of St Mary's.

Disaster struck again in 1644, when Dowsing and his men smashed windows, ornaments and statues, blasted the wooden angels in the roof with hundreds of bullets and used the nave as a stable, with tethering rings screwed into the pillars of the nave. Luckily, the bench-end carvings escaped the desecration, not being labelled idolatrous. These depict the Labours of the Months, and the Seven Deadly Sins. Blythburgh also has a Jack o'the Clock, a brother of the figure at Southwold, and the priest's chamber over the south porch has been lovingly restored complete with an altar made with wood from *HMS Victory*. The angels may have survived, but the font was defaced to remove the signs of the sacraments.

A mile south, at the junction of the A12 and the Walberswick road, **Toby's Walks** is an ideal place for a picnic and, like so many places in Suffolk, has its own ghost story. This concerns Tobias Gill, a dragoon drummer who murdered a local girl and was hanged here after a trial at Ipswich. His ghost is said to haunt the heath, but this should not deter picnic-makers.

The Norman Gwatkin Nature Reserve is an area of marsh and fen with two

## SOLE BAY PINE COMPANY

Red House Farm, Blythburgh, Suffolk  IP17 3RF
Tel: 01502 478077
e-mail: upsfurn@aol.com
website: www.solebaypine.co.uk

Not 'just another pine shop', the **Sole Bay Pine Company** is worth a look. Situated just off the A12 south of Blythburgh (well signposted), the extensive showrooms encompass a treasure-trove of locally made home and decorative pine furnishings. This large and welcoming shop also stocks mirrors, lighting (including Tiffany lamps)

and a handsome selection of soft furnishings such as throws, cushions, wall-hangings and more, in a wide variety of beautiful fabrics and colours.

Kidz Klobber is a range of designer clothing for children aged 1 to 9 for sale here; the shop also boasts accessories for the home such as candles, pottery and many other *objets d'art*. The shop is open Monday to Friday 9.30 – 5; Saturday to Sunday 10 – 4. The shop also offers a nation-wide delivery service. Owner Gerard Delaney also manages additional outlets of this excellent shop at Beccles and at Ipswich.

hides, walkways and a willow coppice.

## WENHASTON

**5 miles W of Southwold off the A12**

The church of **St Peter** is well worth a detour. Saxon stones are embedded in its walls, but the most remarkable feature is the Doom (Last Judgement scene), said to have been painted around 1500 by a monk from Blythburgh.

## HALESWORTH

**8 miles W of Southwold on the A144**

Granted a market in 1222, Halesworth reached the peak of its trading importance when the River Blyth was made navigable as far as the town in 1756. A stroll around the streets reveals several buildings of architectural interest. The Market Place has a handsome Elizabethan timber-framed house, but

## THE OLD VICARAGE

Wenhaston, Halesworth, Suffolk  IP19 9EG
Tel: 01502 478339  Fax: 01502 478068
e-mail: Theycock@aol.com
website: www.southwold.blythweb.co.uk/oldvicarage

Hidden away next to the church in pretty, secluded gardens, **The Old Vicarage** offers very comfortable bed and breakfast accommodation in relaxed and welcoming surroundings. Each of the four guest bedrooms is handsomely appointed and tastefully decorated, ensuring a high standard of comfort. Within easy reach of Southwold, Aldeburgh and many other of the region's attractions, it makes an excellent touring base. The owners regret that children under 12 and pets cannot be accommodated. ETC 4 Diamonds.

the chief attraction for the visitor is the **Halesworth and District Museum** at the railway station, in Station Road, where exhibits on local history, railway and rural life can be seen. The station's unique moveable platforms are adjacent to the museum. Local geology and archaeology includes fossils, prehistoric and medieval finds from recent excavations.

Halesworth Gallery, at Steeple End,

holds a collection of contemporary paintings, sculpture and other artwork in a converted row of 17th century almshouses.

### BRAMFIELD

**7 miles SW of Southwold on the A144**

The massive Norman round tower of **St Andrew's** Church is separate from the main building and was built as a defensive structure, with walls over 3 feet

### CHEDISTON POTTERY

The Pottery, The Green, Chediston, Halesworth, Suffolk IP19 0BB
Tel: 01986 785242
e-mail: clayspirit@tiscali.co.uk
website: www.marktitchinerceramics.com

**Chediston Pottery** is housed in a handsome and spacious workshop and showroom situated alongside the large wood-fired kiln - such an important feature of the work of ceramic artist Mark Titchiner. One of only a handful of UK potters who produce large glazed earthenware pieces, Mark has over 30 years' experience. His extensive range covers domestic pottery for the kitchen and table, one off sculptural pieces for interiors, and distinctive large thrown jars for the garden and conservatory. His work can be found in private and public collections including the Fitzwilliam Museum Cambridge.

### P & R ANTIQUES LTD

Fairstead Farm Buildings, Wash Lane, Spexhall, Halesworth, Suffolk IP19 0RF
Tel: 01986 873232  Fax: 01986 874682
e-mail: pauline@prantiques.com
website: www.prantiques.com

Based in handsome refurbished and modernised farm buildings, with four former stable blocks full of antiques, **P & R Antiques** can offer customers an extensive selection of period antiques from the 17th, 18th and 19th centuries. With furniture for every room of the house –

dressers, wardrobes, chests of drawers, bookcases, writing desks, occasional tables, dining tables, chairs and more – visitors are sure to find pieces that meet their taste and pockets here. Over 2,000 square feet of showroom space ensures viewing in a relaxed and informal atmosphere.

Opening times are arranged according to customers' individual needs – please ring for details. The shop also boasts an excellent website, where potential customers can view some of the wonderful pieces for sale here. Situated just two miles northeast of Halesworth (good maps are available from owner Pauline Lewis), this fine establishment is well worth seeking out.

thick. Dowsing ran riot here in 1643, destroying 24 superstitious pictures, one crucifix, a picture of Christ and 12 angels on the roof. The most important monument is one to Sir Arthur Coke, sometime Lord Chief Justice, who died in 1629, and his wife Elizabeth. Arthur is kneeling, resplendent in full armour, while Elizabeth is lying on her bed with a baby in her arms. This monument is the work of Nicholas Stone, the most important English mason and sculptor of his day. The Cokes at one time occupied Bramfield Hall, and another family, in residence for 300 years, were the Rabetts, whose coat of arms in the church punningly depicts rabbits on its shield.

## Dunwich

**5 miles S of Southwold off the B1105**

Surely the hidden place of all hidden places, Dunwich was once the capital of East Anglia, founded by the Burgundian Christian missionary St Felix and for several centuries a major trading port (wool and grain out; wine, timber and cloth in) and a centre of fishing and shipbuilding. The records show that in 1241 no fewer than 80 ships were built here for the king. By the middle of the next century, however, the sea attacked from the east and a vast bank of sand and shingle silted up the harbour. The course of the river was diverted, the town was cut off from the sea and the town's trade was effectively killed off. For the next 700 years the relentless forces of nature continued to take their toll, and all that remains now of ancient Dunwich are the ruins of a Norman leper hospital, the archways of a medieval friary and a buttress of one of the nine churches which once served the community.

Today's village comprises a 19th century church and a row of Victorian cottages, one of which houses the

## Bridge Nurseries

Dunwich, Suffolk IP17 3DZ
Tel/Fax: 01728 648850 or 01728 648941 (tea-room)
website: www.fiskclematis.co.uk

**Bridge Nurseries** are situated in the beautiful and historic coastal village of Dunwich, just a few hundred yards from the beach - but well sheltered from the North Sea breezes. We specialise in growing clematis and we have hundreds of varieties available throughout the year to visitors to the nursery or via our express mail order service. Our plants are based on the original Jim Fisk collection and are grown on the premises. A free clematis catalogue is available on request.

We also supply a full range of unusual perennials, together with shrubs, wild flowers and herbs. During spring and early summer we sell a massive range of hanging basket and container plants - out-of-the-ordinary plants to brighten any garden or terrace. Customers can purchase garden essentials from our small nursery shop.

One of the features of Bridge Nurseries is our tearoom which is open EVERY day of the year. In summer, our south-facing terrace catches the sun all day. In winter, our small tearoom is well-heated on cold wet days. Our food is sourced locally and everything is freshly-made. We offer sandwiches, interesting salads, home-made soup during the chilly months and a wide range of freshly-baked cakes. We can cater for private parties up to 30 people in The Bower - a delightful covered area in our clematis garden. We are open seven days a week - between 10am and 5pm in the summer months and then 10am and 4pm in winter.

*Dunwich Museum*

**Dunwich Museum**. Local residents set up the museum in 1972 to tell the Dunwich story; the historical section has displays and exhibits from Roman, Saxon and medieval times, the centrepiece being a large model of the town at its 12th century peak. There are also sections devoted to natural history, social history and the arts.

Experts have calculated that the main part of old Dunwich extended up to seven miles beyond its present boundaries, and the vengeance of the sea has thrown up inevitable stories of drama and mystery. The locals say that when a storm is threatening, the sound of submerged church bells can still be heard tolling under the waves as they shift in the currents. Other tales tell of strange lights in the ruined priory and the eerie chanting of long-gone monks.

**Dunwich Forest**, immediately inland from the village, is one of three – the others are further south at Tunstall and Rendlesham – named by the Forestry Commission as Aldewood Forest. Work started on these in 1920 with the planting of Scots pine, Corsican pine and some Douglas fir; oak and poplar were tried but did not thrive in the sandy soil. The three forests, which between them cover nearly 9,000 acres, were almost completely devastated in the hurricane of October 1987, Rendlesham alone losing more than a million trees. Replanting will take many years to be established.

South of the village lies **Dunwich Heath**, one of Suffolk's most important conservation areas, comprising the beach, splendid heather, a field study centre, a public hide and an information

centre and restaurant in converted coastguard cottages. 1998 marked the 30th anniversary of the heath being in the care of the National Trust.

Around Dunwich Heath are the attractive villages of Westleton, Middleton, Theberton and Eastbridge.

In **Westleton**, the 14th century thatched church of St Peter, built by the monks of Sibton Abbey, has twice seen the collapse of its tower. The first fell down in a hurricane in 1776; its smaller wooden replacement collapsed when a bomb fell during the Second World War. The village is also the main route of access to the RSPB-managed **Minsmere Bird Sanctuary**, the most important sanctuary for wading birds in eastern England. The marshland was flooded during the Second World War, and nature and this wartime emergency measure created the perfect habitat for innumerable birds. More than 100 species nest here, and a similar number of birds visit throughout the year. It is thus a birdwatcher's paradise, with many hides, and the **Suffolk Coastal Path** runs along the foreshore.

A little way inland from Westleton lies **Darsham**, where another nature reserve is home to many varieties of birds and flowers.

## YOXFORD

### 10 miles SW of Southwold on the A12

Once an important stop on the London-to-Yarmouth coaching route, Yoxford now attracts visitors with its pink-washed cottages and its arts and crafts, antiques and food shops. Look for the cast-iron signpost outside the church, with hands pointing to London, Yarmouth and Framlingham set high enough to be seen by the driver of a stagecoach.

### SUFFOLK HOUSE ANTIQUES

High Street, Yoxford, Suffolk IP17 3EP
Tel: 01728 668122
e-mail: andrew.singleton@suffolk-house-antiques.co.uk
website: www.suffolk-house-antiques.co.uk

Situated on the junction of the A12 and A1120 roads just north of Ipswich, in the attractive Suffolk village of Yoxford, **Suffolk House Antiques** was established more than 12 years ago by Andrew Singleton. One of the country's leading dealers in early oak, walnut and country furniture, the shop boasts nine showrooms and stock stretches to more than 300 pieces. Prices range from under £100 to over £50,000. Andrew, as a long-standing member of the British Antiques Dealers Association, has supplied pieces to many of the leading collectors of early furniture in the UK and abroad.

Most items of early furniture can be found here – dressers, cupboards, chests of drawers, boxes and coffers and tables and chairs. The 'miscellaneous' collection includes stools, settles and bureaux as well as metalwork and carvings, and there is also a range of mirrors, ceramics (mostly delftware) and tapestries. Andrew is always happy to search for particular pieces for clients. Parking is available, or clients can be collected from nearby Darsham Station. Open Monday, Tuesday, Thursday, Friday and Saturday 10-1 and 2.15-5.15, or at other times by appointment.

## THE GRIFFIN INN

The High Street, Yoxford, Suffolk IP17 3EP
Tel: 01728 668229  Fax: 01728 667040
e-mail: inquiries@thegriffin.co.uk
website: www.thegriffin.co.uk

Set in Yoxford High Street, **The Griffin Inn** is a lovely little country inn and restaurant with letting rooms occupying a listed building dating back to 1358. With a long and distinguished history as a house, manorial court and a busy coaching inn, it was reputedly a haunt of smugglers in the 18th century. Handy for Minsmere, Southwold, Framlingham, Aldeburgh and other points of interest, this charming establishment has three comfortable and handsome guest bedrooms with exposed beamwork, tasteful décor and

furnishings and a warm and welcoming ambience.

The restaurant serves food every day from 12.00-2.00 and 7.00 to 9.00 p.m. Medieval and Tudor dishes make up part of the menu – dishes such as cod in an oatmeal batter, venison steak with redcurrant and red wine sauce, and balls of minced beef with herbs and spices – share space with more modern alternatives like grilled trout, homemade steak, kidney, mushroom and Adnams pie, and more. There is also a very good bar snacks menu and a choice of mouth-watering desserts. To drink, there are three real ales – Adnams and changing guest ales – together with a good selection of wines, spirits, lagers, cider, stout and soft drinks. 3 Diamonds ETC.

## PARK FARM B & B AND COTTAGES

Sibton, Saxmundham, Suffolk IP17 2LZ
Tel: 01728 668324
e-mail: margaret.gray@btinternet.com
website: www.farmstayanglia.co.uk/ParkFarm

Dating back to the 1600s, **Park Farm** is a handsome and welcoming traditional farmhouse offering excellent accommodation. Named for its proximity to Sibton Park, the three lovely guest bedrooms command good views over the park, and guests can partake of private fishing in the park's lakes. The rooms boast lovely décor and furnishings, and personal touches like the handmade quilts. Guests are welcome to use the gracious lounge and large games room.

Behind the main house there are four charming and spacious self-catering cottages. One sleeps two, the others sleep four. All have wide doors to accommodate wheelchair-users, and one is specially equipped for guests with disabilities. All are beautifully decorated and furnished, and boast every amenity including well-equipped kitchen, shared separate laundry room, and individual patio garden. Open for weekly lets (Saturday to Saturday) from April to October, they are also available for winter breaks of three days or more November to Easter.

## Sibton

**12 miles SW of Southwold on the A1120**

Two miles west of Yoxford, on the A1120, Sibton is known chiefly for its abbey (only the ruins remain), the only Cistercian house in Suffolk. The church of St Peter is certainly not a ruin, however, and should be seen for its fine hammerbeam and collar roof.

## Saxmundham

**12 miles SW of Southwold off the A12**

A little town that was granted its market charter in 1272. On the font of the church in Saxmundham is the carving of a 'woodwose' - a tree spirit or green man. He, and others like him, have given their name to a large number of pubs in Suffolk and elsewhere.

## Bruisyard

**4 miles NW of Saxmundham off the B1119**

Just west of this village is the **Bruisyard**

**Vineyard, Winery and Herb Centre**, a complex of a 10-acre vineyard with 13,000 Müller Thurgau grape vines, a wine-production centre, herb and water gardens, a tea shop and a picnic site.

## Peasenhall

**6 miles NW of Saxmundham on the A1120**

A little stream runs along the side of the main street in Peasenhall, whose buildings present several styles and ages. Most distinguished is the old timbered **Woolhall**, splendidly restored to its 15th century grandeur. The oddest is certainly a hall in the style of a Swiss chalet, built for his workers by James Josiah Smyth, grandson of the founder of James Smyth & Sons. This company, renowned for its agricultural drills, was for more than two centuries the dominant industrial presence in Peasenhall. On the south side of St Michael's churchyard stands the 1805 drill-mill where James Smyth

## Palmer & Burnett

30 High Street, Saxmundham, Suffolk IP17 1AB
Tel: 01728 603016

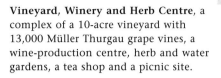

**Palmer & Burnett** was created five years ago, when Sandra Burnett and Susan Palmer joined forces from their varying backgrounds in flowers and antiques. They now have three shops, two in Aldeburgh and

one here in Saxmundham's High Street. At 46 High Street

Aldeburgh, customers will find an original mix of furniture from the 19th Century to the 1950's, plus unusual home accessories. Their other shop at 138 High Street stocks a wide range of kitchen and cookware items.

This most recently opened shop in Saxmundham, a former victorian saddlery, sells french skincare and body products, gifts, candles and vases all complimented by beautiful exotic and seasonal fresh flowers. Their reputation for exquisite hand tied bunches and arrangements extends well beyond this small market town. As well as supplying local restaurants and hotels, they also do weekly flowers for some of the most prestigious locations in the City of London.Why not arrange for a pre-booked flowers delivery whilst staying in the area, perhaps celebrating a special occasion or anniversary, or just to spoil yourself!

## THE OLD CHEQUERS RESTAURANT

Aldeburgh Road, Friston, nr Aldeburgh, Suffolk IP17 1NP
Tel: 01728 688270
e-mail: oldchequers@btopenworld.com

**The Old Chequers Restaurant**, just five minutes from Aldeburgh
and Snape Maltings, boasts an outstanding menu created by
renowned chef Justin Ainsworth, who has worked at Conran's
and many top hotels in the region. His imaginative range of
French and English fare includes fresh fish and seafood dishes,
locally-sourced meats, game in season and more. The wine list is superb; there's also a good range of
local real ales, and excellent champagnes and brandies. The interior is handsome and welcoming, the
ambience always relaxed and informal. Open for lunch only Tuesday to Sunday. Booking required.

manufactured his Nonpareil seed drills,
one of which is on display in
Stowmarket's museum.

## FRISTON

### 3 miles SE of Saxmundham off the A1094

Friston's post mill, the tallest in England,
is a prominent sight on the Aldeburgh-
Snape road, moved from Woodbridge in
1812 just after its construction. It worked
by wind until 1956, then by engine until
1972. St Mary's Church dates from the
11th century.

## LEISTON

### 4 miles E of Saxmundham off the B1119

The first **Leiston Abbey** was built on
Nunsmere marshes in 1182, but in 1363
the Earl of Suffolk rebuilt it on its
present site. It became one of the largest
and most prestigious monasteries in the
country, and its wealth probably spelled

its ruin, as it fell within Henry VIII's plan
for the Dissolution of the Monasteries. A
new abbey was built near the ruins of the
old, and the restored old hall is used as a
base for PROCORDA, a group promoting
musical excellence.

For 200 years the biggest name in
Leiston was that of Richard Garrett, who
founded an engineering works here in
1778 after starting a business in
Woodbridge. In the early years ploughs,
threshers, seed drills and other
agricultural machinery were the main
products, but the company later started
one of the country's first production
lines for steam machines. The Garrett
works are now the **Long Shop Museum**,
the factory buildings having been
lovingly restored, and many of the
Garrett machines are now on display,
including traction engines, a steam-
driven tractor and a road roller. There's

## ALDRINGHAM ARTS & CRAFTS MARKET

Aldeburgh Road, Aldringham, nr Leiston, Suffolk IP16 4PY
Tel/Fax: 01728 830397

The **Aldringham Arts & Crafts Market** is a treasure trove of
the finest work of local artists in three galleries, with a
wonderful range of photos, paintings, prints, excellent local
history books, pottery, glass vases, goblets, costume jewellery,
leatherwork, walking sticks, baskets, toys, clothing, greeting
cards and collectables, pot-pourri, doll's house miniatures,
home-made jams and preserves, and much more. Outside,
plants and pots are sold, and there's also a marvellous coffee shop on site, selling a tempting range of
home-made cakes. Open Monday to Saturday 10-5.30; Sunday 2-5.30.

also a section where the history and workings of steam engines are explained. A small area of the museum recalls the USAAF's 357th fighter group, who flew from an airfield outside Leiston during the Second World War. One of their number, a Captain Chuck Yeager, was the first man to fly faster than the speed of sound

The Garrett works closed in 1980, but what could have been a disastrous unemployment situation was alleviated to some extent by the nuclear power station at **Sizewell**. The coast road in the centre of Leiston leads to this establishment, where visitors can take tours - on foot with access to buildings at Sizewell, A or by minibus, with a guide and videos, round Sizewell B.

## Aldringham

**4 miles E of Saxmundham on the B1122**

Aldringham's church is notable for its superb 15th century font, and the village inn was once a haunt of smugglers. It now helps to refresh the visitors who flock to the **Aldringham Craft Market**, founded in 1958 and extending over three galleries, with a serious selection of arts and crafts, clothes and gifts, pottery, basketry, books and cards.

## Thorpeness

**6 miles E of Saxmundham on the B1353**

Thorpeness is a unique seaside village with a charm all of its own. Buying up a considerable packet of land called the Sizewell estate in 1910, the architect, barrister and playwright Glencairn Stuart Ogilvie created what he hoped would be a fashionable resort with cottages, some larger houses and an atmospheric and lovely 65-acre boating and pleasure lake called the Meare, which is 1 metre in depth throughout and fed by the River Hundred.

## The Meare Shop & Tearoom

Thorpeness, nr Aldeburgh,
Suffolk IP16 4NW
Tel/Fax: 01728 452156
e-mail: meareshop@lycos.co.uk
website: www.meareshop.co.uk

Fresh produce on sale at **The Meare Shop & Tearoom** includes jams, chutneys biscuits, cakes and savouries; the shop also sells paintings, gifts, cards, ornaments, books on

local history and much more. Owner Elizabeth Everett is an expert on Thorpeness history; she and her friendly, helpful staff are happy to offer advice on the many items for sale.

Pies and pasties are baked daily on the premises, and complement a menu bursting with delicious home-made soups, jumbo filled rolls, fish cakes, salads and snacks, together with a range of wonderful ice creams and puddings. Cream teas are a speciality. These are served with a variety of teas, coffees, soft drinks, beers or wines. Set alongside the Meare, the surroundings are picturesque. There are lovely walks to be had around the lake, boats for hire, and the site is just 100 yards from the seashore and beach.

## THORPENESS COUNTRY CLUB APARTMENTS & DOLPHIN INN

Lakeside Avenue, Thorpeness, Aldeburgh, Suffolk IP16 4NH

Tel: 01728 452176  Fax: 01728 453868
e-mail: info@thorpeness.co.uk
website: www.thorpeness.co.uk

Thorpeness, a pretty hamlet on the Suffolk Heritage Coast near Aldeburgh, is home to **Thorpeness Country Club Apartments**, 11 luxury seaside self-catering apartments and houses set within the original Edwardian Country Club buildings. Individually owned and uniquely furnished in a stylish mix of 2- and 3-bedroom units, they are

situated adjacent to the beach. Membership of the Country Club and the Golf Club are included in the tariff. Short breaks of four days or more are also available, as are winter weekend breaks by arrangement. Well-behaved pets are welcome.

**The Dolphin Inn** is a charming and welcoming hostelry where the finest local produce is used to create traditional and innovative dishes that will tempt every palate. The two traditional bars serve up a range of real ales and fine wines, while the garden offers a relaxing place to enjoy the excellent food and drink in summer. The inn also boasts three en suite guest bedrooms which have won the coveted *Sunday Times* Golden Pillow Award for comfort and value.

## THE THORPENESS HOTEL AND GOLF CLUB

Lakeside Avenue, Thorpeness, Aldeburgh, Suffolk  IP16 4NH
Tel: 01728 452176  Fax: 01728 453868
e-mail: info@thorpeness.co.uk
website: www.thorpeness.co.uk

Unique among holiday villages in the UK, **The Thorpeness Hotel and Golf Club** has stood the test of time since G S Ogilvie set out his vision of a holiday paradise in the Suffolk dunes in the early 1900s.

The Golf Club boasts a challenging 18-hole links course designed by James Braid in 1922; the Hotel and Country Club retain their period charm while offering every modern comfort and amenity. The Hotel has 30 spacious and well-appointed en suite guest bedrooms, ideal for couples or families planning a short break or longer stay.

Adjacent to the third tee there's a restaurant offering a varied menu of tempting dishes, the friendly bar serves light lunches, and the stylish lounge overlooks landscaped gardens leading down to the Meare boating lake, where guests can take out a punt or brightly coloured row boat and head for one of the islands for a spot of fishing or a picnic.

*The House in the Clouds*

visitor centre.

Every August, in the week following the Aldeburgh Carnival, a regatta is held on the Meare, culminating in a splendid fireworks show.

## ALDEBURGH

**6 miles SE of Saxmundham on the A1094**

And so down the coast road to Aldeburgh, another coastal town that once prospered as a port with major fishing and shipbuilding industries. Drake's *Greyhound* and *Pelican* were built at Slaughden, now taken by the sea, and during the 16th century some 1,500 people were engaged in fishing. Both industries declined as shipbuilding moved elsewhere and the fishing boats became too large to be hauled up the shingle. Suffolk's best-known poet, George Crabbe, was born at Slaughden in 1754 and lived through the village's hard times. He reflected the melancholy of those days when he wrote of his fellow townsmen:

The 85-foot water tower, built to aid in the lake's construction, looked out of place, so Ogilvie disguised it as a house. Known ever since as the **House in the Clouds**, it is now available to rent as a holiday home. The neighbouring mill, moved lock, stock and millstones from Aldringham, stopped pumping in 1940 but has been restored and now houses a

## THE BRUDENELL HOTEL

The Parade, Aldeburgh, Suffolk IP15 5BU
Tel: 01728 452071 Fax: 01728 454082
e-mail: info@brudenellhotel.co.uk website: www.brudenellhotel.co.uk

Set right on the beach at the south end of Aldeburgh, close to the yacht club, **The Brudenell Hotel** is a large and impressive hotel perfect for family holidays. Distinctive and handsome, the hotel boasts 47 en suite bedrooms offering views over either the sea, marshland or the river. A lift is provided for easy access. A happy marriage of style and tradition, the décor and furnishings are supremely comfortable, while the rooms are large enough to accommodate families.

At the Ocean Bar, cool sea-blues and sunshine yellows bring the seaside indoors to your table. The adjoining terrace is ideal for al fresco dining, including summer barbecues. The hotel's relaxed and spacious dining room has lovely waterside views, and menus offering a tempting range of high-quality dishes using the very finest local ingredients. Two-night stays and other tempting short breaks are available.

## OCEAN HOUSE

25 Crag Path, Aldeburgh, Suffolk IP15 5BS
Tel: 01728 452094
e-mail: jbreroh@aol.com

Pamper yourself with a visit to **Ocean House**, a charming red-brick mid-Victorian building right on the seafront in Aldeburgh and offering superior bed and breakfast accommodation. Large and impressive without losing any of its comfort or cosiness, its ambience is always quiet and relaxed (strategically-placed bollards preventing the passing of traffic). Simply and beautifully decorated with period furniture and luxurious touches such as open fireplaces and Turkish rugs, there are two en suite guest bedrooms on the first floor – a twin and a double – with bay windows overlooking the beach, and a top-floor studio room with a grand piano and panoramic views.

The cellar boasts table tennis equipment and a selection of old bikes which guests can borrow to help in their exploration of the surrounding countryside. In 'the *Country Living* loo', the walls are covered with pages from *Country Living* magazines past! The hearty breakfast features organic yoghurt, fruits, the full English cooked breakfast or vegetarian selection, and homemade bread and scones with homemade marmalade and preserves.

*Here joyless roam a wild amphibious race,*
*With sullen woe displayed in every face;*
*Who far from civil arts and social fly,*
*And scowl at strangers with suspicious eye.*

He was equally evocative concerning the sea and the river, and the following lines written about the River Alde could apply to several others in the county:

*With ceaseless motion comes and goes the tide*
*Flowing, it fills the channel vast and wide;*
*Then back to sea, with strong majestic sweep*
*It rolls, in ebb yet terrible and deep;*
*Here samphire-banks and salt-wort bound the flood*
*There stakes and seaweed withering on the mud;*
*And higher up, a ridge of all things base,*
*Which some strong tide has rolled upon the place.*

It was Crabbe who created the character of the solitary fisherman Peter Grimes, later the subject of an opera composed by another Aldeburgh resident, Benjamin Britten.

Aldeburgh's role gradually changed into that of a holiday resort, and the Marquess of Salisbury, visiting early in the 19th century, was one of the first to be attracted by the idea of sea-bathing without the crowds. By the middle of the century the grand houses that had sprung up were joined by smaller residences, the railway had arrived, a handsome water tower was put up (1860) and Aldeburgh prospered once more. There were even plans for a pier, and construction started in 1878, but the

## 152 ALDEBURGH

152 High Street, Aldeburgh, Suffolk IP16 5AX
Tel: 01728 454594  website: www.152aldeburgh.co.uk

Occupying a prominent corner position leading from the High Street via one of the town's attractive archways, **152 aldeburgh** is a distinctive contemporary restaurant owned and run by Andrew Lister and acclaimed chef, Garry Cook. Andrew came to Aldeburgh with an impressive pedigree in restaurant management. He was at Hintlesham Hall, at the Crown and Castle in nearby Orford and will be fondly remembered as an energetic, lively front-of-house at Aldeburgh's Regatta wine bar and restaurant. The catering at Norwich Football Club, the brainchild of Delia Smith, had Andrew's confident hand on it, working with the Divine Delia for its success. Garry has worked in the kitchens of some of the finest hotels in the country, including Hartwell House in Aylesbury, the famed Lygon Arms in Broadway and Hanbury Manor in Hertfordshire. From this experience and his own talent, Garry creates exciting menus, using, where possible the best of local and seasonal produce.

152 aldeburgh opens for morning coffee at 10, which can be accompanied by an organic pastry or tasty muffin. Next come delicious lunches, served from noon till 3. These are light, expertly prepared dishes, and a number of courses can be varied for all appetites. Try the Suffolk ham or Cheddar melts

or Garry's own take on fish and chips! The kitchen blossoms in the evening to offer a menu du jour and full a la carte sending out a choice of starters, seven main courses and six desserts, and featuring rich traditional ingredients blended together to make innovative and tempting creations. Wild sea bass, salmon with fennel, ragout of vegetables in ginger and coriander nage or crisp confit duck leg are just a sample of what is in store for the lucky diner. 152 aldeburgh offers too an excellent wine list, and you must be sure to leave room for one of the delectable desserts

## THE WHITE LION HOTEL

Market Cross Place, Aldeburgh, Suffolk  IP15 5BJ
Tel: 01728 452720  Fax: 01728 452986
e-mail: whitelionaldeburgh@btinternet.com  website: www.whitelion.co.uk

Set in the heart of Aldeburgh just opposite the shingle beach, **The White Lion** is the town's oldest hotel; a recent facelift guarantees the highest standards of quality and comfort. There are 38 en suite guest bedrooms, with some commanding sea views and furnished with four-poster beds. There is a

stair-lift for guests' use. Attention to detail shows in the touches of luxury in every room, while the staff are always courteous, friendly and helpful.

The hotel bar overlooks the sea, while the oak-panelled Restaurant 1563 – named for the year in which the hotel was built – offers elegant dining amid handsome surroundings, with a menu boasting seafood dishes, traditional roasts and vegetarian meals. During the Aldeburgh Festival and the August proms at Snape, guests can enjoy pre-concert meals or late suppers at the hotel. Hampers are also provided during the proms.

## ORLANDO'S OF ALDEBURGH

30 Crabbe Street, Aldeburgh, Suffolk  IP15 5BN
Tel: 01728 452977

**Orlando's of Aldeburgh** is located in the centre of the town, and is the shop nearest the beach and seafront. The cream-coloured painted brick exterior, fuchsia-pink door and pale blue trim are eye-catching and cheerful – and good harbingers of what awaits inside. Filled with clothing, and accessories; imaginative and colourful apparel sourced from around the world can be found here: Cut Loose linen clothing from San Francisco, Scottish and South American knitwear, 100%

authentic East African Kikoy bags trouser wraps and robes, woven in beautiful bands of colour, Spanish suede loafers and 'Johnnie Loves Rosie' shoes and hair accessories, Out of Xile and Flax, all combine to give this excellent shop it's distinctive range.

For anyone who is looking for something different, this is the place to shop. Owners Jock and Nova Williamson have combined their many creative talents to give Orlando's fun, flair and style.

project proved too difficult or too expensive and was halted, the rusting girders being removed some time later.

One of the town's major benefactors was Newson Garrett, a wealthy businessman who was the first mayor under the charter of the Local Government Act of 1875. This colourful character also developed the **Maltings at Snape**, but is perhaps best remembered through his remarkable daughter Elizabeth, who was the first woman doctor in England (having qualified in Paris at a time when women could not qualify here) and the first woman mayor (of Aldeburgh, in 1908). This lady married the shipowner James Skelton Anderson, who established the golf club in 1884.

If Crabbe were alive today he would have a rather less cantankerous opinion of his fellows, especially at carnival time on a Monday in August when the town celebrates with a colourful procession of floats and marchers, a fireworks display and numerous other events.

As for the arts, there is, of course, the **Aldeburgh Festival**, started in 1948 by Britten and others; the festival's main venue is Snape Maltings, but many performances take place in Aldeburgh itself.

The town's maritime connections remain very strong. There has been a lifeboat here since 1851, and down the years many acts of great heroism have been recorded. The very modern lifeboat station is one of the town's chief

## WENTWORTH HOTEL AND RESTAURANT

Wentworth Road, Aldeburgh,
Suffolk IP15 5BD
Tel: 01728 452312 Fax: 01728 454343
e-mail: stay@wentworth-aldeburgh.co.uk
website: www.wentworth-aldeburgh.com

Distinguished and impressive, **The Wentworth Hotel and Restaurant** is everything a seaside hotel should be. Large and gracious, this excellent establishment in the heart of Aldeburgh is a happy blend of the traditional and contemporary. Handsomely appointed and furnished throughout, the hotel boasts 30 bedrooms in the main building -

18 with wonderful sea views - and seven additional rooms in Darfield House, opposite the main hotel, with secluded patio garden. Five of the bedrooms are situated on the ground floor, for easy access.

The spacious lounges are the perfect place to unwind in comfort, reading or watching the promenaders on the seafront. The service is always friendly and attentive without being intrusive. The restaurant offers diners the best in English and French cuisine, with menus that include the best local produce, served in graceful surroundings. Guests can also enjoy a sandwich in the bar or a light lunch on the terrace. Lovely whatever the season, this superior hotel and restaurant is well worth seeking out.

## Iken - Snape

| | |
|---|---|
| **Distance:** | 5.3 miles (8.53 kilometres) |
| **Typical time:** | 150 mins |
| **Height gain:** | 12 metres |
| **Map:** | Explorer 212 |
| **Walk:** | www.walkingworld.com ID:640 |
| **Contributor:** | Brian and Anne Sandland |

### Access Information:

From Woodbridge take the A1152 eastwards. When the road forks (still on the A1152) bear left towards Snape. At Tunstall, just after the right-angled bend, turn left onto the B1069 ('Snape'). After you pass through the northern end of the Tunstall Forest the road from Blaxhall comes in from the left. Ignore this, but take the next turn right (to Orford/Iken). At the next left ('Iken 2') turn left and in 150 yards look for a picnic site sign left. This takes you down a narrow track to the picnic site at Iken Cliff with glorious views over the Alde. Park here.

### Description:

Wildlife and birds abound. There is also varied plantlife. A visit to St Botolph's Church can be included and after the walk through the forest you can see the wonderful variety of attractions at Snape Maltings. These include an internationally famous concert hall, Henry Moore sculpture, galleries full of furniture, books, pictures, crafts, antiques and food. There is a restaurant and even a small garden centre.

### Features:

Toilets and tea and shops are only available if you include Snape Maltings, River, Church, Wildlife, Birds, Flowers, Great Views

### Walk Directions:

1 Head down into the right-hand corner of the picnic site.

2 Take the footpath which leads along the Alde to Cliff Reach. Continue close to the river finally turning away from the river to reach a road.

3 Leave the river area by steps and walk to the road. If you want to visit the church turn left and in 75 yards left again (signed Iken Church). There are superb views along and across the Alde from the churchyard. Return to the point where you first joined the road then continue, rising slightly. Go left at the junction (signed to Sandy Lane). Pass a number of cottages and after the one named "The Drift", where the road bends sharp left, go right along a track.

4 Follow this signposted track. At trees on the right bear right. Then go left following the edge of the trees (ignore track off left through the trees) to arrive at a broad cross-track. Go slightly right then left along another track, to continue in your original direction, this time with trees on your right. When trees on the right end, go right and then left with the track and exit carefully through bushes onto the road. Cross the road and at a broad cross-track, go right for thirty yards.

5 Turn left at the yellow waymark. Now walk between young pine trees on either side (planted after the devastation of the hurricane of 1987). At next fork bear right along a narrower path. DO

NOT follow main track with yellow waymark. In 150 yards reach another wide cross-track. Cross straight over and follow the track leading straight ahead, which is now wider than the footpath you have just left. Carry on in this direction, ignoring all turns off to the right and left until you suddenly and unexpectedly come across a house on your right (Heath Cottages). Join its drive and walk on to a junction. Take the right turn following the direction of a sign with the number 24. (Do not take the track immediately right).

**6** Despite what the map indicates here, there is no fire tower. After a hundred yards or so the broad track bears right and runs straight into the distance. Leave it and take the narrower grass track which snakes off left. A white waymark should be visible on a post at the intersection. You will soon pass through a clearing. Once again ignore tuns off to right and left and carry on to meet a road.

**7** Turn right and follow this exceedingly pleasant, narrow metalled lane, which bisects the forest, until you reach a crossroads. Cross over and continue straight ahead until you reach the picnic place sign, pointing left to your car and the start point.

**8** If you wish to visit the Maltings, with all its attractions, descend to the bottom left of the picnic site this time. Then follow the footpath left along the Alde. To return retrace your steps. (If you have had enough walking you could, of course take your car to the Maltings. There is ample free parking).

attractions for visitors, and there are regular practice launches from the shingle beach. A handful of fishermen still put out to sea from the beach, selling their catch from their little wooden huts, while a thriving yacht club is the base for sailing on the Orde and, sometimes, on the sea.

At the very southern tip of the town, the Martello tower serves as a reminder of the power of the sea: old pictures show it standing well back from the waves, but now the seaward side of the moat has disappeared and the shingle is constantly being shored up to protect it. Beyond it, a long strip of marsh and shingle stretches right down to the mouth of the river at Shingle Street.

Back in town there are several interesting buildings, notably the **Moot Hall** and the parish church of **St** Peter and St Paul. The Moot Hall is a 16th century timber-framed building that was built in what was once the centre of town. It hasn't moved, but the sea long ago took away several houses and streets. Inside the Hall is a museum of town history and finds from the nearby Snape burial ship. Britten set the first scene of Peter Grimes in the Moot Hall. A sundial on the south face of the Hall proclaims, in Latin, that it only tells the time when the sun shines.

*Aldeburgh Beach*

## SNAPE MALTINGS

Snape, nr Aldeburgh, Suffolk  IP17 1SR
Tel: 01728 688305  Fax: 01728 688930
e-mail: info@snapemaltings.co.uk
website: www.snapemaltings.co.uk

One of Suffolk's premier attractions, **Snape Maltings** was built during the mid-19th century to malt barley for the brewing industry. Now a wonderful collection of shops and galleries on Snape Quay – long a thriving port on the River Alde - it includes House & Garden (for furnishings, kitchenware and fine foods), Snape Craft Shop, Period Home Centre, Books & Cards, Countryware, Snape Antiques and Collectors Centre

and Little Rascals. The Gallery specialises in contemporary paintings and prints from East Anglian artists, while a variety of solo and group exhibitions are held in the Pond Gallery during the summer months. Painting and craft courses are offered from May to September.

Visitors can take morning coffee, lunchtime snacks or afternoon tea in the relaxed rustic atmosphere of the Granary Tea Shop.

**The Plough & Sail** is a light and airy pub that is justly popular with concert-goers and all visitors to Snape Maltings. The rambling interior includes a bar and restaurant. The menu offers an excellent range of local produce throughout the year, from soups, sandwiches and pâtés to traditional roasts and innovative dishes making use of fresh local fish and game.

The **Holiday Cottages** at Snape Maltings comprise three cottages and one flat, which have been carefully and tastefully converted to create four superb self-catering units. Surrounding the main arch through which the railway link used to run, Clock Tower, Garett Cottage and Kiln Cottage sleep six, while the Smugglers Cottage sleeps two. Ranging from the cosy to the spacious, all are very comfortable, with tasteful décor and furnishings, and provide views over either the top of the Maltings and out to the River Alde, or the gardens. Homely and charming, they are fully equipped with every amenity. Available to let all year round.

The church, which stands above the town as a very visible landmark for mariners, contains a memorial to George Crabbe and a beautiful stained-glass window, the work of John Piper, depicting three Britten parables: *Curlew River*, *The Burning Fiery Furnace* and *The Prodigal Son*. Britten is buried in the churchyard, part of which is set aside for the benefit of wildlife.

Aldeburgh has a number of good hotels and fine restaurants specialising in locally-caught fish and shellfish.

## SNAPE

**3 miles S of Saxmundham on the A1094**

This 'boggy place' has a long and interesting history. In 1862 the remains of an Anglo-Saxon ship were discovered here, and since that time regular finds have been made, with some remarkable cases of almost perfect preservation. Snape, like Aldeburgh, has benefited over the years from the philanthropy of the Garrett family, one of whose members built the primary school and set up the Maltings, centre of the Aldeburgh Music Festival.

The last 30-odd years have seen the development of the **Snape Maltings Riverside Centre** (see panel opposite), a group of shops and galleries located in a complex of restored Victorian granaries and malthouses that is also the setting for the renowned Aldeburgh festival.

The Maltings began their designated task of converting grain into malt in the 1840s, and continued thus until 1965, when the pressure of modern techniques brought them to a halt. There was a real risk of the buildings being demolished, but George Gooderham, a local farmer, bought the site to expand his animal feeds business and soon saw the potential of the redundant buildings (his son Jonathan is the current owner of the site).

The Concert Hall came first, in 1967, and in 1971 the Craft Shop was established as the first conversion of the old buildings for retail premises. Conversion and expansion continue to this day, and in the numerous outlets visitors can buy anything from fudge to country-style clothing, from herbs to household furniture, silver buttons to top hats. Plants and garden accessories are also sold, and art galleries feature the work of local painters, potters and sculptors. The Centre hosts regular painting, craft and decorative art courses, and more recent expansion saw the creation of an impressive country-style store.

A short distance west of Snape, off the B1069, lies Blaxhall, famed for its growing stone. The **Blaxhall Stone**, which lies in the yard of Stone Farm, is

*Snape Maltings*

## FRIDAY STREET FARM SHOP & TEAROOM

Farnham, Saxmundham, Suffolk IP17 1JX
Tel/Fax: 01728 602783
e-mail: fridaystreetfarm@btopenworld.com

Set between Woodbridge and Lowestoft at the junction of the A12 and A1094 near Aldeburgh, **Friday Street Farm Shop and Tearoom** is open seven days a week 9-5.30, selling a wonderful range of local produce, seasonal home-grown fruit and vegetables, pick-your-own and local pottery and craftware. This spacious establishment boasts shelves and shelves of jams and preserves, wines, dry goods, meats (wild boar, duck, sausages, game, chicken), fish (fresh and smoked), ice-cream, cheeses and other dairy products, chocolate, breads and the freshest fruit, vegetables and other farm produce. In season, visitors can

gather their own asparagus, runner beans, courgettes, soft fruits, sprouts and more.

Throughout the summer there is a maze – made of maize! – popular with children and adults alike. In season there is a pumpkin-carving competition for all age groups. The friendly, helpful staff are happy to create an individualised fruit basket or bouquet, suggest a recipe for seasonal foods, or even do your shopping for you while you relax at the attractive and comfortable tearoom. Here, home-made cakes and lunches highlight a menu of cream teas, light lunches and luxury desserts.

## ASPENS JEWELLERS

6 The Thoroughfare, Woodbridge, Suffolk IP12 1AG
Tel: 01394 383614
website: www.aspenjewellers.com

Owned and run by Daniel and Matthew Morton – whose family have been jewellers for three generations – **Aspens Jewellers** in Woodbridge is a superior shop selling an excellent range of high-quality pieces for every occasion and pocket. Together they also run a sister shop in Ipswich at the Cattle Market; both shops stock watches, jewellery, giftware, tankards and goblets, Cross pens and pencils and other fine goods.

One speciality of this fine shop is its pieces crafted in amber – an ancient gem formed from fossilised pine resin and dating back some 40-60 million years – together with a fine range of gold and silver, including a selection of second-hand and

antique bracelets. The display cases are attractive, and evaluations are always available. Made-to-order rings can be requested here, and there's a full repair service for rings, bracelets and beaded necklaces. Jewellery cases are also sold here. Helpful and friendly service is always on hand, and the shop is open Monday-Saturday from 9-5. Member of the National Association of Goldsmiths and the Guild of Master Craftsmen.

reputed to have grown to its present size (5 tons) from a comparative pebble the size of a football, when it first came to local attention 100 years ago. Could there be more 'Blarney' than Blaxhall at work here?

# WOODBRIDGE

Udebyge, Wiebryge, Wodebryge, Wudebrige ... just some of the ways of spelling this splendid old market town since it was first mentioned in writing back in AD970. As to what the name means, it could simply be 'wooden bridge' or 'bridge by the wood', but the most likely and most interesting explanation is that it is derived from Anglo-Saxon words meaning 'Woden's (or Odin's) town'.

Standing at the head of the Deben estuary, it is a place of considerable charm with a wealth of handsome, often historic buildings and a considerable sense of history, as both a market town and a port.

The shipbuilding and allied industries flourished here, as at most towns on the Suffolk coast, and it is recorded that both Edward III, in the 14th century, and Drake in the 16th sailed in Woodbridge ships. There's still plenty of activity on and by the river, though nowadays it is all leisure-orientated. The town's greatest benefactor was Thomas Seckford, who rebuilt the abbey, paid for the chapel in the north aisle of St Mary's Church and founded the original almshouses in Seckford Street. In 1575 he gave the town the splendid Shire Hall on Market

## YE OLDE BELL & STEELYARD

New Street, Woodbridge, Suffolk IP12 1DZ
Tel: 01394 382933
website: www.yeoldbell.co.uk

The oldest pub in Woodbridge, **Ye Olde Bell & Steelyard** is a distinctive 16th century inn serving up excellent ales and traditional English fayre. With one of the two remaining steelyards in England - the word derives from the German for a weighbridge, used to ensure that wagon weights of barley and rye did not exceed 3 tonnes - the pub has won the Cask Marque award. The extensive menu of home-cooked dishes includes a taste of Anglia in the shape of steaks, casseroles, lamb chops, local sausages, fish pie, vegetarian dishes and much more.

## SPICE BAR, RESTAURANT & CAFÉ

17 The Thoroughfare, Woodbridge, Suffolk IP12 1AA
Tel/Fax: 01394 382557

Set in the centre of town in the middle of Woodbridge's main shopping street, **Spice Bar, Restaurant & Café** is a first-floor restaurant. Featured in *Time Out and Rough Guide* as best restaurant in Woodbridge, this excellent place boasts a lively atmosphere and is decorated in bright, attractive colours. Malaysian and New World cooking feature on the menu, with dishes such as

Malacca duck, stir-fried king prawns and Kari Kambing (Malaysian lamb curry), all expertly prepared and presented. Open Monday to Saturday, booking is advised for evening meals.

Hill. Originally used as a corn exchange, it now houses the **Suffolk Punch Heavy Horse Museum**, with an exhibition devoted to the Suffolk Punch breed of heavy working horse, the oldest such breed in the world. The history of the breed and its rescue from near-extinction in the 1960s is covered in fascinating detail, and there's a section dealing with the other famous Suffolk breeds – the Red Poll cattle, the Suffolk sheep and the Large Black pigs. Opposite the Shire Hall is **Woodbridge Museum**, a treasure trove of information on the history of the town and its more notable residents; from here it is a short stroll down the cobbled alleyway to the magnificent

*Tide Mill and Harbour, Woodbridge*

parish church of St Mary, where Seckford was buried in 1587.

Seckford naturally features prominently in the museum, along with the painter Thomas Churchyard, the map-maker Isaac Johnson and the poet

---

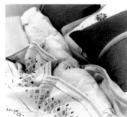

### THE COTTON TREE

Design Boutique, 40 Market Hill, Woodbridge, Suffolk IP12 4LU
Tel/Fax:  01394 388988
e-mail:info@thecottontree.co.uk  website: www.thecottontree.co.uk

As a successful Interior Design group, The Cotton Tree specialises is the creation of remarkable rooms, all with the 'comfortable' hallmark of the proprietor, Jules O'Dowd.  Nestled in the heart of Woodbridge, often described as a small 'Faberge Egg' is an interiors store bursting with design ideas and home inspiration.  Browse the collection of traditional and contemporary furniture, stunning lamps, beautiful fabrics and wallpapers.  Let the resident Interior Designer assist you in creating a unique space in your home.  The Cotton Tree also has stores in both Ipswich and Southwold that offer a tremendous selection of home wares and design led giftware.

---

### MELTON HALL

Woodbridge, Suffolk  IP12 1PF
Tel: 01394 388138  e-mail: delarue@meltonh.fsnet.co.uk
Fax: 01394 388982  website: www.meltonhall.co.uk

**Melton Hall** is a distinctive and gracious Georgian residence set in 7½ acres of grounds that include a walled vegetable and fruit garden, meadows and woodland. Dating back to the 1750s, the hall boasts handsome and spacious rooms and is tastefully decorated and furnished throughout. The guests' sitting room has comfortable, overstuffed settees and French windows leading out to the lovely gardens. The three guest bedrooms (2 doubles – one with four-poster bed – and one single) offer luxuries such as embroidered linen and fresh flowers. The atmosphere is relaxed, peaceful and welcoming.

## THE TURKS HEAD

Low Road, Haskerton, Woodbridge, Suffolk  IP13 6JG
Tel: 01394 382584

More like a charming family home than a pub, **The Turks Head** is a welcoming and charming, cosy little brickbuilt 16th century low house. This traditional rural pub – voted Best Rural Pub of the Year in Suffolk in 2002 – is a relaxed and friendly place to enjoy an excellent range of real ales, specially chosen wines and home-cooked food. The excellent English fare served at lunch and dinner includes venison on special occasions, fresh fish, local beef and more. Special themed evenings feature foods from around the world. This charming pub also has space in its 6½ acres of grounds for five caravans.

Edward Fitzgerald. 'Old Fitz' was something of an eccentric and, for the most part, fairly reclusive. He loved Woodbridge and particularly the River Deben, where he often sailed in his little boat *Scandal*.

Woodbridge is lucky enough to have two marvellous mills, both in working order, and both great attractions for the visitor. The **Tide Mill**, on the quayside close to the town centre, dates from the late 18th century (though the site was mentioned 600 years previously) and worked by the power of the tide until 1957. It has been meticulously restored and the waterwheel still turns, fed by a recently created pond which replaced the original huge mill pond when it was turned into a marina. **Buttrum's Mill**, named after the last miller, is a tower mill standing just off the A12 bypass a mile west of the town centre. A marvellous sight, its six storeys make it the tallest surviving tower mill in Suffolk. There is a ground-floor display of the history and workings of the mill.

Many of the town's streets are traffic-free, so shopping is a real pleasure. If you should catch the Fitzgerald mood and feel like 'a jug of wine and a loaf of bread', Woodbridge can oblige with a good variety of pubs and restaurants.

## AROUND WOODBRIDGE

### SUTTON HOO
**1 mile E of Woodbridge off the B1083**

A mile or so east of Woodbridge on the opposite bank of the Deben is **Sutton Hoo** (see panel on page 148), sometimes known as 'page one of the history of England'. A unique and fascinating place to visit, the discovery of ship rivets in an ancient burial mound in 1939 led to one of the most amazing finds in the nation's history. This, the ship burial of an Anglo-Saxon warrier king and his most treasured possessions, had lain undisturbed for more than 1,300 years. The permanent display in the special exhibition hall reveals how Anglo-Saxon nobles lived, went to war and founded a kingdom in East Anglia. Here visitors can discover how the famous helmet and exquisite gold jewellery were made and used. A second hall houses an exhibition investigating the Anglo-Saxon thirst for imported luxuries from the Mediterranean and elsewhere. Visitors can also take the short walk to the burial mounds to see for themselves the site where the ship and treasures were found. It is now believed that the ship was the burial place of Raedwald, of the Wuffinga

## SUTTON HOO

© NTPL

Tranmer House, Sutton Hoo, Woodbridge, Suffolk IP12 3DJ
Tel: 01394 389700  Fax: 01394 389702

At **Sutton Hoo** you can get close to one of the most important archaeological finds in this country's history - a fascinating story of Anglo-Saxon pagan kings, ship burials, treasure and warriors.

Close to the sea, one of several large mounds was excavated in 1939 revealing the now famous treasures, including a warrior's helmet, shield, gold ornaments and byzantine silver in the remains of a burial chamber of a 90ft ship.

The site has recently been developed by the National Trust and offers extensive new visitor facilities including an exhibition hall, restaurant, shop and walks. The permanent display tells the story of the Anglo-Saxon kings and the excavation of the mounds over fifty years and looks at other aspects of Anglo-Saxon life such as craftsmanship, life, death in the seventh century and the importance of ships for this island nation. The centrepiece is a full-size reconstruction of King Raedwald's burial chamber. The Treasury Room houses a temporary exhibition

© NTPL

(20 March – 30 Sept) with some of the original artefacts on loan from the British Museum for the first time since their discovery. Summer 2004 exhibition: 'Animals in Anglo-Saxon Art'

Location Off B1083 Woodbridge to Bawdsey Road. Follow signs from the A12. Car park charge when visitor facilities and exhibition are closed.

## THE GREYHOUND INN

The Street, Pettistree, Wickham Market,
Suffolk  IP13 0HP
Tel/Fax: 01728 746451

A country restaurant more than just a pub, **The Greyhound Inn** offers excellent home-cooked food from an imaginative menu. Booking is advised at this fine inn, where classic dishes such as fish pie and tarragon chicken vie with more innovative creations expertly prepared and presented, along with game dishes in season and, for afters, a range of mouth-watering puddings and speciality Italian coffees. All dishes make use of the freshest ingredients from local suppliers such as Brom and May (fishmongers), Hamish Johnson (cheeses) and Metfield Bakery (for fresh breads daily).

Here in this pretty village off the A12 near Framlingham Castle and Wickham Market, and just 15 minutes from Woodbridge, this handsome inn is gracious and elegant inside and out. Tasteful and traditional, the cosy bar and dining room offer the perfect ambience for thoroughly enjoying an excellent meal. Owner Deborah Mary trained at Prue Leith's Cookery School in Kensington – and her passion for quality and superb culinary skills have rubbed off on her experienced, attentive staff.

dynasty, King of East Anglia from about 610 to 625. Access to the site is on foot from the B1083. The site's extensive facilities include a restaurant, shop, children's play area and variety of walks in the surrounding countryside. There is good access for visitors with disabilities to all of the site.

## WICKHAM MARKET

**5 miles N of Woodbridge off the A12**

Places to see in this straggling village are the picturesque watermill by the River Deben and All Saints Church, whose 137-foot octagonal tower has a little roof to shelter the bell. At Boulge, a couple of miles southwest of Wickham Market, is the grave of Edward Fitzgerald, whose free translation of *The Rubaiyat of Omar Khayyam* is an English masterpiece. Tradition has it that on his grave is a rose bush grown from one found on Omar Khayyam's grave in Iran.

## UFFORD

**3 miles NE of Woodbridge off the A12**

Pride of place in a village that takes its name from Uffa (or Wuffa), the founder of the leading Anglo-Saxon dynasty, goes to the 13th century **Church of the Assumption**. The font cover, which telescopes from 5 feet to 18 feet in height, is a masterpiece of craftsmanship, its elaborate carving crowned by a pelican. Many 15th century benches have survived, but Dowsing smashed the organ and most of the stained glass – what's there now is mainly Victorian, some of it a copy of 15th century work at All Souls College, Oxford.

Ufford is where the Suffolk Punch originated, Crisp's 404 being, in 1768, the progenitor of this distinguished breed of horses.

## KITTY'S HOMESTORE

46 High Street, Wickham Market, Woodbridge, Suffolk IP13 0QS
Tel/Fax: 01728 748370
e-mail: info@kittyshomestore.com
website: www.kittyshomestore.com

A treasure-trove of everything for the home, **Kitty's Homestore** is a charming place filled with tasteful

and distinctive homeware and giftware. This mini-department store features

home furnishings and more: wonderful handbags, jewellery, belts, gift wrap and cards, beautiful scarves, fragrances, gift ideas – along with everything for enhancing your home and garden. The carefully chosen items are designed to give any home those lovely little touches that make it unique and welcoming.

The staff are always polite and friendly, and are happy to leave customers to browse or offer knowledgeable help when it comes to choosing from among the range of tableware, crockery, candlesticks, garden furniture, vases, bread bins, linens, lamps, soft furnishings such as rugs, cushions and throws, and much more. Set in the town square, this pretty and welcoming shop is well worth a look for its range of traditional and modern items and its excellent customer service.

## BROMESWELL

**3 miles NE of Woodbridge off the B1084**

This quiet village occupies a scenic setting. Bromeswell's church has a 12th century archway at its entrance, a 15th century font and an unusual Flemish well. The angels in the hammerbeam roof are plastic replicas of the originals, whose wings were clipped by Cromwell's men.

## CAMPSEA ASHE

**6 miles NE of Woodbridge on the B1078**

On towards Wickham Market the road passes through Campsea Ashe in the parish of Campsey Ashe. The 14th century church of St John the Baptist has an

interesting brass showing one of its first rectors in full priestly garb.

## RENDLESHAM

**5 miles NE of Woodbridge on the A1152**

The church of **St Gregory the Great** dates from the 14th century, but there is evidence (not physical, unfortunately) of an earlier Christian presence in the shape of Raedwald's palace.

**Rendlesham Forest**, part of the Forest of Aldewood, was ravaged by the great hurricane of October 1987. Seven years before that, on Christmas night, another visitation had occurred. Security guards at RAF Woodbridge, at that time a front

## BUTLEY POTTERY, GALLERY & BARN CAFÉ

Mill Lane, Butley, Woodbridge, Suffolk IP12 3PA
Tel: 01394 450785
e-mail: honorhussey@btconnect.com

A group of sensitively converted farm buildings incorporate **Butley Pottery**, the Barn Café and a summer artist's gallery. The showroom displays studio pottery, individual pieces with slip or majolica designs, sculpture in various media and Dan Hussey's unique and beautiful hand crafted range of steam bent coppiced ash furniture. There are changing exhibitions in the gallery, during the summer by contemporary artists. Self-catering bed and breakfast is also available here, in a charming apartment.

**The Barn Café (Tel: 01394 450800/382332)** specializes in innovative cuisine, using locally produced meat and vegetables, and an abundance of fresh herbs. Unusual vegetarian creations are always on the menu. Lunch bookings advisable, evening parties by arrangement. This is a delightful area of the coast, offering many hidden attractions. Cycle routes, footpaths and bird reserves abound, the river Ore and historic places such as Sutton Hoo, Orford castle and medieval woods are close by.

line NATO base, spotted strange lights in the forest and went to investigate. They came upon a nine-foot high triangular object with a series of lights around it. As they approached, it did what all good UFOs do and flew off before it could be photographed. The next day the guards returned to the spot where it had landed and found three depressions in the ground. The UFO was apparently sighted again two days later, and security in the area was heightened. No explanation has ever been forthcoming about the incident, but interest in it continues and from time to time guided walks to the landing site are arranged.

## BUTLEY

### 5 miles E of Woodbridge on the B1084

At the northern edge of Rendlesham Forest, the village of Butley has a splendid 14th century gatehouse, all that remains of **Butley Priory**, an Augustinian priory founded by Ranulf de Glanville in 1171. The gatehouse is, by itself, a fairly imposing building, with some interesting flintwork on the north façade (1320) and baronial carvings. Butley's parish church is Norman, with a 14th century tower.

There are some splendid country walks

here, notably by **Staverton Thicks**, which has a deer park and woods of oak and holly. The oldest trees date back more than 400 years. Butley Clumps is an avenue of beech trees planted in fours, with a pine tree at the centre of each clump – the technical term for such an arrangement is a *quincunx*. Butley was long renowned for its oysters, and the beds have recently been revived.

## CHILLESFORD

### 6 miles E of Woodbridge on the B1084

Brick was once big business here, and while digging for clay the locals made many finds, including hundreds of varieties of molluscs and the skeleton of an enormous whale. Chillesford supplies some of the clay for Aldeburgh brickworks.

## ORFORD

### 12 miles E of Woodbridge at the end of the B1084

Without doubt one of the most charming and interesting of all the places in Suffolk, Orford has something to please everyone. The ruins of one of the most important castles in medieval England are a most impressive sight, even though the keep is all that remains of the original building commissioned by Henry II in 1165. The walls of the keep are 90 foot high and 10 foot deep, and behind them are many rooms and passages in a remarkable state of preservation. A climb up the spiral staircase to the top provides splendid views over the surrounding countryside and to the sea.

*Orford Castle*

**St Bartholomew's Church** was built at the same time, though the present church dates from the 14th century. A wonderful sight at night when floodlit, the church is regularly used for the performance of concerts and recitals, and many of Benjamin Britten's works were first heard here. At the east end lie the still-splendid Norman remains, all that is left of the original chancel.

These two grand buildings indicate that Orford was a very important town at one time. Indeed it was once a thriving port, but the steadily growing shingle bank of Orford Ness gradually cut it off from the sea, and down the years its appeal has changed. The sea may have gone but the river is still there, and in summer the quayside is alive with yachts and pleasure craft. On the other side of the river is **Orford Ness**, the

largest vegetated shingle spit in England which is home to a variety of rare flora and fauna. The lighthouse marks the most easterly point (jointly with Lowestoft) in Britain.

Access to the spit, which is in the hands of the National Trust, is by ferry from Orford quay. For many years the Ness was out of bounds to the public, being used for various military purposes, including pre-war radar research under Sir Robert Watson-Watt. Boat trips also leave Orford quay for the RSPB reserve at **Havergate Island**, haunt of avocet and tern (the former returned in 1947 after being long absent).

The Dunwich Underwater Exploration Exhibition in Front Street features exhibits on marine archaeology, coastal erosion and more, gleaned from the exploration of the ruins of the former

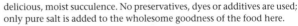

## HOLIDAY COTTAGE

47 Daphne Road, Orford, Suffolk IP12 2NU
Tel: 01394 450714

As its name tells us, the **Holiday Cottage** is a charming hideaway ideal for the perfect break. This handsome and distinctive brickbuilt cottage has three comfortable and welcoming bedrooms, a sitting room/dining area and galley-style kitchen. The quay and Orford Castle are within easy walking distance and there is an interesting choice of pubs in the village as well as the Orford Oysterage Restaurant. There is a well stocked village shop and a good butcher.

There's some excellent walking in the area, and many of the attractions and sights of this area are just a short drive away. Children and pets welcome by arrangement.

town of Dunwich, now largely claimed by the sea.

Back in the market square are a handsome town hall, two pubs with a fair quota of smuggling tales, a well-loved restaurant serving Butley oysters and a smokehouse where kippers, salmon, trout, ham, sausages, chicken and even garlic are smoked over Suffolk oak.

### HOLLESLEY

**5 miles SE of Woodbridge off the B1083**

The Deben and the Ore turn this part of Suffolk almost into a peninsula, and on the seaward side lie Hollesley and Shingle Street. The latter stands upon a shingle bank at the entrance to the Ore and comprises a row of little houses, a coastguard cottage and a Martello tower. Its very isolation is an attraction, and the sight of the sea rushing into and out of the river is worth the journey.

Brendan Behan did not enjoy his visit. Brought here on a swimming outing from the Borstal at Hollesley, he declared that the waves had 'no limit but the rim of the world'. Looking out to the bleak North Sea, it is easy to see what he meant.

### BAWDSEY

**7 miles SE of Woodbridge on the B1083**

The B1083 runs from Woodbridge through farming country and several attractive villages (Sutton, Shottisham, Alderton) to Bawdsey, beyond which lie the mouth of the River Deben, the end of the Sussex Coastal Path, and the ferry to Felixstowe. The late-Victorian Bawdsey Manor was taken over by the Government and became the centre for radar development when Orford Ness was deemed unsuitable. By the beginning of the Second World War there were two dozen secret radar stations in Britain, and radar HQ moved from Bawdsey to Dundee. The manor is now a leisure centre.

### RAMSHOLT

**7 miles SE of Woodbridge off the B1083**

Ramsholt is a tiny community on the north bank of the Deben a little way up from Bawdsey. The pub is a popular port of call for yachtsmen, and half a mile from the quay, in quiet isolation, stands the Church of All Saints with its round tower. Road access to Ramsholt is from the B1083 just south of Shottisham.

# LOCATOR MAP

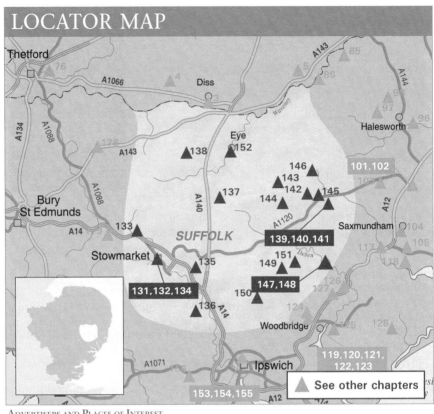

Thetford

A1066    Diss

A143

Eye

A143    ▲138    ○152

Bury
St Edmunds

Stowmarket    133▲

SUFFOLK

▲135

Saxmundham

Halesworth

146▲
143▲
142▲    145
144    ▲

**101,102**

**139,140,141**

151
149    ▲

**147,148**

150

136
▲

Woodbridge

**131,132,134**

A1071    Ipswich

**119,120,121,
122,123**

**153,154,155**

▲ **See other chapters**

ADVERTISERS AND PLACES OF INTEREST

| | | |
|---|---|---|
| 131 Verandah House, Stowmarket | Page 155 | |
| 132 Tot Hill House, Tot Hill, Stowmarket | Page 156 | |
| 133 Redhouse Farm, Haughley, Stowmarket | Page 157 | |
| 134 Museum of East Anglian Life, Stowmarket | Page 157 | |
| 135 Alder Carr Farm Shop & Crafts, Creeting St Mary, Needham Market | Page 158 | |
| 136 Baylham House Rare Breeds Farm, Baylham | Page 159 | |
| 137 Step House, Wetheringsett, Stowmarket | Page 160 | |
| 138 The Forge Café, Restaurant & Gift Shop, Thornham Magna, Eye | Page 161 | |
| 139 Shawsgate Vineyard, Framlingham | Page 162 | |
| 140 Sleeping Partners, Framlingham | Page 162 | |
| 141 Bed Bazaar, Framlingham | Page 162 | |

142 Tannington Hall, Framlingham    Page 163
143 White Hall Plants, Worlingworth, Framlingham    Page 164
144 Abbey House, Monk Soham, Woodbridge    Page 164
145 Grange Farm, Dennington, Framlingham    Page 165
146 Woodlands Farm, Brundish, Framlingham    Page 165
147 Easton Farm Park Holiday Cottages, Easton, Woodbridge    Page 166
148 Easton Farm Park, Easton, Woodbridge    Page 166
149 The Stables at Ivy Lodge Barn, Hoo, Woodbridge    Page 167
150 The Crockery Barn, Ashbocking, Ipswich    Page 168
151 Church Farm, Kettleburgh, Framlingham    Page 169
152 Beards of Eye, Eye    Page 171

# CENTRAL SUFFOLK 5

Inland Suffolk has few peers in terms of picturesque countryside and villages, and the area of central Suffolk between the heathland and the coast is a delightful place for getting away from it all to the real countryside, with unchanged ancient villages, gently flowing rivers and rich farm land. The Rivers Deben and Gipping run through much of the region, which also boasts its fair share of churches, museums, markets, fayres and festivals. The little market towns of Stowmarket and Needham Market are full of interest, and in this part of Suffolk some of the best-preserved windmills and watermills are to be found. Several examples of both types of mills survive, and the village of Pakenham is lucky in having a splendid example of each.

*Willy Lotts Cottage, Flatford Mill*

## STOWMARKET

The largest town in the heart of Suffolk, Stowmarket enjoyed a period of rapid growth when the River Gipping was still navigable to Ipswich and when the railway arrived. Much of the town's history and legacy are brought vividly to life in the splendid **Museum of East Anglian Life** (see panel on page 157), situated in the centre of town to the west of the marketplace (where markets are held twice a week), in a 70-acre meadowland site on the old Abbot's Hall Estate (the aisled original barn dates from the 13$^{th}$ century). Part of the open-air section features several historic buildings that have been moved from elsewhere in the region and carefully re-erected on site. These include an engineering workshop from the 1870s, part of a 14$^{th}$ century farmhouse, a watermill from Alton and a wind pump which was rescued in a collapsed state at Minsmere in 1977. There's also a collection of working steam engines,

---

VERANDAH HOUSE

29 Ipswich Road, Stowmarket, Suffolk IP14 1BD
Tel: 01449 676104   e-mail: info@verandahhouse.co.uk
Fax: 01449 616127   website: www.verandahhouse.co.uk

Set in a quarter-acre of delightful walled gardens with a pond and mature magnolias and eucalyptus trees, **Verandah House** is a large and gracious restored and renovated Georgian and Victorian Grade II listed property offering guests a warm welcome. With a wide choice of beautiful single, double and family rooms – including a ground-floor twin/double – this family-run establishment is well worth seeking out. An excellent touring base, the house is a two minute walk from Stowmarket town centre and within easy reach of the Heritage Coast, the Dedham Vale and Constable Country. 4 Diamonds ETB.

## TOT HILL HOUSE

Tot Hill, Stowmarket, Suffolk  IP14 3QH
Tel/Fax: 01449 673375
website: www.tothillhouse.co.uk

Covered in Virginia Creeper and surrounded by pleasant gardens and grounds that include an open-air swimming pool, **Tot Hill House** is a large and impressive restaurant with rooms dating back to the 1560s. Here, guests can enjoy Modern English cuisine with an emphasis on the freshest produce. The seasonally-changing menu offers up the very best in locally-sourced ingredients creatively combined to produce tempting dishes – be it fish,

fowl, meat or vegetarian, all the dishes are expertly prepared and presented. The wine list is extensive with all wines being available by the glass, and the drinks menu includes a selection of 30 malt whiskies.

There are four guest bedrooms, one boasting a four-poster bed. Three are en suite and one has use of a private bathroom, and all are decorated and furnished to a high standard of quality and comfort. Located on the A14, it is within easy reach of Stowmarket and the many sights and attractions of this part of the county.

farm animals and year-round demonstrations of all manner of local arts and crafts, from coopering to chandlery, from sheep shearing to saddlery. Stowmarket's church of St Peter and St Mary acquired a new spire in 1994, replacing the 1715 version (itself a replacement) which was dismantled on safety grounds in 1975.

The town certainly merits a leisurely stroll, while for a peaceful picnic the riverbank beckons. Serious scenic walkers should make for the **Gipping Valley River Park** walk, which follows the former towpath all the way to Ipswich.

## AROUND STOWMARKET

### ELMSWELL

**7 miles NW of Stowmarket off the A14**

Clearly visible from the A14, the impressive church of St John the Baptist

with its massive flint tower stands at the entrance to the village, facing Woolpit across the valley. A short drive north of Elmswell lies **Great Ashfield**, an unspoilt village whose now disused airfield played a key role in both World Wars. In the churchyard of the 13th century All Saints is a memorial to the Americans who died during the Second World War, as attested to by the commemorative altar. Some accounts say that Edmund was buried here in AD903 after dying at the hands of the Danes; a cross was put up in his memory. The cross was replaced in the 19th century and now stands in the garden of Ashfield House.

### HAUGHLEY

**4 miles NW of Stowmarket off the A14**

On the run into Stowmarket, Haughley once had the largest motte-and-bailey castle in Suffolk. All that now remains is a mound behind the church. **Haughley**

## REDHOUSE FARM

Station Road, Haughley, Stowmarket, Suffolk IP14 3QP
Tel: 01449 673323 Fax: 01449 675413

Set in spacious gardens and grounds, **Redhouse Farm** is a taste of luxury happily married to home comforts. There are four lovely guest bedrooms, all en suite, and a well-appointed and comfortable guests' sitting room and dining room. Peace, relaxation and a genuinely warm welcome await guests here. Handy for shopping in Stowmarket and enjoying the many scenic attractions of this part of the county, the farm also boasts a self-catering cottage and small caravan site within the grounds. 4 Diamonds ETB. Early booking is advised to avoid disappointment.

Park is a handsome Jacobean redbrick manor house set in eight acres of gardens and surrounding woodland featuring ancient oaks and splendid magnolias. Woodland paths take the visitor past a half-mile stretch of rhododendrons, and in springtime the bluebells and lilies of the valley are a magical sight. The gardens are open on Tuesdays between May and September, the house by appointment only.

## HARLESTON

**4 miles NW of Stowmarket off the A14**

The churches of Shelland and Harleston lie in close proximity on a minor road between Woolpit and Haughley picnic site. At Shelland, the tiny church of King Charles the Martyr is one of only four in England to be dedicated to King Charles I. The brick floor is laid in a herringbone pattern, there are high box pews and a triple-decker pulpit, but the most unusual feature is a working barrel organ dating from the early 19th century.

The church of St Augustine at Harleston stands all alone among pine trees and is reached by a track across a field. It has a thatched roof, Early English windows and a tower with a single bell.

## BUXHALL

**3 miles W of Stowmarket just off the B1115**

The village church here is notable for its six heavy bells, but the best-known landmark in this quiet village is undoubtedly the majestic tower mill, without sails since a gale removed them

## MUSEUM OF EAST ANGLIAN LIFE

Stowmarket, Suffolk IP14 1DL
Tel: 01449 612229  Fax: 01449 672307
website: www.suffolkcc.gov.uk/central/meal

**The Museum of East Anglian Life** occupies a 70-acre site in the heart of Stowmarket. Its rich collections of social, rural and industrial history

include a number of historic buildings such as a working watermill, a smithy, a chapel and a 13th century farmhouse. There is something for the whole family to enjoy with a variety of farm animals, adventure playground, picnic sites, café and gift shop.

Throughout the year the Museum holds special events as well as demonstrations of crafts and engines in steam. The Museum is open from April to October.

in 1929 but still standing as a silent, sturdy reminder of its working days. This is good walking country, with an ancient wood and many signposted footpaths.

## NEEDHAM MARKET
### 4 miles SE of Stowmarket off the A14

A thriving village whose greatest glory is the wonderful carvings on the ceiling of the church of **St John the Baptist**. The church's ornate double hammerbeam roof is nothing short of remarkable, especially when bathed in light from the strategically placed skylight. The roof is massive, as high as the walls of the church itself; the renowned authority on Suffolk churches, H Munro Cautley, described the work at Needham as 'the culminating achievement of the English carpenter'. The village also boasts some excellent examples of Tudor architecture.

The River Gipping flows to the east of the High Street and its banks provide miles of walks: the towpath is a public right of way walkable all the way from Stowmarket to Ipswich. On the riverbank at Needham is a 25-acre picnic site and a nature reserve.

Monthly farmers' markets are held at Alder Carr Farm, where there is also a pottery, crafts centre and farm shop.

Nearby **Barking**, on the B1018 south of Needham, was once more important than its neighbour, being described in 1874 as 'a pleasant village ... including the hamlet of Needham Market'. This explains the fact that Barking's church is exceptionally large for a village house of worship: it was the mother church to Needham Market and was used for Needham's burials when Needham had no burial ground of its own.

## ALDER CARR FARM SHOP & CRAFTS

Creeting St Mary, Needham Market, Suffolk  IP6 8LX
Tel/Fax: 01449 720820
website: www.aldercarrfarm.co.uk

Family run, **Alder Carr Farm Shop & Crafts** is several specialist shops in one: The **Country Studio, Sugarcraft Studio, farm shop and tea room**, together with a pick-your-own service featuring the very best of farm-fresh vegetables and fruits. Here in this pretty village south of Stowmarket, all three attract a discerning clientele from far and wide. The Country Studio hosts paintings by Resident Artist Wendy Beck, along with jewellery and floral decor. The Sugarcraft Studio specialises in handcrafted and individually designed Wedding and Celebration cakes made to order.

At the pick-your-own, the fields are filled to bursting with strawberries, raspberries, gooseberries, sweetcorn and more of Nature's harvest. Produce at the farm shop includes meats, vegetables, juices – and celebrated home-made ice creams in a tempting variety of traditional and innovative flavours such as Gooseberry and Elderflower, and Stem Ginger and Rhubarb. The licensed tea room offers homemade cakes and scones with a fresh daily menu using seasonal produce from the farm shop, which includes delicious soups, open tarts, baked Suffolk Ham and much more. The staff are friendly and helpful.

## BAYLHAM

**7 miles SE of Stowmarket off the B1130**

The Roman site of Combretrovium is home to **Baylham House Rare Breeds Farm** (see panel), and visitors (April-early October) will find displays and information relating to both Rome and rare animals. The farm's chief concern is the survival of rare breeds, and there are breeding groups of cattle, sheep, pigs, goats and poultry.

## EARL STONHAM

**5 miles E of Stowmarket on the A1120**

A scattered village set around three greens in farming land, Earl Stonham's church of St Mary the Virgin boasts one of Suffolk's finest single hammerbeam roofs, and is also notable for its Bible scene murals, the 'Doom' (Last Judgement scene) over the chancel arch and a triple hour-glass, presumably to record just how protracted were some of the sermons.

## STONHAM ASPAL

**6 miles E of Stowmarket on the A1120**

On the other side of the A140 lies Stonham Aspal, where in 1962 the remains of a Roman bath-house were unearthed. The parish church has an unusual wooden top to its tower, a necessary addition to house the ten bells that a keen campanologist insisted on installing. At Stonham Barns, the **British Birds of Prey and Nature Centre** is

### BAYLHAM HOUSE RARE BREEDS FARM

Mill Lane, Baylham, Suffolk IP6 8LG
Tel: 01473 830264
website: www.baylham-house-farm.co.uk

**Baylham House Rare Breeds Farm** is a wonderful place to take children. Previous visitors have described it as having a unique and magical quality not found elsewhere. The primary aim of the farm is to help maintain the national stock of endangered rare breed farm animals, providing the best possible care in a traditional and sympathetic way. The secondary aim is to provide people, particularly children, with an opportunity to meet healthy, contented and friendly farm animals. Four different breeds of cattle and six small flocks of rare sheep can be seen at Baylham House. The pig collection includes some very friendly

Maori pigs from New Zealand called Kune Kunes and Large Blacks, one of the rarest of British pigs. The farm also keeps poultry and pygmy goats.

The farm is situated within a significant Roman site, scheduled as an Ancient Monument and includes two military forts and a large civilian settlement. Information and artefacts are displayed at the Visitors' Centre. Whilst here you can also take a walk along the lovely riverside path and spend a day in the countryside within the Gipping Valley. When you've had your fill of fresh air, you can recover with some refreshments at the Visitors' Centre, which also sells souvenirs and gifts.

home to every species of British owl, together with raptors from Britain and around the world. These wonderful birds flap their wings in regular flying displays, and in the Pets Paradise area children can meet and greet hamsters and horses, mice and meerkats, parrots and piglets.

## MENDLESHAM

**6 miles NE of Stowmarket off the A140**

On the green in Old Market Street, Mendlesham, lies an enormous stone which is said to have been used as a preaching stone, mounted by itinerant Wesleyan preachers. In the Church of St Mary there is a collection of parish armour assembled some 400 years ago,

## STEP HOUSE

Hockey Hill, Wetheringsett, nr Stowmarket, Suffolk  IP14 5PL
Tel/Fax: 01449 766476
e-mail: stephouse@tiscali.co.uk

Set amid beautiful gardens, **Step House** is a wonderful 15th century Grade II listed timber-frame former Hall House. Located in the heart of Suffolk, just half a mile from the A140, it makes an excellent base for exploring the coast. Heavily oak-beamed and with wattle-and-daub walls and other original features such as the inglenook fireplaces, the accommodation at this characterful and elegant place comprises three guest bedrooms, two with private sitting room and bath. 4 Diamonds ETB.

and also some fine carvings. The least hidden local landmark is a 1,000-ft TV mast put up by the IBA in 1959.

## WETHERINGSETT
**7 miles NE of Stowmarket off the A140**

On the other side of the A140, Wetheringsett is where visitors will find **Mid-Suffolk Light Railway Museum**, open on summer Sundays and during school holidays.

Wetheringsett has had two well-known rectors, famous for very different reasons. Richard Hakluyt, incumbent from 1590 to 1616, is remembered for his major work *Voyages* (full title *Principal Navigation, Voyages, Traffiques and Discoveries of the English Nation*). The rector between 1858 and 1883 was a certain George Wilfrid Ellis, sometime tailor and butler, and finally a bogus clergyman. After he was unmasked as a sham, a special Act of Parliament was needed to validate the marriage ceremonies he had illegally performed, and to legitimise the issue of those marriages.

## COTTON
**5 miles N of Stowmarket off the B1113**

South of Finningham, where Yew Tree House displays some fine pargetting, and just by Bacton, a lovely village originally built around seven greens, lies the village of Cotton, which should be visited for several reasons, one of which is to see the splendid 14th century flint church of St Andrew, impressive in its dimensions and notable for its double hammerbeam roof with carved angels.

Cotton's **Mechanical Music Museum & Bygones** has an extensive collection that includes gramophones, music boxes, street pianos, fairground organs and polyphons, as well as the marvellous Wurlitzer Theatre pipe organ.

## THORNHAM MAGNA & PARVA
**10 miles N of Stowmarket off the A140**

The **Thornham Walks and Field Centre**, with 12 miles of walks and a herb garden and nursery, cater admirably for hikers, horticulturists and lovers of the countryside. The tiny thatched church of St Mary at Thornham Parva houses a considerable treasure in the shape of an exquisite medieval altar painting, known as a *retable*, with a central panel depicting the Crucifixion and four saints on each side panel. Its origins are uncertain, but it was possibly the work of the Royal Workshops at Westminster Abbey and made for Thetford Priory, or for a nearby Dominican monastery. Also to be admired is the 14th century octagonal font and a series of fascinating wall paintings. In the churchyard is a monument to Sir Basil Spence (1907-76), architect of Coventry Cathedral.

## THE FORGE CAFÉ, RESTAURANT & GIFT SHOP

Red House Yard, Thornham Walks, Thornham Magna,
Eye, Suffolk IP23 8HH
Tel: 01379 783035  Fax: 01379 783015
website: www.forgerestaurant.co.uk

You will receive a warm welcome from Laura and Richard at **The Forge Café, Restaurant and Gift Shop**. Richard, originally from Durban, South Africa, has many years' experience in hotel and catering management, and together with Laura has made this establishment a great success. Set in a former forge, the café/restaurant serves up dishes using the freshest ingredients, locally sourced whenever possible and all cooked to order. Open (winter) Wednesday to Sunday and Friday and Saturday evenings, and in summer 7 days a week and Friday and Saturday evenings, the menu boasts tempting morsels such as pan-fried swordfish, vegetable jambalaya and a full range of sandwiches, salads and snacks, which can be accompanied by wine,

beer, soft drinks or a variety of coffees. The ambience is always welcoming, the surroundings attractive and comfortable.

Opposite the café/restaurant stands the craft and giftshop, where a delightful variety of giftware and collectibles are sold: pictures and prints, books, hand-crafted wooden knick-knacks, cushion covers, hand-made wrought iron pieces created by local artists, trinket boxes, cards, gift wrap, and much more. The Forge is situated at the entrance to the famous Thornham Walks, and makes an excellent place to stop and enjoy a relaxed snack or meal, or do a bit of shopping, while exploring the area.

## YAXLEY

**12 miles N of Stowmarket on the A140**

Yaxley's church of **St Mary** offers up more treasures. One is an extremely rare sexton's wheel, which hangs above the south door and was used in medieval times to select fast days in honour of the Virgin. When a pair of iron wheels were spun on their axle, strings attached to the outer wheel would catch on the inner, stopping both and indicating the chosen day. The 17$^{th}$ century pulpit is one of the finest in the country, with the most glorious, sumptuous carvings.

Yaxley's most famous son is Sir Frederick Ashton, who is buried in the churchyard.

# FRAMLINGHAM

The marvellous **Castle**, brooding on a hilltop, dominates this agreeable market

town, as it has since Roger Bigod, 2$^{nd}$ Earl of Norfolk, built it in the 12$^{th}$ century (his grandfather built the first a century earlier, but this wooden construction was soon demolished). The Earls and Dukes of Norfolk, the Howards, were here for many generations before moving to Arundel in 1635. The castle is in remarkably good condition, partly because it was rarely attacked – though

*Framlingham Church*

## SHAWSGATE VINEYARD

Badingham Road, Framlingham, Woodbridge, Suffolk  IP13 9HZ
Tel: 01728 724060  e-mail: wines@shawsgate.co.uk
Fax: 01728 723232  website: www.shawsgate.co.uk

Established for more than 25 years, **Shawsgate Vineyard** produces fine English wines and has won over 30 awards in competition with both English and international wines. The 21-acre vineyard contains over 20,000 vines. Six grape varieties are grown on a medium clay loam, benefiting from Suffolk's warm, dry climate. Varieties include Bacchus, Seyval Blanc, Reichensteiner and Muller Thurgau, used to make white wines. Unusually for an English vineyard, they also produce a red wine, using the Rondo grape. Visitors are welcome to take a tour to see vineyards at different stages of maturity, from newly planted ones to those laid down when the vineyard first became established.

Through the unique 'vine-leasing scheme', customers can lease a row or more of vines, effectively becoming wine-producers and therefore benefiting from the duty-free and VAT-free allowances, enabling them to secure home-grown English wines for a third of the normal price. Located a mile from the Norman Castle in Framlingham, Shawsgate can be reached by following the brown tourist signs from the A12/B1116 Saxmundham bypass, the A1120/B1120 from Badingham, and the B1119/B1120 from Framlingham. Customers are also more than welcome to shop and buy online, using the vineyard's secure e-commerce system.

## SLEEPING PARTNERS

The Old Station, Station Road, Framlingham, Suffolk  IP13 9EE
Tel: 01728 724944  Fax: 01728 724626

At the **Sleeping Partners** factory showroom, traditional high-quality mattresses are hand-crafted to any size or shape, made to order. Established by the Bed Bazaar to complement its antique bedstead business, this specialist showroom is regularly chosen to supply mattresses to interior designers, hoteliers and bedstead retailers large and small. Horsehair insulation, layers of super-cotton, lambswool and Belgium ticking cover are used to create a range of supremely comfortable pocket-sprung and open-coil mattresses, including premier Backcare varieties. Nationwide delivery.

## BED BAZAAR

The Old Station, Station Road, Framlingham, Suffolk  IP13 9EE
Tel: 01728 723756  Fax: 01728 724626

With over 2,000 genuine antique wooden and metal bedsteads in stock, plus a vast array of period reproduction bedsteads, **Bed Bazaar** has earned a well-deserved reputation for quality and value. With sizes from 2'6 to 6' wide, hand-made mattresses and quilts, and luxury bed linen from the French Linen Company, there's everything required for a wonderful night's sleep for many years to come. They can also undertake restoration and repair work. Delivery anywhere in the UK.

King John put it under siege in 1215. Its most famous occupant was Mary Tudor, who was in residence when proclaimed Queen in 1553. During the reign of Elizabeth I it was used as a prison for defiant priests and, in the 17th century after being bequeathed to Pembroke College, Cambridge, it saw service as a home and school for local paupers. Nine of the castle's 13 towers are accessible - the climb up the spiral staircase and walk round the battlements are well worth the effort. On one side the view is of the Meres, a bird sanctuary. In the north wing is the **Lanman Museum**, devoted to agricultural, craftsman's tools and domestic memorabilia.

The castle brought considerable prestige and prosperity to Framlingham, evidence of which can be found in the splendid church of **St Michael**, which has two wonderful works of art. One is the tomb of Henry Fitzroy, bastard son of Henry VIII, beautifully adorned with scenes from Genesis and Exodus and in a superb state of repair. The other is the tomb of the 3rd Duke, with carvings of the apostles in shell niches. Also of note is the Carolean organ of 1674, a gift of Sir Robert Hitcham, to whom the Howards sold the estate. Cromwell and the Puritans were not in favour of organs in churches, so this instrument was lucky to have escaped the mass destruction of organs at the time of the Commonwealth. Sir Robert is buried in the church.

# AROUND FRAMLINGHAM

### SAXTEAD GREEN

**2 miles W of Framlingha off the A1120**

One of the prettiest sights in Suffolk is the white **18th century mill** that stands on the marshy green in Saxtead. This is a wonderful example of a post mill,

### TANNINGTON HALL

Nr Framlingham, Suffolk IP13 7NH
Tel/Fax: 01728 627999
e-mail: enquiries@tanningtonhall.com
website: www.tanningtonhall.com

A taste of old-world luxury awaits guests at **Tannington Hall**, a magnificent Tudor farmhouse set in 10 acres of meadows and scented gardens amid a further 2,000 acres of arable farmland. Famous for its horse and carriage tours, this gracious, charming place offers excellent accommodation in three comfortable and elegant oak-beamed en suite bedrooms enjoying views of the garden. The moats remain traditionally stocked with fish, and guests are welcome to bring their rods.

Locally grown food and homemade seasonal specialities are the base for breakfast and suppers.Private horse drawn carriages can be easily arranged to transport guests to local inns for drinks or meals or longer tours of the Suffolk countryside.

Handy for Framlingham, Sutton Hoo, Easton Farm Park and other sights and attractions of the region, this superb establishment makes a relaxing and welcoming place to serve as a base while in the area.

## White Hall Plants

Southolt Road, Worlingworth,
nr Framlingham, Suffolk IP13 7HW
Tel: 01728 628490  Fax: 01728 628160
e-mail: charleswalker@suffolkonline.net

At **White Hall Plants** of Worlingworth, Suffolk, herbaceous perennials, grasses and unusual plants are among the specialities set in 1½ acres of grounds covered with stock beds and tunnels. Over 2,000 plant species and varieties can be found here, carefully tended and clearly labelled. Featured in Suffolk Magazine and praised by renowned garden designers, this excellent nursery also boasts a large sales area with inspirational plants for cottage gardens, dramatic borders and perennial gardens. Open March to October 7 days a week 10-6; other times by prior arrangement.

perhaps the best in the world, dating back to 1796 and first renovated in the 19th century. It worked until 1947 and has since been kept in working order, with the sails turning even though the mill no longer grinds. In summer, visitors can climb into the buck (body) of this elegant weatherboarded construction and explore its machinery.

## Earl Soham

**3 miles W of Framlingham on the A1120**

Earl Soham comprises a long, winding street that was once part of a Roman road. It lies in a valley, and on the largest of its three greens the village sign is a carved wooden statue of a falconer given as a gift by the Women's Institute in 1953. The 13th century church of St Mary is well worth a visit.

## Abbey House

Monk Soham, Woodbridge, Suffolk IP13 7EN
Tel: 01728 685225

Surrounded on all sides by mature gardens and pastureland, **Abbey House** is a haven of peace and tranquillity. There are three guest bedrooms – a twin and a double both with en suite bathrooms and a double with a private bathroom. The delicious breakfast is prepared to individual requirements; the guests' dining room and drawing room are attractively and comfortably furnished. Sheep and cows roam the grounds, and local sights and attractions include Southwold, Aldeburgh, Lavenham and Minsmere.

## Debenham

**6 miles W of Framlingham on the B1077**

Debenham is a sizable village of architectural distinction, with a profusion of attractive timber-framed buildings dating from the 14th to the 17th centuries. The River Deben flows beside and beneath the main street and, near one of the little bridges, weavers still practise their craft. There is also a pottery centre. St Mary's Church is unusual in having an original Saxon tower, and the roof alternates hammerbeams with crested tie beams.

## Dennington

**2 miles N of Framlingham on the B1116**

The pretty little village of Dennington boasts one of the oldest post offices in

## GRANGE FARM

Dennington, Framlingham, Suffolk IP13 8BT
Tel: 01986 798388  Mobile: 07774 182835
website: www.framlingham.com/grangefarm

Situated in the handsome village of Dennington off the main A1120, **Grange Farm** is an enchanting moated farmhouse dating back to the 13th century. Every room in this characterful home is beamed, and in winter cosy log fires burn in the sitting rooms, where guests can enjoy rest and relaxation, a game of billiards, quiet reading or some television. There are three supremely comfortable guest bedrooms, all looking out over the very pretty and extensive (two-and-a-half-acre) gardens, which are full of birdlife and where guests are welcome to wander.

The grounds include an all-weather tennis court. Owner Libby Hickson has lived at the farm since 1971. Farming ceased in 1992; now the house and grounds make for a charming rural hideaway. The choice of breakfasts includes local produce and home-made bread and marmalade, while the honey is locally produced. The surrounding countryside is perfect for walking and cycling, while Snape, Minsmere, the seaside and a wealth of historic and picturesque attractions are within easy reach. For a true taste of rural bliss, look no further.

the country, this one having occupied the same site since 1830. The village church has some very unusual features, none more so than the hanging 'pyx' canopy above the altar. A pyx served as a receptacle for the Reserved Sacrament, which would be kept under a canopy attached to weights and pulleys so that the whole thing could be lowered when the sacrament was required for the sick and the dying.

The church also has many interesting carvings, the most remarkable being that of a skiapod, the only known representation in this county of a mythical creature of the African desert, humanoid but with a huge boat-shaped foot with which it could cover itself against the sun. This curious beast was 'known' to Herodotus and to Pliny, who remarked that it had 'great pertinacity in leaping'. In the chapel at the top of the

## WOODLANDS FARM

Brundish, nr Framlingham, Suffolk IP13 8BP
Tel: 01379 384444   e-mail: jillatwoodlands@aol.com
website: www.smoothhound.co.uk/hotels/woodlandsfarm.html

For 25 years, Jill Graham has been providing excellent bed and breakfast accommodation at **Woodlands Farm**, a charming and supremely comfortable farmhouse surrounded by lovely grounds featuring an orchard, ponds and local wildlife. Gracious and cosy, this excellent house – handy for exploring Framlingham, Sutton Hoo, Bressingham Gardens and the coast - offers three beautifully-appointed and furnished guest bedrooms. The breakfast is hearty and delicious, and Jill is happy to recommend one of several excellent local inns for evening meals. 4 Diamonds AA. No smoking.

south aisle stands the tomb of Lord Bardolph, who fought at Agincourt, and of his wife, their effigies carved in alabaster.

## PARHAM

**2 miles SE of Framlingham on the B1116**

**Parham Airfield** is now agricultural land, but in the control tower and an adjacent hut can be found memorabilia of the 390th Bomb Group of the USAAF.

## EASTON

**5 miles S of Framlingham off the B1078**

A scenic drive leads to the lovely village of Easton, one of the most colourful, flower-bedecked places in the county. A remarkable sight to the west of the village is the two-mile-long **Crinkle-Crankle Wall** that surrounds Easton Park. This extraordinary type of wall, also known as a ribbon wall, weaves snake-like in and out and is much

## EASTON FARM PARK HOLIDAY COTTAGES

Easton Farm Park, Easton, Woodbridge, Suffolk IP13 0EQ
Tel: 01728 746475  e-mail: fionakerr@suffolkonline.net
Fax: 01728 747861  website: www.eastonfarmpark.co.uk

With access to all the sights and attractions of the Farm, **Easton Farm Park Holiday Cottages** have recently been refurbished to Grade 4 Standard by the English Tourist Board. Here, superior self-catering accommodation is available. 'The Duke' has two double bedrooms and a twin, sleeping up to six adults and four children, while 'The Duchess' sleeps up to five adults and one child. Both have fully fitted kitchens and are charming and cosy, with a separate laundry room. The cottages are available for weekly bookings or, in low season, mid-week and weekend breaks.

## EASTON FARM PARK

Easton, Woodbridge, Suffolk IP13 0EQ
Tel: 01728 746475  Fax: 01728 747861
e-mail: easton@eastonfarmpark.co.uk
website: www.eastonfarmpark.co.uk

Comprising 35 acres of woodland walks, meadows and farmland, with the River Deben flowing through on its way to Woodbridge and the sea, **Easton Farm Park** is a marvellous day out, and one of Suffolk's greatest attractions. Suffolk Punch horses, rare breed cattle, sheep, goats, rabbits, poultry and more can be found here. Local traditional crafts are showcased in the woodwright's and blacksmith's, while the café and gift shop provide a range of tempting wares.

Bikes are available to hire at the Farm, and there are pleasant walks to be had along the

River Deben. Children will enjoy the Pets Paddock, feeding time for the farm animals, the chick nursery, riding ponies and the adventure playground. Farmers' markets are held monthly on the fourth Saturday in the month.

Other special events are hosted throughout the year – please telephone or consult the website for more details. The Farm is open daily to the public from March to September and during school half-term holidays from 10.30 a.m. to 6 p.m.

## THE STABLES AT IVY LODGE BARN

Hoo, nr Woodbridge, Suffolk IP13 7QF
Tel: 01473 737422

**The Stables** is set in lovely grounds including open fields, paddocks with rare breed sheep, ornamental pond, copse, natural ponds and a box rose garden. It offers excellent comfortable self-catering accommodation for 4. The recent conversion includes double and twin bedrooms, fully equipped kitchen and special touches earning it a 4 star ETB rating. Towels, linen, electricity and heating are included. No smoking, pets or children under 5. Open all year. A welcoming and tranquil base for exploring the region.

stronger than if it were straight. This particular wall, said to be the world's longest, was built by Lord of the Manor, the Earl of Rochford, in the 1820s.

### CHARSFIELD

#### 5 miles S of Framlingham off the B1078

A minor road runs from Framlingham through picturesque Kettleburgh and Hoo to Charsfield, best known as the inspiration for Ronald Blyth's book *Akenfield*, later memorably filmed by Sir Peter Hall. A cottage garden in the village displays the Akenfield village sign and is open to visitors in the summer.

### OTLEY

#### 7 miles SW of Framlingham on the B1079

The 15th century **Moated Hall** in Otley is open to the public at certain times of the year. Standing in ten acres of gardens that include a canal, a nuttery and a knot garden, the hall was long associated with the Gosnold family, whose coat of arms is also that of the village. The best-known member of that family was Bartholomew Gosnold, who sailed to the New World, coined the named 'Martha's Vineyard' for the island off the coast of Massachusetts, discovered Cape Cod and founded the settlement of Jamestown, Virginia. The 13th century church of St Mary has a remarkable baptistry font

measuring 6 feet in length and 2 feet 8 inches in depth. Though filled with water, the font is not used and was only discovered in 1950 when the vestry floor was raised. It may have been used for adult baptisms.

### HELMINGHAM

#### 7 miles SW of Framlingham on the B1077

Another moated hall, this one a Tudor construction, stands in Helmingham. Although the house is not open to the public, on Sundays in summer the gardens can be visited; attractions include herbaceous and spring borders, many varieties of roses, safari rides, and deer, Highland cattle and Soay sheep. The Tollemache family were here for many years - and one of their number founded a brewery, which, after a merger, became the Tolly Cobbold brewery, based in Ipswich.

### FRAMSDEN

#### 7 miles SW of Framlingham on the B1077

The scenery in these parts is real picture-postcard stuff, and in the village of Framsden the picture is completed by a fine **Post Mill**, built high on a hill in 1760, refitted and raised in 1836 and in use until 1934. The milling machinery is still in place and the mill is open for visits (at weekends, by appointment only).

## THE CROCKERY BARN

Ashbocking, Ipswich, Suffolk  IP6 9JS
Tel/Fax: 01473 890123
e-mail: info@thecrockerybarn.co.uk
website: www.thecrockerybarn.co.uk

**The Crockery Barn** in Ashbocking is a cornucopia of everything needed to grace your kitchen, table or any room you please, or to find the perfect gift. Tableware, cookware – all manner of beautiful and practical treasures can be found here. Flamboyant, lavish, homely and eye-catching pots, plates, tea cups, mugs, teapots, candelabra and more, fashioned in clay, earthenware, china, brass and stainless steel, to name but a few of the variety of wares sold here – are displayed in tidy rows throughout this wonderful barn space.

Set in a tastefully and handsomely converted former farm building in the midst of unspoilt open scenery, there is plenty of room to browse at your leisure among the many fine pieces on display. Owner Trish Sargent has been running this thriving concern since 1993. Ceramics from Portugal, France, Italy and the Far East – together with work from named potters throughout the UK, such as Portmeiron, Spode, Poole Pottery, Queens, Aga, Mason & Cash, Cloverleaf, Emma Bridgewater and Nicholas Mosse – grace the many shelves brimming with expertly crafted and designed pieces. All these well-known names and many other superior makes are here in great quantity and a wealth of colours, shapes, sizes and styles, across the range of the best tableware and cookware available.

Trish and her husband Michael travel regularly to mainland Europe in search of the most exciting and beautiful examples of the potter's and metalsmith's art. The white china imported from Sri Lanka is inn particularly great demand by many hotels and restaurants throughout the region and nationwide, as it is justly prized for its durability and classic style. Wholesale enquiries are just as welcome as retail ones. Much of the stock is imported direct from manufacturers, so that the extra choice and value are passed on to customers. Also on site is the Long Barn, where you will find a range of plant pots,

basketware (hampers, log baskets) and all kinds of unique hand-woven goods together with changing specialist stock such as Italian copperware. At the Barnyard Café, tempting bistro-style snacks and speciality teas and coffees are available – and it's just the place to relax over a quiet cuppa and a cake or hot or cold snack after a few hours' happy browsing and shopping through the Crockery Barn's elegant and practical wares. The Crockery Barn is open Monday to Saturday from 10 – 5, Sundays 11 – 4 (closed for two weeks at Christmas), and is located just six miles north of Ipswich on the B1077.

## CHURCH FARM

Kettleburgh, Nr Framlingham, Suffolk IP13 7LF
Tel: 01728 732532
e-mail: jbater@suffolkonline.net
website: aa.com/getway

Home to Anne and John Bater, **Church Farm** is a beautiful 450-year-old farmhouse that combines luxury accommodation with a relaxed, homely feel that makes every guest feel welcome. This oak-beamed home commands delightful views over the water to the 13th century village church.

There are three good-sized bedrooms – a double downstairs and two twin rooms on the first floor. All rooms are tastefully furnished and decorated. The rose-filled patio area leads to the lovely lawned gardens. The guests' dining room is spacious and attractive, and the meals – served at breakfast and dinner – are exceptional. Home-cooking at its very best awaits guests here.

Handy for many sights and attractions in the region – Framlingham Castle, Easton Farm Park, Aldeburgh (and other points along the coast), Minsmere RSPB Reserve and the delights of Constable Country – and guests can also enjoy clay-pigeon shooting, fishing or walking. Children and pets are welcome. Open all year long. 3 Diamonds ETB & AA.

Also on-site is space for five caravan pitches, with electricity and water available.

### CRETINGHAM

**4 miles SW of Framlingham off the A1120**

The village sign is the unusual item here, in that it has two different panels: one shows an everyday Anglo-Saxon farming scene, the other a group (of Danes?) sailing up the River Deben, with the locals fleeing. The signs are made from mosaic tiles.

### BRANDESTON

**3 miles SW of Framlingham off the A1120**

A further mile to the east, through some charming countryside, Brandeston is another delightful spot, with a row of beautiful thatched cottages and the parish church of All Saints with its 13th century font. The best-known vicar of Brandeston was John Lowes (1572-1646) who was accused of witchcraft by the villagers, interrogated by Witchfinder

General Matthew Hopkins and hanged at Bury St Edmunds. His sad end was made even sadder by the fact that before being strung up he had to read out the burial service of a condemned witch himself, as no priest was allowed to conduct the service. Hopkins made a handsome living out of this bizarre business, preying on the superstitions of the times and using the foulest means to obtain confessions. One account of Hopkins' end is that he himself was accused of being a witch and hanged. The less satisfactory alternative is that he died of tuberculosis.

## EYE

The name of this excellent little town is derived from the Saxon for an island, as Eye was once surrounded by water and marshes. The church of **St Peter and St Paul** stands in the shadow of a mound

# *Eye*

| | |
|---|---|
| **Distance:** | 3.5 miles (5.64 kilometres) |
| **Typical time:** | 90 mins |
| **Height gain:** | 10 metres |
| **Map:** | Explorer 230 |
| **Walk:** | www.walkingworld.com ID:1484 |
| **Contributor:** | Joy & Charles Boldero |

## Access Information:

For buses ring Travel Line 0545 583358. You can start this walk in Eye and point 7*. The car park at the Pennings picnic site car park is just outside the town. This is where the walk starts . The car park is situated on a country lane south of the B1117 just east of Eye. Eye is situated on the B1077 off the A140, 4 miles southeast of Diss.

## Additional Information:

Eye Town Moor Wood has a lot of unusual features in it. The pond you pass has conical structures in it and beside it a lovers seat.

Eye has many beautiful buildings, one the 15th century Guildhall by the church, which is said to be one of the finest in the county. Near the church is the old castle. The Queen's

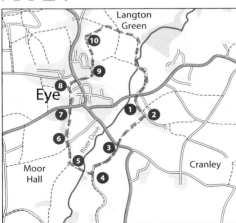

Head has an excellent menu but does not serve food on Mondays.

At point 10 there was once a Priory, built in about 1080 by Robert Malet, Lord of Eye, in memory of his father, William, a Norman baron. There were fish ponds near by, now they are a wild life habitat, kingfishers can be seen there. To the right is the 16th century brick building, which became part of a farm complex, milling, malting and brewing beer. Opposite is the 'Abbey'. The 18th century red brick front hides a mediaeval timber farmed building in which the Prior lived.

## Description:

This walk is mostly across meadows, along tracks and through woodland and touches the fine old town of Eye which has so many lovely and ancient buildings. The route uses part of the Mid-Suffolk designated paths.

## Features:

Lake/Loch, Pub, Toilets, Church, Castle, Wildlife, Birds, Flowers, Great Views, Butterflies, Food Shop

## Walk Directions:

**1** From the car park turn right along the country lane.

**2** Turn right at the finger post and cross meadows going over stiles.

**3** Cross the road and continue along the track opposite, Park Lane. Go under a barrier where the track becomes grassy.

**4** Turn right towards an iron bar and cross a stile to its left. Cross a meadow keeping a copse on the left. Go over a concrete humped bridge and climb a stile in the corner. Cross a second meadow and an earth bridge, then cross a third meadow to a stile ahead.

**5** After climbing this stile and crossing a bridge turn right along a fourth meadow keeping to its left-hand side. Climb the stile and turn right along the track.

**6** At the finger post turn left along the field edge. This path goes into the wood. Cross the bridge and take the right fork. By the pond ignore a path on the right.

Keep along the main path to the notice board, ignoring all paths left off it.

**7** Turn right over the bridge and turn left along the gravel track. Turn right along the pavement. Turn left at the road junction. At the Town Hall * turn left to the Queens Head and then turn right. By the alms houses cross the road.

**8** Turn right at the finger post along a driveway. The path keeps right by a stream over grass lawn. At the end turn left, then left again along a lane with houses.

**9** Cross the road and go along a signed path opposite. Keep on through a newish housing estate.

**10** Soon after house No. 3 turn right along a track; it becomes a grassy one. Climb the stile, cross a meadow and go through a gate. Turn left along the track. Climb a stile and continue along a track. Cross the road and continue along a driveway opposite. Turn right over the stile and cross a meadow. Climb a stile and go along a path under trees then turn right along a country lane to the car park.

on which a castle once stood (the remains are worth a look and the mound offers a panoramic view of the town – almost a bird's eye view, in fact). The church's 100-foot tower was described by Pevsner as 'one of the wonders of Suffolk' and the interior is a masterpiece of restoration, with all the essential medieval features in place. The rood screen, with painted panels depicting St Edmund, St Ursula, Edward the Confessor and Henry VI, is particularly fine.

Other interesting Eye sights are the ornate redbrick Town Hall; the timbered Guildhall, with the archangel Gabriel carved on a corner post; a 'crinkle-crankle' (serpentine) wall fronting Chandos Lodge, where Sir Frederick Ashton once lived; and a thriving theatre, one of the smallest professional theatres in the country.

## BEARDS OF EYE

39 Church Street, Eye, Suffolk  IP23 7BD
Tel: 01379 870383
e-mail: beards@eye-town.fsnet.co.uk

**Beards of Eye** is three excellent businesses in one: a delicatessen, a traditional tearoom, and accommodation in the form of three guest bedrooms.

Owned and personally run by Michael and Margaret-Ann Beard, who bought the premises back in 1986, when the building – a medieval hall house dating back to 1350 and a Grade II listed building - was almost derelict, they have carefully restored and renovated it to make it the success it is today, building

at the same time a reputation for outstanding quality and service. The deli specialises in home-cooked savouries and deserts and local produce such as 50-60 different cheeses, meats, olives, quiches, honey, ice-cream and much more. Some of these delicacies are also sold next door in the tearoom, together with a range of light lunches and afternoon teas. The deli and tearoom are open 9 until 5.30, Monday, Wednesday, Thursday, Friday and Saturday. The accommodation comprises two charming double rooms and one single. Guests are welcome to use the tearoom in the evenings as a lounge.

# AROUND EYE

## HOXNE
### 4 miles NE of Eye on the B1118

Palaeolithic remains indicate the exceptionally long history of Hoxne (pronounced Hoxon), which stands along the banks of the River Waveney near the Norfolk border. It is best known for its links with King Edmund, who was reputedly killed here, though Bradfield St Clare and Shottisham have rival claims to this distinction. The Hoxne legend is that Edmund was betrayed to the Danes by a newlywed couple who were crossing the Goldbrook bridge and spotted his golden spurs reflected from his hiding place below the bridge. Edmund put a curse on all newlyweds crossing the bridge, and to this day some brides take care to avoid it.

The story continues that Edmund was tied to an oak tree and killed with arrows. That same oak mysteriously fell down in 1848 while apparently in good health, and a monument at the site is a popular tourist attraction. In the church of St Peter and St Paul an oak screen (perhaps that very same oak?) depicts scenes from the martyr's life. A more cheerful event is the Harvest Breakfast on the village green that follows the annual service.

## HORHAM
### 6 miles E of Eye on the B1117

Three distinct musical connections distinguish this dapper little village. The Norman church has had its tower strengthened for the rehanging of the peal of eight bells, which is believed to be the oldest in the world. Benjamin Britten, later associated with the Aldeburgh Festival, lived and composed in Horham for a time, and on a famous day during the Second World War, Glenn Miller brought his band here to celebrate the 200th flying mission to set out from the American aerodrome.

## WORLINGWORTH
### 8 miles SE of Eye off the B1118

It's well worth taking the country road to Worlingworth, a long, straggling village whose church of St Mary has a remarkable font cover reaching up about 30 feet. It is brilliantly coloured and intricately carved, and near the top is an inscription in Greek which translates as 'wash my sin and not my body only.' Note, too, the Carolean box pews, the carved pulpit and an oil painting of Worlingworth's Great Feast of 1810 to celebrate George III's jubilee.

## WINGFIELD
### 6 miles E of Eye off the B1118

**Wingfield College** is one of the country's most historic seats of learning, founded in 1362 as a college for priests with a bequest from Sir John de Wingfield, Chief Staff Officer to the Black Prince. Sir John's wealth came from ransoming a French nobleman at the Battle of Poitiers in 1356. Surrendered to Henry VIII at the time of the Dissolution, the college became a farmhouse and is now in private hands. The façade is now Georgian, but the original medieval Great Hall still stands, and the college and its three acres of gardens are open to the public at weekends in summer. Attractions include regular artistic events and printing demonstrations.

The church of St Andrew was built as the collegiate church and has an extra-large chancel to accommodate the college choir. The church contains three really fine monuments: to Sir John (in stone); to Michael de la Pole, 2nd Earl of Suffolk (in wood); and to John de la

*Hevenham Hall*

Pole, Duke of Suffolk (in alabaster). In the churchyard there is a 'hudd' – a shelter for the priest for use at the graveside in bad weather.

On a hill outside the village are the imposing remains of a castle built by the 1st Earl.

## FRESSINGFIELD

**10 miles E of Eye on the B1116**

Fressingfield's first spiritual centre was the church of St Peter and St Paul. It has a superb hammerbeam roof and a lovely stone bell tower that was built in the 14th century. On one of the pews the initials A P are carved. These are believed to be the work of Alice de la Pole, Duchess of Norfolk and grand-daughter of Geoffrey Chaucer. Was this a work of art or a bout of vandalism brought on by a dull sermon?

At nearby **Ufford Hall** lived the Sancroft family, one of whom became Archbishop of Canterbury. He led the revolt of the bishops against James II and was imprisoned in the Tower of London.

Released by William IV and sacked for refusing to swear the oath of allegiance, he returned home and is entombed by the south porch of the church.

The village sign is a pilgrim and a donkey, recording that Fressingfield was a stopping place on the pilgrim route from Dunwich to Bury St Edmunds.

## LAXFIELD

**12 miles E of Eye on the B1117**

**Laxfield & District Museum**, in the 16th century Guildhall, gives a fine insight into bygone ages with geology and natural history exhibits, agricultural and domestic tools, a Victorian kitchen, a village shop and a costume room. The museum is open on Saturday and Sunday afternoons in summer.

All Saints Church is distinguished by some wonderful flint 'flushwork' (stonework) on its tower, roof and nave. In the 1808 Baptist church is a plaque remembering John Noyes, burnt at the stake in 1557 for refusing to take Catholic vows. History relates that the villagers - with a single exception - dowsed their fires in protest. The one remaining fire, however, was all that was needed to light the stake.

A couple of miles east of Laxfield, **Heveningham Hall** is a fine Georgian mansion, a model of classical elegance designed by James Wyatt with lovely grounds by Capability Brown. As it runs through the grounds, the River Blyth widens into a lake.

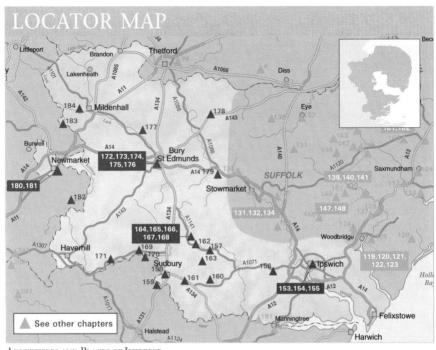

# LOCATOR MAP

See other chapters

ADVERTISERS AND PLACES OF INTEREST

| | | |
|---|---|---|
| 153 Salthouse Harbour Hotel, Ipswich | Page 176 | |
| 154 The Cotton Tree, Ipswich | Page 177 | |
| 155 Ipswich Transport Museum, Ipswich | Page 179 | |
| 156 Chilli & Chives, Hintlesham, Ipswich | Page 183 | |
| 157 Corncraft and The Summer House, Monks Eleigh, Hadleigh | Page 183 | |
| 158 Gainsborough's House, Sudbury | Page 188 | |
| 159 Bulmer Brick & Tile Co. Ltd., Bulmer, Sudbury | Page 189 | |
| 160 Green Lawn Bonsai, Boxford, Sudbury | Page 191 | |
| 161 Wheldons Farm Shop & Pick Your Own, Newton, Sudbury | Page 191 | |
| 162 Hedgerows Farm Shop & Nursery, Brent Eleigh, Lavenham | Page 193 | |
| 163 Milden Hall Farmhouse, Milden, Lavenham | Page 193 | |
| 164 The Avocet Collection, Lavenham | Page 194 | |
| 165 The Guildhall, Lavenham, Lavenham | Page 195 | |
| 166 Vintage Pink, Lavenham | Page 195 | |
| 167 Gallery 48, Lavenham | Page 195 | |
| 168 Fisks Restaurant, Lavenham | Page 196 | |

| | |
|---|---|
| 169 The George, Cavendish, Sudbury | Page 199 |
| 170 Fiddlesticks B&B, Pentlow, Clare | Page 200 |
| 171 Clare Castle Country Park, Clare | Page 200 |
| 172 Clarice House Hotel & Spa, Bury St Edmunds | Page 202 |
| 173 Romark Jewellers, Bury St Edmunds | Page 203 |
| 174 St Edmunsbury Cathedral, Bury St Edmunds | Page 204 |
| 175 Northgate House, Bury St Edmunds | Page 205 |
| 176 The Angel Hotel, Bury St Edmunds | Page 206 |
| 177 West Stow Anglo-Saxon Village, West Stow, Bury St Edmunds | Page 207 |
| 178 Wyken Vineyard, Stanton, Bury St Edmunds | Page 210 |
| 179 Elm Tree Gallery, Woolpit, Bury St Edmunds | Page 212 |
| 180 Coffee & Co, Newmarket | Page 217 |
| 181 National Horseracing Museum, Newmarket | Page 218 |
| 182 Hill Farm B&B, Kirtling, Newmarket | Page 219 |
| 183 The Golden Boar Inn, Freckenham, Bury St Edmunds | Page 221 |
| 184 Worlington House, Worlington | Page 222 |

# SOUTH AND WEST SUFFOLK 6

Much of Suffolk's character comes from its rivers, and in the part of the county surrounding Ipswich, the Orwell and the Stour mark the boundaries of the Shotley Peninsula. The countryside here is largely unspoilt, with wide-open spaces between scattered villages. The relative flatness of Suffolk gives every encouragement for motorists to leave their machines, and the peninsula, still relatively peaceful, is ideal for a spot of walking or cycling, or even boating. Southeast of Ipswich, the peninsula created by the River Deben and the River Orwell is one of the prettiest areas in Suffolk, its winding lanes leading through a delightful series of quiet rural villages and colourful riverside communities.

John Constable, England's greatest landscape painter, was born at East Bergholt in 1776 and remained at heart a Suffolk man throughout his life. He was later to declare *'I associate my careless boyhood with all that lies on the banks of the Stour. Those scenes made me a painter and I am grateful.'* He painted the occasional portrait and even attempted a couple of religious works, but he concentrated almost entirely on the scenes that he knew and loved as a boy. The Suffolk tradition of painting continues to this day,

*Willy Lots Cotttage, Dedham Vale*

with many artists drawn particularly to Walberswick and what is known as 'Constable country'. Its beauty is not always that easy to appreciate when crowds throng the Stour valley at summer weekends, but at other times the peace and beauty are much as they were in Constable's day.

Cambridgeshire, Norfolk, the A134 and the A14 frame the northern part of West Suffolk, which includes Bury St Edmunds, a pivotal player in the country's religious history, and Newmarket, one of the major centres of the horseracing world. Between and above them are picturesque villages, bustling market towns, rich farming countryside, the fens, and the expanse of sandy heath and pine forest that is Breckland. The area south and west of Bury towards the Essex border contains some of Suffolk's most attractive and peaceful countryside. The visitor will come upon a succession of picturesque villages, historic churches, remarkable stately homes, heritage centres and nature reserves. In the south, along the River Stour, stand the historic wool towns of Long Melford, Cavendish and Clare.

# IPSWICH

History highlights Ipswich as the birthplace of Cardinal Wolsey, but the story of Suffolk's county town starts very much earlier than that. It has been a port since the time of the Roman occupation, and by the 7th century the Anglo-Saxons had expanded it into the largest port in the country. King John granted a civic charter in 1200, confirming the townspeople's right to their own laws and administration, and for several centuries the town prospered as a port, exporting wool, textiles and agricultural products.

Thomas Wolsey arrived on the scene in 1475, the son of a wealthy butcher. Educated at Magdalen College, Oxford, he was ordained a priest in 1498 and rose quickly in influence, becoming chaplain to Henry VII and then Archbishop of York, a cardinal, and Lord Chancellor under Henry VIII. He was quite indispensable to the king and had charge of foreign policy as well as powerful sway over judicial institutions. He also managed to amass enormous wealth, enabling him to found a grammar school in Ipswich and Cardinal's College (later Christ Church) in Oxford. Wolsey had long been hated by certain nobles for his low birth and arrogance, and they were easily able to turn Henry against him when his attempts to secure an annulment from the Pope of the king's marriage to Catherine of Aragon met with failure. Stripped of most of his offices following a charge of overstepping his authority as a legate, he was later charged with treason, but died while travelling from York to London to face the king. His death put an end to his plans for the grammar school - all that remains now is a red-brick gateway.

When the cloth market fell into

## The Cotton Tree

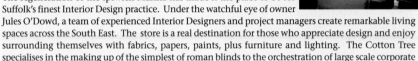

Ipswich Marina, No 5 Christie's Warehouse, Wherry Quay, Ipswich, Suffolk IP4 1LG
Tel: 01473 287474 Fax: 01473 284080
e-mail: info@thecottontree.co.uk website:www.thecottontree.co.uk

The regeneration of the Ipswich Marina has made it the place to be for Suffolk's finest Interior Design practice. Under the watchful eye of owner Jules O'Dowd, a team of experienced Interior Designers and project managers create remarkable living spaces across the South East. The store is a real destination for those who appreciate design and enjoy surrounding themselves with fabrics, papers, paints, plus furniture and lighting. The Cotton Tree specialises in the making up of the simplest of roman blinds to the orchestration of large scale corporate projects and this store is particularly good for designing kitchens and bathrooms.

decline in the 17th century, a respite followed in the following century, when the town was a food-distribution port during the Napoleonic Wars. At the beginning of the 19th century the risk from silting was becoming acute at a time when trade was improving and industries were springing up. The Wet Dock, constructed in 1842, solved the silting problem and, with the railway arriving shortly after, Ipswich could once more look forward to a safe future. The Victorians were responsible for considerable development: symbols of their civic pride include the handsome **Old Custom House** by the Wet Dock, the Town Hall, and the splendid **Tolly Cobbold** brewery, rebuilt at the end of the 19th century, 150 years after brewing started on the site. Victorian enterprise depleted some of the older buildings, but a number survive, notably the house where Wolsey was born, the Ancient House with its wonderful pargetting, and the fine former Tudor merchants' houses which grace the town's historic waterfront, such as Isaac Lord's and The Neptune (the latter was once home of Thomas Eldred, who circumnavigated the world with Thomas Cavendish

shortly after Drake). A dozen medieval churches remain, of which St Margaret's is the finest, boasting some very splendid flintwork and a double hammerbeam roof. Another, St Stephen's, today houses the town's Tourist Information Centre.

**Christchurch Mansion** is a beautiful Tudor home standing in 65 acres of attractive parkland, a short walk from the town centre. Furnished as an English country house, it contains a major collection of works by Constable and Gainsborough, as well as many other paintings, prints and sculptures by Suffolk artists from the 17th century onwards.

Wolsey Art Gallery is a purpose-built space entered through Christchurch Mansion which features changing

*Christchurch Mansion*

*Ornate Plaster Work, Ipswich*

displays including touring and national exhibitions.

**Ipswich Museum** is in a Victorian building in the High Street. Displays include a natural history gallery, a wildlife gallery complete with a model of a mammoth, a reconstruction of a Roman villa, and replicas of Sutton Hoo treasures. A recent addition is a display of elaborately carved timbers from the homes of wealthy 17th century merchants. There is also a rolling programme of exciting temporary exhibitions, events and displays.

In a former trolleybus depot on Cobham Road is the **Ipswich Transport Museum**, a fascinating collection of vehicles, from prams to fire engines, all made or used around Ipswich.

Ipswich's position at the head of the River Orwell has always influenced the town's fortunes; today, a stroll along the waterfront should be included in any visit. Tudor houses and medieval churches stand alongside stylish new apartments which overlook the new marinas. An art gallery and choice of eateries enhance the experience, and there are regular pub cruises, leaving the Ipswich waterfront and travelling the Orwell (recently voted one of the prettiest rivers in England) as far as Felixstowe harbour.

On the outskirts of town, signposted from Nacton Road, is **Orwell Country Park**, a 150-acre site of wood, heath and reedbeds by the Orwell estuary. At this point the river is crossed by the imposing Orwell Bridge, a graceful construction in pre-stressed concrete that was completed in 1982 and is not far short of a mile in length.

Notables from the world of the arts with Ipswich connections include Thomas Gainsborough, who got his first major commissions here to paint portraits of local people; David Garrick, the renowned actor-manager, who made his debut here in 1741 as Aboan in Thomas Southerne's *Oroonoko*; and the peripatetic Charles Dickens, who stayed at the Great White Horse while still a young reporter with the *Morning Chronicle*. Soon afterwards, he featured the tavern in *The Pickwick Papers* as the place where Mr Pickwick wanders inadvertently into a lady's bedroom. Sir V S Pritchett was born in Ipswich, while Enid Blyton trained as a kindergarten teacher at Ipswich High School.

## AROUND IPSWICH

### BRAMFORD

#### 1 mile NW of Ipswich off the A14

Bramford has a pretty little church, St Mary's, with a 13th century stone screen.

# IPSWICH TRANSPORT MUSEUM

Old Trolleybus Depot, Cobham Road,
Ipswich, Suffolk IP3 9JD
Tel: 01473 715666
website: www.ipswichtransportmuseum.co.uk

The **Ipswich Transport Museum** is dedicated to preserving the transport and engineering heritage of the Ipswich area. The collection is believed to be the largest in the country devoted to just one area and is an entirely volunteer run and funded museum, housed in a former trolleybus depot. The building has been altered to include a gift shop, tearoom and outdoor picnic area.

Among the more unusual exhibits are a monorail for transporting spoil, a road sweeper conversion from a Morris car, a petrol roller for rolling grass runways, a horse-drawn tower wagon for maintaining overhead wires, the oldest trolleybus in the world (Ipswich no. 2, built by Railless in 1923), and a collection of wheelchairs. There are additional exhibition rooms covering air, water and rail transport of the Ipswich area, with exhibits and photographs. The Ipswich area was the hub of experimentation in the 1930's with research bases for fixed wing aircraft, seaplanes and bombing ranges. Radar was developed nearby at Bawdsey Manor.

Ipswich was an engineering town throughout the 19th and 20th centuries. The museum commemorates this heritage through its collection of Ipswich-made exhibits, which include lawnmowers, mobile cranes, fork lift trucks and factory trucks. Photographs depict the huge Walking Draglines built in Ipswich, weighing up to 2,000 tons.

It was once an important spot on the river route, when barges from Ipswich stopped to unload corn; the walls of the old lock are still visible. In the vicinity is **Suffolk Water Park**, where the lake welcomes canoeists and windsurfers.

## NACTON

**4 miles SE of Ipswich off the A14**

South of Nacton's medieval church lies **Orwell Park House**, which was built in the 18th century by Admiral Edward Vernon, sometime Member of Parliament for Ipswich. The admiral, who had won an important victory over the Spanish in the War of Jenkins Ear, was known to his men as 'Old Grog' because of his habit of wearing a cloak of coarse grogram cloth. His nickname passed into the language when he ordered that the rum ration dished out daily to sailors should be diluted with water to combat the drunkenness that was rife in the service. That was in 1740, but this allotted ration of 'grog' was officially issued to sailors right up until 1970.

George Tomline bought Orwell Park House in 1857 and made it even more splendid, adding a conservatory, a ballroom and towers. He also changed the façade along handsome Georgian lines. The house became the setting for some of the grandest shooting parties ever seen in this part of the world, and such was the power of the Tomlines that they were able to move the village away from the house to its present site.

**Nacton Picnic Site** in Shore Lane (signposted from the village) commands wonderful views of the Orwell and is a prime spot in winter for birdwatchers. The birds feed very well off the mud flats.

## LEVINGTON

**5 miles SE of Ipswich off the A14**

A pretty village on the banks of the Orwell. Fisons established a factory here in 1956, and developed the now famous Levington Compost. On the foreshore below the village is an extensive marina which has brought a bustling air to the area. The coastal footpath along the bank of the Orwell leads across the nature reserve of **Trimley Marshes** and on to Felixstowe.

## TRIMLEY ST MARY & TRIMLEY ST MARTIN

**6 miles SE of Ipswich off the A14**

Twin villages with two churches in the same churchyard, famous Trimley residents have included the Cavendish family, whose best-known member was the adventurer Thomas Cavendish. In 1590 he became the second man to sail round the world. Two years later he died while embarked on another voyage. He is depicted on the village sign. **Trimley Marshes** were created from farmland and comprise grazing marsh, reed beds and wetland that's home to an abundance of interesting plant life and many species of wildfowl, waders and migrant birds. Access is on foot from Trimley St Mary.

## NEWBOURNE

**7 miles E of Ipswich off the A12**

A small miracle occurred here on the night of the hurricane of October 1987. One wall of the ancient St Mary's Church was blown out, and with it the stained glass, which shattered into fragments. One piece, showing the face of Christ, was found undamaged and was later incorporated into the rebuilt wall.

Two remarkable inhabitants of Newbourne were the Page brothers, who both stood over 7 feet tall; they enjoyed a career touring the fairs, and are buried in Newbourne churchyard.

## WALDRINGFIELD

**7 miles E of Ipswich off the A12**

Waldringfield lies on a particularly beautiful stretch of the Deben estuary, and the waterfront is largely given over to leisure boating and cruising. The quay was once busy with barges, many of them laden with coprolite. This fossilised dung, the forerunner of today's fertilisers, was found in great abundance in and around Waldringfield, and a number of exhausted pits can still be seen.

## FELIXSTOWE

**12 miles SE of Ipswich off the A14**

Until the early 17th century, Felixstowe was a little-known village - but it was the good Colonel Tomline of Orwell Park who put it on the map by creating a port to rival its near neighbour Harwich. He also started work on the Ipswich-Felixstowe railway (with a stop at Nacton for the guests of his grand parties), and 1887 saw the completion of both projects. Tomline also developed the resort aspects of Felixstowe, rivalling the amenities of Dovercourt, and when he died in 1887 most of his dreams had become reality. (He was, incidentally, cremated, one of the first in the county to be so disposed of in the modern era.) What he didn't live to see was the pier, opened in 1904 and still in use.

The town has suffered a number of ups and downs since that time, but continues to thrive as one of England's busiest ports, having been much extended in the 1960s. The resort is strung out round a wide, gently curving bay, where the long seafront road is made even prettier with trim lawns and gardens.

The Martello tower is a noted landmark, as is the **Pier**, which was once long enough to merit an electric tramway. It was shortened as a security measure during the Second World War.

All kinds of attractions are provided for holidaymakers, including one very unusual one. This is the **Felixstowe Water Clock**, a curious piece assembled from dozens of industrial bits and pieces.

The original fishing hamlet from which the Victorian resort was developed lies beyond a golf course north of the town. This is **Felixstowe Ferry**, a cluster of holiday homes, an inn, a boatyard, fishing sheds and a Martello tower. The sailing club is involved mainly with dinghy racing, and the whole place becomes a hive of activity during the class meetings. A ferry takes foot passengers (plus bicycles) across to Bawdsey.

At the southernmost tip of the peninsula is **Landguard Point**, where a nature reserve supports rare plants and migrating birds.

Just north on this shingle bank is **Landguard Fort**, built in 1718 (replacing an earlier construction) to protect Harwich harbour. It is now home to **Felixstowe Museum**. The museum is actually housed in the Ravelin Block (1878), which was used as a mine storage depot by the army when a mine barrier was laid across the Orwell during the First World War. A fascinating variety of exhibits includes local history, model aircraft and model paddle steamers, Roman coins and the history of the fort itself, which was the scene of the last invasion of English soil, by the Dutch in 1667. Beyond the fort is an excellent viewing point for watching the comings and goings of the ships.

## FRESTON

**3 miles S of Ipswich off the B1080**

Freston is an ancient village on the south bank of the Orwell, worth visiting for some fine old buildings and some curiosities. The most curious and best known of these buildings is the six-storey Tudor tower by the river in **Freston Park** (it's actually best viewed from across the river). This red-brick house, built around 1570, has just six rooms, one per storey. It might be a folly, but it was probably put up as a lookout tower to warn of enemies sailing up the river. The nicest theory is that it was built for Ellen, daughter of Lord Freston, to study a different subject each day, progressing floor by floor up the tower (and with Sundays off, presumably). A 4,000-year-old archaeological site at Freston was revealed by aerial photography.

## WOOLVERSTONE

**4 miles S of Ipswich on the B1456**

Dating back to the Bronze Age, Woolverstone has a large marina along the banks of the Orwell. One of the buildings in the complex is **Cat House**, where it is said that a stuffed white cat placed in the window would be the all-clear sign for smugglers. **Woolverstone House** was originally St Peter's Home for 'Fallen Women', run by nuns. It was designed by Sir Edwin Lutyens and has its own chapel and bell tower.

## TATTINGSTONE

**4 miles S of Ipswich off the A137**

**Tattingstone Wonder**, on the road between Tattingstone and Stutton, looks like a church from the front, but it isn't. It was built by a local landowner to provide accommodation for estate workers. He presumably preferred to look at a church from his mansion than some plain little cottages. Tattingstone lies at the western edge of Alton Water, a vast man-made lake created as a reservoir in the late 1970s. A footpath runs round the perimeter, and there's a wildlife sanctuary. On the water itself all sorts of leisure activities are on offer, including angling, sailing and windsurfing.

## CHELMONDISTON

**5 miles S of Ipswich on the B1456**

The church here is modern, but incorporates some parts of the original, which was destroyed by a flying bomb in 1944. In the same parish is the tiny riverside community of **Pin Mill**, a well-known beauty spot and sailing centre. The river views are particularly lovely at this point, and it's also a favourite place for woodland and heathland walks. Pin Mill was once a major manufacturer of barges, and those imposing craft can still be seen, sharing the river with sailing boats and pleasure craft. Each year veteran barges gather for a race that starts here, at Buttermans Bay, and ends at Harwich. Arthur Ransome, author of *Swallows and Amazons*, stayed here and had boats built to his specifications. His *We Didn't Mean to Go to Sea* starts aboard a yacht mooring here.

The local hostelry is the 17th century Butt & Oyster, much visited, much painted and one of the best-known pubs in the county. To the east of the Quay is Cliff Plantation, an ancient coppiced wood of alder and oak.

## STUTTON

**6 miles S of Ipswich on the B1080**

The elongated village of Stutton lies on the southern edge of Alton Water. The *Domesday Book* records six manor houses standing here, and there are still some grand properties down by the Stour. St Peter's Church stands isolated overlooking Holbrook Bay, and a footpath from the church leads all the way along the river to Shotley Gate. A little way north, on the B1080, Holbrook is a large village with a brook at the bottom of the hill. Water from the brook once powered Alton Mill, a weatherboarded edifice on a site occupied by watermills for more than 900 years. The mill is now a restaurant.

## ERWARTON

**6 miles S of Ipswich off the B1456**

An impressive red-brick Jacobean gatehouse with a rounded arch, buttresses and pinnacles is part of **Erwarton Hall**, the family home of the Calthorpes. Anne Boleyn was the niece of Philip Calthorpe, and visited as a child and as queen. Just before her execution Anne apparently requested that her heart be buried in the family vault at St Mary's Church. A casket in the shape of a heart was found there in 1836, but when opened contained only dust that could not be positively identified. The casket was resealed and laid in the Lady Chapel.

## SHOTLEY

**8 miles S of Ipswich on the B1456**

Right at the end of the peninsula, with the Orwell on one side and the Stour on the other, Shotley is best known as the home of *HMS Ganges*, where generations of sailors received their training. The main feature is the 142-foot mast, up which trainees would shin at the passing-out ceremony. A small museum records the history of the establishment from 1905 to 1976, when it became a police academy. At the very tip of the peninsula is a large marina where a classic boat festival is an annual occasion.

## HINTLESHAM

**7 miles W of Ipswich on the A1071**

Hintlesham's glory is a magnificent hall dating from the 1570s, when it was the home of the Timperley family. It was considerably altered during the 18th century, when it acquired its splendid Georgian façade. For some years the hall was owned by the celebrated chef Robert Carrier, who developed it into the county's leading restaurant. It still functions as a high-class hotel and restaurant.

## CHILLI & CHIVES

George Street, Hintlesham, Ipswich, Suffolk IP8 3NH
Tel: 01473 652020  Fax: 01473 652886

**Chilli & Chives** is *the* place for quality and luxury foods. Situated in the heart of Hintlesham village on the A1071, this excellent shop sells a wide range of dishes, such as seafood pancakes, vanilla raspberry bavarois, North African lamb, cakes and brownies, all made on the premises. These are complimented by a range of locally produced meats, ice-creams, cheeses and pâtés. Relax and enjoy a coffee or cake whilst choosing your dishes. Functions and deliveries catered for. Open Tuesday to Friday 9am -5,30pm; Saturday 9am -1pm.

## MONKS ELEIGH

**16 miles W of Ipswich on the A1141**

The setting of thatched cottages, a 14th century church and a pump on the village green is so traditional that Monks Eleigh was regularly used on railway posters as a lure to this wonderful part of the country.

## BILDESTON

**14 miles W of Ipswich on the B1115**

More fine old buildings here, including timber-framed cottages with overhanging upper floors. The Church of St Mary has a superb carved door and a splendid hammerbeam roof. A tablet inside the church commemorates

## CORNCRAFT AND THE SUMMER HOUSE

Monks Eleigh, Hadleigh, Suffolk IP7 7AY
Tel: 01449 740456
e-mail: rwgage@lineone.net
website: www.corncraft.co.uk

**Corncraft** brings together some of East Anglia's most creative artists and craftspeople, in converted farm buildings where a variety of traditional corn dollies, pottery, ceramics, tea pots, cards, calendars and much more can be found. The centre's showrooms include a flower shop selling dried and silk flowers and loose bunches of dried floral arrangements in baskets. In the spacious and charming tea room, visitors

can enjoy a range of delectable cakes, biscuits and light snacks all day.

Also on site is **The Summer House**, a specialist source of beautiful accessories and original design for home and garden. Continental furniture, French quilts, cushions and leather accessories for the home are just some of the exquisite pieces on display. Among the many practical and unusual items for the garden are wire garden furniture, statuary, garden-inspired giftware and more. This fine shop also offers an interior design service and a specialist 'house-dressing' service for properties going onto the market.

Captain Edward Rotherham, Commander of the *Royal Sovereign* at the Battle of Trafalgar. He died in Bildeston while staying with a friend, and is buried in the churchyard.

## CONSTABLE COUNTRY

England's greatest landscape painter was born at East Bergholt in 1776 and remained at heart a Suffolk man throughout his life. His father, Golding Constable, was a wealthy man who owned both Flatford Mill and

*Flatford Mill*

Dedham Mill, the latter on the Essex side of the Stour. The river was a major source of inspiration to the young John Constable, and his constant involvement in country matters gave him an expert knowledge of the elements and a keen eye for the details of nature. He was later to declare 'I associate my careless boyhood with all that lies on the banks of the Stour. Those scenes made me a painter and I am grateful.' His interest in painting developed early and was fostered by his friendship with John Dunthorne, a local plumber and amateur artist. Constable became a probationer at the Royal Academy Schools in 1799, and over the following years developed the technical skills to match his powers of observation. He painted the occasional portrait and even attempted a couple of religious works, but he concentrated almost entirely on the scenes that he knew and loved as a boy.

The most significant works of the earlier years were the numerous sketches in oil which were forerunners of the major paintings of Constable's mature years. He had exhibited at the Royal Academy every year since 1802, but it was not until 1817 that the first of his important canvases, *Flatford Mill on the River Stour*, was hung. This was succeeded by the six large paintings which became his best-known works. These were all set on a short stretch of the Stour, and all except *The Hay Wain* show barges at work. These broad, flat-bottomed craft were displayed in scenes remarkable for the realism of the colours, the effects of light and water and, above all, the beautiful depiction of clouds. His fellow-artist Fuseli declared that whenever he saw a Constable painting he felt the need to reach for his coat and umbrella. Though more realistic than anything that preceded them, Constable's paintings were never lacking soul, and his work was much admired by the painters of the French Romantic School.

Two quotations from the man himself reveal much about his aims and philosophy:

*'In a landscape I want to give one brief moment caught from fleeting time a lasting and sober existence.'*

*'I never saw any ugly thing in my life; in fact, whatever may be the shape of an object, light, shade or perspective can always make it beautiful.'*

At the time of his death in 1837, Constable's reputation at home was relatively modest, though he had many followers and admirers in France. Awareness and understanding of his unique talent grew only in the ensuing years, so that, today, his place as England's foremost landscape painter is rarely disputed.

Suffolk has produced many other painters of distinction. Thomas Gainsborough, born in Sudbury in 1727, was an artist of great versatility, innovative and instinctive, and equally at home with portraits and landscapes. He earned his living for a while from portrait painting in Ipswich before making a real name for himself in Bath. His relations with the Royal Academy were often stormy, however, culminating in 1784 in a major dispute over the height at which a painting should be hung. He withdrew his intended hangings from the exhibition and never again showed at the Royal Academy.

A man of equally indomitable spirit was Sir Alfred Munnings, born at Mendham in the north of Suffolk in 1878. The last of the great sporting painters in the tradition of Stubbs and Marshall, Munnings was outspoken in his opinions on modern art. In 1949, as outgoing President of the Royal Academy, he launched an animated attack on modern art as 'silly daubs' and 'violent blows at nothing'. The occasion was broadcast on the radio; in response many listeners complained about the 'strong language' Munnings had used. In 1956, Munnings jolted the art world again by describing that year's Summer Exhibition as 'bits of nonsense' hung on the wall.

Mary Beale, born at Barrow in 1633, was a noted portrait painter and copyist; some of her work has been attributed to Lely and Kneller, and it was rumoured that Lely was in love with her.

Philip Wilson Steer (1860-1942) was among the most distinguished of the many painters who were attracted to Walberswick. He studied in Paris and acquired the reputation of being the best of the English impressionist painters.

The Suffolk tradition of painting continues to this day, with many artists drawn to this part of the county. While nowadays crowds congregate throughout the Stour valley at summer weekends, at other times the tranquillity and loveliness are just as unmatched as they were in Constable's day.

## CAPEL ST MARY

**6 miles SW of Ipswich on the A12**

Constable sketched here, but modern building has more or less overrun the old. A feature of the Church of St Mary is the 'weeping chancel' - a slight kink between the nave and the chancel that is meant to signify Christ's head leaning to the right on the cross.

## BRANTHAM

**8 miles SW of Ipswich on the A137**

Also known as 'Burnt Village' – possibly because it was sacked during a Danish invasion 1,000 years ago – Brantham's Church of St Michael owns one of the only two known religious paintings by Constable, *Christ Blessing the Children*, which he executed in the style of the American painter Benjamin West. It is kept in safety in Ipswich Museum. Just off the junction of the A137 and the B1070 is **Cattawade Picnic Site**, a small area on the edge of the Stour estuary. It's a good spot for birdwatching, and redshanks, lapwings and oystercatchers all breed on the well-known Cattawade Marshes. Fishing and canoeing are available, and there are public footpaths to Flatford Mill.

## EAST BERGHOLT

**8 miles SW of Ipswich on the B1070**

Narrow lanes lead to this picturesque and much-visited little village. The **Constable Country Trail** starts here, where the painter was born, and passes through Flatford Mill and on to Dedham in Essex. The actual house where he was born no longer stands, but the site is marked by a plaque on the fence of its successor, a private house called Constables. A little further along Church Street is Moss Cottage, which Constable once used as his studio. **St Mary's** is one of the many grand churches built with the wealth brought by the wool trade. This one should have been even grander, with a tower to rival that of Dedham across the river.

The story goes that Cardinal Wolsey pledged the money to build the tower, but fell from grace before the funds were forthcoming. The tower got no further than did his college in Ipswich, and a bellcage constructed in the churchyard as a temporary house for the bells became their permanent home, which it remains to this day. In this unique timber-framed structure the massive bells hang upside down and are rung by hand by pulling on the wooden shoulder stocks - an arduous task, as the five bells are among the heaviest in England.

The church is naturally something of a shrine to Constable, his family and his friends. There are memorial windows to the artist and to his beloved wife Maria Bicknell, who bore him seven children and whose early death was an enormous blow to him. His parents, to whom he was clearly devoted, and his old friend

Willy Lott, whose cottage is featured famously in *The Hay Wain*, are buried in the churchyard.

East Bergholt has an interesting mix of houses, some dating back as far as the 14th century. One of the grandest is **Stour House**, once the home of Randolph Churchill. Its gardens are open to the public, as is **East Bergholt Place Garden** on the B1070.

A leafy lane leads south from the village to the Stour, where two of Constable's favourite subjects, **Flatford Mill** and **Willy Lott's Cottage**, both looking much as they did when he painted them, are to be found. Neither is open to the public, and the brick watermill is run as a residential field study centre.

Nearby Bridge Cottage at Flatford is a restored 16th century building housing a Constable display, a tea room and a shop. There's also a restored dry dock, and the whole area is a delight for walkers; it is easy to see how Constable drew constant inspiration from the wonderful riverside setting.

## NAYLAND

**14 miles SW of Ipswich on the B1087**

On a particularly beautiful stretch of the Stour in Dedham Vale, Nayland has charming colour-washed cottages in narrow, winding streets, as well as two very fine 15th century buildings in Alston Court and the Guildhall. Abels Bridge, originally built of wood in the 15th century by wealthy merchant John Abel, divides Suffolk from Essex. In the 16th century a hump bridge replaced it, allowing barges to pass beneath. The current bridge carries the original keystone, bearing the initial A. In the Church of St James stands an altarpiece by Constable entitled *Christ Blessing the Bread and Wine*.

*Church of St Mary, Stoke by Nayland*

One mile west of Nayland, at the end of a track off the Bures road, stands the Norman Church of St Mary at Wissington. The church has a number of remarkable features, including several 13th century wall paintings, a finely carved 12th century doorway and a tiebeam and crown post roof.

## STRATFORD ST MARY

**10 miles SW of Ipswich off the A12**

Another of Constable's favourite locations, Stratford St Mary is the most southerly village in Suffolk. *The Young Waltonians* and *A House in Water Lane* (the house still stands today) are the best known of his works set in this picturesque spot. The village church is typically large and imposing, with parts dating back to 1200. At the top of the village are two splendid half-timbered cottages called the **Ancient House** and the **Priest's House**. Stratford was once on the main coaching route to London, and the largest of the four pubs had stabling for 200 horses. It is claimed that Henry Williamson, author of *Tarka the Otter*, saw his first otter here.

## STOKE BY NAYLAND

**12 miles SW of Ipswich on the B1087**

The drive from Nayland reveals quite stunning views, and the village itself has a large number of listed buildings. The magnificent **Church of St Mary**, with its 120-foot tower, dominates the scene from its hilltop position. This church also dominates more than one Constable painting, the most famous showing the church lit up by a rainbow. William Dowsing destroyed 100 'superstitious pictures' here in his Puritan purges, but plenty of fine work is still to be seen, including several monumental brasses.

The Guildhall is another very fine building, now private residences but in the 16th century a busy centre of trade and commerce. When the wool trade declined, so did the importance of the Guildhall, and for a time this noble building saw service as a workhouse.

The decline of the cloth trade in East Anglia had several causes. Fierce competition came from the northern and western weaving industries, which generally had easier access to water supplies for fulling; the wars on the continent of Europe led to the closure of some trading routes and markets; and East Anglia had no supplies of the coal that was used to drive the new steam-powered machinery. In some cases, as at Sudbury, weaving or silk took over as smaller industries.

## POLSTEAD

**11 miles SW of Ipswich off the B1068**

Polstead is a very pretty village set in wooded, hilly countryside, with thatched, colour-washed cottages around the green and a wide duck pond at the bottom of the hill. Standing on a rise above the pond are Polstead Hall, a handsome Georgian mansion, and the 12th century Church of St Mary. The church has two features not found elsewhere in Suffolk – a stone spire and the very early bricks used in its construction. The builders used not only these bricks, but also tiles and tufa, a soft, porous stone much used in Italy. In the grounds of the hall stand the remains of a 'Gospel Oak' said to have been 1,300 years old when it collapsed in 1953. Legend has it that Saxon missionaries preached beneath it in the 7th century; an open-air service is still held here annually.

Polstead has two other claims to fame. One is for Polstead Blacks, a particularly tasty variety of cherry which was cultivated in orchards around the village and which used to be honoured with an annual fair. The other is much less agreeable, for it was here that the notorious Red Barn murder hit the headlines in 1827. A young girl called Maria Marten, daughter of the local molecatcher, disappeared with William Corder, a farmer's son who was the girl's lover and father of her child. It was at first thought that they had eloped, but Maria's stepmother dreamt three times that she had been murdered and buried in a red barn. A search of the barn soon revealed this to be true. Corder was tracked down to Middlesex, tried and found guilty of Maria's murder and hanged. His skin was used to bind a copy of the trial proceedings and this, together with his scalp, is on display at Moyse's Hall in Bury St Edmunds. The incident aroused a great deal of interest; today's visitors to the village will still find reminders of the ghastly deed: the thatched cottage where Maria lived stands, in what is now called Marten's Lane, and the farm where the murderer lived, now called Corder's Farm.

## Boxford

**12 miles W of Ipswich on the A1071**

A gloriously unspoilt weaving village, downhill from anywhere, surrounded by the peaceful water meadows of the River Box, Boxford's St Mary's Church dates back to the 14th century. Its wooden north porch is one of the oldest of its kind in the country. In the church is a

## Gainsborough's House

46 Gainsborough Street, Sudbury, Suffolk CO10 2EU
Tel: 01787 372958  Fax: 01787 376991
e-mail: mail@gainsborough.org
website: www.gainsborough.org

**Gainsborough's House** is the birthplace museum of Thomas Gainsborough (1727-1788), one of England's most celebrated artists. An exceptional collection of his paintings, drawings and prints is on display in this charming town house with a Georgian façade built by the artist's father. Around 25 oil paintings are on show, including a magnificent landscape of 1782 and a touching miniature of his wife, and among the Gainsborough memorabilia to be seen in the house are the artist's studio cabinet, his swordstick and his pocket watch. Two galleries and the garden showcase contemporary art and craft, and the print workshop hosts evening classes and summer courses in the techniques of etching, screenprinting, stone lithography and relief printing.

touching brass in memory of David Byrde, son of the rector, who died a baby in 1606. At the other end of the continuum is Elizabeth Hyam, four times a widow, who died in her 113th year.

### EDWARDSTONE

**14 miles W of Ipswich off the A1071**

Just to the north of Boxford and close to Edwardstone Hall and the Temple Bar Gate House, Edwardstone is now a 700-acre estate originally home to the Winthrop family. Winthrop was born in Edwardstone and emigrated to the New World, eventually becoming Governor of Massachusetts.

### BURES

**17 miles W of Ipswich on the B1508**

At this point the River Stour turns sharply to the east, creating a natural boundary between Suffolk and Essex. The little village of Bures straddles the river, lying partly in each county. Bures St Mary in Suffolk is where the church is, overlooked by houses of brick and half-timbering.

Bures wrote itself very early into the history books when on Christmas Day AD855 it is thought that our old friend Edmund the Martyr, the Saxon king, was crowned at the age of 15 in the Chapel of St Stephen. For some time after that momentous occasion, Bures was the capital seat of the East Anglian kings.

Bures also has a long connection with the Waldegrave family, possibly from as far back as Chaucer's day. One of the Waldegrave memorials shows graphically the results of a visitation by Dowsing and the Puritan iconoclasts: all the figures of the kneeling children have had their hands cut off.

## SUDBURY

Sudbury is another wonderful town, the largest of the 'wool towns' and still home to a number of weaving concerns. Unlike Lavenham, Sudbury kept its industry because it was a port, and the result is a much more varied architectural picture. The surrounding countryside is some of the loveliest in Suffolk, and the River Stour is a further plus, with launch trips and fishing available.

Sudbury boasts three medieval churches, but what most visitors make a beeline for is **Gainsborough's House** (see panel opposite) on Gainsborough Street. The painter Thomas Gainsborough was born here in 1727 in the house built by his father John. More of the artist's work is displayed in this Georgian-fronted

### BULMER BRICK & TILE CO. LTD

Brickfields, Hedingham Road, Bulmer, Sudbury, Suffolk CO10 7EF
Tel: 01787 269232  Fax: 01787 269040
e-mail: bbt@bulmerbrickandtile.co.uk

A brickworks has stoon on the site of **Bulmer Brick & Tile** since the 15th century. The skilled staff produce hand-moulded facings and specials to nearly 5,000 patterns, together with a range of terracotta pieces. The specialise in purpose-made bricks for restoration, using London Bed clay to

produce the mellow reds seen in the nation's finest buildings, as in their restoration work at Hampton Court and Windsor Castle.

# The Waldingfields

| | |
|---|---|
| **Distance:** | 3.1 miles (4.83 kilometres) |
| **Typical time:** | 60 mins |
| **Height gain:** | 15 metres |
| **Map:** | Explorer 196 |
| **Walk:** | www.walkingworld.com ID:1876 |
| **Contributor:** | Brian and Anne Sandland |

## Access Information:

To reach the church at Great Waldingfield turn south east off the B1115.

## Description:

This walk visits two churches and quaint old Suffolk villages. There are picturesque cottages and excellent paths, tracks and lanes on the way. The walk can be combined with another which starts from Great Waldingfield Church and visits Acton as well as reaching the outskirts of Little Waldingfield.

## Features:

Pub, Church, Wildlife, Birds, Flowers, Great Views, Butterflies, Woodland

## Walk Directions:

**1** Starting from the Church take the road signposted No through road - Footpath to Little Waldingfield. After a descent on the track to Hole Farm look for a signposted footpath on the right just before the farm.

**2** Turn right and before long follow a stream beside a wood (left), then take a signposted footpath left over a bridge and through the wood.

**3** After the wood cross a footbridge, then continue beside a very large field (on your left). When you reach a lane by the road to Archers Farm turn left along it. Pass the church at Little Waldingfield then turn left at the T-junction with the B 1115 (past the Swan Inn).

**4** Just beyond the thatched cottage The Grange (left) take the right hand of two signposted footpaths off left. At the far end of the field cross a footbridge, then follow signs (and a concrete roadway) around Hole Farm before reaching the lane you used at the start of your walk and ascending it to reach Great Waldingfield church again.

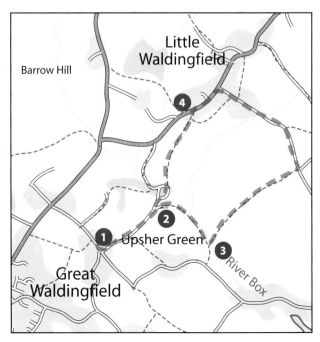

house than in any other gallery, and there is also assorted 18<sup>th</sup> century memorabilia and furnishings. A changing programme of contemporary art exhibitions includes fine art, photography and sculpture, highlighting East Anglian artists in particular. A bronze statue of Gainsborough stands in the square.

About those churches: All Saints dates from the 15th century and has a glorious carved tracery pulpit and screens; 14<sup>th</sup> century St Gregory's is notable for a wonderful medieval font; and St Peter's has some marvellous painted screen panels and a piece of 15<sup>th</sup> century embroidered velvet.

Other buildings of interest are the **Victorian Corn Exchange**, now a library; **Salter's Hall**, a 15<sup>th</sup> century timbered house (sadly no longer open to the public); and the **Quay Theatre**, a thriving centre for the arts.

# AROUND SUDBURY

## HADLEIGH

**12 miles E of Sudbury on the A1071**

The old and not-so-old blend harmoniously in a variety of architectural styles in Hadleigh. Timber-framed buildings, often with elaborate plasterwork, stand in the long main street as a reminder of the prosperity generated by the wool trade in the 14th to 16th centuries, and there are also some fine houses from the Regency and Victorian periods. The 15<sup>th</sup> century **Guildhall** has two overhanging storeys, and together with the Deanery Tower and the church makes for a magnificent trio of huge appeal and contrasting construction – timber for the Guildhall, brick for the tower and flint for the church.

Guthrun, the Danish leader who was

### GREEN LAWNS BONSAI

Hadleigh Road, Boxford, Sudbury, Suffolk CO10 5JH
Tel: 01787 210501
website: www.greenlawns.co.uk

Open Tuesday to Saturday 9 – 5, Sundays and Bank Holiday Mondays 10 – 4, **Green Lawns Bonsai** can be found just three miles from Hadleigh on the A1071. This two-acre site boasts probably the largest bonsai nursery in East Anglia. Indoor and outdoor bonsai, outdoor starter trees, pots, tools, compost and more await visitors here, and there are regularly scheduled workshops comprising half- and full-day sessions, where participants can bring their own trees to work on or purchase a starter tree or trees from the nursery.

### WHELDONS FARM SHOP & PICK YOUR OWN

Newton, Sudbury, Suffolk, CO10 0QE
Tel: 01787 374322

For over 70 years, **Wheldons** have been growing fruit near Sudbury, supplying the public and many of the finest supermarkets. The Pick Your Own is open early June to mid September 7 days a week from 10am to 5 or 6pm selling a range of the freshest fruits in season- strawberries, blackberries, gooseberries, loganberries, red and blackcurrants, plums and apples and pears- whatever takes your fancy you'll find delicious varieties of it here. The farm shop is open Monday to Friday 10am to 4pm from mid September to May and sells apples and pears, jams, honey, fruit juices, puddings and cakes. Wheldons is signed off the A134 between Sudbury and Newton Green.

captured by Alfred and pardoned on condition that he became a Christian, made Hadleigh his HQ and lived here for 12 years. He was buried in the church, then a wooden construction but subsequently twice rebuilt. In the south chapel of the present church is a 14th century bench-end carving depicting the legendary scene of the wolf guarding the head of St Edmund. The wolf is wearing a monk's habit, indicating a satirical sense of humour in the carpenter. Also of interest is the **Clock Bell**, which stands outside the tower.

A famous resident of Hadleigh was the rector Dr Rowland Taylor, who was burnt at the stake on Aldham Common for refusing to hold a mass. A large stone, inscribed and dated 1555, marks the spot.

There are two good walks from Hadleigh, the first being along the Brett with access over medieval **Toppesfield Bridge**. The other is a walk along the disused railway line between Hadleigh and Raydon through peaceful, picturesque countryside. At Raydon a few buildings survive from the wartime base of the 353rd, 357th and 358th Fighter Groups of the USAAF.

Two miles east of Hadleigh is **Wolves Wood**, an RSPB reserve with woodland nature trails - and no wolves!

*Kersey Water Splash*

### KERSEY
**11 miles E of Sudbury off the A1141**

The ultimate Suffolk picture-postcard village, Kersey boasts a wonderful collection of timbered merchants' houses and weavers' cottages with paint and thatch. The main street has a **Water Splash**, which, along with the 700-year-old Bell Inn, has featured in many films and travelogues. The Church of St Mary, which overlooks the village from its hilltop position, is of massive proportions, testimony to the wealth that came with the wool and cloth industry. Kersey's speciality was a coarse twill broadcloth much favoured for greatcoats and army uniforms. Headless angels and mutilated carvings are reminders of the Puritans' visit to the church, though some treasures survive, including the ornate flintwork of the 15th century south porch.

Traditional craftsmanship can still be seen in practice at the Kersey Pottery, which sells many items of stoneware plus paintings by Suffolk artists.

### CHELSWORTH
**10 miles NE of Sudbury off the A1141**

Chelsworth is an unspoilt delight in the lovely valley of the River Brett, which is crossed by a little double hump-backed bridge. The timbered houses and thatched cottages look much the same as when they were built, and every year the villagers open their gardens to the public.

## Hedgerows Farm Shop & Nursery

Brent Eleigh, Lavenham, Suffolk CO10 9NU
Tel: 01787 247772

Set in beautiful countryside, **Hedgerows Farm Shop & Nursery** offers a wide range of unusual and well-priced plants, including hardy perennials, geraniums, grasses, home-grown vegetables in season, free-range eggs, pick-your-own soft fruit, 20 varieties of tomatoes, six varieties of apples – including Katie, Discovery and Fiesta - and more. From August to Halloween there are 20 varieties of pumpkins and squash, including Turks Turbans, Butternut and Yellow Crookneck. Expert advice on hand.

## Brent Eleigh

**8 miles NE of Sudbury off the A1141**

The church at Brent Eleigh, on a side road off the A1141, is remarkable for a number of quite beautiful ancient wall paintings, discovered during maintenance work as recently as 1960. The most striking and moving of the paintings is one of the Crucifixion.

## Lavenham

**6 miles N of Sudbury on the A1141**

An absolute gem of a town, the most complete and original of the medieval 'wool towns', with crooked timbered and whitewashed buildings lining the narrow streets. From the 14th to the 16th centuries Lavenham flourished as one of the leading wool and cloth-making

## Milden Hall Farmhouse & Barn Bed & Breakfast & Self-catering

Milden Hall, nr Lavenham, Sudbury,
Suffolk  CO10 9NY
Tel/Fax: 01787 247235
e-mail: hawkins@thehall-milden.co.uk
website: www.thehall-milden.co.uk

A listed 16th-century hall farmhouse with Georgian additions found down a quiet drive, just three miles from Lavenham, **Milden Hall** is surrounded by ancient wildflower meadows, walled garden and hedged countryside. Offering superior bed

and breakfast accommodation, the house is filled with beautiful period furniture, wall hangings and tapestries in the three spacious guest bedrooms and charming, sunny sitting room. All rooms boast fabulous views. The delicious breakfast includes free-range bantam eggs from the farm, local bacon

and sausages or home-grown fruit compote. Evening meals are available by arrangement.

For groups, the aisled Tudor barn offers self-catering for up to 20 guests, alongside ample camping space.

Among the many activities and attractions on-site include planned nature trails and walks, cycle hire, and car-free planned itineraries to Lavenham, Kersey, Long Melford and Constable Country. There are also castle earthworks, ancient barns and the beginnings of a farm museum with farm finds and memorabilia to explore.

*Little Hall, Lavenham*

medieval character remains: there was simply not enough money for the rebuilding and development programmes that changed many other towns, often for the worse. The medieval street pattern still exists, complete with market place and market cross.

More than 300 of Lavenham's buildings are officially listed as being of architectural and historical interest, and none of them is finer than the **Guildhall**. This superb 16th century timbered building was originally the meeting place of the Guild of Corpus Christi, an organisation that regulated the production of wool. It now houses exhibitions of local history and the wool trade, and has a walled garden

centres in the land. With the decline of that industry, however, the prosperous times soon came to an end. It is largely due to the fact that Lavenham found no replacement industry that so much of its

## THE AVOCET COLLECTION

16a High Street, Lavenham, Suffolk CO10 9PT
Tel: 01787 247347
e-mail: avocet@boxvalley.fsnet.co.uk

Selling beautiful gifts and decorative accessories for home and garden, **The Avocet Collection** offers an outstanding range of choice. Dee Abrey and her daughter Claire have owned and run this business since 1999, opening this shop here in Lavenham in 2003. Their passion for beautiful and well-made pieces is infectious, and they've a wealth of knowledge and experience. Elegance and taste are the bywords here, where reasonable prices combine with high quality.

Classic traditional and stylish, modern accoutrements – from gifts and garden furniture to cushions and soft furnishings – are displayed here, together with French glassware, Limoges porcelain, Dresden collectables, textiles from Scandinavia and England and more. This large shop also features a selection of handsome silver photo frames, limited edition paintings, greeting cards and more. The atmosphere is always relaxed and informal, and the staff informed, friendly and helpful. Customers will be sure to find something fresh and exciting within the unusual and diverse range offered by this superior shop. Open: Monday-Saturday 10-5; Sunday 11-4.

## THE GUILDHALL, LAVENHAM

Market Place, Lavenham,
Suffolk CO10 9QZ
Tel: 01787 247646
e-mail: almjtg@smtp.ntrust.org.uk

**The Guildhall**, built around 1530 by the prosperous Corpus Christi religious guild, has been at the heart of village life ever since. It is a fine example of close-studded timber framing, with exuberant carvings that show off the impressive skills of the carpenters of the time. In 1547, when religious guilds were abolished as part of the Reformation, the Guildhall became parish property and in the ensuing centuries was put to various uses, including a house of correction, parish workhouse, home for WWII evacuees, Red Cross restaurant and nursery school. In 1951 it was vested in the National Trust and now houses a local history museum that includes exhibitions on the cloth industry, farming and the railway. The peaceful walled garden contains examples of the plants that were used to dye cloth in medieval times.

with a special area devoted to dye plants.

**Little Hall** is hardly less remarkable, a 15th century hall house with a superb crown post roof. It was restored by the Gayer Anderson brothers, and has a fine collection of their furniture. The Church of St Peter and St Paul dominates the town from its elevated position. It's a building of great distinction, perhaps the greatest of all the 'wool churches' and declared by the 19th century architect August Pugin to be the finest example of Late Perpendicular style in the world. It was built, with generous help from wealthy local families (notably the Spryngs and

## VINTAGE PINK

4 High Street, Lavenham, Suffolk CO10 9PX
Tel: 01787 247546

Vintage Pink is a real treasure trove, owned and run by Sarah Cornwell, who also owns Gallery 48. In contrast to the modern designs of the gallery, Vintage Pink oozes decadence and indulgence! The main clothing range is by British company Out of Xile and is accompanied by beautiful jewellery, scarves and bags by well known labels such as Johnny Loves Rosie and Adele Marie. Silk nightwear and beautiful bedding are displayed alongside evocative toiletries and decorative items. Rustic lanterns, zinc planters and carrot hand cream help create a country living lifestyle. Vintage Pink also has a junior section which includes decorative nursery items.

## GALLERY 48

48 High Street, Lavenham, Suffolk CO10 9PY
Tel: 01787 248542

This small but friendly gallery is a colourful showcase for UK artists and craftspeople. Specialising in graduates and newcomers, it shows an eclectic range of contemporary crafts and applied arts. Gallery 48 has established an enviable reputation for its selection of contemporary jewellery made using materials as diverse as rubber and melted carrier bags, as well as the usual mediums of silver and gold. One can also find here decorative ceramics, beautiful textiles, turned wood, glassware and a huge selection of handmade cards. The work of renowned Norfolk artist, Lucy Clibbon, whose magical paintings transport you into a world of childhood memories, is available as paintings, prints, cards and ceramics.

## FISKS RESTAURANT

2 Church Street, Lavenham, Suffolk CO10 9QT
Tel: 01787 248512  Fax: 01787 249612
website: www.fisks@lavenham.co.uk

**Fisks Restaurant** is an exquisite and venerable place which has been
carefully and sensitively restored and redecorated in keeping with
the historic Suffolk village where it makes its home. The traditional
ceiling and wall beams have been restored, together with the original
fireplace. But it's not just the handsome décor and ambience that
attracts diners, but the extensive menu of delicious traditional and innovative dishes such as filet
steaks, venison sausages, griddled tuna steaks and filo parcels of chargrilled vegetables. *Serving:* Tuesday-
Saturday 12.00-14.00 and 18.30-21.00. and Sunday lunches from 12.00-14.00.

the de Veres) in the late 15$^{th}$ and early
16$^{th}$ centuries to celebrate the end of the
Wars of the Roses. Its flint tower is a
mighty 140 feet in height, and it's
possible to climb to the top to take in the
glorious views over Lavenham and the
surrounding countryside. Richly carved
screens and fine (Victorian) stained glass
are eye-catching features within.

**The Priory** originated in the 13th
century as a home for Benedictine
monks; the beautiful timber-framed
house on the site dates from about 1600.
In the original hall, at the centre of the
building, is an important collection of
paintings and stained glass. The
extensive grounds include a kitchen
garden, a herb garden and a pond.

John Constable went to school in
Lavenham, where one of his friends was
Jane Taylor, who wrote the words to
'Twinkle Twinkle Little Star'.

## LONG MELFORD

**2 miles N of Sudbury off the A134**

The heart of this atmospheric wool town
is its very long and, in stretches, fairly
broad main street, set on an ancient
Roman site in a particularly beautiful
part of south Suffolk. In Roman times
the Stour was a navigable river, and trade
flourished. Various Roman finds have
been unearthed, notably a blue glass vase
which is now on display in the British
Museum in London. The street is filled
with antiques shops, book
shops and art galleries,
and is a favourite place
for collectors and
browsers. Some of the
houses are washed in the
characteristic Suffolk
pink, which might
originally have been
achieved by mixing ox
blood or sloe juice into
the plaster.

**Holy Trinity Church**,
on a 14-acre green at the
north end of Hall Street,
is a typically exuberant
manifestation of the

*Lavenham Village*

*Long Melford*

the overall impression that stays in the memory, and the sight of the building floodlit at night is truly spectacular. The distinguished 20th century poet Edmund Blunden spent his last years in Long Melford and is buried in the churchyard. The inscription on his gravestone reads 'I live still to love still things quiet and unconcerned.'

**Melford Hall**, east of town beyond an imposing 16th century gateway, was built around 1570 by Sir William Cordell on the site of an earlier hall that served as a country retreat, before the Dissolution of the Monasteries, for the monks of St Edmundsbury Abbey. There exists an account of Cordell entertaining Queen Elizabeth I at the Hall in 1578, when she was welcomed by '200 young gentlemen in white velvet, 300 in black and 1,500 serving men'. Much of the fine work of Sir William (whose body lies in Holy Trinity Church) has been altered in restoration, but the pepperpot chimneys are original, as is the panelled banqueting hall. The rooms are in various styles, some with ornate walnut furniture, and there's a notable collection of Chinese porcelain on show. Most delightful of all is the Beatrix Potter room, with some of her watercolours, first editions of her books and, among the toys, the original of Jemima Puddleduck. She was a frequent visitor here (her cousins, the Hyde Parkers, were then the owners), bringing small animals to draw. The Jeremy Fisher illustrations were mostly drawn at Melford Hall's fishponds, and the book is dedicated to Stephanie Hyde Parker. The Hall, which is a National Trust property, stands in a

wealth of the wool and textile trade. It's big enough to be a cathedral, but served (and still serves) comparatively few parishioners. John Clopton, grown rich in the woollen business, was largely responsible for this magnificent Perpendicular-style edifice, which has a 180-foot nave and chancel and half timbers, flint 'flushwork' (stonework) of the highest quality, and 100 large windows to give a marvellous sense of light and space. Medieval glass in the north aisle depicts religious scenes and the womenfolk of the Clopton family. There are many interesting monuments and brasses, and in the chantry entrance is a bas relief of the Three Wise Men, the Virgin and Child, and St Joseph. In the Lady Chapel, reached by way of the churchyard, a children's multiplication table written on one wall is a reminder that the chapel served as the village school for a long period after the Reformation.

John Clopton's largesse is recorded rather modestly in inscriptions on the roof parapets. His tower was struck by lightning in the early 18th century; the present brick construction dates from around 1900. The detail of this great church is of endless fascination, but it's

*Kentwell Hall*

**5 miles NW of Cavendish on the B1065**

Driving into Glemsford, the old Church of St Mary makes an impressive sight on what, for Suffolk, is quite a considerable hill. Textiles and weaving have long played a prominent part in Glemsford's history, and thread from the silk factory, which opened in 1824 and is still going strong, has been woven into dresses and robes for various members of the royal family, including the late Princess Diana's wedding dress. During the last century several factories produced matting from coconut fibres, and in 1906 Glemsford was responsible for the largest carpet in the world, used to cover the floor at London's Olympia. To this day one factory processes horse hair for use in judges' wigs, sporrans and busbies.

CAVENDISH
**5 miles W of Sudbury on the A1092**

A most attractive village, where the Romans stayed awhile - the odd remains have been unearthed - and the Saxons settled. Cavendish is splendidly traditional, with its church, thatched cottages, almshouses, Nether Hall and the **Sue Ryder Foundation Museum** spread around the green. The last, in a 16th century rectory by the pond, illustrates the work of the Sue Ryder Foundation, and was formally opened by Queen Elizabeth II in 1979. Once a refuge for concentration camp victims, it houses abundant war photographs and memorabilia. Nether Hall is a well-restored 16th century building and the headquarters of **Cavendish Vineyards**.

In the church of **St Mary**, whose tower has a pointed bellcote and a room inside complete with fireplace and shuttered windows, look for the two handsome lecterns, one with a brass eagle (15th century), the other with two chained

lovely garden with some distinguished clipped box hedges. William Cordell was also responsible for the red-brick almshouses, built in 1593 for '12 poor men', which stand near Holy Trinity.

**Kentwell Hall** is a red-brick Tudor moated mansion approached by a long avenue of limes. Its grounds include a unique Tudor rose maze, and are set out to illustrate and re-create Tudor times, with a walled garden, a bakery, a dairy and several varieties of rare-breed farm animals. The buildings include a handsome 14th century aisle barn. The Hall was the setting for a film version of *Toad of Toad Hall*.

Long Melford is a great place for leisurely strolls, and for the slightly more energetic there's a scenic 3-mile walk along a disused railway track and farm tracks that leads straight into Lavenham.

## THE GEORGE

The Green, Cavendish, Sudbury, Suffolk CO10 8BA
Tel: 01787 280248 Fax: 01787 281703
e-mail: reservations@georgecavendish.co.uk
website: www.georgecavendish.co.uk

**The George** is a handsome and traditional inn, memorable for its
excellent food, drink and accommodation. The extensive menu boasts
a range of modern English dishes at lunch and dinner – meat and poultry,
fish and shellfish, pastas and salads, all are expertly prepared and
presented, fresh to order and delicious. The early dining special (served
between 6 and 7 p.m.) is available Monday to Friday – booking essential.
The five guest bedrooms are spacious and supremely comfortable.

books; and for the Flemish and Italian
statues. In 1381 Wat Tyler, leader of the
Peasants' Revolt, was killed at Smithfield,
in London, by John Cavendish, son of
Sir John Cavendish, then lord of the
manor and Chief Justice of England. Sir
John was then hounded by the peasants,
who caught him and killed him near
Bury St Edmunds. He managed en route
to hide some valuables in the belfry of St
Mary's here in Cavendish, and
bequeathed to the church £40, sufficient
to restore the chancel. A later Cavendish
– Thomas – sailed round the world in the
1580s and perished on a later voyage. In
the shadow of the church, on the edge of
the village green, is a cluster of
immaculate thatched cottages at a spot
known as Hyde Park Corner. Pink-

washed and pretty as a picture, they look
almost too good to be true – and they
almost are, having been rebuilt twice
since the Second World War due to
unhappy forces that included fires
and dilapidation.

## CLARE

**7 miles W of Sudbury on the A1092**

A medieval wool town of great
importance, Clare repays a visit today
with its fine old buildings and some
distinguished old ruins. Perhaps the most
renowned tourist attraction is **Ancient
House**, a timber-framed building dated
1473 and remarkable for its pargetting.
This is the decorative treatment of
external plasterwork, usually by dividing
the surface into rectangles and
decorating each panel. It was
very much a Suffolk
speciality, particularly in the
16th and 17th centuries, with
some examples also being
found in Cambridgeshire and
Essex. The decoration could
be simple brushes of a comb,
scrolls or squiggles, or more
elaborate, with religious
motifs, guild signs or family
crests. Some pargetting is
incised, but the best is in
relief – pressing moulds into
wet plaster or shaping it by

*Cavendish Church*

## FIDDLESTICKS B&B

Pentlow, Nr Clare, Suffolk CO10 7JW
Tel/Fax: 01787 280154
e-mail: sarah@fiddlesticks.biz
website: www.fiddlesticks.biz

**Fiddlesticks B&B** is a handsome and modern bungalow where
guests enjoy their own private entrance and terrace. Created
with the needs of the elderly and disabled particularly in mind,
this fine B&B has full disabled access and facilities. The double
guest bedroom connects to a carer's suite. Facilities include a wheel-in shower chair and mobile hoist.
The room also boasts a fridge, microwave, kettle, china, cutlery, glassware, hairdryer and radio alarm.
Newspapers and a hair-dresser are also available. The breakfast choice is excellent; evening meals
available by arrangement. ETC 4 Diamonds Silver Award.

hand. Ancient House sports some splendid entwined flowers and branches, and a representation of two figures holding a shield. The best-known workers in this unique skill had their own distinctive styles, and the expert eye could spot the particular 'trademarks' of each man (the same is the case with the master thatchers). Ancient House is now a museum, open during the summer months and housing an exhibition on local history.

Another place of historical significance is **Nethergate House**, once the workplace of dyers, weavers and spinners. The Swan Inn, in the High Street, has a sign which lays claim to being the oldest in the land. Ten feet in length and carved from a solid piece of wood, it portrays the arms of England and France. **Clare Castle** was a motte-and-bailey fortress that sheltered a household of 250. **Clare Castle Country Park** (see panel below), with a visitor centre in the goods shed of a disused railway line, contains the remains of the castle and the moat, the latter now a series of ponds and home to varied wild life.

At the Prior's House, the original cellar and infirmary are still in use. Established in 1248 by Augustine friars and used by them until the Dissolution of 1538, the priory was handed back to that order in 1953 and remains their property.

A mile or so west of Clare on the A1092 lies **Stoke-by-Clare**, a pretty village on one of the region's most picturesque routes. It once housed a Benedictine priory,

## CLARE CASTLE COUNTRY PARK

Maltings Lane, Clare, Suffolk CO10 8NJ
Tel: 01787 277491

**Clare Castle Country Park** is open daily throughout the year and offers
the visitor a variety of attractions. Within the country park can be found

the remains of Clare Castle and Clare Railway Station. The former railway goods shed is now a visitor centre (open April - September). There is ample open space for picnics and games, while children can enjoy an adventure playground. Wander along the riverside path and old railway line or follow the nature and history trails to learn more about the country park's wildlife and heritage.

whose remains are now in the grounds of a school. There's a fine 15<sup>th</sup> century church and a vineyard: **Boyton Vineyards** at Hill Farm, Boyton End, is open early April-end October for a tour, a talk and a taste.

### KEDINGTON

**12 miles W of Sudbury on the B1061**

Haverhill intrudes somewhat, but the heart of the old village of Kedington gains in appeal by the presence of the River Stour. Known to many as the 'Cathedral of West Suffolk', the church of **St Peter and St Paul** is the village's chief attraction. Almost 150 feet in length, it stands on a ridge overlooking the Stour Valley. It has several interesting features, including a 15<sup>th</sup> century font, a Saxon cross in the chancel window, a triple-decker pulpit (with a clerk's desk and a reading desk) and a sermon-timer, looking rather like a grand egg-timer. The foundations of a Roman building have been found beneath the floorboards.

The Bardiston family, one of the oldest in Suffolk, had strong links with the village and many of the family tombs are in the church. In the church grounds is a row of ten elm trees, each, the legend says, with a knight buried beneath its roots.

Following the Stour along the B1061, the visitor will find a number of interesting little villages. In Little Wratting, Holy Trinity Church has a shingled oak-framed steeple (a feature more usually associated with Essex churches). John Sainsbury was a local resident, while in Great Wratting another magnate, W H Smith, financed the restoration of St Mary's Church in 1887. This church boasts some diverting topiary in the shape of a church, a cross and – somewhat comically - an armchair.

### HAVERHILL

**14 miles W of Sudbury on the A604**

Notable for its fine Victorian architecture, Haverhill also boasts one fine Tudor gem. Although many of Haverhill's buildings were destroyed by fire in 1665, the **Anne of Cleves House** was restored and is well worth a visit. Anne was the fourth wife of Henry VIII and, after a brief political marriage, she was given an allowance and spent the remainder of her days at Haverhill and Richmond. **Haverhill Local History Centre**, in the Town Hall, has an interesting collection of memorabilia, photographs and archive material.

**East Town Park** is an attractive and relatively new country park on the east side of Haverhill.

### GREAT AND LITTLE THURLOW

**15 miles W of Sudbury on the B1061**

Great and Little Thurlow form a continuous village on the west bank of the River Stour a few miles north of Haverhill. Largely undamaged thanks to being in a conservation area, together they boast many 17<sup>th</sup> century cottages and a Georgian manor house. In the main street is a schoolhouse built in 1614 by Sir Stephen Soame, one-time Lord Mayor of London, whose family are commemorated in the village church.

A short distance further up the B1061 stands the village of **Great Bradley**, divided in two by the River Stour, which rises just outside the village boundary. Chief points of note in the tranquil parish church are a fine Norman doorway sheltering a Tudor brick porch and some beautiful stained glass poignantly depicting a soldier in the trenches during the First World War. The three bells in the tower include one cast in the 14<sup>th</sup> century, among the oldest in Suffolk.

# BURY ST EDMUNDS

A gem among Suffolk towns, rich in archaeological treasures and places of religious and historical interest, Bury St Edmunds takes its name from St Edmund, who was born in Nuremberg in AD841 and came here as a teenager to become the last King of East Anglia. He was a staunch Christian, and his refusal to deny his faith caused him to be tortured and killed by the Danes in AD870. Legend has it that although his body was recovered, his head (cut off by the Danes) could not be found. His men searched for it for 40 days, then heard his voice directing them to it from the depths of a wood, where they discovered it lying protected between the paws of a wolf. The head and the body were seamlessly united and, to commemorate the wolf's deed, the crest of the town's armorial bearings depicts a wolf with a man's head.

Edmund was possibly buried first at Hoxne, the site of his murder, but when he was canonised in about AD910 his remains were moved to the monastery at Beodricsworth, which changed its name to St Edmundsbury. A shrine was built in his honour, later incorporated into the Norman Abbey Church after the monastery was granted abbey status by King Canute in 1032. The town soon became a place of pilgrimage, and for many years St Edmund was the patron saint of England, until replaced by St George. Growing rapidly around the great abbey, which became one of the largest and most influential in the land, Bury prospered as a centre of trade and commerce, thanks notably to the cloth industry.

The next historical landmark was reached in 1214, when on St Edmund's Feast Day the then Archbishop of Canterbury, Simon Langton, met with

## CLARICE HOUSE HOTEL AND HEALTH SPA

Horringer Court, Horringer Road, Bury St Edmunds, Suffolk IP29 5PH
Tel: 01284 705550  Fax: 01284 716120
e-mail: cdk@netcomuk.co.uk
website: www.clarice.co.uk

Established in 2001 and family run, **Clarice House Hotel and Health Spa** combines gracious accommodation and service with a friendly, welcoming atmosphere perfect for total relaxation of body and mind. Located just three miles south of Bury on the A143, this excellent hotel boasts 13 luxurious guest rooms, a superb restaurant, and a wide range of day treatments including massage, facials, body wraps, manicure and pedicure, reflexology, Indian head massage and more. Guests can of course also make full use of the state-of-

the-art gym, pool, sauna, steam room and health club, and take one of the variety of classes in health-enhancing practices such as yoga, Pilates, Callenetics and more.

In the restaurant, special dietary requirements are happily catered for and the menu provides an extensive choice of delicious dishes made to order with the freshest ingredients.

Set in 20 acres of delightful wooded grounds, this haven of peace and good health will replenish you physically and mentally.

*Abbey Ruins*

Gardens beyond the splendid Abbey Gate and Norman Tower. **St Edmundsbury Cathedral** (see panel on page 204) was originally the Church of St James, built in the 15th/16th century and accorded cathedral status (alone in Suffolk) in 1914. The original building has been much extended over the years (notably when being adapted for its role as a cathedral) and outstanding features include a magnificent hammerbeam roof, whose 38 beams are decorated with angels bearing the emblems of St James, St Edmund and St George. The monumental Bishop's throne depicts wolves guarding the crowned head of St Edmund, and there's a fascinating collection of 1,000 embroidered kneelers.

**St Mary's** Church, in the same complex, is also well worth a visit: an equally impressive hammerbeam roof, the detached tower standing much as Abbot Anselm built it in the 12th century, and several interesting monuments, the most important commemorating Mary Tudor, sister of Henry VIII, Queen of France and Duchess of Suffolk. Her remains were moved here when the Abbey was suppressed; a window in the Lady Chapel recording this fact was the gift of Queen Victoria.

the Barons of England at the high altar of the Abbey and swore that they would force King John to honour the proposals of the Magna Carta. The twin elements of Edmund's canonisation and the resolution of the Barons explain the motto on the town's crest: *sacrarium regis, cunabula legis* – 'shrine of a king, cradle of the law'.

Rebuilt in the 15th century, the Abbey was largely dismantled after its Dissolution by Henry VIII, but imposing ruins remain in the colourful Abbey

The **Abbey Gardens**, laid out in 1831, have as their central feature a great circle of flower beds following the pattern of

## ST EDMUNDSBURY CATHEDRAL

Angel Hill, Bury St Edmunds, Suffolk IP33 1LS
Tel: 01284 754933  Fax: 01284 768655
website: www.stedscathedral.co.uk

The site of Suffolk's Cathedral has been one of pilgrimage and worship for almost 1,000 years. One church within the precinct of a Norman Abbey was built by Abbot Anselm in the 12th century and was dedicated to St James.

The nave of today's church, started in 1503, is the successor to that church, and though little remains of the abbey following the dissolution in 1539, St James' Church has continued to grow over the years and in 1914 it became the Cathedral Church of the Diocese of Saint Edmundsbury and Ipswich. The last 40 years have seen several additions to the church as well as the building of the Cathedral Centre, which houses the Song School, the refectory and meeting rooms. Outstanding features of the Cathedral include a magnificent hammerbeam roof and a monumental bishop's throne.

the Royal Botanical Gardens in Brussels. Some of the original ornamental trees can still be seen, and other - later - features include an Old English rose garden, a water garden and a garden for the blind where fragrance counts for all. Ducks and geese live by the little River Lark, and there are tennis courts, putting and bowls greens and children's play equipment.

Bury is full of fine non-ecclesiastical buildings, many with Georgian frontages concealing medieval interiors. Among the most interesting are the handsome **Manor House Museum** with its collection of clocks, paintings, furniture, costumes and objets d'art; the **Victorian Corn Exchange** with its imposing colonnade; the Athenaeum, hub of social life since Regency times and scene of Charles Dickens's public readings; **Cupola House**, where Daniel Defoe once stayed; the **Angel Hotel**, where Dickens

and his marvellous creation Mr Pickwick stayed; and the **Nutshell**, owned by Greene King Brewery and probably the smallest pub in the country. The **Theatre Royal**, now in the care of the National Trust, was built in 1819 by William Wilkins, who was also responsible for the National Gallery in London. It once staged the premiere of *Charley's Aunt*, and still operates as a working theatre.

One of Bury's oldest residents and newest attractions is the **Greene King Brewery Museum and Shop**. Greene King has been brewed here in

*The Nutshell Pub*

Bury since 1799; the museum's informative storyboards, artefacts, illustrations and audio displays bring the history and art of brewing to life. Brewery tours include a look round the museum and beer-tasting. The shop sells a variety of memorabilia, souvenirs, gifts and clothing – as well, of course, as bottles and cans of the frothy stuff.

The **Bury St Edmunds Art Gallery** is housed in one of Bury's noblest buildings, built to a Robert Adam design in 1774. It has filled many roles down the years, and was rescued from decline in the 1960s to be restored to Adam's original plans. It is now one of the county's premier art galleries, with eight exhibitions each year and a thriving craft shop.

Perhaps the most fascinating building of all is **Moyse's Hall Museum**, located at one end of the Buttermarket. Built of flint and limestone about 1180, it has claims to being the oldest stone domestic building in England. Originally a rich man's residence, it later saw service as a tavern, gaol, police station and railway parcels office, but since 1899 it has been a museum, and has recently undergone total refurbishment. It houses some 10,000 items, including many important archaeological collections, from a Bronze Age hoard, Roman pottery and Anglo-Saxon jewellery to a 19th century doll's house and some grisly relics of the notorious Red Barn murder. A new wing contains the Suffolk Regiment collection and education room.

Outside the Spread Eagle pub on the western edge of town is a horse trough erected to the memory of the Victorian romantic novelist 'Ouida' (Maria Louisa Ramee, 1839-1908).

Steeped though it is in history, Bury also moves with the times, and its sporting, entertainment and leisure

## Northgate House

8 Northgate Street, Bury St Edmunds,
Suffolk IP33 1HQ
Tel: 01284 760469  Fax: 01284 724008
e-mail: northgate_hse@hotmail.com
website: www.northgatehouse.com

Awarded 5 Diamonds by the English Tourism Council – their highest accolade – **Northgate House** in Bury is an outstanding Grade I listed house offering superb bed and breakfast accommodation. The present building dates from 1713 and was built over two medieval houses with cellars thought to connect via tunnels to the Abbey of St Edmund. Behind its impressive Georgian façade lies a true architectural gem. The unaltered Queen Anne west façade is shaded by two vast London Plane trees – the tallest in the borough. The four en suite bedrooms are spacious and boast original panelling; they are

furnished with antiques and the bathrooms contain restored original period fittings. Polished floors, four-poster beds and elegant decorative touches ensure a luxuriously comfortable experience.

In the oak-panelled breakfast room, overlooking the lovely garden, guests can enjoy a full English breakfast using organic or local produce. A country house in the heart of the town, just a stone's throw from the Abbey precincts and historic centre of this thriving town, there are at least 15 good restaurants within walking distance and the house makes an excellent base from which to explore East Anglia.

## THE ANGEL HOTEL

Angel Hill, Bury St Edmunds, Suffolk IP33 1LT
Tel: 01284 714000 Fax: 01284 714001
e-mail: sales@theangel.co.uk
website: www.theangel.co.uk

**The Angel** is a beautiful and historic coaching inn that dates back to 1452. Originally three inns serving the pilgrims visiting the great Abbey of St Edmundsbury, it has a long and impressive history as host to scores of artists, renowned writers including Charles Dickens (who wrote part of *The Pickwick Papers* whilst in residence) and members of the Royal Family.

Noted for its beautiful location on Angel Hill, it is set in one of the prettiest squares in the country. It has been in the Gough family for over 30 years, and enjoys a well-earned reputation for quality and service. The warm, relaxed atmosphere is enhanced by the friendly service and truly lovely surroundings.

Each room contains interesting collections of antiques, art and photographs reflecting the hotel's rich heritage. There is a choice of two restaurants, a superb guests' lounge and the convivial Pickwick Bar. Meals range from brasserie-style informal dishes to local specialities and a range of imaginative and delicious English and Continental delights. The wine list provides a variety of Old and New World vintages. The guest bedrooms are exquisitely appointed and furnished in individual styles, including some with four-poster beds and some suitable for families.

facilities are impressive. A mile and a half outside town on the A14 (just off the East Exit) is **Nowton Park**, 172 acres of countryside landscaped in Victorian style and supporting a wealth of flora and fauna; the avenue of limes, carpeted with daffodils in the spring, is a particular delight. There's also a play area and a ranger centre.

Bury's disciplined network of streets (the layout was devised in the 11th century) provides long, alluring views. A great fire destroyed much of Bury in 1608, but it was rebuilt using traditional timber-framing techniques. Arriving here in 1698, Celia Fiennes, the inveterate traveller and architecture critic, was uncharacteristically favourable in her remarks about Cupola House, which had just been completed at the time of her visit. William Cobbett (1763-1835), a visitor when chronicling his Rural Rides, did not disagree with the view that Bury

St Edmunds was 'the nicest town in the world' - a view which would be endorsed by many of today's inhabitants and by many of the millions of visitors who have been charmed by this jewel in Suffolk's crown.

# AROUND BURY ST EDMUNDS

## ICKLINGHAM

**8 miles NW of Bury St Edmunds on the A1101**

The village of Icklingham boasts not one but two churches - the parish church of St James (mentioned in the *Domesday Book*) and the deconsecrated thatched-roofed All Saints, with medieval tiles on the chancels and beautiful east windows in the south aisle. At the point where the Icknield Way crosses the River Lark, Icklingham has a long history, brought to light in frequent archaeological finds, from pagan bronzes to Roman coins. The place abounds in tales of the supernatural, notably of the white rabbit who is seen at dusk in the company of a witch, causing – it is said - horses to bolt and men to die.

Just south of Icklingham, at the A1101, is **Rampart Field** picnic site, where pleasant walks through gorse-filled gravel workings reveal the varied plant life of a typical Breckland heath.

## West Stow

**4 miles NW of Bury St Edmunds off the A1101**

The villages of West Stow, Culford, Ingham, Timworth and Wordwell were for several centuries part of a single estate covering almost 10,000 acres. Half the estate was sold to the Forestry Commission in 1935 and was renamed the King's Forest in honour of King George V's Jubilee in that year.

An Anglo-Saxon cemetery was discovered in the village in 1849; subsequent years have revealed traces of Roman settlements and the actual layout of the original **Anglo-Saxon Village** (see panel below). A trust was established to investigate further the Anglo-Saxon way of life and their building and farming techniques. Several buildings were constructed using, as accurately as could be achieved, the tools and methods of the 5th century. The undertaking has become a major tourist attraction, with assistance from guides both human (in Anglo-Saxon costume) and in the form of taped cassettes. There are pigs and hens, growing crops, craft courses, a Saxon market at Easter, a festival in August and special events all year round. This fascinating village, which is entered through the Visitor Centre, is part of **West Stow Country Park**, a large part of

## West Stow Anglo-Saxon Village

The Visitor Centre, Icklingham Road, West Stow, Bury St Edmunds, Suffolk IP28 6HG
Tel: 01284 728718 Fax: 01284 728277
website: www.stedmundsbury.gov.uk/weststow.htm

Between 1965 and 1972 the low hill by the River Lark in Suffolk was excavated to reveal several periods of occupation, but in particular, over 70 buildings from an early Anglo Saxon village. There was also information from about 100 graves in the nearby cemetery. It was decided that such extensive evidence about these people should be used to carry out a practical experiment to test ideas about the buildings that formed the elements of the original village.

Part of the Anglo Saxon Village has been reconstructed on the site where the original (inhabited from around AD420 - 650) was excavated. The reconstructions have been built over a period of more than 20 years. Each of the eight buildings is different, to test different ideas, and each has been built using the tools and techniques available to the early Anglo Saxons. Exploring the houses is an excellent way of finding out about the Anglo Saxons who lived at West Stow. Costumed "Anglo Saxons" bring the village to life at certain times, especially at Easter and during August. The new Anglo Saxon Centre is an exciting addition to the site, housing the original objects found there and at other local sites. Many of the objects have never been seen by the public before. The displays show aspects of village life and the focal point is a series of life size reconstructions of costume, based upon the grave finds.

West Stow Anglo Saxon Village lies in the middle of a beautiful 125 acre Country Park, part of which is a Site of Special Scientific Interest. The park has a number of different habitats, including woodland, heathland, a lake and a river. There is a play area, a bird feeding area and bird hides. The Park is open daily all year, from 9am-5pm in winter, 9am-8pm in summer. Entry to the park is free.

which is designated a Site of Special Scientific Interest (SSSI). Over 120 species of birds and 25 species of animals have been sighted in this Breckland setting, and a well-marked 5-mile nature trail links this nature reserve with the woods, a large lake and the River Lark..

## HENGRAVE

### 3 miles NW of Bury St Edmunds on the A1101

A captivating old-world village of flint and thatch, excavations and aerial photography indicate that there has been a settlement at Hengrave since Neolithic times. Those parts of the village that are of archaeological interest are now protected. The chief attraction is **Hengrave Hall**, a rambling Tudor mansion built partly of Northamptonshire limestone and partly of yellow brick by Sir Thomas Kytson, a wool merchant. A notable visitor in the early days was Elizabeth I, who brought her court here in 1578.

Several generations of the Gage family were later the owners of Hengrave Hall - one of them, with a particular interest in horticulture, imported various kinds of plum trees from France. Most of the bundles were properly labelled with their names, but one had lost its label. When it produced its first crop of luscious green fruit, someone had the bright idea of calling it the green Gage.

The name stuck, and the descendants of these trees, planted in 1724, are still at the Hall, which may be visited by appointment. In the grounds stands a lovely little church with a round Saxon tower and a wealth of interesting monuments. The church was for some time a family mausoleum; restored by Sir John Wood, it became a private chapel and now hosts services of various denominations.

## FLEMPTON

### 4 miles NW of Bury St Edmunds on the A1101

An interesting walk from this village just north of the A1101 follows the **Lark Valley Park** through Culford Park, providing a good view of Culford Hall, which has been a school since 1935. A handsome cast-iron bridge dating from the early 19th century - and recently brought to light from amongst the reeds - crosses a lake in the park.

## LACKFORD

### 6 miles NW of Bury St Edmunds on the A1101

More interest here for the wildlife enthusiast. Restored gravel pits have been turned into a reserve for wildfowl and waders. Two hides are available.

## EUSTON

### 9 miles N of Bury St Edmunds on the A1088

**Euston Hall**, on the A1088, has been the seat of the Dukes of Grafton for 300 years. It's open to the public on Thursday afternoons and is well worth a visit, not least for its portraits of Charles II and its paintings by Van Dyck, Lely and Stubbs. In the colourful landscaped grounds is an ice-house disguised as an Italianate temple, the distinguished work of John Evelyn and William Kent.

Euston's church, in the grounds of the Hall, is the only one in the county dedicated to St Genevieve. It's also one of only two Classical designs in the county, being rebuilt in 1676 on part of the original structure. The interior is richly decorated, with beautiful carving on the hexagonal pulpit, panelling around the walls and a carved panel of the Last Supper. Parts of this lovely wood carving are attributed by some to Grinling Gibbons. Behind the family pew is a marble memorial to Lord Arlington, who built the church.

Euston's watermill was built in the 1670s and rebuilt in 1730 as a Gothic church.

## PAKENHAM

### 4 miles NE of Bury St Edmunds off the A143

On a side road just off the A143 (turn right just north of Great Barton) lies the village of Pakenham, whose long history has been unearthed in the shape of a Bronze Age barrow and kiln, and another kiln from Roman times.

Elsewhere in Pakenham are the 17th century **Nether Hall**, from whose lake in the park the village stream flows through the fen into the millpond. From the same period dates **Newe House**, a handsome Jacobean building with Dutch gables and a two-storey porch. The Church of St Mary has an impressive carved Perpendicular font, and in its adjacent vicarage is the famous Whistler Window - a painting by Rex Whistler of an 18th century parish priest. The fens were an important source of reeds, and many of Pakenham's buildings show off the thatcher's art.

Pakenham's current unique claim to fame is in being the last parish in England to have a working watermill *and* windmill, a fact proclaimed on the village sign. The **Watermill** was built around 1814 on a site mentioned in the *Domesday Book* (the Roman excavations suggest that there could have been a mill here as far back as the 1st century AD). The mill, which is fed from Pakenham fen, has many interesting features, including the Blackstone oil engine, dating from around 1900, and the Tattersall Midget rollermill from 1913, a brave but ultimately unsuccessful attempt to compete with the larger roller mills in the production of flour. The mill and the neighbouring recreation park are well worth a visit.

No less remarkable is the **Windmill**, one of the most famous in Suffolk. The black-tarred tower was built in 1831 and was in regular use until the 1950s. One of the best preserved mills in the county, it survived a lightning strike in 1971.

Both mills lie on the village's circular walks, and fresh flour is available from both.

## IXWORTH

### 5 miles NE of Bury St Edmunds on the A143

Ixworth played its part as one of the Iceni tribe's major settlements, with important Roman connections and, in the 12th century, the site of an Augustinian priory. The remains of the priory were incorporated into a Georgian house known as Ixworth Abbey, which stands among trees by the River Blackbourne. The village has many 14th century timber-framed dwellings, and the Church of St Mary dates from the same period, though with many later additions.

A variety of circular walks take in lovely parts of the village, which is also the staring point of the Miller's Trail cycle route.

A little way north of the village, on the A1088, are a nature trail and bird reserve at Ixworth Thorpe Farm. At this point a brief diversion northwards up the A1088 is very worth while.

## BARDWELL

### 7 miles NE of Bury St Edmunds just off the A1088

Bardwell offers another tower windmill. This one dates from the 1820s and was worked by wind for 100 years, then by an oil engine until 1941. It was restored in the 1980s, only to suffer severe damage in the great storm of October 1987, when its sails were torn off. Stoneground flour is still produced by an auxiliary engine, and there's an on-site bakery.

### WYKEN VINEYARDS

Stanton, Bury St Edmunds, Suffolk IP31 2DW
Tel: 01359 250287  Fax: 01359 252372
Directions: Follow brown signs for Wyken Vineyards from
A143 at Ixworth, 8 miles N.E. of Bury St Edmunds

At the heart of a quintessential Suffolk estate that was first settled 6,000 years ago stands Wyken Hall, a romantic Elizabethan manor house owned by Englishman Sir Kenneth Carlisle and his American wife Carla. Their collaboration has produced a garden which has something to delight every visitor: blue rocking chairs on a Southern-style verandah, a dog chapel and a US mailbox typify the American humour, while a herb garden, knot garden, nuttery and rose garden planted with old-fashioned roses, hardy geraniums and delphiniums assert the Englishness of the setting. And everywhere, Carla's eye for design and instinct for colour are in evidence.

A stroll through ancient woodland brings visitors to **Wyken Vineyards**, set in seven acres on a south-facing slope where it may well be that Romans were the first to plant vines. The present enterprise started in 1988, since when it has been producing grapes for some of the very best wines in England. Wyken Bacchus, a dry white, has won the English Vineyard Association's Wine of the Year award, and the full, dark red is establishing an excellent and well-deserved reputation.

Inspired by the viticultural traditions of California's Napa Valley, Carla has converted the impressive 400-year-old flint barn on the estate into the Leaping Hare Vineyard Restaurant, where Wyken wines accompany dishes that are in tune with the seasons, the land and guests' appetites. Only the best and freshest of local ingredients find their way into the kitchen, including fruits, vegetables and herbs from the kitchen garden. The style is mainly English (salmon fishcakes are among the specialities) with influences from France and California. An adjacent café serves teas, coffees, cakes and light lunches. There is a weekly Farmers' Market selling a range of locally-grown farm produce.

Alongside these, the Leaping Hare Country Store is committed to selling the best of everything that is both special and useful: the eclectic range runs from Suffolk and Norfolk crafts to women's

clothing, American quilts, French grape-picking baskets and English bicycles.

**Opening times:**

**Restaurant, cafe & shop:**

Everyday 10-6, Friday and Saturday evenings for dinner from 7pm (advisable to book for restaurant, no bookings in cafe).

**Garden:**

Open 1st April-1st October, 2 until 6, Sunday - Friday (closed Saturday).

**Farmers Market:**

Every Saturday 9am until 1pm.

Also in this delightful village are a 16th century inn and the Church of St Peter and St Paul, known particularly for its medieval stained glass.

## HONINGTON

**7 miles NE of Bury St Edmunds on the A1088**

Back on the A1088, the little village of Honington was the birthplace of the pastoral poet Robert Bloomfield (1766-1823), whose best known work is *The Farmer's Boy*. The house where he was born is now divided, one part called Bloomfield Cottage, the other Bloomfield Farmhouse. A brass plaque to his memory can be seen in All Saints Church, in the graveyard of which his parents are buried.

## BARNINGHAM

**8 miles NE of Bury St Edmunds on the B1111**

Near the Norfolk border, Barningham was the first home of the firm of Fisons, which started in the late 18th century. Starting with a couple of windmills, they later installed one of the earliest steam mills in existence. The engine saw service for nearly 100 years and is now in an American museum; the mill building exists to this day, supplying animal feed.

This is marvellous walking country, and **Knettishall Heath Country Park**, on 400 acres of prime Breckland terrain, is the official starting place of the Peddars Way National Trail to Holme-next-Sea and of the Angles Way Regional Path that stretches 77 miles to Great Yarmouth by way of the Little Ouse and Waveney valleys.

## STANTON

**7 miles NE of Bury St Edmunds on the A143**

Stanton is mentioned in the *Domesday Book*; before that, the Romans were here. A double ration of medieval churches - All Saints and St John the Baptist - will satisfy the ecclesiastical scholar, while for

more worldly indulgences **Wyken Vineyards** (see panel opposite) will have a strong appeal. Four acres of gardens - herb, knot, rose, kitchen and woodland - are on the same site, and the complex also includes an Elizabethan manor house, a 16th century barn, a country shop and a café. There's also a splendid woodland walk.

## WALSHAM-LE-WILLOWS

**9 miles NE of Bury St Edmunds off the A143**

A pretty name for a pretty village, with weatherboarded and timber-framed cottages along the willow-banked river which flows throughout its length. **St Mary's** church is no less pleasing to the eye, with its sturdy western tower and handsome windows in the Perpendicular style. Of particular interest inside is the superb tie and hammerbeam roof of the nave, and (unique in Suffolk, and very rare elsewhere) a tiny circular medallion which hangs suspended from the nave wall, known as a 'Maiden's Garland' or 'Virgin's Crant'. These marked the pew seats of unmarried girls who had passed away, and the old custom was for the young men of the village to hang garlands of flowers from them on the anniversary of a girl's death. This particular example celebrates the virginity of one Mary Boyce, who died (so the inscription says) of a broken heart in 1685, just 20 years old. There is also a carving on the rood screen which looks rather like the face of a wolf: this may well be a reference to the benevolent creature that plays such an important role in the legend of St Edmund. A museum by the church has changing exhibitions of local history.

## REDGRAVE

**13 miles NE of Bury St Edmunds on the B1113**

Arachnophobes beware! Redgrave and Lopham Fens form a 360-acre reserve of reed and sedge beds where one of the most interesting inhabitants is the Great Raft Spider. The village is the source of the Little Ouse and Waveney rivers, which rise on either side of the B1113 and set off on their seaward journeys in opposite directions.

### THELNETHAM

**12 miles NE of Bury St Edmunds off the B111**

West of Redgrave between the B1113 and the B1111 lies Thelnetham – which boasts a windmill of its own. This one is a tower mill, built in 1819 to replace a post mill on the same site, and worked for 100 years. It has now been lovingly restored. Stoneground flour is produced and sold at the mill. If you wish to visit you should set sail on a summer Sunday or Bank Holiday Monday; other times by appointment.

### RICKINGHALL

**12 miles NE of Bury St Edmunds on the A143**

More timber-framed buildings, some thatched, are dotted along the streets of the two villages, Superior and Inferior, which follow an underground stream running right through them. Each has a church dedicated to St Mary and featuring fine flintwork and tracery. The upper church, now closed, was used as a school for London evacuees during the Second World War.

### HESSETT

**4 miles E of Bury St Edmunds off the A14**

Dedicated to St Ethelbert, King of East Anglia, Hessett's church has many remarkable features, particularly some beautiful 16th century glass and wall paintings, both of which somehow escaped the Puritan wave of destruction. Ethelbert was unlucky enough to get on the wrong side of the mighty Offa, King of the Mercians, and was killed by him at Hereford in AD794.

### WOOLPIT

**6 miles E of Bury St Edmunds on the A14**

The church of St Mary the Virgin is Woolpit's crowning glory, with a marvellous porch and one of the most magnificent double hammerbeam roofs in the county.

Voted winner of Suffolk Village of the Year in 2000, the village was long famous for its brick industry, and the majority of the old buildings are faced with 'Woolpit Whites'. This yellowish-white brick looked very much like more expensive stone, and for several centuries was widely exported. Some was used in the building of the Senate wing of the Capitol Building in Washington DC. Red bricks were also produced, and the village **Museum**, open in summer, has a brick-making display and also tells the story of the evolution of the village.

### ELM TREE GALLERY

The Street, Woolpit, Bury St Edmunds, Suffolk IP30 9QG
Tel: 01359 240255

**Elm Tree Gallery** in Woolpit, just off the A14 between Bury and Stowmarket, features a variety of hand-crafted pieces from the likes of Moorcraft pottery, Caithness paperweights, Clarecraft (creators of figures such as characters from Terry Prachett's Discworld and Faerie Realm) and Harmony Kingdom. The range of crafts and giftware also includes wooden and soft toys, jewellery, fine toiletries and greetings cards, many of which are hand-made. Open Monday to Saturday 10 – 6; Sundays in December 10 – 5. Teas, coffees and homemade cakes also served.

Woolpit also hosts an annual music festival.

Nearby is a moated site known as **Lady's Well**, a place of pilgrimage in the Middle Ages. The water from the spring was reputed to have healing properties, most efficacious in curing eye troubles.

A favourite Woolpit legend concerns the *Green Children*, a brother and sister with green complexions who appeared one day in a field, apparently attracted by the church bells. Though hungry, they would eat nothing until some green beans were produced. Given shelter by the lord of the manor, they learned to speak English and said that they came from a place called St Martin. The boy survived for only a short time, but the girl thrived, lost her green colour, was baptised and married a man from King's Lynn – no doubt leaving many a Suffolk man green with envy!

## THE BRADFIELDS
### 7 miles SE of Bury St Edmunds off the A134

The Bradfields - St George, St Clare and Combust - and Cockfield thread their way through a delightful part of the countryside and are well worth a little exploration, not only to see the picturesque villages themselves but for a stroll in the historic **Bradfield Woods**. These woods stand on the eastern edge of the parish of Bradfield St George and have been turned into an outstanding nature reserve, tended and coppiced in the same way for more than 700 years, and home to a wide variety of flora and fauna. They once belonged to the Abbey of St Edmundsbury, and one area is still today called Monk's Park Wood.

Coppicing involves cutting a tree back down to the ground every ten years or so. Woodlands were managed in this way to provide an annual crop of timber for local use and fast regrowth. After coppicing, as the root is already strongly

established, regrowth is quick. Willow and hazel are the trees most commonly coppiced. Willow is often also pollarded, a less drastic form of coppicing where the trees are cut far enough from the ground to stop grazing animals having a free lunch.

Bradfield St Clare, the central of the three Bradfields, has a rival claim to that of Hoxne as the site of the martyrdom of St Edmund. The St Clare family arrived with the Normans and added their name to the village, and to the church, which was originally All Saints but was then rededicated to St Clare; it is the only church in England dedicated to her. Bradfield Combust, where the pretty River Lark rises, probably takes it curious name from the fact that the local hall was burnt to the ground during the 14th century riots against the Abbot of St Edmundsbury's crippling tax demands. Arthur Young (1741-1820), noted writer on social, economic and agricultural subjects, is buried in the village churchyard.

## COCKFIELD
### 8 miles SE of Bury St Edmunds off the A1141

Cockfield is perhaps the most widely spread village in all Suffolk, its little thatched cottages scattered around and between no fewer than nine greens. Great Green is the largest, with two football pitches and other recreation areas, while Parsonage Green has a literary connection: the **Old Rectory** was once home to a Dr Babbington, whose nephew Robert Louis Stephenson was a frequent visitor and who is said to have written *Treasure Island* while staying there.

Cockfield also shelters one of the last windmills to have been built in Suffolk (1891). Its working life was very short but the tower still stands, now in use as a private residence.

## Thorpe Morieux

**9 miles SE of Bury St Edmunds off the B1071**

St Mary's Church in Thorpe Morieux is situated in as pleasant a setting as anyone could wish to find. With water meadows, ponds, a stream and a fine Tudor farmhouse to set it off, this 14th century church presents a memorable picture of old England. Look at the church, then take the time to wander round the peaceful churchyard with its profusion of springtime aconites, followed by the colourful flowering of limes and chestnuts in summer.

## Great Welnetham

**2 miles S of Bury St Edmunds off the A134**

One of the many surviving Suffolk windmills is to be found here, just south of the village. The sails were lost in a gale 80 years ago, but the tower and a neighbouring old barn make an attractive sight.

## Hawkedon

**9 miles S of Bury St Edmunds off the A143**

Hawkedon is designated a place of outstanding natural beauty. Here the Church of St Mary is located atypically in the middle of the village green. The pews and intricately carved bench-ends take the eye here, along with a canopied stoup (a recess for holding holy water) and a Norman font. There is a wide variety of carved animals, many on the bench-ends but some also on the roof cornice. One of the stalls is decorated with the carving of a crane holding a stone in its claw: legend has it that if the crane were on watch and should fell asleep, the stone would drop and the noise would wake it.

## Wickhambrook

**9 miles S of Bury St Edmunds on the B1063**

Wickhambrook is a series of tiny hamlets with no fewer than 11 greens and three manor houses. The greens have unusual names - Genesis, Nunnery, Meeting, Coltsfoot - whose origins keep local historians busy. One of the two pubs has the distinction of being officially half in Wickhambrook and half in Denston.

## Alpheton

**10 miles S of Bury St Edmunds on the A134**

There are several points of interest in this little village straddling the main road. It was first settled in AD991 and its name means 'the farm of Aefflaed'. That lady was the wife of Ealdorman Beorhtnoth of Essex, who was killed resisting the Danes at the Battle of Maldon and is buried in Ely Minster.

The hall, the farm and the church stand in a quiet location away from the main road and about a mile from the village. This remoteness is not unusual: some attribute it to the villagers moving during times of plague, but the more likely explanation is simply that the scattered cottages, originally in several tiny hamlets, centred on a more convenient site than that of the church. Equally possible is that the church was located here to suit the local landed family (who desired to have the church next door to their home). The main features at the church of **St Peter and St Paul** are the flintwork around the parapet (the exterior is otherwise fairly undistinguished), the carefully restored 15th century porch and some traces of an ancient wall painting of St Christopher with the Christ Child. All in all, it's a typical country church of unpretentious dignity and well worth a short detour from the busy main roads.

Back in the village, two oak trees were planted and a pump installed in 1887, to commemorate Queen Victoria's 50th year on the throne. Another of the village's claims to fame is that its American airfield was used as the setting for the classic film *Twelve o'Clock High*, in which Gregory Peck memorably plays a Second World War flight commander cracking under the strain of countless missions. Incidentally, one of the reasons for constructing the A134 was to help in the development of the airfield. The A134 continues south to Long Melford. An alternative road from Bury to Long Melford is the B1066, quieter and more scenic, with a number of pleasant places to visit en route.

## SHIMPLING
### 9 miles S of Bury St Edmunds off the B1066

Shimpling is a peaceful farming community whose church, St George's, is approached by a lime avenue. It is notable for Victorian stained glass and a Norman font, and in the churchyard is the **Faint House**, a small stone building where ladies overcome by the tightness of their stays could decently retreat from the service. The banker Thomas Hallifax built many of Shimpling's cottages, as well as the village school and Chadacre Hall, which Lord Iveagh later turned into an agricultural college (a role it ceased to hold in 1989 - the Hall is today again in private hands).

## LAWSHALL
### 8 miles S of Bury St Edmunds off the A134

A spread-out village first documented in AD972 but regularly giving up evidence of earlier occupation, Lawshall was the site where a Bronze Age sword dated at around 600BC was found (the sword is now in Bury Museum). The Church of All Saints, Perpendicular with some Early English features, stands on one of the highest points in Suffolk. Next to it is Lawshall Hall, whose owners once entertained Queen Elizabeth I. Another interesting site in Lawshall is the **Wishing Well**, a well-cover on the green put up in memory of Charles Tyrwhitt

Drake, who worked for the Royal Geographic Society and was killed in Jerusalem.

## HARTEST
### 9 miles S of Bury St Edmunds on the B1066

Hartest, which has a history as long as Alpheton's, celebrated its millennium in 1990 with the erection of a village sign (the hart, or stag). It's an agreeable spot in the valley, with colour-washed houses and chestnut trees on the green. Also on the green are All Saints Church (mentioned in the *Domesday Book*) and a large glacial stone, the **Hartest stone**, which was dragged by a team of 45 horses from where it was found in a field in neighbouring Somerton. From 1789 until the 1930s, Hartest staged a St George's Day Fair, an annual event celebrating King George III's recovery from one of his spells of illness. Just outside the village is **Gifford's Hall**, a smallholding which includes 14 acres of nearly 12,000 grapevines, as well as a winery producing white and rosé wines and fruit liqueurs. There are also organic vegetable gardens, wildflower meadows, black St Kilda sheep, black Berkshire pigs, goats and free-range fowl, together with a trailer ride ('The Grape Express') and children's play area. The Hall is particularly famous for its sweet peas and roses, and an annual festival is held on the last weekend in June. Open from Easter to the end of October.

## HORRINGER
### 3 miles SW of Bury St Edmunds on the A143

Rejoining the A143 by Chedburgh, the motorist will soon arrive at Horringer, whose village green is dominated by the flintstone Church of St Leonard. Beside the church are the gates of one of the country's most extraordinary and fascinating houses, now run by the National Trust. **Ickworth House** was the

*Ickworth House*

brainchild of the eccentric 4th Earl of Bristol and Bishop of Derry, a collector of art treasures and an inveterate traveller (witness the many Bristol Hotels scattered around Europe). His inspiration was Belle Isle, a house built on an island in Lake Windermere, and the massive structure is a central rotunda linking two semi-circular wings. It was designed as a treasure house for his art collection, and work started in 1795. Sadly, the first collection of the Earl's treasures was seized by Napoleon in 1798, so never reached England.

Derry died in 1803 and his son, after some hesitation, saw the work through to completion in 1829. Its chief glories are some marvellous paintings by Titian, Gainsborough, Hogarth, Velasquez, Reynolds and Kauffman, but there's a great deal more to enthral the visitor: late Regency and 18th century French furniture, a notable collection of Georgian silver, friezes and sculptures by John Flaxman, frescoes copied from wall paintings discovered at the Villa Negroni in Rome in 1777. The Italian garden, where Mediterranean species have been bred to withstand a distinctly non-Mediterranean climate, should not be missed, with its hidden glades, orangery

and temple rose garden, and in the park landscaped by Capability Brown there are designated walks and cycle routes, bird hides, a deer enclosure and play areas. More recent attractions include the vineyard and plant centre. The House is open from Easter until the end of October, while the park and gardens are open throughout the year.

Arable land surrounds Horringer, with a large annual crop of sugar beet grown for processing at the factory in Bury, the largest of its kind in Europe.

## NEWMARKET

On the western edge of Suffolk, Newmarket is home to some 16,000 human and 3,000 equine inhabitants. The historic centre of British racing lives and breathes horses, with 60 training establishments, 50 stud farms, the top annual thoroughbred sales and two racecourses (the only two in Suffolk). Thousands of the population are involved in the trade, and racing art and artefacts fill the shops, galleries and museums; one of the oldest established saddlers even has a preserved horse on display - 'Robert the Devil', runner-up in the Derby in 1880.

History records that Queen Boudicca of the Iceni, to whom the six-mile Devil's Dyke stands as a memorial, thundered around these parts in her lethal chariot behind her shaggy-haired horses. She is said to have established the first stud here. In medieval times the chalk heathland was a popular arena for riders

*National Stud, Newmarket*

to display their skills. In 1605, James I paused on a journey northwards to enjoy a spot of hare coursing. He enjoyed the place and said he would be back. By moving the royal court to his Newmarket headquarters, he began the royal patronage which has remained strong throughout the years. James' son, Charles I, maintained the royal connection, but it was Charles II who really put the place on the map when he, too, moved the Royal court here in the spring and autumn of each year. He initiated the Town Plate, a race which he himself won twice as a rider and which, in a modified form, still exists.

One of the racecourses, the **Rowley Mile**, takes its name from Old Rowley, a favourite horse of the Merry Monarch. Here the first two classics of the season, the 1,000 and 2,000 Guineas, are run, together with important autumn events including the Cambridgeshire and the

## COFFEE & CO

12 Palace Street, Newmarket, Suffolk CB8 8EP
Tel: 01638 611000  Fax: 01638 612612

Pristine and welcoming with its own distinctive charm, Newmarket's **Coffee & Co** is just the place to take a well-earned break from exploring the town and region and savour an excellent meal and drink. Open Monday to Saturday from 8.30 until 4 p.m., the menu offers a tempting range of breakfast and lunch dishes – speciality sandwiches made with granary baguettes,

ciabattas, foccacia, herb pockets, panini and more, filled with a selection of meats, cheeses and other delicious fillings, in any combination, made to order from the freshest ingredients.

Along with this there's a mouth-watering variety of home-made cakes and other desserts – and, of course, a wide range of coffees, lattes, teas, thick milk shakes and much more. This family-run establishment, found just two minutes' walk from the centre of town, next to the Tourist Information Centre, is modern, stylish and comfortable, with indoor and outdoor seating for up to 30 guests.

Cesarewich. There are some 18 race days at this track, while on the leafy July course, with its delightful garden-party atmosphere, a similar number of race days take in all the important summer fixtures.

The visitor to Newmarket can learn almost all there is to know about flat racing and racehorses by making the grand tour of the several establishments open to the public (sometimes by appointment only). **The Jockey Club**, which was the first governing body of the sport and, until recently, its ultimate

## NATIONAL HORSERACING MUSEUM

99 High Street, Newmarket, Suffolk  CB8 8JL
Tel: 01638 667333  Fax: 01638 665600
website: www.nationalstud.co.uk

"The Newmarket Experience" comprises two separate attractions: **The National Horseracing Museum** and **The National Stud**. The story of racing throughout the ages is told through the Museum's permanent collections, featuring the horses, people, events and scandals that make the sport so colourful.

Highlights include the head of Persimmon, a great Royal Derby winner in 1896; a special display about Fred Archer, the Victorian jockey who committed suicide after losing the struggle to keep his weight down; the skeleton of Eclipse, ancestor of 90 per cent of modern thoroughbreds; items associated with Red Rum, Lester Piggott, Frankie Dettori and other heroes of the Turf. In the Practical Gallery, visitors can learn everything there is to know about the horse and jockey, and experience the thrill of riding on the horse simulator. The Gallery is staffed by retired jockeys and trainers, who make the world of racing come alive. Special exhibitions have included "*Why* did you get that hat?", a display

of Gertrude Shilling's outrageous Ascot outfits. Mrs Shilling (1910-1999) was one of the most colourful and eccentric personalities ever to grace the sport.

The Museum also boasts a range of exciting temporary exhibitions, including paintings and other works of art with a racing theme. The daily minibus tours of working establishments in Newmarket are another treat, offering visitors a chance to see horses at close quarters and meet stable staff in a two-hour tour, as well as horses training on the gallops, the horses' swimming pool and a training yard, together with the historic town itself.

The National Stud extends a warm welcome to all its visitors. Breeding top-class thoroughbreds, the 500-acre site has 12 yards, 9 miles of roads and tracks, 60 miles of post and rail fencing, 21 houses, a feedmill and storage for 50 tons of hay and straw - all

purpose built between 1963 and 1967. The Stud year follows a set pattern, with the breeding season officially beginning on 15th February, and ending with the annual National Stud Fair and Stallion Parade held over the first week in December. Any tour, which will vary depending on the season, takes in the superb Stallion Unit, along with the stallions in residence, Nursery Yards and mares and foals in their paddocks. The helpful, informative tour guides offer a full insight into the workings of a modern stud.

The Stud provides training courses on horse husbandry and stud management for students who wish to make their careers in the thoroughbred breeding industry.

authority, was formed in the mid-18th century and occupies an imposing building which was restored and rebuilt in Georgian style in the 1930s. Originally a social club for rich gentlemen with an interest in the turf, it soon became the all-powerful regulator of British racing, owning all the racing and training land. When holding an enquiry the stewards sit round a horseshoe-shaped table while the jockey or trainer under scrutiny faces them on a strip of carpet by the door - hence the expression 'on the mat'.

Next to the Jockey Club in the High Street is the **National Horseracing Museum** (see panel opposite). Opened by the Queen in 1983, its five galleries chronicle the history of the Sport of Kings from its royal beginnings through to the top trainers and jockeys of today. Visitors can ride a mechanical horse, try on racing silks, record a race commentary, ask questions and enjoy a snack in the café, whose walls are hung with murals of racing personalities. The chief treasures among the art collection are equine paintings by Alfred Munnings, while the most famous item is probably the skeleton of the mighty Eclipse, whose superiority over his contemporaries gave rise to the saying 'Eclipse first, the rest nowhere.'

A few steps away is **Palace House**, which contains the remains of Charles II's palace and which, as funds allow, has

been restored over the years for use as a visitor centre and museum. In the same street is **Nell Gwynn's House**, which some say was connected by an underground passage beneath the street to the palace. The diarist John Evelyn spent a night in (or on?) the town during a royal visit, and declared the occasion to be 'more resembling a luxurious and abandoned rout than a Christian court'. The palace is the setting for the Newmarket Tourist Information Centre.

Other must-sees on the racing enthusiast's tour are **Tattersalls**, where leading thoroughbred sales take place from April to December; the **British Racing School**, where top jockeys are taught the ropes; the **National Stud**, open from March till the end of September (plus race days in October - booking essential); and the **Animal Health Trust** based at Lanwades Hall, where there's an informative Visitor Centre. The National Stud at one time housed no fewer than three Derby winners - Blakeney, Mill Reef, and Grundy.

Horses aren't all about racing, however. One type of horse you won't see in Newmarket is the wonderful Suffolk Punch, a massive yet elegant working horse which can still be seen at work at Rede Hall Park Farm near Bury St Edmunds and at Kentwell Hall in Long

Melford. All Punches descend from Crisp's horse, foaled in 1768. The Punch is part of the Hallowed Trinity of animals at the very centre of Suffolk's agricultural history; the others being the Suffolk Sheep and the Red Poll Cow. It is entirely appropriate that the last railway station to employ a horse for shunting wagons should have been at Newmarket. That hardworking one-horse-power shunter retired in 1967.

Newmarket also has things to offer the tourist outside the equine world, including the churches of **St Mary and All Saints**, and **St Agnes**, and a landmark at each end of the High Street - a Memorial Fountain in honour of Sir Daniel Cooper and the Jubilee Clock Tower commemorating Queen Victoria's Golden Jubilee.

# AROUND NEWMARKET

### EXNING

**2 miles NW of Newmarket on the A14**

A pause is certainly in order at this ancient village, whether on your way from Newmarket or arriving from Cambridgeshire on the A14. Anglo-Saxons, Romans, the Iceni and the Normans were all here, and the *Domesday Book* records the village under the name of Esselinga. The village was stricken by plague during the Iceni occupation, so its market was moved to the next village along - thus Newmarket acquired its name.

Exning's written history begins when Henry II granted the manor to the Count of Boulogne, who divided it between four of his knights. References to them and to subsequent Lords of the Manor are to be found in the little church of **St Martin**, which might well have been founded by the Burgundian Christian

missionary monk St Felix in the 7th century. Water from the well used by that saint to baptise members of the Saxon royal family is still used for baptisms by the current vicar.

### KENTFORD

**5 miles E of Newmarket by the A14**

At the old junction of the Newmarket-to-Bury road stands the grave of a young boy who hanged himself after being accused of sheep-stealing. It was a well-established superstition that suicides should be buried at a crossroads to prevent their spirits from wandering. Flowers are still sometimes laid at the **Gypsy Boy's Grave**, sometimes by punters hoping for good luck at Newmarket races.

### MOULTON

**4 miles E of Newmarket on the B1085**

This most delightful village lies in wonderful countryside on chalky downland in farming country; its proximity to Newmarket is apparent from the racehorses which are often to be seen on the large green. The River Kennett flows through the green before running north to the Lark, a tributary of the Ouse. Flint walls are a feature of many of the buildings, but the main point of interest is the 15th century four-arch **Packhorse Bridge** on the way to the church.

### DALHAM

**5 miles E of Newmarket on the B1063**

Eighty per cent of the buildings in Dalham are thatched (the highest proportion in Suffolk) and there are many other attractions in this pretty village. Above the village on one of the county's highest spots stands **St Mary's** church, which dates from the 14th century. Its spire toppled over during the gales which swept the land on the night that Cromwell died, and was replaced by a tower in 1627. Sir Martin Stutteville was the leading light behind this reconstruction; an inscription at the back of the church notes that the cost was £400. That worthy's grandfather was Thomas Stutteville, whose memorial near the altar declares that 'he saw the New World with Francis Drake.' (Drake did not survive that journey - his third to South America.) Thomas' grandson died in the fullness of his years (62 wasn't bad for those times) while hosting a jolly evening at The Angel Hotel in Bury St Edmunds. **Dalham Hall** was constructed in the first years of the 18th century at the order of the Bishop of Ely, who decreed that it should be built up until Ely Cathedral could be seen across the fens on a clear day. That view was sadly cut off in 1957 when a fire shortened the hall to only two storeys high. Wellington lived here for some years, and much later it was bought by Cecil Rhodes, who unfortunately died before taking up residence. His brother Francis erected the village hall in the adventurer's memory, and he himself is buried in the churchyard.

All in all, Dalham is a place of charm and interest - clearly no longer resembling the place described in *The Times* in the 1880s as full of ruffians and drunks, where the vicar felt obliged to give all the village children boxing lessons to increase their chances of survival.

## MILDENHALL

**8 miles NE of Newmarket off the A11**

On the edge of the Fens and Breckland, Mildenhall is a town which has many links with the past. It was once a port for the hinterlands of West Suffolk, though

## THE GOLDEN BOAR INN

The Street, Freckenham, Bury St Edmunds, Suffolk IP28 8HZ
Tel: 01638 723000 Fax: 01638 721166
e-mail: thegoldenboarinn@aol.com

**The Golden Boar Inn** is a superior inn offering great food, drink and hospitality. Originally known as The Golden Board – the name for the most inland herring port in the nation, until Dutch settlers drained the Fens – the last 'd' in this fine inn's name was dropped sometime during its 500-year history. It has been owned and run by Kate and Alan Strachan since 1996. The large and impressive exterior is adorned with flower baskets and the interior has been refurbished to a high standard of comfort and quality. The central brick and wood square bar has a carpeted area with a beamed ceiling and a rustic wall surrounding a lovely open fireplace with an old timbered lintel. The stones around the fireplace came from an old monastery dating the building to 1540.

The restaurant is large and welcoming, tastefully decorated and furnished. Double doors and a ramp for people with disabilities lead to the tiled patio area outside with picnic tables and pleasant views over an adjoining field and the delightful parish church. Renowned for its excellent food, the

menus feature a range of freshly prepared dishes created by the two qualified chefs, who use local produce whenever possible – veal escalopes, roast breast of duck and filled tortellini are just a small sample of the many choices. To drink there are four real ales along with lager, cider, stout, soft drinks and a selection of over 40 wines. To the front there is a large car-parking area; to the rear guests can enjoy a secure enclosed garden – lawned and tree-fringed, with a handsome rose bed, picnic tables and a children's play area including a roundabout, swings, slide and Wendy house.

Mildenhall Road, Worlington, Suffolk  IP28 8RX
Tel: 01636 711993

**Worlington House** is an elegant 16th century former manor house which epitomises traditional country grace and charm. Set in beautiful grounds and gardens, which, like the house, have been restored tastefully to their original splendour, there are three individually designed guest bedrooms, all en suite. Uniformly charming and comfortable, one of the rooms is in fact a suite with sitting room. The home-cooked breakfast is delicious and satisfying. For a taste of true luxury, look no further.

the River Lark has long ceased to be a trade route. Most of the town's heritage is recorded in the excellent **Mildenhall & District Museum** in King Street. Here will be found exhibits of local history (including the distinguished RAF and USAAF base), crafts and domestic skills, the natural history of the Fens and Breckland and, perhaps most famously, the chronicle of the 'Mildenhall Treasure'. This was a cache of 34 pieces of 4th century Roman silverware - dishes, goblets and spoons - found by a ploughman in 1946 at Thistley Green and now on display in the British Museum in London, while a replica makes its home here where it was found. There is evidence of much earlier occupation than the Roman era, with flint tools and other artefacts being unearthed in 1988 on the site of an ancient lake.

The parish of Mildenhall is the largest in Suffolk, so it is perhaps fitting that it should boast so magnificent a parish church as **St Mary's**, built of Barnack stone; it dominates the heart of the town and indeed its west tower commands the flat surrounding countryside. Above the splendid north porch (the largest in Suffolk) are the arms of Edward the Confessor and of St Edmund. The chancel, dating back to the 13th century, is a marvellous work of architecture, but pride of place goes to the east window,

divided into seven vertical lights. Off the south aisle is the Chapel of St Margaret, whose altar, itself modern, contains a medieval altar stone. At the west end, the font, dating from the 15th century, bears the arms of Sir Henry Barton, who was twice Lord Mayor of London and whose tomb is located on the south side of the tower. Above the nave and aisles is a particularly fine hammerbeam roof whose outstanding feature is the carved angels. Efforts of the Puritans to destroy the angels failed, though traces of buckshot and arrowheads remain and have been found embedded in the woodwork.

Sir Henry North built a manor house on the north side of the church in the 17th century. His successors included a dynasty of the Bunbury family, who were Lords of the Manor from 1747 to 1933. Sir Henry Edward Bunbury was the man chosen to let Napoleon Bonaparte know of his exile to St Helena, but the best-known member of the family is Sir Thomas, who in 1780 tossed a coin with Lord Derby to see whose name should be borne by a race to be inaugurated at Epsom. Lord Derby won, but Sir Thomas had the satisfaction of winning the first running of the race with his colt, Diomed.

The other focal point in Mildenhall is the Market Place, with its 16th century timbered cross.

## WORLINGTON

**2 miles W of Mildenhall on the B1102**

Worlington is a small village near the River Lark, known chiefly as the location of **Wamil Hall**, an Elizabethan mansion which stands on the riverbank. Popular lore has it that a person called Lady Rainbow haunts the place, though the spot she once favoured for appearances, a flight of stairs, was destroyed in one of the many fires the mansion has suffered. Cricket is very much part of the village scene (there's a splendid village green), and has been since the early days of the 19th century.

## BRANDON

**9 miles NE of Mildenhall on the A1065**

On the edge of **Thetford Forest** by the Little Ouse, Brandon was long ago a thriving port, but flint is what really put it on the map. The town itself is built mainly of flint, and flint was mined from early Neolithic times to make arrowheads and other implements and weapons of war. The gun flint industry brought with it substantial wealth, and a good flint-knapper could produce up to 300 gun flints in an hour. The invention of the percussion cap killed off much of the need for this type of work, however, so they turned to shaping flints for church buildings and ornamental purposes. **Brandon Heritage Centre**, in a former fire station in George Street, provides visitors with a splendid insight into this industry, while for an even more tangible feel, a visit to **Grime's Graves**, just over the Norfolk border, reveals an amazing site covering 35 acres and 300 pits (one of the shafts is open to visitors). With the close proximity of numerous warrens and their rabbit population, the fur trade also flourished here, and that, too, along with forestry, is brought to life in the Heritage Centre.

The whole of this northwestern corner of Suffolk, known as **Breckland**, offers almost unlimited opportunities for touring by car, cycling or walking. A mile south of town on the B1106 is **Brandon Country Park**, a 30-acre landscaped site with a tree trail, forest walks, a walled garden and a visitor centre. There's also an orienteering route leading on into Thetford Forest, Britain's largest lowland pine forest. The **High Lodge Forest Centre**, near Santon Downham (off the B1107), also attracts with walks, cycle trails and adventure facilities.

## ELVEDEN

**8 miles NE of Mildenhall on the A11**

**Elveden Hall** became more remarkable than its builders intended when Prince Duleep Singh, the last Maharajah of Punjab and a noted sportsman, crack shot and the man who handed over the Koh-I-Noor diamond to Queen Victoria, arrived on the scene. Exiled to England with a handsome pension, he bought the Georgian house in 1863 and commissioned John Norton to transform it into a palace modelled on those in Lahore and Delhi. Although it is stated that in private Duleep Singh referred to Queen Victoria as 'Mrs Fagin ... receiver of stolen goods', he kept close contact with the royal household and the Queen became his son's godmother. The Guinness family (Lord Iveagh) later took the Hall over and joined in the fun, adding even more exotic adornments including a replica Taj Mahal, while at the same time creating the largest arable farm in the whole of the country. In recent times, Stanley Kubrick's last film, *Eyes Wide Shut*, was shot here, as was *Tomb Raider*.

# LOCATOR MAP

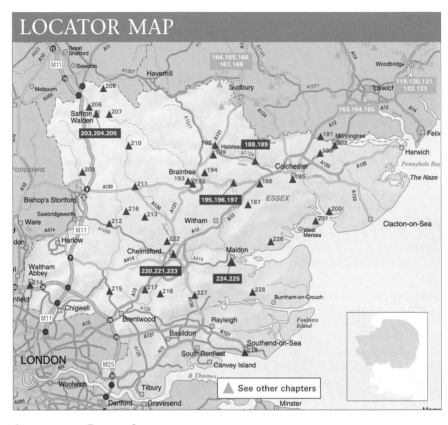

## ADVERTISERS AND PLACES OF INTEREST

185 Colchester Castle, Colchester — Page 228

186 Poplar Nurseries, Garden Centre & Restaurant, Markstey, Colchester — Page 231

187 Crispins Restaurant & Rooms, Messing, Tiptree — Page 233

188 East Anglian Railway Museum, Chappel, Colchester — Page 234

189 Chappel Galleries, Chappel, Colchester — Page 234

190 Green Island, Ardleigh, Colchester — Page 235

191 Gaye Drummond Flowers, Dedham — Page 236

192 Braintree District Museum, Braintree — Page 237

193 The Old House, Bocking, Braintree — Page 238

194 Ballaglass, Stisted, Braintree — Page 239

195 Baumanns Brasserie, Coggleshall — Page 240

196 Out of the Blue, Coggleshall — Page 240

197 Dutch Nursery, Coggleshall — Page 241

198 Head Street Gallery, Halstead — Page 244

199 Rare View B&B, Gosfield, Halstead — Page 245

200 Paxton Dene, Brightlingsea — Page 250

201 Mersea Island Vineyard, East Mersea, Colchester — Page 252

202 North House Gallery, Manningtree — Page 255

203 Kims Coffee House, Saffron Walden — Page 256

204 Sceptred Isle Food Company, Saffron Walden — Page 257

205 Saffron Walden Antiques Centre, Saffron Walden — Page 258

206 The Chaff House, Littlebury Green, Saffron Walden — Page 259

207 Redgates Farmhouse, Seward End, Saffron Walden — Page 260

208 Yardleys, Orchard Pittle, Hadstock — Page 260

209 Mountfitchet Castle & Norman Village, Stansted — Page 263

210 The Thaxted Garden for Butterflies, Thaxted — Page 265

211 Delicious Delicatessen, Great Dunmow — Page 265

212 Peacock's Country Flower & Gift Store, White Roding — Page 267

213 The White Horse Pleshey, Pleshey, Chelmsford — Page 268

214 Royal Gunpowder Mills, Waltham Abbey — Page 271

Northeast Essex has the true feel of East Anglia, particularly around the outstanding villages of the Stour Valley - which has come to be known as Constable Country, a soubriquet it shares with its neighbour, Suffolk. The inland villages and small towns here are notably historic and picturesque, offering very good touring and walking opportunities. A plethora of half-timbered medieval buildings, farms and churches mark this region out as of particular historical interest. Monuments to engineering feats past and present include Hedingham Castle, Chappel Viaduct and the postmill at Bocking Church Street. Truly lovely villages abound, rewarding any journey to this part of the county. There are also many lovely gardens to visit, and the region's principal town,

*Arkesden Village*

Colchester, is a mine of interesting sights and experiences.

The North Essex Coast has a distinguished history and a strong maritime heritage, as exemplified in towns like Harwich, Manningtree and Mistley. Further examples are the fine Martello Towers - circular brick edifices built to provide a coastal defence against Napoleon's armies - along the Tendring coast at Walton, Clacton, Jaywick and Point Clear. Dating from 1808 to 1812,

### ADVERTISERS AND PLACES OF INTEREST

215 Kelvedon Hatch Secret Nuclear Bunker,
     Brentwood                                   Page 274
216 Maidens Barn, High Easter, Chelmsford  Page 275
217 Ingatestone Hall, Ingatestone            Page 277
218 Bear Restaurant & Bar, Stock,
     Chelmsford                                  Page 278
219 Bizarre Alternative Gifts,
     Southend-on-Sea                            Page 284
220 Bookleaf Café & Bookshop, Chelmsford  Page 286
221 Waterfront Place Restaurant,
     Chelmsford                                  Page 287

222 Rue Gavaret, Broomfield                   Page 288
223 Chelmsford Museum & Essex Regiment
     Museum, Chelmsford                         Page 289
224 Mulberry House, Maldon                    Page 292
225 Topsail Charters, Maldon                   Page 293
226 Essex Kilns, Tollesbury, Maldon          Page 294
227 RHS Garden Hyde Hall, Rettendon,
     Chelmsford                                  Page 296
228 Wrekin Farmfoods, Althorne,
     Burnham-on-Crouch                          Page 297

each is mounted with a gun on the roof.

The Tendring Peninsula, which takes its name from the old Tendring Hundred (a name that reflects the county divisions of Saxon times, of which Tendring was a centre), has a rich and varied heritage ranging from prehistoric remains to medieval churches and elegant Victorian villas. The Tendring Coast contains an interesting mix of extensive tidal inlets, sandy beaches and low cliffs, and the Tendring District Council publishes a series of 'Tendring Trails' beginning at Mistley, Manningtree, Debenham, Ardleigh and other places along the North Essex Coast.

The Stour Estuary, Hamford Water and Colne Estuary are all renowned for seabirds and other wildlife. Many areas are protected nature reserves. The Manningtree-Ramsey road passes through some of the best coastal scenery in Essex, with some outstanding views of the Suffolk shore.

This is, of course, also the part of the county known as 'the sunshine holiday coast'. Resorts, both boisterous and more tranquil, dot the landscape here: Clacton-on-Sea, Frinton-on-Sea and Walton-on-the-Naze to name but three - offering many opportunities for relaxation and recreation.

*Vineyards, Felstead*

The small northwest Essex towns of Saffron Walden, Thaxted, Great Dunmow and Stansted Mountfichet are among the most beautiful and interesting in the nation. This area is also home to a wealth of picturesque villages boasting weatherboarded houses and pargeting. The quiet country lanes are perfect for walking, cycling or just exploring. This area also retains three beautiful and historic windmills, at Stansted Mountfichet, Aythorpe Roding and Thaxted. Visitors to southwest Essex and the Epping Forest will find a treasure-trove of woodland, nature reserves, superb gardens and rural delights. The Epping Forest dominates much of the far western corner, but all of this part of Essex is rich in countryside, forests and parks, including the magnificent Lee Valley Regional Park, Thorndon Country Park at Brentwood, and Weald Country Park at South Weald. Many of these parks arrange special events during the year. Southwest Essex also has major attractions in Audley End House and Waltham Abbey.

Bordering the north bank of the Thames, the borough of Thurrock has long been a gateway to London but also affords easy access to southwest Essex and to Kent. This thriving borough encompasses huge swathes of greenbelt country, and along its 18 miles of Thames frontage there are many important marshland wildlife habitats. History, too, abounds in this part of the county. Henry VIII built riverside Block Houses at East and West Tilbury, which later became Coalhouse Fort and Tilbury Fort. It was at West Tilbury that Queen Elizabeth I gave her most famous speech to her troops, gathered to meet the Spanish Armada threat. Both forts also played an important defensive role during the two World Wars. At the extreme southeast of the county, Southend is a popular and friendly seaside resort with a wealth of sights and amenities. There are also smaller seaside communities which repay a visit. The area surrounding the Rivers Blackwater and Crouch contains a wealth of ancient woodland and other natural beauties, particularly along the estuaries and the Chelmer and Blackwater Canal. This corner of Essex is ideal for those who enjoy any kind of watersports activities. The island of Northey near Maldon is owned by the National Trust and is a haven for wildlife.

There are hundreds of acres of ancient woodland, much of it coppiced, which is the traditional woodland-management technique which encourages a vast array of natural flora and fauna. This stretch of Essex affords some marvellous walking, cycling, birdwatching and other treats for everyone who loves the great outdoors.

## COLCHESTER

This ancient market town and garrison stands in the midst of rolling East Anglian countryside. England's oldest recorded town, it has over 2,000 years of history, there to be discovered by visitors. First established during the 7th century BC, west of town there are the remains of the massive earthworks built to protect Colchester in pre-Roman times. During the 1st century, Colchester's prime location made it an obvious target for invading Romans. The Roman Emperor Claudius accepted the surrender of 11 British Kings in Colchester. In AD60, Queen Boudicca helped to establish her place in history by taking revenge on the Romans and burning the town to the ground, before going on to destroy London and St Albans. Here in this town that was once

*Dutch Quarter, Colchester*

capital of Roman Britain, Roman walls - the oldest in Britain - still surround the oldest part of town. Balkerne Gate, west gate of the original Roman town, is the largest surviving Roman gateway in the country, and remains magnificent to this day.

Today the town is presided over by its lofty town hall and enormous Victorian water tower, nicknamed 'Jumbo' after London Zoo's first African elephant, an animal sold to P T Barnum (causing some controversy) in 1882. The tower has four massive pillars made up of one-and-a-quarter million bricks, 369 tons of stone and 142 tons of iron, all working to support the 230,000-gallon tank.

The town affords plenty to see and explore. There are many guided town walks available, as well as bus tours. The local Visitor Information Centre on Queen Street has details of the many places to visit. Market days in this thriving town are Friday and Saturday.

A good place to start any exploration of the town is **Colchester Castle** (see panel below) itself and its museum. When the Normans arrived, Colchester (a name given the town by the Saxons) was an important borough. The Normans built

## COLCHESTER CASTLE

Castle Park, High Street, Colchester
Tel: 01206 282939
website: www.colchestermuseums.co.uk

**Colchester Castle** is undeniably one of the most important historic buildings in the country, and today, a thousand years after it was built, it is still a living, vibrant place, a potent symbol of Britain's oldest recorded town. Colchester was the first capital of Britain and beneath the Castle's foundations are the remains of one of the most renowned Roman buildings, the Temple of Claudius. To the Romans it was the symbol of their power and success, but to the native Britons it was a symbol of oppression.

The temple became a main target of the rebels led by Queen Boudicca (Boadicea) who attacked the Roman town in AD60. The town's citizens barricaded themselves in the temple but after two days they were all killed. It is estimated that as many as 30,000 could have been killed during the sacking of Colchester. After the revolt had been suppressed the town and the temple were rebuilt.

Around 1076 King William I ordered a royal fortress to be built at Colchester, and the great stone base of the now ruined temple was an obvious foundation for the central tower or keep of the new castle. The great size of the temple dictated that of the keep, which was the largest ever built in Britain.

For most of its life the Castle was used as a prison; one of the most infamous episodes in its history occurred in 1645 when Matthew Hopkins, the self-styled Witchfinder General, used the Castle to imprison and interrogate suspected witches. The Castle first opened its doors in the role of Museum in 1860 and today features many hands-on displays to help explain the town-people's experience of Colchester's varying fortunes. Visitors can slip into a toga, feel the weight of Roman armour, try on medieval hats and shoes and see treasures like the Roman bronze statue of Mercury and the Colchester Vase, one of the finest examples of Roman pottery found in Britain.

*Castle Museum*

their castle on the foundations of the Roman temple of Claudius. Having used many of the Roman bricks in its construction, it boasts the largest Norman keep ever built in Europe - the only part still left standing. The keep houses the **Castle Museum**, one of the most exciting hands-on historical attractions in the country. Its fascinating collection of Iron Age, Roman and medieval relics is one of the most important in the country. There are tombstones carved in intricate detail and exquisite examples of Roman glass and jewellery. Visitors can try on Roman togas and helmets, touch some of the 2,000-year-old pottery unearthed nearby, and experience the town's murkier past by visiting the Castle prisons, where witches were interrogated by the notorious Witchfinder General Matthew Hopkins.

**Hollytrees Museum** in the High Street is located in a fine Georgian home dating back to 1718. This award-winning museum can be found on the edge of Castle Park and houses a wonderful

collection of toys, costumes, curios and antiquities from the last two centuries. Purchased for the town by Viscount Cowdray it first opened as a museum in 1920. Also nearby, housed in the former All Saints' Church, is the **Natural History Museum**, with exhibits and many hands-on displays illustrating the natural history of Essex from the Ice Age right up to the present day.

Housed in the Minories Art Gallery, **First Site** is a recent addition to Colchester's fine choice of art institutes, and features changing exhibitions of contemporary visual art, housed in a converted Georgian town house with beautiful walled garden. An arch in Trinity Street leads to **Tymperleys Clock Museum**, the 15th century timber-framed home of William Gilberd, who entertained Elizabeth I with experiments in electricity. Today this fine example of architectural splendour houses a magnificent collection of 18th and 19th century Colchester-made clocks. The **Colchester Arts Centre**, not far from Balkerne Gate, features a regular programme of visual arts, drama, music, poetry and dance; the **Mercury Theatre** is the town's premiere site for stage dramas, comedies and musical theatre.

Dutch Protestants arrived in Colchester in the 16th century, fleeing Spanish rule in the Netherlands, and revitalised the local cloth industry. The houses of these Flemish weavers in the **Dutch Quarter** to the west of the castle, and the Civil War scars on the walls of Siege House in East Street, bear testimony to their place in the town's history. The Dutch Quarter west of the castle remains a charming and relatively quiet corner of this bustling town.

Close to the railway station are the ruins of **St Botolph's Priory**, the oldest Augustinian priory in the country. Its remains are a potent reminder of the bitterness of Civil War times, as it was here that Royalists held out for 11 weeks during the siege of Colchester, before finally being starved into submission.

On Bourne Road, south of the town centre just off the B1025, there's a striking stepped-and-curved gabled building known as **Bourne Mill**, now owned by the National Trust. Built in 1591 from stone taken from the nearby St John's Abbeygate, this delightful restored building near a lovely millpond was originally a fishing lodge, later converted (in the 19th century) into a mill - and still in working order.

**Colchester Zoo**, just off the A12 outside the town, stands in the 40-acre park of Stanway Hall, with its 16th century mansion and church dating from the 14th century. Founded in 1963, the Zoo has a wide and exciting variety of attractions. The Zoo has gained a well-deserved reputation as one of the best in Europe. Its award-winning enclosures allow visitors closer to the animals and provide naturalistic environments for the 170 species. There are 15 unique daily displays including opportunities to feed an African elephant, bear, chimp or alligator, stroke a snake and watch a penguin parade.

Colchester has been famous in its time for both oysters and roses. Colchester oysters are still cultivated on beds in the lower reaches of the River Colne, which skirts the northern edge of town. A visit to the **Oyster Fisheries** on Mersea Island is a fascinating experience, and the tour includes complimentary fresh oysters and a glass of wine.

Just north of the centre of town, **High Woods Country Park** offers 330 acres of woodland, grassland, scrub and farmland. A central lake is fed by a small tributary of the River Colne. The land originated as three ancient farms, and forms part of a Royal hunting forest.

Large numbers of musket balls dating from the Civil War period have been unearthed, indicating that the woods served as a base for the Roundheads.

# AROUND COLCHESTER

## WIVENHOE
### 4 miles SE of Colchester off the A133

This riverside town on the banks of the River Colne was once renowned as a smugglers' haunt, and there is a very pretty quayside that is steeped in maritime history. There are still strong connections with the sea, with boat-building having replaced fishing as the main industry. The pretty church, with its distinctive cupola atop a sturdy tower, stands on the site of the former Saxon church and retains some impressive 16th century brasses.

The small streets lead into each other and end at the picturesque waterfront, where fishing boats and small sailing craft bob at their moorings. On the Quay visitors will find the **Nottage Institute**, the River Colne's nautical academy; classes here teach students about knots, skippering and even how to build a boat! It is open to visitors on Sundays in summer. The Wivenhoe Trail, by the river, is an interesting cycle track starting at the railway station and continuing along the river to Colchester Hythe. Wivenhoe Woods is dotted with grassy glades set with tables, the perfect place for a picnic.

East of the Quay, the public footpath takes visitors to the Tidal Surge Barrier, one of only two in the country. Volunteers run a ferry service operating across the River Colne between the Quay at Wivenhoe, Fingringhoe and Rowhedge. Nearby Wivenhoe Park has been the site of the campus for the University of Essex since 1962. Visitors are welcome to stroll around the grounds.

## ABBERTON

**3 miles S of Colchester off the B1026**

Two natural beauties are within reach of this village. **Abberton Reservoir Nature Reserve** is a 1,200 acre reservoir and wildlife centre, ideal for birdwatching. A site of international importance, home to 700 goldeneye, 8,000 wigeon and nearly 500 gadwall and shovellers, as well as a resting colony of cormorants, the site features a conservation room, shop, toilets and hides.

Four miles further east, **Fingringhoe Wick Nature Reserve** offers visitors 125 acres of woodland and lakes by the Colne estuary.

## COPFORD

**3½ miles SW of Colchester off the B1022**

Copford is home to the wonderful Norman church of **St Michael and All Angels**, with its magnificent, well-restored medieval wall paintings, whilst Copford Green, a lovely and peaceful village, is home to **Springfields at Copford** with 17 acres of gardens and parkland. Here visitors will find old established south gardens with roses and shrubbery, as well as a parterre planted in 1997 with 330 rose bushes. Other attractions include a rare Maidenhair Gingko tree, ancient mulberry, woodland walks spring-fed water gardens and lake, and croquet and putting greens. The church of **St Mary the Virgin** also repays a visit.

## LAYER BRETON

**5½ miles SW of Colchester off the B1026**

On the right side of Layer Breton Heath there's **Stamps and Crows**, a must for gardening enthusiasts. Two and a half acres of moated garden surrounding a 15th century farmhouse. The farmhouse is not open to the public, but the

## POPLAR NURSERIES, GARDEN CENTRE & RESTAURANT

Coggeshall Road, Marks Tey, Colchester, Essex CO6 1HR
Tel: 01206 210374  Fax: 01206 211783
e-mail: info@poplarnurseries.co.uk
website: www.poplarnurseries.co.uk

**Poplar Nurseries,Garden Centre and Restaurant** is a 3rd generation family-run business with more than 65 years' experience in horticulture. Perennials and annuals, the range of plants is impressive, and include a large choice of frost-resistant varieties and trees, shrubs and flowers to suit every garden.

There is a theme house with oriental plants, palms and other tropical varieties. There are landscaped gardens to walk in and a play area for the children. In addition a large choice of frost-resistant pots, garden furnishings, tools and a wide selection of gifts complete the comprehensive selection of items available.

What better after a few hours' browsing through the nurseries than a relaxing cup of tea or coffee, cakes, breakfast, lunch or dinner in the licensed restaurant, known far and wide for the quality of its menu.

# Layer Breton

| | |
|---|---|
| **Distance:** | 4.0 miles (6.44 kilometres) |
| **Typical time:** | 90 mins |
| **Height gain:** | 10 metres |
| **Map:** | Explorer 184 |
| **Walk:** | www.walkingworld.com ID:1458 |
| **Contributor:** | Brian and Anne Sandland |

### Access Information:

The walk starts in the car park of Layer Breton church.

### Additional Information:

Layer Marney Tower was built around 1520 for Henry VIII's Privy Seal, it is the tallest Tudor Tower and has a magnificent residence, farm and gardens attached.

### Description:

Following field paths and country lanes this walk takes you through three small, out-of-the-way settlements, past two churches, a deer compound and a magnificent Tower.

### Features:

Toilets, Museum, Play Area, Church, Wildlife, Birds, Flowers, Butterflies, Good for Kids, Mostly Flat, Ancient Monument

### Walk Directions:

**1** From Layer Breton church car-park take the road south then the first road right (signposted Layer Marney and Tiptree). Follow Shatters Road past a pond and then a junction left. Where the road goes sharp right take a signposted footpath left.

**2** Follow the path, which bends right then follows the right hand edge of a field and heads in a dead straight line to the right of Layer Marney Tower and Church. When you reach a road go left. At the entrance to Layer Marney Tower car-park go right.

**3** Pass the entrance to the Tower, then the Church (right) and continue on a broad grass track which bends left then right (signposted)

beside a deer compound, carrying on ahead when the wire fence bends left to pass through a hedge and cross a ditch by a footbridge. Continue along the right hand edge of another huge field to a gap in the hedge (right), then pass a garage (left) and use the drive of a house to reach the road at a junction where you go right.

**4** Just after the road bends right and before houses on the right take a footpath left.

**5** Cross the stile and head straight across the field to a gap in the hedge between two telegraph poles. Bear half right to head for a stile next to a gate with houses beyond. At the road go right then continue ahead (signposted Messing, Kelvedon and Colchester). Continue to a path off right through trees where the road begins a sharp left hand bend.

**6** Follow the path to the B1022 and turn right. When this road goes sharp left take a signposted footpath right (through a lay-by) to keep a hedge on your right.

**7** Continue to a stile through the hedge on the right. Cross this, turn left and carry on to another stile, which you cross to reach a road.

**8** Cross the road and take a signposted footpath over a stile. Cross a small field and another signposted stile and footbridge, and follow a clear path ahead to a track on a bend where you continue ahead passing a reservoir on your left . Ignore a track off left. Your track passes 2 lonely oak trees then heads towards houses. Just beyond Briar Cottage turn right on a tarmac lane past housing on both sides.

**9** You pass houses on your left and trees and a tall hedge right, then when you reach another road you turn right to return to the Church car-park at Layer Breton.

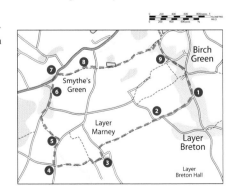

gardens boast herbaceous borders, mixed shrubs, old roses and good ground cover. There is also a recently created bog garden and dovecote.

## LAYER MARNEY

**6 miles SW of Colchester off the B1022**

The mansion, which was planned to rival Hampton Court, was never completed, but its massive 8-storey Tudor gatehouse, known as **Layer Marney Tower**, is very impressive. Built between 1515 and 1525, it is one of the most striking examples of 16th century architecture in Britain. Its magnificent four red brick towers, covered in 16th century Italianate design, were built by Lord Marney, Henry VIII's Lord Privy Seal. As well as spectacular views from the top of the towers, they are surrounded by formal gardens designed at the turn of the century, with lovely roses, yew hedges and herbaceous

borders. There is also on site a rare breeds farm, farm shop and tea room.

## TIPTREE

**7 miles SW of Colchester on the B1023**

As all true jam-lovers will know, Tiptree is famed as the home of the **Wilkin and Son Ltd** jam factory, a Victorian establishment which now boasts a fascinating visitors' centre in the grounds of the original factory.

## ALDHAM

**4 miles W of Colchester off the A604**

This picturesque village was, for a time, home to the famous Essex historian Philip Morant, who held the post of vicar here. He is buried in the local churchyard. **Old Hill House** in Aldham is a one-acre garden with mixed shrubs, herbaceous borders and formal herb garden for year-round interest.

## CHAPPEL
### 5 miles W of Colchester off the A604

Here, on a 4-acre site beside Chappel and Wakes Colne Station, is the **East Anglian Railway Museum** (see panel), a comprehensive collection spanning 150 years of railway history, with period railway architecture, engineering and memorabilia in beautifully restored station buildings.

For every railway buff, young or old, this is the place to try your hand at being a signalman and admire the handsome restored engines and carriages. There is also a delightful miniature railway. Special steam days and other events are held throughout the year.

## EAST ANGLIAN RAILWAY MUSEUM

Chappel Station, nr Colchester, Essex CO6 2DS
Tel/Fax: 01206 242524

The **East Anglian Railway Museum** is a fascinating and comprehensive collection of period railway architecture, engineering and memorabilia housed in beautifully restored station buildings. A grand day out for railway buffs young and old, this is the place to try your hand at being a signalman and to admire the

handsome engines and carriages. There is also a delightful miniature railway. Special steam days and events are held throughout the year.

The dramatic 32-arched **Chappel Viaduct** standing 75 feet above the Colne Valley, a designated European

## CHAPPEL GALLERIES FINE ART

15 Colchester Road, Chappel, Colchester, Essex CO6 2DE    Tel/Fax: 01206 240326
e-mail: chappelgalleries@btopenworld.com
website: www.chappelgalleries.com

Just six miles west of Colchester, in the Colne Valley, **Chappel Galleries Fine Art** boasts four spacious, light and airy rooms in which changing exhibitions feature the work of established 20th- and 21st-century artists. The yearly programme is packed with exciting shows, and for 17 years this gallery has showcased the work of a range of notable artists – 2004 will see the work of Ronald Ronaldson, who works in oils and creates landscapes and

*by Glyn Morgan*

still lifes, Cyril Deakins (1916-2000), landscape painters Glyn Morgan and Sargy Mann, John Atkins' sculpture and drawings, figurative artist John Lessore, Nicholas Simington, Mike Pope, Michael Collins, Katherine Hamilton, Mary Griffiths and more - in one-person shows that highlight the unique gifts of each artist.

Paintings, sculpture and mixed media pieces will delight art-lovers of every kind. Owner Wladyslaw Mirecki is an acclaimed artist in his own right, and can provide expert knowledgeable advice. Open: Tuesday to Saturday 10 – 5.

*by W Mirecki "Tollesbury Pier"*

Monument, was begun in 1846 and opened in 1849.

## ARDLEIGH

**3 miles NE of Colchester off the A137**

Tendring's westernmost village comprises an attractive group of 16th and 17th century cottages grouped around the fine 15th century **Butterfield Church**. **Spring Valley Mill**, a now privately owned 18th century timber-framed and weatherboarded edifice, was once a working watermill, later adapted to steam. Day and half-day canoeing and sailing lessons can be taken at the **Ardleigh Outdoor Education Centre**.

Nearby is **Ardleigh Reservoir**, offering up many opportunities for water sports and trout fishing.

## DEDHAM

**6 miles NE of Colchester off the A14**

This is true Constable country, along the border with Suffolk, the county's prettiest area. The village has several fine old buildings, especially the 15th century flint church, its pinnacled tower familiar from so many Constable paintings. There's also the school Constable went to, and good walks through the protected riverside meadows of Dedham Vale to **Flatford**, where **Bridge Cottage** is a restored thatched 16th century building housing a display about Constable, who featured this cottage in several of his paintings (his father's mill is across the river lock in Dedham).

**Dedham Vale Family Farm** on Mill Street is a nicely undeveloped 16-acre

## GREEN ISLAND

Park Road, Ardleigh, Colchester,
Essex CO7 7SP
Tel/Fax: 01206 230455
e-mail: andrewedmond105@aol.com

**Green Island** is an outstanding designed by Fiona Edmond, a professional garden designer who qualified at the Inchbold School of Design in 1989. She runs the garden, nursery and design centre here. Situated in 20 acres of woodland, this wonderful informal garden boasts a huge variety of unusual plants offering all year round colour and scent. Main features include the terrace, mixed borders, Japanese garden, woodland walks, and seaside

garden, gravel garden, bamboo dell, water garden, tree house and sculpture trail by Clare Iles.

The house was built in 1958 and designed by Raymond Erith, and the garden was originally part of the orchard belonging to Ardleigh Park. Fiona and her husband bought the house and 20-acre site in 1996, and the gardens have been Fiona's labour of love since 1997. The nursery offers unusual perennials, and there is a garden design exhibition. Teas are sold on Sundays. The garden can be reached by taking the B1029 from the centre of Ardleigh towards Bromley. Park Road is the second right after the level crossing.

farm boasting a comprehensive collection of British farm animals, including many different breeds of livestock such as pigs, sheep, cattle, Suffolk horses, goats and poultry. Children may enter certain of the paddocks to stroke and feed the animals (bags of feed provided).

The **Art & Craft Centre** on Dedham's High Street is well worth a visit. **Marlborough Head**, a wool merchant's house dating back to 1475, is now a pub. The **Toy Museum** has a fascinating collection of dolls, teddies, toys, games, doll houses and other artefacts of childhoods past.

At **Castle House**, approximately three-quarters of a mile from the village centre on the corner of East Lane and Castle Hill, The **Sir Alfred Munnings Art Museum** is housed in the former home, studios and grounds of the famous painter, who lived here between 1898

*River Stour, Dedham Vale*

### GAYE DRUMMOND FLOWERS

The White House, High Street, Dedham, Essex  CO7 6HL
Tel/Fax: 01206 322360
e-mail: gaye@gayedrummond.com
website: www.gayedrummond.com

Original floral designs using the finest, freshest materials can be found at **Gaye Drummond Flowers**, a distinctive specialist florist set in the heart of Dedham.

Named for its owner – a gifted trained florist who has many years' experience of creating beautiful floral arrangements – and who is well worth seeking out. Gaye ensures she has the

freshest flowers and plants to create decorations for churches and marquees, bridal bouquets and more. Exquisite wreathes, baskets and other floral arrangements – in traditional and more modern styles – will suit every taste and budget. Each one is a unique expression of the florist's art, and will grace every occasion. Delivery available. For more information, please consult the excellent website.

and 1920. The museum prides itself on the diversity of paintings and sculptures on view. The house itself is a mixture of Tudor and Georgian periods, carefully restored. Munnings' original furniture is still in place. The spacious grounds boast well-maintained gardens.

# BRAINTREE

This town, along with its close neighbour Bocking, are sited at the crossing of two Roman roads and were brought together by the cloth industry in the 16th century. Flemish weavers settled here, followed by many Huguenots. One, Samuel Courtauld, set up a silk mill in 1816 and, by 1866, employed over 3,000 Essex inhabitants.

The magnificent former Town Hall is

one of the many Courtauld legacies in the town. It was built in 1928 with panelled walls, murals by Grieffenhagen showing stirring scenes of local history, and a grand central tower with a five-belled striking clock. A smaller but no less fascinating reminder of Courtauld's generosity is the 1930s bronze fountain, with bay, shell and fish, near St Michael's Church.

Huguenot names such as Courtauld are connected with international enterprises to this day. Their reason for coming to Britain is a fascinating and poignant tale. Formed in France in 1559 as an organised Protestant group taking direction from Calvin and the Calvinistic Reformation in Geneva, the Huguenots were at first allowed to live and worship freely. However, as political and religious

## BRAINTREE DISTRICT MUSEUM

The Town Hall Centre, Market Place,
Braintree, Essex CM7 3YG
Tel: 01376 328868  Fax: 01376 344345
e-mail: jean@bdcmuseum.demon.co.uk
website: www.braintree.gov.uk/museum

In the historic market square (market days Wednesday and Saturday), **Braintree District Museum** is housed in a beautifully converted Victorian school. Visitors are assured of a warm welcome at this award-winning museum, whose elegant exhibition areas are in contrast to the somewhat stern Victorian façade; the exception

to this is the faithfully re-created Victorian classroom, where nostalgia lovers will be in their element and where role-play lessons are provided for schools on a daily basis.

Braintree was the centre of the medieval wool trade in north Essex and gained international fame when Courtaulds evolved their revolutionary silk industry in the town. The permanent galleries tell the fascinating story of this industry and also of the development of engineering design - Braintree was also the home of Crittalls. Country crafts such as straw plaiting are featured, along with the rural artists who made their home in Great Barfield and became pivotal in the development of fine and decorative arts in the 1950s and 1960s. John Ray, often considered the father of English natural history, has a dedicated gallery to his ground-breaking research in the 17th century.

A feature of the Museum is the programme of changing exhibitions, often with a craft base such as ceramics, decorative arts and particularly textiles. Friendly staff are pleased to welcome visitors with a free Soundalive audio tour and explain the wide range of craft items available in the shop.

## THE OLD HOUSE

11 Bradford Street, Bocking, Braintree,
Essex CM7 9AS
Tel: 01376 550457  Fax: 01376 343863
e-mail: old_house@talk21.com
website: www.theoldhousebraintree.co.uk

A spacious 16th-century Grade II listed house set
near the town centre with its own half-acre of
grounds, **The Old House** is a gracious and
charming family-run hotel. Set in a handsome
road lined with timber-framed houses, it makes a
wonderful retreat. Single, double, twin and family
rooms are available, and the lovely panelled bar/lounge area features an inglenook fireplace and is a
cosy and welcoming place to relax over a quiet drink.

Open all year round, most rooms are en suite and some
are on the ground floor. One boasts a four-poster bed.
Breakfast is a hearty and delicious affair, and evening meals
and packed lunches can be provided by arrangement.

Just off the B1053, it is within easy reach of Braintree,
golfing, horse-riding facilities, tennis courts, indoor
swimming, fishing and shooting at Fennes Estate,
Constable Country, Castle Hedingham, Finchingfield,
Thaxted, the area's nature reserves and many other sights
and attractions. 3 Diamonds ETC.

rivalries grew in France, the Catholic
majority started to persecute them; a
century of war, massacre and bloodshed
followed. Finally in 1685 all their rights
were stripped. In the chaos that ensued,
many died and thousands fled. It was to
turn out to be France's loss, for the
Huguenots were among the most
industrious and economically advanced
elements in French society. Others
gained at France's expense; Huguenots
poured into England, and especially East
Anglia, where their skills soon made
them welcome and valued members of
the community.

The **Braintree District Museum** on
Manor Street tells the story of Braintree's
diverse industrial heritage and traditions.
The **Town Hall Centre** is a Grade II
listed building housing the Tourist
Information Centre and the Art Gallery,
which boasts a continuous changing
programme of exhibitions and works.

## AROUND BRAINTREE

### FAIRSTEAD

**4 miles S of Braintree off the A131**

Fairstead (or Fairsted) is an undulating
parish about three miles east of the
A131, some four miles northwest of
Witham. The **Church of St Mary and St
Peter** is an ancient building of flint, in
the Norman style, consisting of chancel,
nave, north porch and a western tower
with a lofty shingled spire with four
bells, one of which dates back to before
the Reformation. During restoration in
the late 1800s various handsome mural
paintings were discovered, including,
over the chancel arch, those entitled *Our
Lord's Triumphal Entry into Jerusalem, The
Last Supper, The Betrayal, Our Lord being
crowned with thorns,* and *Incidents on the
way to Calvary*. The hamlet of Fuller
Street lies 1 mile west of the church.

## CRESSING

**4 miles SE of Braintree off the B1018**

**Cressing Temple Barns**, set in the centre of an ancient farmstead, are two splendid medieval timber barns commissioned in the 12th century by the Knights Templar. They contain the timber of over 1,000 oak trees; an interpretive exhibition explains to visitors how the barns were made, as a special viewing platform brings visitors up into the roof of the magnificent Wheat Barn for a closer look. There's also a beautiful walled garden re-creating the Tudor style, with an arbour, fount and physic garden. Special events are held throughout the year.

## COGGESHALL

**5 miles E of Braintree on the A120**

This medieval hamlet, a pleasant old cloth and lace town, has some very fine timbered buildings. **Paycocke's House** on West Street, a delightful timber-framed medieval merchant's home dating from about 1500, boasts unusually rich panelling and wood carvings, and is owned by the National Trust. Inside there's a superb carved ceiling and a display of Coggeshall lace. Outdoors there's a lovely garden. The village also has some good antique shops and a working pottery.

Located in Stoneham Street, **Coggeshall Heritage Centre** displays items of local interest and features changing exhibitions on themes relating to the past of this historic wool town. There's an authentic, working wool loom on site.

The National Trust also owns the restored **Coggeshall Grange Barn**, which dates from around 1140 and is the oldest surviving timber-framed barn in Europe. Built for the monks of the nearby Cistercian Abbey, it is a magnificent

---

## BALLAGLASS

Coggeshall Road, Stisted, Braintree,
Essex CM77 8AB
Tel: 01376 331409  Fax: 01376 331405
e-mail: ballaglass@btinternet.com

Ideally placed for touring the picturesque Essex villages and Constable Country, **Ballaglass** is set in two acres of gardens and is close to many local amenities. This purpose-built self-contained accommodation comprises a large lounge/dining area with French doors leading onto the patio area. Equipped to a very high standard with electric oven and hob, microwave, fridge/

freezer and washing machine, the décor and furnishings throughout provide luxurious holiday accommodation.

The well-appointed lounge includes two sofa beds, while the double bedroom is bright, elegant and spacious. Cosy and welcoming, the owners make every effort to ensure that all their guests have a relaxing and enjoyable stay, offering extras such as arranging for your groceries to be delivered to await your arrival and providing all towels and bed linen. The gardens boast three large ponds and a summerhouse which guests are welcome to enjoy. No smoking. Children over 5 welcome. Mobility friendly

## BAUMANNS BRASSERIE

4-6 Stoneham Street, Coggeshall, Essex CO6 1TT
Tel: 01376 561453 e-mail: food@baumannsbrasserie.co.uk
Fax: 01376 563762 website: www.baumannsbrasserie.co.uk

Situated in the historic and picturesque market town of Coggeshall, **Baumanns Brasserie** is an absolute must for food lovers. The menu changes regularly and is incredibly varied. Old favourites include dishes as diverse as pan-fried medallions of venison with sweet and sour leeks, to caviar and chips.

Owned by internationally acclaimed Master Chef, Mark Baumann, this bright 16th century brasserie offers a truly relaxed dining experience. Former chef at Langan's Brasserie, Coggeshall, Mark took over the restaurant following the tragic death of eccentric Irish entrepreneur Peter Langan in 1988. While the brasserie has retained all its original charm and character, it is the restaurant's fine cuisine that has earned it such a wide acclaim. Featured in every major food guide in Great Britain, Baumanns Brasserie is famous for its innovative cuisine and A La Carte menu. Trained at the Royal Champagne (France) owned by Moet & Chandon, Mark applies the same attention to detail when cooking for patrons of his brasserie as when he has cooked for royalty.

Tourists can have a light lunch following a visit to nearby Marks Hall Estate and Arboretum, one of a number of country parks in the surrounding area. After lunch a short trip to Colchester Castle, a stroll round the many local antiques shops and boutiques, or a walk along the awesome and varied Essex coastline might conclude the perfect day out. A former location for the BBC series Lovejoy, Coggeshall is steeped in English history and is home to several National Trust properties.

## OUT OF THE BLUE

15 Church Street, Coggeshall, Colchester,
Essex CO6 1TU
Tel/Fax: 01376 564229

A collection of exquisite bags, evening wear, casual clothing, accessories, jewellery and more can be found at **Out of the Blue**, a charming emporium of unusual fashion. Anyone looking for something completely original and different should visit this boutique where owner Henrietta Lyttelton is happy to showcase the work of some of the country's top emerging designers.

Exquisite beaded dresses, tops and skirts, luxurious chenilles and velvets, handmade bags, suede skirts and coats, silk scarves, jewellery made with freshwater pearls, semi-precious stones and dichroic glass and fashions from Aftershock, Patric Casey, Out of Xile, Flax and Rene Derhy are just some of the gorgeous items in this excellent shop where you will be sure to find the perfect outfit for anyone with unusual taste.

example of this type of architecture.

**MarksHall** is an historic estate and arboretum that began life in Saxon times, and is mentioned in the *Domesday Book*. In the 15th century, then-owner Sir Thomas Honywood was a leading Parliamentarian who commanded the Essex Regiment during the Civil War. Local legend has it that the two artificial lakes on the grounds were dug by Parliamentary troops during the siege of Colchester in 1648. One of his successors, General Philip Honywood, in 1758 forbade (under the terms of his will) any of his successors to fell timber - thus his lasting legacy of avenues of mature oaks, limes and horse chestnuts, surrounded by one of the largest continuous areas of ancient woodland in the county.

The estate fell on hard times in the 19th and early 20th century, but owner Thomas Phillips Price began an

*Victorian Clock Tower, Coggeshall*

## DUTCH NURSERY

West Street, Coggeshall, Colchester, Essex CO6 1NT
Tel: 01376 561287  Fax: 01376 561423
e-mail: robert@dutchnursery.co.uk
website: www.dutchnursery.co.uk

A family nursery that has been a thriving concern for over 50 years, Dutch Nursery has branches in Hertfordshire and here in Coggeshall. Run by Robert and Nicole Henn, this fine nursery and garden centre has a complete A – Z of seasonal plants, shrubs, trees, perennials, herbaceous plants and more. Information sheets and guides help you with advice on planting and siting, while the friendly, knowledgeable staff are more than happy to assist. Garden implements and ornaments include terracotta pots, furniture, aquatics, vases, essential gardening clothing and more.

Gifts for the garden and home include greeting cards, indoor plants, silk flowers and a range of everything needed to create and maintain the perfect garden. The site also comprises a wonderful coffee shop where you can enjoy a hot or cold drink and a tempting range of home-made cakes, sandwiches and light meals after a leisurely browse through the nursery, and a children's play area. Set against the backdrop of the River Blackwater, the new landscaped garden area showcases border displays with seasonal plants in bloom – inspiration for any garden can be found here.

association with Kew Gardens and left the estate to be held and used for 'advancement in the National interest of Agriculture, Aboriculture and Forestry'. The Thomas Phillips Price Trust was formed and registered as a charity in 1971, and a major programme of revitalisation and restoration began. The estate now flourishes with native plants and wildlife, ornamental lakes, a 17th century walled garden, cascades, Coach House and Information Centre. This last is housed in a painstakingly refurbished 15th century barn, and features informative displays as well as a gift shop and tea room.

Plans for the on-site arboretum were first drawn up in the late 1980s, to cover 120 acres. Still being established, it will contain a collection of trees from all over the world, laid out in geographical themes - Europe, Asia, America, and the southern hemisphere.

## KELVEDON
**6 miles SE of Braintree off the A12**

This village alongside the River Blackwater houses the **Feering and Kelvedon Museum**, which is dedicated to manorial history and houses artefacts from the Roman settlement of Canonium, agricultural tools through the ages and other interesting exhibits.

## FEERING
**6 miles E of Braintree off the A12**

**Feeringbury Manor** near Feering has a fine, extensive riverside garden with ponds, streams, a little waterwheel, old-fashioned plants and bog gardens, and fascinating sculpture by artist Ben Coode-Adams.

## BLAKE END
**3 miles W of Braintree off the A120**

**The Great Maze** at Blake End is one of the most challenging in the world. Set in over 10 acres of lovely North Essex farmland, it is grown every year from over half a million individual maize and sunflower seeds, and is open every summer. Continuing innovations bring with them extra twists and turns, making this wonderful maze, with more than five miles of pathways, even more of a brain teaser. A viewing platform makes it easy to help anyone hopelessly lost! Ten per cent of all profits go to the Essex Air Ambulance service.

**Blake House Craft Centre** comprises carefully preserved farm buildings centred round a courtyard. One of the county's prettiest craft centres, visitors will find a fine array of craft shops and a restaurant serving breakfast and morning coffee, lunch and afternoon tea.

## GREAT SALING
**4 miles NW of Braintree off the A120**

**Saling Hall Garden** is a 12-acre garden including a walled garden dating from 1698. The small park boasts a collection of fine trees, and there are ponds, a water garden and an extensive collection of unusual plants with an emphasis on rare trees.

## WETHERSFIELD
**5 miles NW of Braintree on the B1053**

**Boydells Dairy Farm** is a working farm where visitors are welcome to join in with tasks such as milking, feeding and more. A guided tour mixes fun with education, and all questions are most welcome. From bees to llamas, just about every kind of farm animal can be found here. Goat rides and donkey cart rides, a lovely picnic area and refreshments such as 'Yoggipops' (sheep's milk yogurt ice-lollies made on site) make for a most enjoyable day out. Open to the public April to September.

ESSEX

## FINCHINGFIELD
### 6 miles NW of Braintree off the B1053

This charming village is graced with thatched cottages spread generously around a sloping village green that dips to a stream and duck pond at the centre of the village. Nearby stands an attractive small 18th-century Post Mill with one pair of stones and tailpole winding. Extensively restored, today's visitors can climb up the first two floors.

Just up the hill, visitors will find the Norman church of **St John the Baptist**, and the **Guildhall** (mentioned in the *Domesday Book*), which has a small museum open Sundays and also houses a local heritage centre with displays of artwork, paintings, pottery, sewing and weaving.

Finchingfield is easily one of the most picturesque and most photographed villages in Essex, featured in many television programmes and the home of the series *Lovejoy*. Here visitors will also find the privately owned Tudor stately home, **Spains Hall**, which has a lovely flower garden containing a huge Cedar of Lebanon planted in 1670 and an Adams sundial. Many good roses surround the kitchen garden, which contains an ancient Paulonia tree and a bougainvillea in the greenhouse. The garden is generally open on Sunday afternoons in summer.

Finchingfield also has an easily followed path along the Finchingfield Brook leading from the village to Great Bardfield.

## GREAT BARDFIELD
### 6 miles NW of Braintree off the B1053

This old market town on a hill above the River Pant is a pleasant mixture of cottages and shops, nicely complemented by the 14th century church of **St Mary the Virgin**. Perhaps Great Bardfield's most notable feature is, however, a restored windmill that goes by the unusual name of 'Gibraltar'.

Here in one of the prettiest villages in all of Essex, the **Great Bardfield Museum** occupies a 16th century charity cottage and 19th century village lockup, and features exhibits of mainly 19th and 20th century domestic and agricultural artefacts and some fine examples of rural crafts such as corn-dollies and straw-plaiting.

## GOSFIELD
### 4 miles N of Braintree off the A1017

**Gosfield Lake Leisure Resort**, the county's largest freshwater lake, lies in the grounds of Gosfield Hall. This Tudor mansion was remodelled in the 19th century by its owner Samuel

*Finchingfield Village*

Courtauld. He also built the attractive mock-Tudor houses in the village.

# HALSTEAD

The name 'Halstead' comes from the Anglo-Saxon for *healthy place*. Like Braintree and Coggeshall, Halstead was an important weaving centre. **Townsford Mill** is certainly the most picturesque reminder of Halstead's industrial heritage. Built in the 1700s, it remains one of the most handsome buildings in a town with a number of historic buildings. This white, weatherboarded three-storey mill across the River Colne at the Causeway was once a landmark site for the Courtauld empire, producing both the famous funerary crepe and rayon. Today the Mill is an antiques centre, one of the largest in Essex, with thousands of items of furniture, porcelain, collectibles, stamps, coins, books, dolls, postcards, costume, paintings, glass and ceramics, old lace and clocks.

There are a number of historic buildings in the shopping centre of Halstead, which is part of a designated conservation area. Markets are held every Tuesday, Friday and Saturday, and each year in March the town hosts the Grand Prix of Essex - an international cycle race through Halstead and the surrounding area. The prestigious Dynes Hall International Horse Trials are held nearby.

Though it may now seem somewhat improbable, Halstead's most famous product was once mechanical elephants. Life-sized and weighing half a ton, they were built by one W Hunwicks. Each one consisted of 9,000 parts and could carry a load of eight adults and four children at speeds of up to 12 miles per hour. Rather less unusual is the Tortoise

## HEAD STREET GALLERY

1 Head Street, Halstead, Essex CO9 2AT
Tel: 01787 472705
e-mail: information@headstreetgallery.co.uk

**Head Street Gallery** is relaxed, affordable and accessible, with friendly staff offering a wide range of fine art and hand crafted gifts to suit all tastes and budgets.

Take time to browse around the 3 gallery rooms and enjoy the quality and variety of works on offer. Combining painting and sculpture with

ceramics, glass, jewellery, toys, hand made gifts and cards, a wide selection of work is always on display. Exhibitions of paintings change every 8 weeks throughout the year.

With a coffee bar serving freshly ground coffee and other beverages, why not browse through the gallery's own art library or take advantage of the gift wrapping service?

Head Street Gallery is on the A131 just beyond the top of Halstead High Street, directly opposite St Andrews Church. Open daily, excluding Wednesdays, Sundays and Bank Holidays, 9am-5.30pm.

## RARE VIEW B&B AND SELF-CATERING

Sharlowes Farm, Gosfield, Halstead, Essex CO9 1PZ
Tel: 01787 474696
website: www.countryholidays.co.uk ref 16350, 16351 and 17143

With full facilities for guests with disabilities, **Rare View B&B and Self-catering** cottages offer three excellent properties for that perfect get-away-from-it-all break.

Originally calf-rearing barns, The Bullock Lodge, The Calf Lodge and The Cottage have been tastefully and sensitively converted to provide marvellous holiday accommodation in a peaceful setting on rolling farmland. The farm, which is listed in the Domesday Book, commands 36 acres of unspoilt land that guests are welcome to roam, and is just half a mile from Gosfield's village shops and pubs.

Nearby attractions include a golf course and lake for fishing or water-skiing. Within an hour's drive from Colchester and Cambridge, the charming villages of Lavenham, Clare, Kersey and Long Melford are also within easy reach, and Stansted is just 35 minutes away. The Bullock and Calf lodges sleep up to six, while the Cottage sleeps 2 – 4. All are beautifully decorated and furnished to provide every comfort.

Foundry Company, remembered for its warm 'tortoise stoves'.

forced King John to accept the Magna Carta. Amongst those entertained at the castle were Henry VII and Elizabeth I.

# AROUND HALSTEAD

### CASTLE HEDINGHAM

**3 miles NW of Halstead off the B1058**

This town is named for its Norman **Castle**, which dominates the landscape. One of England's strongest fortresses in the 11th century, even now it is impossible not to sense its power and strength. The impressive stone keep is one of the tallest in Europe, with four floors and rising over 100 feet, with 12-ft thick walls. The banqueting hall and minstrels' gallery can still be seen. It was owned by the Earls of Oxford, the powerful de Veres family, one of whom was among the barons who

*Castle Hedingham*

The village itself is a maze of narrow streets radiating from Falcon Square, named after the half-timbered Falcon Inn. Attractive buildings include many Georgian and 15th century houses comfortably vying for space, and the **Church of St Nicholas**, built by the de Veres, which avoided Victorian 'restoration' and is virtually completely Norman, with grand masonry and interestingly carved choir seats. There is a working pottery in St James' Street.

At the **Colne Valley Railway and Museum**, a mile of the Colne Valley and Halstead line between Castle Hedingham and Great Yeldham has been restored and now runs steam trains operated by enthusiasts. These lovingly restored Victorian railway buildings feature a collection of vintage engines and carriages; short steam train trips are available. **Colne Valley Farm Park**, set in 30 acres of traditional river meadows, is open from April to September.

The B1058 towards Sudbury, then left through Gestingthorpe and the Belchamps, makes for a pleasant excursion.

## SIBLE HEDINGHAM

**3 miles NW of Halstead off the A1017**

Mentioned in the *Domesday Book* as the largest parish in England, Sible Hedingham was the birthplace of Sir John Hawkwood, one of the 14th century's most famous soldiers of fortune. He led a band of mercenaries to Italy, where he was paid to defend Florence and where he also died. There is a monument to him in the village church, decorated with hawks and various other beasts.

Swan Street is the main artery of this charming village, boasting several delightful establishments devoted to providing visitors and natives of the town with places to shop, dine, enjoy a quiet drink and even stay for the night.

## GESTINGTHORP

**5 miles N of Halstead off the A131**

The Church of **St Mary the Virgin** in Gestingthorp is distinctive in many respects. Witness to centuries of Christian worship, the *Domesday Book* of 1086 tells that 'Ghestingetorp' was held by Ledmer the priest before 1066. The oldest part extant of the existing building is the blocked-up lancet window in the north wall of the chancel, which dates back to the 1200s. Apart from this, most of the chancel, nave and south aisle dates from the 14th century. The tower, constructed in about 1500, is 66 feet high. Of the six bells hung in the tower, four were cast in 1658-9 by Miles Gray, a Colchester bellfounder. The 16th century fifth and sixth bells were cast in Bury St Edmunds, and recast in 1901. The west door, set in a stepped brick arch, is the original. The unusual tracery in the East window consists of arches placed atop the apexes of the arches beneath them. The late 15th century/early 16th century nave roof is of the double hammer-beam type, and one of the finest in Essex. The font is late 14th century. One of the church's handsome memorials commemorates Captain L E G Oates, who died in an attempt to save the lives of his companions on an ill-fated expedition to the Antarctic in 1912.

# THE NORTH ESSEX COAST

## CLACTON-ON-SEA

**16 miles SE of Colchester on the A133**

Clacton is a traditional sun-and-sand family resort with a south-facing, long sandy beach, lovely gardens on the seafront and a wide variety of shops and places to explore. It also boasts a wide variety of special events and entertain-ments taking place throughout the year.

Settled by hunters during the Stone Age - which is borne witness to by the wealth of flint implements and the fossilised bones of the cave lion, straight-tusked elephant and wild ox unearthed on the Clacton foreshore and at Lion Point - the town grew over the centuries from a small village into a prosperous seaside resort in the 1800s, when the craze for the health benefits of coastal air and bathing was at its peak. The Pier was constructed in 1871; at first paddle steamers provided the only mode of transport to the resort, the railway arriving in 1882. **The Pier** was widened from 30 to over 300 foot in the 1930s. On the pier, apart from the marvellous traditional sideshows, big wheel, restaurants and fairground rides, there is the fascinating **Seaquarium and Reptile Safari**.

Amusement centres include the arcades and **Clacton Pavilion**. The two theatres, Princes Theatre and West Cliff, are open all year. Clacton Pavilion boasts a range of attractions, including crazy golf, dodgems and a rock & roll Fun House. The **Clifftop Public Gardens** also repay a visit.

**Great Clacton** is the oldest part of town, comprising an attractive grouping of shops, pubs and restaurants within the shadow of the 12th century parish church.

A walk round the town rewards the visitor with some very handsome sights. There are three Martello Towers along this bit of the Essex coast. Just south of the town, **Jaywick Sands** is the ideal spot for a picnic by the sea, boasting one

*Clacton-on-Sea*

of the finest natural sandy beaches in the county.

## LITTLE CLACTON

### 3 miles NW of Clacton off the A133

Though it shares its name with its near neighbour, this is a town apart. Quiet and secluded, multiple-winner of the Best Kept Village award, Little Clacton features a lovely **Jubilee Oak**, planted to celebrate Victoria's 50th year on the throne.

The fine church of **St James** has been described as one of the most beautiful medieval churches in Essex, and sits at the heart of the village

**Oakwood Crafts Resource Centre** in Little Clacton provides an environment for people with learning disabilities to learn and develop work skills, motivation, responsibility, team spirit, self-esteem and confidence through horticulture, woodwork, ceramics, crafts and catering. Set in three acres of land, it opened in 1975 and, as a horticultural centre, sells a wide range of bedding plants, shrubs and hanging baskets seasonally, along with a selection of wooden garden implements, furnishings and other items, and ceramics. Teas and coffees are available.

## WEELEY

### 5 miles NW of Clacton off the A133

**St Andrew's** is the handsome parish church just south of the centre of this picturesque village. There is a lovely tree-lined path that passes Weeleyhall Wood and Weeley Lodge, with its beautifully kept gardens. Here visitors will also pass a navigational beacon that forms part of Aircraft Flight Operations for both civil and military flights.

A mile south, off the B1411, Weeley Heath is a small and attractive community boasting a lovely village green and stunning surrounding countryside.

## TENDRING

### 7 miles NW of Clacton off the A133

This village that gives its name to both the peninsula and the district council contains the handsome church of **St Edmund** with its elegant spire which can be seen for miles around. The church is dedicated to the last King of independent East Anglia, martyred by the Danes in the 9th century.

## BEAUMONT-CUM-MOZE

### 7 miles NW of Clacton off the B114

This small village once had a quay

originally constructed for loading and unloading the vessels plying the Walton backwaters. The disused **Trading Quay** was rebuilt in 1832 using stone from the old London Bridge. The 11th century parish church of **St Leonard** contains the grave of Viscount Byng of Vimy, one-time Governor General of Canada.

## HOLLAND-ON-SEA

### 1½ miles NE of Clacton off the B1032

This attractive community is home to **Holland Haven Country Park**, 100 acres of open space near the seashore, ideal for watching the marine birds and other wildlife of the region. Throughout the area there are a number of attractive walks which take full advantage of the varied coastal scenery.

## FRINTON-ON-SEA

### 3 miles NE of Clacton off the B1032

Once a quiet fishing village, this town was developed as a select resort by Sir Richard Cooper, and expanded in the 1880s to the genteel family resort it is today. Situated on a long stretch of sandy beach, Frinton remains peaceful and unspoilt. The tree-lined residential avenues sweep elegantly down to the Esplanade and extensive clifftop greensward. Along its main shopping street in **Connaught Avenue**, the 'Bond Street' of the East Coast, shopkeepers maintain a tradition of friendly and courteous service. Summer theatre and other open-air events take place throughout the season, and there are also some excellent tennis and golf clubs in the town. The grace and elegance of this sophisticated resort is evidenced all round, as are hints of its distinguished past: Victorian beach huts

*Frinton-on-Sea*

still dot the extensive beach.

The area south of **Frinton Gates** has a unique local character, being laid out with detached houses set along broad tree-lined avenues.

The **Church of Old St Mary** in the town contains some panels of stained glass in the East window designed by the Pre-Raphaelite artist Burne Jones.

A good example of 20th century English vernacular architecture is **The Homestead** at the corner of Second Avenue and Holland Road, built in 1905 by C F Voysey.

*Walton-on-the-Naze*

## KIRBY-LE-SOKEN

**5 miles NE of Clacton off the B1034**

There is a footpath in this attractive village which begins to the west of the 14th century Ship Inn and affords views of the backwaters of Hamford Water, with views of Horsey and Hedge End Islands in the middle distance.

## WALTON-ON-THE-NAZE

**8 miles NE of Clacton on the B1034**

Walton is all the fun of the fair. It is a traditional, singular and cheerful resort which focuses on the pier and all its attractions, including a ten-pin bowling alley. The gardens at the seafront are colourful and the beach has good sand. **The Backwaters** to the rear of Walton are made up of a series of small harbours and saltings, which lead into Harwich harbour. Walton has an outstanding sandy beach. The town's seafront was developed in 1825 and provides a fine insight into the character of an early Victorian seaside resort. The charming narrow streets of the town contain

numerous shops, restaurants and pubs overlooking the second longest pier in the country. **Marine Parade**, originally called The Crescent, was built in 1832. **The Pier**, first built in 1830, was originally constructed of wood and measured 330 feet long. It was extended to its present length of 2,610 feet in 1898, at the same time as the electric train service began.

The wind-blown expanse of **The Naze** just north of Walton is an extensive coastal recreation and picnic area, pleasant for walking, especially out of season when the visitor is likely to have all 150 acres virtually to him- or herself, with great views out over the water. The shape of the Naze is constantly changing, eroded by wind, water and tide.

The year 1796 saw the demise of the medieval church, and somewhere beyond the 800-foot pier lies medieval Walton. The sandstone cliffs are internationally important for their shell fossil deposits. Inhabitants have been enjoying the bracing sea air at Walton since before Neolithic times: flint-shaping instruments have been found here, and the fossil teeth and the ears of sharks and whales have been discovered in the Naze's red crag cliffs. The **Naze Tower** is brickbuilt and octagonal in shape, originally built as a beacon in 1720 to warn seamen of the West Rocks off shore. A nature trail has been created nearby, and the Essex Skipper butterfly and Emperor moth can be seen here.

The **Old Lifeboat House Museum** at East Terrace, in a building over 100 years old, houses an interpretive museum of local history and development, rural and maritime, covering Walton, Frinton and the Sokens.

### BRIGHTLINGSEA

**7 miles W of Clacton on the B1029**

Brightlingsea enjoys a long tradition of shipbuilding and seafaring. In 1347, 51 men and five ships were sent to the siege of Calais. Among the crew members of Sir Francis Drake's fleet which vanquished the Spanish Armada was one 'William of Brightlingsea'. Brightlingsea

has the distinction of being the only limb of the Cinque Ports outside Kent and Sussex.

The 13th century **Jacobes Hall** in the town centre is one of the oldest occupied buildings in Essex. It is timber-framed with an undulating tile roof and an external staircase. Used as a meeting hall during the reign of Henry III, its name originates from its first owner, Edmund, Vicar of Brightlingsea, who was known locally as Jacob le Clerk.

**All Saints Church**, which occupies the highest point of the town on a hill about a mile from the centre, is mainly 13th century. Here are to be found some Roman brickwork and a frieze of ceramic tiles commemorating local residents whose lives were lost at sea. Its 97-foot tower can be seen from 17 miles out to sea. A light was once placed in the tower to guide the town's fishermen home

The **Town Hard** is where you can see

### PAXTON DENE

Strangers Corner, Church Road,
Brightlingsea, Essex  CO7 0QT
Tel/Fax: 01206 304560
Fax: 01206 304809

**Paxton Dene** offers attractive, spacious cottage-style accommodation. It is set in half an acre of well maintained gardens, in this historic Cinque Port town, on the B1029 approach road to Brightlingsea just half a mile from the village church of All Saints. An

excellent base for touring, with private parking facilities on site, this beautiful and comfortable place has two  tastefully decorated and furnished en suite guest bedrooms, (double/twin and family room), with colour TV, hospitality tray, hair dryer and radio alarm clock. A hearty and delicious breakfast is efficiently served in the charming dining room between 7.30 and 9.00am in a relaxed and friendly atmosphere. 4 Diamonds ETC, this is a non smoking establishment.

all the waterfront comings and goings, including the activities of the Colne Smack Preservation Society, which maintains a seagoing link with the past.

**Brightlingsea Museum** in Duke Street offers an insight into the lives, customs and traditions of the area, housing a collection of exhibits relating to the town's maritime connections and the oyster industry.

There are plenty of superb walks along Brightlingsea Creek and the River Colne, which offer a chance to watch the birdlife on the saltings and the plethora of boats on the water. Today the town is a haven for the yachting fraternity and is the home of national and international sailing championships, with one of the best stretches of sailing on the East Coast. Day and half-day sailing and canoeing sessions are held at the **Brightlingsea Outdoor Education Centre**.

## GREAT BENTLEY
### 4 miles N of Brightlingsea off the A133

Reputed to have the largest village green in England, this lovely village has a number of shops, a pub with a restaurant, a beautiful church and a chapel.

## ELMSTEAD MARKET
### 6 miles N of Brightlingsea off the A120

The Church of **St Anne and St Lawrence** to the north of this village has a rare carved oak, recumbent effigy of a knight in armour.

Elmstead Market is perhaps best known as the location of **Beth Chatto Gardens**, at White Barn House, designed and still presided over by the famous gardener herself. Here visitors will find five acres of landscaped gardens including extensive water gardens, shady walks and a Mediterranean-style garden where aromatic drought-loving plants

thrive. The adjoining nursery contains a wide variety of plants for sale. Close by is the **Rolts Nursery Butterfly Farm**.

## THORRINGTON
### 3 miles NW of Brightlingsea off the AB1027

**Thorrington Tide Mill**, built in the early 19th century, is the only remaining Tide Mill in Essex, and one of very few left in East Anglia. It has been fully restored, and although no longer in use, the Wheel can be run for guided groups. There is a public footpath which runs along the creek here.

**China Maroc Bonsai** is a specialist nursery, part of which is devoted to a peaceful Japanese garden with a waterfall and pool, where one can enjoy the tranquil atmosphere and the many fascinating outdoor bonsai. Crossing the bridge over the pool, one enters a tropical tunnel containing hundreds of indoor bonsai, many of which are imported from the hotter regions of the world, as well as bonsai and seedlings grown and cultivated on the premises.

## POINT CLEAR
### 2 miles SE of Brightlingsea off the B1027

The **East Essex Aviation Society & Museum**, located in the Martello Tower at Point Clear, not only retains its original flooring and roof, but today contains interesting displays of wartime aviation, military and naval photographs, uniforms and other memorabilia with local and US Air Force connections. There are artefacts on show from the crash sites of wartime aircraft in the Tendring area, including the engine and fuselage section of a recovered P51D Mustang fighter. The museum also explores civil and military history from both World Wars. There are very good views from the tower over the Colne Estuary and Brightlingsea.

## St Osyth

**3 miles SE of Brightlingsea off the B1027**

This pretty little village has a fascinating history and centres around its Norman church and the ancient ruins of **St Osyth Priory**, founded in the 12th century. The village and Priory were named by Augustinian Canons after St Osytha, martyred daughter of Frithenwald, first Christian King of the East Angles, who was beheaded by Diceian pirates AD 653. Little of the original Priory remains, except for the magnificent late 15th century flint gatehouse, complete with battlements.

The village is centred on a crossroads and contains an attractive group of shops and restaurants. The Church of **St Peter and St Paul** in the village centre has unusual internal red brick piers and

arches. The nearby creek has a small boatyard.

## Mersea Island

**2 miles SW of Brightlingsea off the B1025**

Much of this island is a **National Nature Reserve**, home to its teeming shorelife. The island is linked to the mainland by a narrow causeway which is covered over at high tide. The towns of both East and West Mersea have excellent facilities for sailing enthusiasts. East Mersea is also a haven for birdwatchers.

**Cudmore Grove Country Park** on Bromans Lane, East Mersea, boasts fine views across the Colne and Blackwater estuaries. Grassland adjoining a sandy beach, it's an ideal spot for shore walks and picnics. There's also a pathway on the sea wall and a birdwatching hide.

### Mersea Island Vineyard and Accommodation

Rewsalls Lane, East Mersea, Colchester, Essex  CO5 8SX
Tel: 01206 385900
Fax: 01206 383600
e-mail: accommodation@merseawine.com
website: www.merseawine.com

A unique opportunity to stay on a working vineyard awaits guests at **Mersea Island Vineyard and Accommodation**. With stunning views across the estuaries of the Rivers Blackwater and Colne, in the newly constructed house there are three ground-floor en suite guest bedrooms (two doubles and a twin) and two charming self-catering cottages. These are available for weekly lets or short breaks out of season.

The island is tranquil and lovely, with excellent walks and sailing available. The vineyard is 20 years old, and produces a range of white wines from sparkling varieties to dessert wines.

The Vineyard has a retail shop where guests can sample and purchase its produce. Winners of East Anglian Wine of the Year Award and Gold and Silver at the UK Vineyard Association awards, these splendid wines are well worth sampling. Tours can be arranged by appointment, and there is an excellent mail-order service available. The on-site shop provides a gift-packaging service.

# HARWICH

Harwich's name probably originates from the time of King Alfred, when 'hare' meant army, and 'wic' a camp. This attractive old town was built in the 13th century by the Earls of Norfolk to exploit its strategic position on the Stour and Orwell estuary; the town has an important and fascinating maritime history, the legacy of which continues into the present.

During the 14th and 15th century French campaigns, Harwich was an important naval base. The famous Elizabethan seafarers Hawkins, Frobisher and Drake sailed from Harwich on various expeditions; in 1561 Queen Elizabeth I visited the town, describing it 'a pretty place and want[ing] for nothing'. Christopher Newport, leader of the *Goodspeed* expedition which founded Jamestown, Virginia, in 1607, and Christopher Jones, master of the Pilgrim ship *The Mayflower*, lived in Harwich (the latter just off the quay in King's Head Street), as did Jones' kinsman John Alden, who sailed to America in 1620. The famous diarist Samuel Pepys was MP for the town in the 1660s, thus it was also during this time headquarters for the King's Navy. Charles II took the first pleasure cruise from Harwich's shores. Other notable visitors included Lord Nelson and Lady Hamilton, who are reputed to have stayed at The Three Cups in Church Street.

Harwich remains popular as a vantage point for watching incoming and outgoing shipping in the harbour and across the waters to Felixstowe. Nowadays, lightships, buoys and miles of strong chain are stored along the front, and passengers arriving on North Sea ferries at Harwich International Port see the 90-foot high, six-sided **High Lighthouse** as the first landmark. Now

*High Lighthouse*

housing the **National Vintage Wireless and Television Museum**, it was built in 1818 along with the **Low Lighthouse**. When the two lighthouses were in line they could indicate a safe shipping channel into the harbour. Each had replaced earlier wooden structures, and were themselves replaced by cast iron structures (both of which still stand on the front in nearby Dovercourt) in 1863 when the shifting sandbanks altered the channel. Shipping now relies on light buoys to find its way. The Low lighthouse is now the town's **Maritime Museum**, with specialist displays on the Royal Navy and commercial shipping.

Two other worthwhile museums in the town are the **Lifeboat Museum** off Wellington Road, which contains the last Clacton offshore 34-foot lifeboat and a history of the lifeboat service in Harwich, and the **Ha'penny Pier Visitor**

Centre on the Quay, with information on everything in Harwich and a small heritage exhibition.

The **Treadwell Crane** now stands on Harwich Green, but for over 250 years it was sited in the Naval Shipyard. It is worked by two people walking in two 16-foot diameter wheels, and is the only known British example of its kind. Amazingly, it was operational up until the 1920s. Another fascinating piece of the town's history is the **Electric Palace Cinema**, built in 1911 and now the oldest unaltered purpose-built cinema in Britain. It was restored by a trust and re-opened in 1981.

The importance of Harwich's port during the 19th century is confirmed by **The Redoubt**, a huge grey fort built between 1808 and 1810. Its design is an enlarged version of the Martello towers which dotted the English coast, awaiting a Napoleonic invasion that never came (some of these towers, of course, still exist). Today the Harwich Society has largely restored it and opened it as a small museum.

The old town also contains many ancient buildings, including the **Guildhall**, which was rebuilt in 1769 and is located in Church Street. The Council chamber, Mayor's Parlour and other rooms may be viewed. The former gaol contains unique graffiti of ships, probably carved by prisoners, and is well worth putting aside a morning to explore (by appointment only).

# AROUND HARWICH

## DOVERCOURT
### 1 mile S of Harwich off the A120

This residential and holiday suburb of Harwich has Market Day on Fridays. With its attractive cliffs and beach, it

also boasts the **Iron Lighthouse** or 'Leading Lights' located just off lower Marine Parade. The town has been settled from prehistoric times, as attested to by the late Bronze Age axe-heads found here (now in Colchester Museum). The Romans found the town a useful source of the stone 'Septaria', taken from the cliffs and used in building. The town that visitors see today developed primarily in Victorian times as a fashionable resort.

## MISTLEY
### 7 miles W of Harwich off the B1352

Here at the gateway to Constable Country, local 18th century landowner and MP Richard Rigby had grand designs to develop Mistley into a fashionable spa to rival Harrogate and Bath, adopting the swan as its symbol. Sadly, all that remains of Rigby's ambitious scheme is the Swan Fountain, a small number of attractive Georgian houses and **Mistley Towers**, the remains of a church (otherwise demolished in 1870) designed by the flamboyant architect Robert Adams. From the waterfront, noted for its colony of swans, there are very pleasant views across the estuary to Suffolk.

**Mistley Quay Workshops** in the High Street feature a pottery workshop, lute/cello maker, harpsichord maker, wood worker, bookbinder, and stained-glass window maker and restorer. There is also a tea-shop on the premises (the key to Mistley Towers can be obtained from the Workshops).

**Mistley Place Park Environmental & Animal Rescue Centre** is 25 acres of parkland affording country walks, wildlife habitats, lake, farm animals and great views across the Stour Estuary. Over 2,000 rescued animals including rabbits, Vietnamese pigs and horses roam free.

## Manningtree

**9 miles W of Harwich off the B1352**

**The Walls**, on the approach to Manningtree along the B1352, offer unrivalled views of the Stour estuary and the Suffolk coast, and the swans for which the area is famous. Lying on the River Stour amid beautiful rolling countryside, the scene has oft been depicted by artists over the centuries.

Back in Tudor times, Manningtree was the centre of the cloth trade, and later a port filled with barges carrying their various cargoes along the coast to London. Water still dominates today and the town is a centre of leisure sailing.

Manningtree has been a market town since 1238, and is still a busy shopping centre. It is the smallest town in Britain, and a stroll through the streets reveals the diversity of its past. There are still traditional (and mainly Georgian) restaurants, pubs and shops, as well as handcraft and specialist outlets. The views over the river are well known to birdspotters, sailors and ramblers. The town has an intriguing past - as a river crossing, market, smugglers' haven and home of Matthew Hopkins, the reviled and self-styled Witchfinder General who struck terror into the local community during the 17th century. Some of his victims were hanged on Manningtree's small village green.

It is believed that the reference in Shakespeare's *Henry IV* to Falstaff as 'that roasted Manningtree ox' relates to the practice of roasting an entire ox, as was known at that time to be done at the town's annual fair.

**Manningtree Museum** in the High Street opened in the late 1980s and mounts two exhibitions a year, together

## North House Gallery

The Walls, Manningtree, Essex CO11 1AS
Tel: 01206 392717 Fax: 01206 390026
e-mail: mail@northhousegallery.co.uk
website: www.northhousegallery.co.uk

Featuring outstanding contemporary art by 20th- and 21st-century artists, **North House Gallery** is set in the ground floor of a Georgian double-fronted brick house overlooking the estuary of the River Stour. Owner Penny Hughes-Stanton, whose father Blair was an acclaimed artist in wood-engraving, linocut, drawing and painting, returned after many years in London to her native Manningtree and established the gallery in her father's former studio. Here she showcases an eclectic mix of work by artists of East Anglian, national and international renown.

The gallery tends to focus on solo exhibitions but with five separate spaces even in the twice-yearly mixed themed shows the work of each individual artist can be displayed to best effect. To the rear, Penny's letterpress workshop features cabinets filled with traditional lead type, racks of letterpress furniture and four presses of different vintages. Open three Saturdays each month and by prior arrangement.

with permanent photographs and pieces relating to the heritage of Manningtree, Lawford, Mistley and the district.

## SAFFRON WALDEN

Named after the Saffron crocus - grown in the area to make dyestuffs and fulfil a variety of other uses in the Middle Ages - Saffron Walden has retained much of its original street plan, as well as hundreds of fine old buildings, many of which are timbered and have overhanging upper floors and decorative plastering (also known as pargetting). Gog and Magog (or, in some versions, folk-hero Tom Hickathrift and the Wisbech Giant) battle forever in plaster on the gable of the **Old Sun Inn**, where, legend has it, Oliver Cromwell and General Fairfax both lodged during the Civil War.

A typical market town, Saffron Walden's centrepiece is its magnificent church. At the **Saffron Walden Museum**, as well as the gloves worn by Mary Queen of Scots on the day she died is a piece of human skin which once coated the church door at Hadstock. The museum first opened to the public at its present location in 1835, and was founded 'to gratify the inclination of all who value natural history'. It remains faithful to this credo, while widening the museum's scope in the ensuing years. The museum has won numerous awards, including joint winner of the Museum of the Year Award for best museum of Industrial or Social History in 1997. At this friendly, family-sized museum visitors can try their hand at corn grinding with a Romano-British quern, see how a medieval timber house would have been built, admire the displays of

### KIM'S COFFEE HOUSE

5 Hill Street, Saffron Walden, Essex CB10 1EH
Tel: 01799 513553
e-mail: info@kimscoffeehouse.co.uk
website: www.kimscoffeehouse.co.uk

Relaxed and welcoming, **Kim's Coffee House** in the centre of Saffron Walden – overlooking Jubilee Gardens and close to the main shopping area – is an ideal place to visit for excellent food and hot or cold drinks ( including wines and beers). Owners Kim and Paul are committed to providing their customers with the freshest food using the best possible ingredients.

They serve over 15 varieties of traditional leaf tea ( including Rose Petal, Jasmine, Earl Grey, Lapsang Souchong and decaffeinated ) as well as the usual cappuccinos, lattes, espressos, mochas and regular 'guest' coffees served in cafetieres. Wherever possible they use local suppliers and the extensive menu includes home-made soup, freshly made home-baked scones, home-made tarts, plus a huge choice of salads, sandwiches, toasties, bagels and cakes. During the summer months, seating is increased by an additional five tables overlooking Jubilee Gardens. Open 9 – 5.30 six days a week.

Native American and West African embroidery, and come face to face with Wallace the Lion, the museum's faithful guardian. Over two floors, exhibits focus on town and country (with a wealth of wooden ploughs and other agricultural artefacts), furniture and woodwork, costumes, ancient Egyptian and Roman artefacts, geology exhibits, and ceramics and glass. In the 'ages of man' gallery, the history of northwest Essex is traced from the Ice Age to the Middle Ages. The ruins of historic Walden Castle are also on-site.

On the local **Common**, once known as Castle Green, is the largest surviving Turf Maze in England. Only eight ancient turf mazes survive in England: though there were many more in the Middle Ages, if they are not looked after they soon become overgrown and are lost. This one is believed to be some 800 years old.

Though many miles from the sea, it

*River Cam, Saffron Walden*

## SCEPTRED ISLE FOOD COMPANY

Lime Tree Court, off King Street, Saffron Walden, Essex  CB10 1HG  Tel: 01799 526288

Every market town should have a food emporium as fabulous as this family-run business! Combining the best of modern retailing with an old-fashioned approach to service, this excellent shop is a foodie's heaven where customers are encouraged to sample the fresh foods in store before purchasing.

**Sceptred Isle Food Company** stocks a wide range of delicious foods, from local organic bread and vegetables to fantastic British cheeses from Neal's Yard Dairy in London, hard-to-obtain Spanish delicacies and superb Italian produce from Carluccio's. Handmade organic cakes and biscuits are available alongside ranges of exquisite chocolates from exclusive British suppliers.

Fresh food is also made daily in store, all to take out. Savoury and sweet tarts are the house speciality and various tasty salads are also available for lunch. Fresh hot soup is made every day in season too. Perfect for an impromptu picnic or for consumption whilst strolling round town! This shop simply has to be on everyone's "must visit" list in this beautiful part of East Anglia.

Open: Monday to Saturday 9 a.m. – 5 p.m.; Fridays until 6.30 p.m.

## SAFFRON WALDEN ANTIQUES CENTRE

1 Market Row, Saffron Walden, Essex CB10 1HA
Tel: 01799 524534
website: www.saffronwaldenantiquescentre.co.uk

Antiques, collectibles and bygones can be found at the marvellous **Saffron Walden Antiques Centre** in the heart of the town. With over 40 dealers under one roof, set on two floors (basement and ground-floor level) customers can choose from a range of wares including everything from fine period furniture, mirrors, clocks, pictures and brassware to jewellery, silver, porcelain, glass, dolls, toys, steam models, railwayana and sporting memorabilia, there's something for every taste and budget. Open seven days a week.

was here that Henry Winstanley - inventor, engineer and engraver, and designer of the first Eddystone Lighthouse at Plymouth - was born in 1644. He is said to have held 'lighthouse trials' with a wooden lantern in the lavishly decorated 15th to 16th century church. The Lighthouse, and Winstanley with it, were swept away in a fierce storm in 1703.

The town was also famous for its resident Cockatrice, which was reputed to have hatched from a cock's egg by a toad or serpent and could, it was said, kill its victims with a glance. The Cockatrice was blamed for any inexplicable disaster in the town. Like Perseus and Medusa the Gorgon, a Cockatrice could be destroyed by making it see its own reflection, thereby turning it to stone. The Saffron Walden Cockatrice's slayer was said to be a knight in a coat of *'cristal glass'*.

To the north of the town are the **Bridge End Gardens**, a wonderfully restored example of early Victorian gardens, complete with the unique Hedge Maze, which is open only by appointment (which can be made at the TIC). A viewing platform was reinstated in 2000 to enhance visitors' enjoyment of these lovely gardens.

Next to the gardens is the **Fry Public Art Gallery**, with a unique collection of work by 20th century artists and designers

who lived in and around Saffron Walden, such as Edward Bawden, Michael Rothenstein, Eric Ravilious, John Aldridge and Sheila Robinson. It also exhibits work by contemporary artists working in Essex today, demonstrating the area's continuing artistic tradition. The gallery was purpose-designed and opened in 1856 to house the collection of Francis Gibson. The gallery also houses the Lewis George Fry RBA, RWA (1860-1933) Collection, which is exhibited each summer, along with works by Robert Fry (1866-1934) and Anthony Fry.

Close to Bridge End is the **Anglo-American War Memorial** dedicated by Field Marshal the Viscount Montgomery of Alamein in 1953 to the memory of all the American flyers of the 65th Fighter Wing who lost their lives in the Second World War.

**Audley End House** was, at one time, home of the first Earl of Suffolk, and at one time home of Charles II. The original early 17th century house, with its two large courtyards, had a magnificence claimed to match that of Hampton Court. Remodelled in the 18th century by Robert Adam, unfortunately the subsequent earls lacked their forebears' financial acumen, and much of the house was demolished as it fell into disrepair. Nevertheless it remains today one of England's most impressive

*Audley End House*

original embroidered drapes. The silver, the Doll's House, the Jacobean Screen and Robert Adam's painted Drawing Room are just among the many sights to marvel at. The natural history collection features more than 1,000 stuffed animals and birds. To complement this, there are paintings by Holbein, Lely and Canaletto. Fascinating introductory talks help visitors get the most from any visit to this, one of the most magnificent houses in England. This jewel also has a kitchen garden and grounds landscaped by Capability Brown, including the 'Temple of Concord' which Brown dedicated to George III. There is a lovely parterre, lake

Jacobean mansions; its distinguished stone façade set off perfectly by Capability Brown's lake. The remaining state rooms retain their palatial magnificence and the exquisite state bed in the Neville Room is hung with the

## THE CHAFF HOUSE

Ash Grove Barns, Littlebury Green,
Saffron Walden, Essex CB11 4XB
Tel: 01763 836278
e-mail: dianaduke@btopenworld.com

For a true taste of traditional country farmhouse living, **The Chaff House** offers guests a beautifully-appointed bedroom with exposed beamwork and an enormous bed. Light, bright

and airy, it is tastefully and comfortably furnished. In

addition there are two more guest bedrooms in a separate building which includes a kitchen and can therefore also be used for self-catering accommodation. Set in a courtyard, there is patio seating and a lovely selection of plants in pots and tubs, making for a charming outdoor space.

Owner Diana Duke lives next door, and takes pride in providing her guests with the very best – everything from the linen and towels to the excellent food is of the very highest quality. This warm and comfortable, sympathetically restored barn conversion is set in 900 acres of beautiful countryside. Convenient for the M11, Stansted, Cambridge and other sights and attractions, it makes an excellent touring base. Dinner available by prior arrangement Monday to Friday.

## REDGATES FARMHOUSE

Redgates Lane, Sewards End, Saffron Walden,
Essex  CB10 2LP
Tel: 01799 516166

Set in pristine lawns amid several acres of countryside,
**Redgates Farmhouse** offers marvellous old-fashioned
hospitality. This charming traditional farmhouse has a
welcoming ambience all its own. The spacious and
comfortable guest bedrooms include one of the only family-
sized guest rooms in the area. All rooms command outstanding views across the open countryside.
Alison is that rarity – a Cordon Bleu-trained chef who can capably turn her hand to hearty meals as
well. Evening meals are available by arrangement. The grounds include a tennis court that guests are
welcome to enjoy. Children and pet dogs welcome.

and Pond Garden. Circular walks help
visitors make the most of all there is to
see. The organic kitchen garden was
recently opened to the public for the first
time in 250 years. The gardens are
managed by the Henry Doubleday
Research Association, who grow and sell
a wide range of organic produce in the
shop, which also features a restaurant.
The Audley End Miniature Railway
(separate admission charge) is 1.5 miles
long and takes visitors along Lord
Braybrooke's private 10¼ inch gauge
railway through the beautiful private
woods of the house.

Within the rolling parkland of the
grounds there are several elegant
outbuildings, some of which were
designed by Robert Adam. Among these
are an icehouse, a circular temple and a
Springwood Column.

## AROUND SAFFRON WALDEN

### RADWINTER
**4 miles E of Saffron Walden off the B1053**

Radwinter boasts a fine church, which
was largely renovated and rebuilt in the
19th century by architect Eden Nesfield
and has a fine 14th century porch. The
village also has cottages and almshouses
designed by Nesfield.

### HADSTOCK
**4 miles N of Saffron Walden off the B1052**

As well as claiming to have the oldest
church door in England, at the parish
**Church of St Botolph**, Hadstock also
has a macabre tale to tell. The church's
north door was once covered with a
piece of human skin, now to be seen in
Saffron Walden Museum. Local legend

## YARDLEYS

Orchard Pightle, Hadstock, Cambridge, Cambridgeshire
CB1 6PQ
Tel: 01223 891822
e-mail: enquiries@b-and-b-yardleys.co.uk
website: www.b-and-b-yardleys.co.uk

Superior accommodation awaits guests at **Yardleys**, in a
tastefully decorated and furnished modern house with three
comfortable, spacious and handsome guest bedrooms (one
double and two twins) with full facilities. Situated in a peaceful rural setting, it is close to Cambridge,
Duxford and the many sights and attractions of this part of Cambridgeshire. Breakfast includes delicious
home-made preserves; evening meals by arrangement. 4 Diamonds/Silver Award ETC.

says it is a 'Daneskin', from a Viking flayed alive.

Lining doors with animal leather was common in the Middle Ages, and many so-called 'Daneskins' are just that. However, the skins at Hadstock - and at Copford, in northeast Essex - are almost certainly human, the poor wretch at Hadstock undoubtedly having his hide nailed there as a warning to others. The door itself is Saxon, as are the 11th century carvings, windows and arches, rare survivors that predate the Norman Conquest.

**Linton Zoo** near the village is a privately owned collection of wild animals set in 10½ acres of gardens. There is a free car park, children's play area, picnic areas and a café on site.

## BARTLOW
### 5 miles NE of Saffron Walden off the B1052

**Bartlow Hills** are reputed to be the largest burial mounds in Europe dating from Roman times. Fifteen metres high, they date back to the 2nd century.

## HEMPSTEAD
### 5 miles E of Saffron Walden off the B1054

The highwayman, Dick Turpin, was born here in 1705. His parents kept the Bell Inn, later renamed the Rose and Crown and more recently known by the sobriquet 'Turpin's Tavern'. Gilt letters announce that *'It is the Landlord's great desire that no one stands before the fire'* over the wide hearth where logs still burn; pictures all around celebrate the infamy of the former innkeeper's son.

Inside the 14th to 15th century village church, an impressively life-like bust carved by Edward Marshall recalls the town's rather worthier son, William Harvey (1578-1657). Harvey was chief physician to Charles I and the discoverer of the circulation of blood, as recorded in his *De Motu Cordis* of 1628.

Like many other villages, Hempstead once boasted a village cockpit; its faint outline can still be traced, though the steep banks are now crowned with trees.

## WIDDINGTON
### 4 miles S of Saffron Walden off the B1383

Covering over 20 acres, **Mole Hall Wildlife Park** offers visitors the chance to come close to a range of wild and domesticated animals. With the private fully-moated 13th century manor house as a backdrop, the wide variety of animals in this excellent park include South American llamas, flamingos, Formosa Sika deer (which are extinct in the wild), chimpanzees, muntjac, Arctic fox, wallabies, red squirrels and much more. Mole Hall is also home to two species of North American otter: Short-clawed and North American. Domesticated animals such as guinea pigs, rabbits, goats, pigs and sheep can also be seen. The Butterfly Pavilion offers a tropical experience where brilliantly coloured butterflies flit about freely. Within the tropical pavilion you can also find lovebirds and small monkeys, along with a variety of snakes, spiders and insects (safe behind glass). The pools are home to goldfish, toads and terrapins.

Widdington is also home to **Priors Hall Barn**, one of the finest surviving medieval 'aisled' barns in all of southeast England, and owned by English Heritage.

## STANSTED MOUNTFITCHET
### 8 miles SW of Saffron Walden off the B1383

Though rather close to **Stansted Airport**, there are plenty of reasons to visit this village. Certainly pilots approaching the airport may be surprised at the sight of a **Norman Village**, complete with domestic animals and the reconstructed motte-and-bailey **Mountfitchet Castle**

# Stansted Mountfitchet

**Distance:** 3.1 miles (4.83 kilometres)

**Typical time:** 60 mins

**Height gain:** 15 metres

**Map:** Explorer 195

**Walk:** www.walkingworld.com
ID:1835

**Contributor:** Brian and Anne Sandland

## Access Information:

Stansted Mountfitchet is close to the M11, the A120 and Stansted Airport. To reach the car park from which the walk begins follow signs for Mountfitchet castle - or use the train; the station is adjacent to the car park.

## Description:

This walk starts from the car park serving the station and visitors to the castle. It takes in one of the main streets of Stansted Mountfitchet before emerging into field paths and continuing to Ugley Green (which certainly deserves a better name!) The return is on more field and farmland paths via Aubrey Buxton (which was once the pleasure park to Norman House). This delightful woodland section passes a number of small lakes before rejoining the outward route.

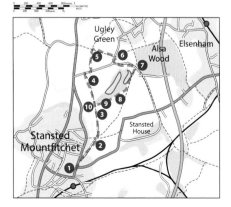

## Features:

Lake/Loch, Pub, Toilets, Play Area, Castle, Wildlife, Birds, Flowers, Great Views, Butterflies, Food Shop, Woodland

## Walk Directions:

**1** From the car park head right past the Queen's head (left). Take a left fork (signposted Quendon and Saffron Walden) then a right fork by the Dog and Duck and continue along Gall End. Take the path to the left of North End House.

**2** Continue following the left edge of a field. Bear right then go left through the hedge.

**3** Continue on the left of another field, climbing briefly to enter and follow the right edge of another field reaching a road. Turn right then at a signposted footpath turn left over a stile.

**4** Continue in the same general direction bearing right and left through a gate.

**5** Cross a track then bear one-third right across a field. Pass through a hedge at the far side (signpost) then cross the field ahead to reach a gate. Follow the path to the right of a thatched cottage then, using its drive, arrive at a road and turn right. Bear left at a junction then take a signposted footpath right.

**6** At the far side of the first field go through a gap then right and left through a metal hurdle barrier. Continue between a hedge left and a wire fence right, then cross a stile and continue ahead, ignoring a signposted footpath left and another right. Soon the path bears right and left to a narrow lane. Go right and left to reach the edge of Aubrey Buxton.

**7** Pass through the gate and follow the earth track, passing lakes on either side, ignoring turns off and bearing right, left and right again. Ignore a way out left into a field and turn right, (slightly downhill).

**8** Join another path and turn left past tall willows then clumps of bamboo (right). Cross a stream, climb slightly, then go left to leave the woodland through a wooden fence.

**9** Follow the left-hand edge of the field, left and right to a T-junction with another path.

**10** Turn left on this path (which is part of your outward route) and retrace your steps back to your car.

*Stanstead Airport*

Good Britain Guide, visitors can take a trip to the top of the siege tower and tiptoe into the baron's bed chamber while he sleeps!

Next door to the castle is **The House on the Hill Museum Adventure**, where there are three museums for the price of one. The Toy Museum is the largest of its kind in the world, and here children of every age are treated to a unique and nostalgic trip back to their childhood. There is every toy imaginable here, many of them now highly prized collectors' items. There is a shop selling new toys and a collectors' shop with many old toys and books to choose from. The Rock 'n' Roll, Film and Theatre Experience and the End-of-the-

(see panel below), standing just two miles from the end of the runway. The original castle was built after 1066 by the Duke of Boulogne, a cousin of the Conqueror. Siege weapons on show include two giant catapults. Voted Essex attraction of the year in 2002 by the

## MOUNTFITCHET CASTLE & NORMAN VILLAGE

Stansted, Essex CM24 8SP
Tel: 01279 813237  Fax: 01279 816391
e-mail: mountfitchetcastle1066@btinternet.com
website: www.gold.enta.net

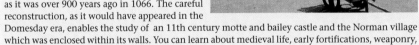

This historic site gives visitors a glimpse into life as it was over 900 years ago in 1066. The careful reconstruction, as it would have appeared in the Domesday era, enables the study of an 11th century motte and bailey castle and the Norman village which was enclosed within its walls. You can learn about medieval life, early fortifications, weaponry, the construction of dwellings and much more.

Many of the animals and birds to be found in the grounds are rescued and represent those which would have been kept for food by the Normans, such as fallow deer, sheep, goats, chickens and geese.

The Castle Shop carries a comprehensive range of gifts and souvenirs and is open March to November 10am-5pm daily, as is the Castle.

Also here you will find the House on the Hill Toy Museum Adventure. An impressive collection of toys, games and books can be enjoyed by children of all ages and the museum has been greatly improved by the addition of sound effects, animation and hands-on opportunities. Permanent displays of film, theatre and rock'n'roll memorabilia have been added in recent years, as has an exhibition of seaside end-of-the-pier amusements.

*Morris Dancers, Thaxted*

Thaxted has numerous attractively pargetted and timber-framed houses, and a magnificent **Guildhall**, built as a meeting-place for cutlers around 1390. The demise of the cutlery industry in this part of Essex in the 1500s led it to becoming the administrative centre of the town. Restored in Georgian times, it became the town's Grammar School, as well as remaining a centre of administration. Once more restored in 1975, the Parish council still holds its meetings here.

The town's famous **Tower Windmill** was built in 1804 by John Webb. In working order until 1907, it had fallen into disuse and disrepair but has now been returned to full working order. It contains a rural life museum, well worth a visit. Close to the windmill are the town's **Almshouses**, which continued to provide homes for the elderly even 250 years after they were built for that purpose.

pier Amusement machine displays also contribute to a grand day out here in Stansted Mountfichet.

**Stansted Windmill** is one of the best-preserved tower mills in the country. Dating back to 1787 and in use until 1910, most of the original machinery has survived. It is open on the first Sunday of each month from April to October; every Sunday in August, and on Bank Holiday Mondays.

### THAXTED

**7 miles SE of Saffron Walden on the B184**

This small country town has a recorded history that dates back to before the *Domesday Book*. Originally a Saxon settlement, it developed around a Roman road. The town's many beautiful old buildings contribute to its unique character and charm. To its credit Thaxted has no need of artificial tourist attractions, and is today what is has been for the last ten centuries: a thriving and beautiful town.

**Thaxted Church** stands on a hill and soars cathedral-like over the town's streets. It has been described as the finest Parish church in the country and, though many towns may protest long and loud at this claim, it certainly is magnificent. It was also the somewhat unlikely setting for a pitched battle in 1921. The rather colourful vicar and secretary of the Church Socialist League, one Conrad Noel, hoisted the red flag of communism and the Sinn Fein flag in the church. Incensed Cambridge students tore them down and put up the Union Jack; Noel in turn ripped that down and, with his friends, slashed the tyres of the students' cars and

## THE THAXTED GARDEN FOR BUTTERFLIES

Aldboro' Lodge, Park Street, Thaxted, Essex CM6 2ND
Tel: 01371 830780

**The Thaxted Garden for Butterflies** is a Help the Aged Millenium award-winning project demonstrating how a retirement hobby garden of one acre could be developed to conserve our native British Butterflies and other local wildlife.

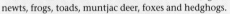

The garden has been developed since 1987 and has proven to have been successful by attracting twenty-three species of butterflies, as well as rare moths, dragonflies, many insects, grass snakes, newts, frogs, toads, muntjac deer, foxes and hedghogs.

Since it was opened to the public in 2000 many people have enjoyed its charm and tranquility, and learned much about butterflies from seeing them, the static exhibits in the garden, as well as the habitat and food plants they and their caterpillars need. Open daily May to October.

motorbikes. A fine bronze in the church celebrates this adventurous man of the cloth.

Conrad Noel's wife is remembered for encouraging Morris dancing in the town. Today, the famous Morris Ring is held annually (usually on the Spring Bank Holiday), attracting over 300 dancers from all over the country, who dance through the streets. Dancing can also be seen around the town on most Bank Holiday Mondays, usually in the vicinity of a pub!

Gustav Holst, composer of, amongst other pieces, the renowned 'Planets' Suite', lived in Thaxted from 1914-1925, and often played the church organ. To celebrate his connection with the town there is a month-long music festival in late June/early July which attracts performers of international repute.

In Park Street, at Aldborough Lodge, the **Thaxted Garden for Butterflies** (see panel opposite) is an unprepossessing garden that has been developed with a view to pleasing birds, butterflies and other wildlife species - including humans. Displays depict the 22 native wild butterfly species that have visited the garden since its inception in 1988.

## GREAT DUNMOW

The town is famous for the 'Flitch of Bacon', an ancient ceremony which

dates back as far as the early 12$^{th}$ century. A prize of a flitch, or side, of bacon was awarded to the local man who, in the words of then-Lord Mayor Robert Fitzwalter;

*'does not repent of his marriage nor quarrel, differ or dispute with his wife within a year and a day after the marriage'.*

Amidst great ceremony, the winning couple would be seated and presented with their prize. The custom lapsed on the Dissolution of the Monasteries, was briefly revived in the 18$^{th}$ century, and became established again after 1885. 'Trials' to test the truth are all in good fun, and carried out every leap year. The successful couple are carried through the streets on chairs and then presented with the Flitch. The 'bacon chair' can be seen in Little Dunmow parish church.

Other places of historical interest include the parish church of St Mary at Church End, Great Dunmow, dating back to 1322. The Clock House, a private residence built in 1589, was the home of St Anne Line, martyred for sheltering a Jesuit priest. The **Great Dunmow Maltings**, opened to the public in 2000 after restoration costing £750,000, is the most complete example of a medieval timber-framed building of its type in the United Kingdom, and a focal point for local history in the shape of Great Dunmow Museum, with changing displays illustrating the history of the town from Roman times to the present day. H G Wells lived at **Brick House** in Great Dunmow, overlooking the **Doctor's Pond**, where in 1784 Lionel Lukin is reputed to have tested the first unsinkable lifeboat.

**The Flitch Way** is a 15-mile country walk along the former Bishop's Stortford-to-Braintree railway, taking in Victorian stations, impressive views, and a wealth of woodland wildlife.

# AROUND GREAT DUNMOW

## LITTLE EASTON
### 2 miles NW of Great Dunmow off the B184

The charming 12$^{th}$ century **Church** in this small village is rich in historic features. Its Maynard Chapel features some outstanding marble monuments of the family that gives the chapel its name, as well as some famous brasses. The church's oldest treasures are, however, a well-preserved and priceless 12$^{th}$ century wall painting and several 15$^{th}$ century frescoes. Two more recent additions, a pair of stained glass windows, were unveiled in 1990. The 'Window of the Crusaders' and the 'Window of Friendship and Peace' are a lasting memorial to the American 386$^{th}$ Bomb Group. Known as 'The Marauders', they were stationed nearby for 13 months and lost over 200 of their number in battle overseas during that short time.

Little Easton Manor boasts extensive gardens, lakes and fountains. The ancient **Barn Theatre** at Little Easton Manor is one of the finest and oldest tithe barns in the country, with magnificent oak timbers and ancient tiled roof. Host to performances by many of the most distinguished actors over the years - including Ellen Terry, Hermione Baddeley, Charlie Chaplin, George Formby and many others - the sympathetic restoration of the facilities has meant its continued use as a setting for special events. Both the Barn Theatre and the Turkey Barn within the grounds are available for private hire. Day-ticket angling can also be arranged.

## GREAT EASTON
### 3 miles NW of Great Dunmow off the B184

Great Easton boasts a wealth of cottages and farmhouses with ornamental plasterwork, clustered Tudor chimneys and half-timbering. Great Easton's well-known and very popular Green Man pub occupies a handsome building dating back to the 15<sup>th</sup> century.

## CHICKNEY

**6 miles NW of Great Dunmow off the B1051**

Here can be found the rustic and remote little Saxon Church of St Mary's, with 1,000 years of history. Delightfully unspoilt inside, it retains its 14<sup>th</sup> century tower with pyramid spire. Craftsmanship on display includes the rare Pre-Reformation altar.

## BROXTED

**6 miles NW of Great Dunmow off the B1051**

The parish **Church of St Mary the Virgin** here in the handsome village of Broxted has two remarkably lovely stained glass windows commemorating the captivity and release of John

McCarthy and the other Beirut hostages, dedicated in January 1993. Though just a few minutes' drive from Stansted Airport off the M11, it is a welcoming haven of rural tranquillity.

**Church Hall Farm Antique and Craft Centre** in Broxted is housed in a magnificent Grade II listed barn flanked by a willow-lined pond with its own resident ducks! The building itself is a miracle of medieval craftsmanship, located just a few yards from Broxted parish church.

## TAKELEY

**4 miles W of Great Dunmow off the A120**

The village is built on the line of the old Roman **Stane Street**. There are plenty of pretty 17<sup>th</sup> century timbered houses and barns to be seen in the village, and the church still has many of its original Norman features along with some

## PEACOCKS COUNTRY FLOWER AND GIFT STORE

Bretts Farm Market, Chelmsford Road,
White Roding, Essex CM6 1RF
Tel: 01279 876796

Set in one of the eight Rodings villages that dot this part of rural Essex, **Peacocks Country Flower and Gift Store** is a specialist shop with a marvellous range of giftware and accessories for the home. Located on the A1106 between Chelmsford and Bishops Stortford, adjacent to a garden centre and coffee shop, visitors here will

find a large selection of dried and silk flowers – over 25 varieties – that change with the seasons and can include lilies, roses and more.

Together with these are other objets d'art such as candles and fragrances from makers such as Crabtree & Evelyn, glassware, Portmeiron pottery, china, Damske silverware, jewellery from the Isle of Bute, perfumes and Norfolk lavender, greetings cards, throws and cushions, picture frames, soft toys, rag dolls and much more. Owner June Peacock has established this wonderful shop over the past 10 years, and she and her staff are experienced, friendly and helpful.

Roman masonry. Rather unusually, it has a modern font that is surrounded by a six-foot-high medieval cover.

## HATFIELD BROAD OAK

### 3 miles SW of Great Dunmow off the B184

This very pretty village has many notable buildings for visitors to enjoy, including a church dating from Norman times, some delightful 18<sup>th</sup> century almshouses and several distinctive Georgian houses.

Nearby **Hatfield Forest** is a rare surviving example of a medieval Royal hunting forest. It has wonderful 400-year-old pollarded trees, two ornamental lakes and an 18<sup>th</sup> century shell house. Guided tours can be arranged. Once covering a great deal more land, the remaining 400 hectares are now protected by the National Trust and offer splendid woodland walks along with good chases and rides.

## AYTHORPE RODING

### 4 miles SW of Great Dunmow off the B184

**Aythorpe Roding Windmill** is the largest remaining post mill in Essex. Four storeys high, it was built around 1760 and remained in use up until 1935. It was fitted in the 1800s with a fantail which kept the sails pointing into the wind. It is open to the public on the last Sunday of each month from April to September, 2-5 p.m.

## PLESHEY

### 5 miles SE of Great Dunmow off the A130

Pleshey, midway between Chelmsford and Great Dunmow, is surrounded by a mile-long earthen rampart protecting the remains of its castle, of which only the motte with its moat and two baileys survive. There are good views from the mound, which – although only 60 feet high – is one of the highest points in

## THE WHITE HORSE PLESHEY

The Street, Pleshey, nr Chelmsford, Essex  CM3 1HA
Tel: 01245 237281
e-mail: thewhitehorse@ukonline.co.uk
website: thewhitehorsepleshey.co.uk

Both food and drink play prominent roles at **The White Horse Pleshey**, a classic country inn dating back to 1483. The interior is gracious and charming, with ancient beams and timbers, brick and tiled floors, and large open fires adding to the inn's cosy ambience and character.

The inn's excellent restaurant has a reputation built up over 20 years for good home-cooked food that is second to none in the area, with a changing menu that features the finest in freshest local ingredients combined in exciting ways to create truly tempting dishes. The menu boasts rabbit, game and venison in season, and the choice of fish dishes is very good. The wine list offers an extensive selection of vintages. In the coffee shop, guests can enjoy morning coffee and afternoon tea all year round.

The White Horse also sells a lovely range of watercolours and oil paintings by local artists, gifts, cards, sweet wines, Suffolk glass, second-hand books and collectibles from the onsite gallery, an added point of interest at this superb inn.

The inn is also an ideal venue for celebrations, large dinner parties and business gatherings, being equipped with several spacious rooms and a large garden that can accommodate a marquee.

*Pleshey Village*

Essex. The village is truly delightful, with a number of thatched cottages, and the area is excellent for walkers and ramblers.

## WALTHAM ABBEY

The town of Waltham began as a small Roman settlement on the site of the present-day Market Square. The early Saxon kings maintained a hunting lodge here; a town formed round this, and the first church was built in the 6th century. By the 8th, during the reign of Cnut, the town had a stone minster church with a great stone crucifix that had been brought from Somerset, were it had been found buried in land owned by Tovi, a trusted servant of the king. This cross became the focus of pilgrims seeking healing. One of those cured of a serious illness, Harold Godwinsson, built a new church, the third on the site, which was dedicated in 1060 - and it was this self-same Harold who became king and was killed in the battle of Hastings six years on. Harold's body was brought back to Waltham to be buried in his church. The church that exists today was built in the

first quarter of the 12th century. It was once three times its present length, and incorporated an Augustinian Abbey, built in 1177 by Henry II. The town became known for the Abbey, which was one of the largest in the country and the last to be the victim of Henry VIII's Dissolution of the Monasteries, in 1540.

The Abbey's Crypt Centre houses an interesting exhibition explaining the history of both the Abbey and the town, highlighting the religious significance of the site. Some visible remains of the Augustinian Abbey include the chapter house and precinct walls, cloister entry and gateway in the surrounding Abbey Gardens. The Abbey Gardens are also host to a Sensory Trail exploring the highlights of hundreds of years of the site's history; there's also a delightful Rose Garden.

Along the Cornhill Stream, crossed by the impressive stone bridge, the town's **Dragonfly Sanctuary** is home to over half the native British species of dragonflies and damselflies. It is noted as the best single site for seeing these species in Greater London, Essex and Hertfordshire.

A Tudor timber-framed house forms part of the **Epping Forest District Museum** in Sun Street. The wide range of displays includes exhibits covering the history of the Epping Forest District from the Stone Age to the 20th century. Tudor and Victorian times are particularly well represented, with some magnificent oak panelling dating from the reign of Henry

VIII, and re-creations of Victorian rooms and shops. There is also an archaeological display and temporary exhibitions covering such subjects as contemporary arts and crafts. The museum has several hands-on displays which help to bring history to life, and features special events and adult workshops throughout the year.

Sun Street is the town's main thoroughfare, and it is pedestrianised. It contains many buildings from the 16th century onwards. The Greenwich Meridian (0 degrees longitude) runs through the street, marked out on the pavement and through the Abbey Gardens.

In spite of its proximity to London and more recent development, the town retains a peaceful, traditional character, with its timber-framed buildings and small traditional market which has been held here since the early 12th century (now every Tuesday and Saturday – there is also a Farmers' Market held every third Thursday of the month, when farm-fresh produce is the order of the day). The whole of the town centre has been designated a conservation area. The Market Square boasts many fine and interesting buildings such as the Lych-gate and The Welsh Harp, dating from the 17th and 16th centuries respectively.

The **Town Hall** offers a fine example of Art Nouveau design, and houses the Waltham Abbey Town Council Offices and Epping Forest District Council Information Desk. The Tourist Information Centre is in Highbridge Street, opposite the entrance to the Abbey Church.

To the west of town, the **Lee Navigation Canal** offers opportunities for anglers, walkers, birdwatching and pleasure craft. Once used for transporting corn and other commercial goods to the growing City of London,

and having associations with the town's important gunpowder industry for centuries, the canal remains a vital part of town life.

Gunpowder production became established in Waltham as early as the 1660s; by the 19th century the **Royal Gunpowder Mills** (see panel opposite) employed 500 workers, and production did not cease until 1943, after which time the factory became a research facility. In the spring of 2000, however, all this changed and the site was opened to the public for the first time. Of the 175 acres the site occupies, approximately 80 have been designated a Site of Special Scientific Interest, as the ecology of the site offers a rare opportunity for study. With two-thirds of the site a Scheduled Ancient Monument, there are some 21 listed buildings to be found here, some of which date from the Napoleonic Wars. The site also contains some of the finest examples of industrial archaeology in the world. Regular events and activities include costumed living history.

**Lee Valley Regional Park** is a leisure area stretching for 26 miles along the River Lea (sometimes also spelled Lee) from East India Dock Basin, on the north bank of the River Thames in East London, to Hertfordshire. There's a range of facilities ideal for anglers, walkers and birdwatchers. The Lee Valley is an important area of high biodiversity, sustaining a large range of wildlife and birds. Two hundred species of birds, including internationally important populations of Gadwall and Shoveler ducks, can be seen each year on the wetlands and water bodies along the Lea. The Information Centre in the Abbey Gardens provides displays and information on a range of countryside pursuits and interests, sport, leisure and heritage facilities and special events. Of

## ROYAL GUNPOWDER MILLS

Powdermill Lane, Waltham Abbey, Essex EN9 1BN
Tel: 01992 767022  Fax: 01992 710341
website: www.royalgunpowdermills.com

The **Royal Gunpowder Mills** in Waltham Abbey is open to the general public after a 300 year history. Thanks to funding from the Heritage Lottery Fund and Ministry of Defence, this secret site which was home to gunpowder and explosive production and research for more than three centuries, has been developed to offer visitors a truly unique day out.

Gunpowder production began at Waltham Abbey in the mid 1660's on the site of a late medieval fulling mill. The gunpowder Mills remained in private hands until 1787, when they were purchased by the crown. From this date, the Royal Gunpowder Mills developed into the pre-eminent powder works in Britain and one of the most important in Europe.

Set in 175 acres of natural parkland and boasting 21 important historic buildings the regenerated site will offer visitors a unique mixture of fascinating history, exciting science and beautiful surroundings. Approximately 70 acres of the site, containing some of the oldest buildings and much of the canal network, will be open for visitors to explore freely. The remaining area of the site including the largest heronry in Essex has been designated as a Site of Special Scientific Interest and will be accessible to the public by way of special guided tours. Open April to September.

national importance for overwintering waterbirds including rare species of bittern and smew, this fine park makes an ideal place for a picnic. Guided tours by appointment.

At the southern end of Lee Valley Park, **The House Mill**, one of two tidal mills still standing at this site, has been restored by the River Lea Tidal Mill Trust. It was built in 1776 in the Dutch style, and was used to grind grain for gin distilling.

**Lee Valley Park Farms**, along Stubbins Hall Lane, boasts two farms on site: **Hayes Hill** and **Holyfield Hall**. At Hayes Hill Farm, visitors can interact with the animals and enjoy a picnic or the children's adventure playground. This traditional farm also boasts old-fashioned tools and equipment, an exhibition in the medieval barn and occasional craft demonstrations. The entry fee to Hayes Hill Farm also covers a visit to Holyfield Hall Farm, a working farm and dairy where visitors can see

milking and learn about modern farming methods. Seasonal events such as sheep-shearing and harvesting are held, and there's an attractive farm tea room and a toy shop. A farm trail is another of the site's attractions, offering wonderful views of the Lee Valley, an expanse of open countryside dotted with lakes and wildflower meadows attracting a wide range of wildlife including otters, bats, dragonfly, kingfisher, great-crested grebe and little-ringed plover. The area is ideal for walking or fishing, and the bird hides are open to all at weekends; permits available for daily access. Guided tours by arrangement.

**Myddleton House Gardens** within Lee Valley Park is the place to see the work of the famous plantsman who created them - E.A. Bowles, the greatest amateur gardener of his time. Breathtaking colours and interesting plantings - such as the National Collection of award-winning bearded iris, the Tulip Terrace and the Lunatic Asylum (home to unusual plants) - are offset by a beautiful carp lake, two conservatories and a rock garden.

# AROUND WALTHAM ABBEY

## EPPING
### 4 miles E of Waltham Abbey off the B182

Just off the B1391, on the outskirts of Epping town centre towards Waltham Abbey, this town's handsome **St John's Church** was designed over 100 years ago by G F Bodley.

## LOUGHTON
### 5 miles SE of Waltham Abbey off the A121

**Corbett Theatre** in Rectory Lane in Loughton is a beautiful Grade I listed converted medieval tithe barn, where classical, modern and musical theatre productions are performed. The theatre is set in a five-acre site with lovely gardens.

Loughton borders **Epping Forest**, a magnificent and expansive tract of ancient hornbeam coppice, mainly tucked between the M25 and London. There are miles of leafy walks and rides (horses can be hired locally), with some rough grazing and occasional distant views.

## ABRIDGE
### 7 miles SE of Waltham Abbey off the A113

The **BBC Essex Garden** at Crowther Nurseries, Ongar Road, is a working garden consisting of a vegetable plot, two small greenhouses, lawns and herbaceous and shrub borders. Sheila Chapman, clematis expert, is also on site, as the garden boasts 600 varieties of clematis. The garden is also home to a range of farmyard animals which visitors are welcome to see and interact with, and there's a delightful tea shop filled with homemade cakes.

## CHIGWELL
### 8 miles SE of Waltham Abbey off the A113

**Hainault Forest Country Park** is an ancient woodland covering 600 acres, with a lake and rare breeds farm, managed by the London Borough of Redbridge and the Woodland Trust for Essex County Council.

## CHINGFORD
### 6 miles S of Waltham Abbey off the A11

**Queen Elizabeth Hunting Lodge** in Ranger's Road, Chingford, is a timber-framed hunting grandstand first built for Henry VIII. This unique Tudor-era survivor boasts exceptional carpentry, and is situated in a beautiful part of Epping Forest with ancient oaks and fine views. The Visitor Centre can be found at High Beach, Epping.

## BROXBOURNE
### 5 miles NW of Waltham Abbey off the A10

At **Broxbourne Old Mill and Millpool**, the remains of the old watermill can be seen, the waterwheel of which has been restored to working order.

## HODDESDON
### 6 miles NW of Waltham Abbey off the A10

**Rye House Gatehouse** in Rye Road was built by Sir Andre Ogard, a Danish nobleman, in 1443. It is a moated building and a fine example of early English brickwork. Now restored, visitors can climb up to the battlements. A permanent exhibition covers the architecture and history of the Rye House Plot to assassinate Charles II in 1683. Guided tours by prior arrangement. The building lies adjacent to a Royal Society for the Protection of Birds reserve. Other features include an information centre, shop, and circular walks around the site.

*Queen Elizabeth Hunting Lodge*

## Harlow

**10 miles NE of Waltham Abbey on the A414**

The 'New Town' of Harlow sometimes gets short shrift, but it is in fact a lively and vibrant place with a great deal more than excellent shopping facilities. There are some very good museums and several sites of historic interest. The **Gibberd Collection** in Harlow Town Hall offers a delightful collection of British watercolours featuring works by Blackadder, Sutherland, Frink, Nash and Sir Frederick Gibberd, Harlow's master planner and the founder of the collection.

**Harlow Museum** in Passmores House, Third Avenue, occupies a Georgian manor house set in picturesque gardens which includes a lovely pond and is home to several species of butterfly. The museum has extensive and important Roman, post-medieval and early 20th century collections, as well as a full programme of temporary exhibitions.

**Mark Hall Cycle Museum and Gardens** in Muskham Road offers a unique collection of cycles and cycling accessories illustrating the history of the bicycle from 1818 to the present day, including one made of plastic, one that folds, and one where the seat tips forward and throws its rider over the handlebars if the brakes are applied too hard. The museum is housed in a converted stable block within Mark Hall manor. Adjacent to the museum are three period walled gardens.

**Gibberd Gardens**, on the eastern outskirts of Harlow in Marsh Lane, Gilden Way, is well worth a visit, reflecting as it does the taste of Sir Frederick Gibberd, the famous architect. This 7-acre garden was designed by Sir Frederick on the side of a small valley, with terraces, wild garden, landscaped vistas, pools and streams and some 80 sculptures. Marsh Lane is a turning off the B183.

**Harlow Study and Visitors Centre** in Netteswellbury Farm is set in a medieval tithe barn and 13th century church. The site has displays outlining the story of Harlow New Town.

**Parndon Wood Nature Reserve**, Parndon Wood Road, is an ancient woodland with a fine variety of birds, mammals and insects. Facilities include two nature trails with hides for observing wildlife, and a study centre.

## Chipping Ongar

**8 miles SE of Harlow on the A414**

Today firmly gripped in the commuter belt of London, Chipping Ongar began

## KELVEDON HATCH SECRET NUCLEAR BUNKER

Kelvedon Hatch Lane, Brentwood,
Essex CM14 5TL
Tel: 01277 364883   Fax: 01277 372562
e-mail: bunker@japar.demon.co.uk
website: www.japar.demon.co.uk

The **Kelvedon Hatch Secret Nuclear Bunker** was built in 1952 as a base from which the government and military commanders could have run operations, had there been a nuclear war. The labyrinth of rooms built into the hillside, 75 feet below ground and encased in 10 foot thick concrete, is cleverly disguised from the outside by a rural bungalow.

Inside the bunker you will be able to see the areas where up to 600 personnel could have been housed, along with all the equipment they would have needed to co-ordinate the survival of civilians. There is a  BBC radio studio, enormous power generators and water filtration system, a radar room and large dormitories and sickbay.

To add to your enjoyment of this attrcation, refreshments are available  and there is  a souvenir shop. Picnics can be taken amid the beautiful woodland setting. Opening times vary according to the time of year - phone for details.

as a Saxon market town protected beneath the walls of a Norman castle. The motte and bailey were built by Richard de Lucy in 1155. Indeed, the town's name comes from 'cheaping', meaning market. Only the mound and moat of the castle remain, but the contemporary **Church of St Martin of Tours** still stands. Built in 1080, it has

fine Norman flint walls and an anchorite's recess. There are several other interesting buildings in the town, some dating from Elizabethan times.

Explorer David Livingstone was a pupil pastor of the town's 19th century United Reform Church, and lived in what are now called **Livingstone Cottages** before his missionary work in Africa began.

## BOBBINGWORTH

### 2 miles NW of Chipping Ongar off the A414

**Blake Hall Gardens** at Bobbingworth near Chipping Ongar incorporates a Tropical House, an Ice House, Bog garden, wild gardens, herbaceous borders, rose garden, sunken garden, duck pond and an ornamental wood. The south wing of Blake Hall itself houses the Airscene Aviation Museum run by local RAF enthusiasts.

## FYFIELD

### 2 miles N of Chipping Ongar off the B184

The name 'Fyfield' means five river meadows. Originally a Saxon enclave, the village church of St Nicholas is Norman. There's a beautiful mill house with flood gates in the village. **Fyfield Hall**, opposite the church, is said to be the oldest inhabited timber frame building in England (it dates from AD870).

## WILLINGALE

### 3 miles NE of Chipping Ongar off the B184

**St Christopher's** and **St Andrew's**, churches of the respective parishes of Willingale Doe and Willingale Spain, stand side by side in the same churchyard in the heart of this lovely village. St Andrew's is the older, dating back to the 12th century; it is protected by the Churches Conservation Trust.

## BEAUCHAMP RODING

### 3 miles NE of Chipping Ongar off the B184

One of the eight Rodings, it was at

Beauchamp Roding that a local farm labourer, Isaac Mead, worked and saved enough to become a farmer himself in 1882. To show his gratitude to the land that made him his fortune, he had a corner of the field consecrated as an eternal resting place for himself and his family. Their graves can still be seen in the undergrowth.

Beauchamp's **Church of St Botolph** stands alone in the fields, marked by a tall 15th century tower and reached by a track off the B184. Inside, the raised pews at the west end have clever space-saving wooden steps, pulled out of slots by means of iron rings.

## GOOD EASTER AND HIGH EASTER

**5 miles NE of Chipping Ongar off the B184**

A quiet farming village, now in the commuter belt for London, Good Easter's claim to fame is the making of a world-record daisy chain (6,980 ft 7 inches) in 1985. The village's interesting name is probably derived from 'Easter', the Old English for 'sheepfolds' and 'Good' from a Saxon lady named Godiva.

Close to Good Easter, and thus named because it stands on higher ground than its neighbour, High Easter is a quiet and very picturesque village not far from the impressive **Aythorpe Post Mill**.

## KELVEDON HATCH

**4 miles S of Chipping Ongar off the A128**

A bungalow in the rural Essex village of Kelvedon Hatch is the deceptively simple exterior for the **Kelvedon Hatch Secret Nuclear Bunker** (see panel opposite).

Built in 1952, 40,000 tons of concrete were used to create a base some 80 feet underground for up to 600 top Government and civilian personnel in the event of nuclear war. Visitors can

## MAIDENS BARN

High Easter, Chelmsford, Essex CM3 1HU
Tel: 01245 231515 Fax: 01245 231075
e-mail: katherine@maidensbarn.com
website: www.maidensbarn.com

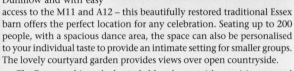

**Maidens Barn** is a friendly family-run business under the ownership of Katherine Little, a charming and welcoming host. Here in this lovely part of the county, just four miles from Dunmow and with easy

access to the M11 and A12 – this beautifully restored traditional Essex barn offers the perfect location for any celebration. Seating up to 200 people, with a spacious dance area, the space can also be personalised to your individual taste to provide an intimate setting for smaller groups. The lovely courtyard garden provides views over open countryside.

The Barn combines the best of old and new, with exquisite exposed beamwork and pitched roof as well as underfloor heating. The facilities include an entrance hall, raised gallery, bar area and fully-equipped kitchen. There is also ample car parking. Guests are welcome to supply their own drink, or Katherine can recommend local contractors to run a bar. There is no corkage charge either way. Guests will have exclusive use of the Barn for the day – as a small family business, the owners are happy to be flexible about the arrangements. Licensed for civil ceremonies, the Barn makes an ideal place for weddings. Farmhouse bed and breakfast is also available – please ring or visit the website for full details.

explore room after room to see communications equipment, a BBC studio, sick bay, massive kitchens and dormitories, power and filtration plant, government administration room and the scientists' room, where nuclear fall-out patterns would have been measured.

### GREENSTED

**1½ miles SW of Chipping Ongar off the A414**

**St Andrew's** in Greensted is the world's oldest wooden church, dating from the 9th-11th centuries, with a later Tudor chancel. It is famous as the only surviving example of a Saxon log church extant in the world, built from split oak logs held together with dowells. Over the centuries the church has been enlarged and restored; later additions include the simple weatherboarded tower, Norman flint walls, the Tudor tiled roof, Victorian stone coping, porch and stained glass windows. The body of King Edmund (later canonised a saint) is believed to have rested here in 1013.

The village also has associations with the Tolpuddle Martyrs - six Dorset farm labourers who were taken to court on a legal technicality because they agitated for better conditions and wages, and formed a Trades Union. After their conviction in 1834 they were condemned to transportation to Australia for seven years. There was a public outcry for their release, and their sentences were commuted in 1837. Unable to return to Dorset, they were granted tenancies in Greensted and High Laver.

One of the martyrs, James Brine, of New House Farm (now Tudor Cottage, on Greensted Green), married Elizabeth Standfield, daughter of one of his fellow victims - the record of their marriage in 1839 can be seen in the parish register.

### NORTH WEALD

**3 miles W of Chipping Ongar off the A414**

**North Weald Airfield Museum and Memorial** at Ad Astra House, Hurricane Way, North Weald Bassett is a small, meticulously detailed 'House of Memories' displaying the history of the famous airfield and all who served at RAF North Weald from 1916 to the present. Collections of photos and artefacts such as uniforms and the detailed records of all flying operations are on display. There is also a video exhibit recounting a day-to-day account of North Weald history. Guided tours of the airfield can be arranged for large groups.

# BRENTWOOD

Brentwood is a very pleasant shopping and entertainment centre, with quite a distinguished past. The town was on the old pilgrim and coaching routes to and from London. Mainly post-war in character, the town is the setting for the UK headquarters of Ford Motors.

**Brentwood Cathedral** on Ingrave Road was built in 1991. This classically-styled church incorporates the original Victorian church that stood on this spot. It was designed by the much-admired architect Quinlan Terry, with roundels by Raphael Maklouf (who also created the relief of the Queen's head used on current coins).

**Brentwood Centre** on Doddinghurst Road is one of the top entertainment venues in the UK, with an extensive programme of concerts, shows, bands and top comedy names. Sport and fitness facilities include pool, health suite and sunbeds.

**Brentwood Museum** at Cemetery Lode in Lorne Road, in the Warley Hill area of Brentwood, is a small and picturesque cottage museum concentrating on local and social interests during the late 19th and early 20th centuries. It is set in an attractive disused cemetery, which is in itself of unique interest and is open on the first Sunday of every month from 2.30-4.30 p.m. and throughout the summer months.

**Thorndon Country Park** boasts historic parkland, lakes and woods. The site, formerly a Royal deer park, also features a wildlife exhibition and attractive gift shop. Fishing is also available.

# AROUND BRENTWOOD

## MOUNTNESSING
**6 miles SE of Chipping Ongar off the A12**

This village has a beautifully restored early 19th century windmill as its main landmark, though the isolated church also has a massive beamed belfry. **Mountnessing Post Mill** in Roman Road is open to the public. This traditional weatherboarded post mill was built in 1807 and restored to working order in 1983. Visitors can see the huge wooden and iron gears; one pair of stones have been opened up for viewing.

## INGATESTONE
**6 miles E of Chipping Ongar off the B1002**

**Ingatestone Hall** on Hall Lane is a 16th century mansion set in 11 acres of grounds. It was built by Sir William Petre, Secretary of State to four monarchs, whose family continue to reside here. Open to the public in summer, the Hall contains family portraits, furniture and memorabilia accumulated over the centuries. Guided tours by prior arrangement.

## BILLERICAY
**6 miles E of Brentwood off the A129**

There was a settlement here as far back as the Bronze Age, though there is to date no conclusive explanation of Billericay's name. There is no question about the attraction of the High Street, though, with its timber weather boarding and Georgian brick. **The Chantry House**, built in 1510, was the home of Christopher Martin, treasurer to the Pilgrim Fathers.

The Peasants' Revolt of 1381 saw the massacre of hundreds of rebels just northeast of the town, at **Norsey Wood**. Today this area of ancient woodland is a country park, managed by coppicing (the

### INGATESTONE HALL

Ingatestone, Essex CM4 9NR
Tel: 01277 353010  Fax: 01245 248979

**Ingatestone Hall** is a 16th century mansion and grounds, built by Sir William Petre, Secretary of State to four Tudor monarchs, and still occupied by his descendants. The house substantially retains its original form and appearance (including two priests' hiding places) and contains furniture, pictures and family memorabilia accumulated over the centuries.

A programme of special events is available on request and there is a gift shop and a tea room in the grounds. A picnic area is sited in Car Park Meadow. The house and/or grounds are available to hire for a variety of events including fairs, exhibitions, concerts, lectures and location filming. Open Saturday, Sunday and Bank Holiday afternoons from Easter to the end of September, plus Wednesdays, Thursdays and Fridays in the school summer holidays.

## BEAR RESTAURANT AND BAR

The Square, Stock, Chelmsford, Essex  CM4 9LH
Tel: 01277 829100  Fax: 01277 841621
e-mail: lee@anderson-frogley.fsnet.co.uk  website: www.thebearinn.biz

**The Bear Restaurant and Bar** is extraordinary for its setting – in an historic 16th-century Grade I Listed building – and for its excellent food, drink and ambience. All of the building's original elegance and charm remains, combined with the very best in modern-day luxury and comfort. The exposed beams and other original features add a charm all their own, while the traditional leather furnishings and partitions ensure an intimate dining experience. Head chef Phil Utz worked for 10 years in some of London's top 5-star hotels and restaurants before coming to this peaceful and charming village to oversee the gastronomic delights that await diners.

Winner of the Gold Award at the 'Parade de Chefs' at the Hotel Olympia in 2000, he brings his

passion and expertise to creating a superb choice of delicious dishes. He and his personally-trained staff are devoted to producing freshly cooked modern European and English food purchased from quality local suppliers. The menu changes monthly, but always includes a choice of 10 starters, 10 main courses and 8 desserts, all freshly cooked or prepared to order. The five fish dishes make best use of the freshest Turbot, John Dory and other catches of the day, while sumptuous choices such as chateaubriand, duck or rack of lamb, whole poached lobster, corn-fed chicken and pumpkin risotto are sure

to please the palate. From start to finish – starters such as terrine of Mediterranean vegetables, home-cured salmon gravadlax, Cornish scallops or Thai crab spring roll to the superb cheeseboard and a range of sweets such as champagne strawberry jelly, banana bread and butter pudding and rum and raison ice-cream – there's something to delight every diner.

All dishes are expertly prepared and presented. A la carte lunches are available Tuesday to Saturday, while on Sunday the traditional lunch is added to the a la carte menu. Dinner is served daily from 7 p.m.

traditional way of ensuring the timber supply), which also encourages plant- and birdlife.

**Barleylands Farm Museum and Visitors' Centre** features a glass-blowing studio, blacksmith's and other craft shops, a wealth of farm animals, chick hatchery, duck pond and one of the largest collections of vintage farm machinery in the country, together with a play area, picnic area and, on Sunday afternoons, a steam railway.

## STOCK
### 6 miles NE of Brentwood off the B1007

Stock boasts a fine early 19th century tower windmill on five floors, with superb late 19th century machinery that has been restored to working order.

Stock's delightful church has a traditional Essex-style wooden belfry and spire, lending character to this pleasant village of well-kept houses.

## GREAT WARLEY
### 1 mile S of Brentwood on the B186

**Warley Place** was formerly home to one of the most famous women gardeners, Ellen Willmott, who died in 1934. She introduced to Warley - and to Britain - many exotic plants. A trail takes visitors through what is now Warley Place Nature Reserve, with 16 acres of what was once domesticated garden but has now reverted to woodland. A fascinating selection of trees, shrubs and wildlife make this well worth a visit.

## SOUTH WEALD
### 2 miles W of Brentwood off the A12

This very attractive village has, at its outskirts, **Weald Country Park**, a former estate with medieval deer park, partially landscaped in the 1700s. Featuring lake and woodland, visitors' centre, landscapes exhibition and gift shop, with

facilities for fishing and horse-riding, there are guided events and activities programmes held throughout the year.

Another good day out in the open air can be had at **Old Macdonald's Educational Farm Park**, where visitors can see the largest selection of pure-bred British farm animals and poultry in the southeast of England. Specialising in native rare-breeds, with nine breeds of pig, 23 of sheep, six of cattle, 30 of poultry and 30 of rabbit to see and learn about, as well as shire horses, deer, owls, otters, goats, ferrets, red squirrels and much more. The farm boasts informative breed labelling and excellent facilities.

# NORTH THAMES CORRIDOR

## GRAYS
### 4 miles E of Brentwood off the M25

**Thurrock Museum** is in the Thameside Complex in Grays. It collects, conserves and displays items of archaeology and local history from prehistoric times to the end of the 20th century. The archaeological items include flint and metal tools of people who lived in prehistoric Thurrock and pottery, jewellery and coins from the Roman and Saxon period.

**Thameside Theatre** in Grays town centre offers a good range of productions throughout the year, with a popular pantomime now 24 years strong.

## WEST THURROCK
### 1½ miles SW of Grays off the A13

Immortalised by the film *Four Weddings and a Funeral*, little **St Clement's Church** occupies a striking location and is one of a number of picturesque ancient churches in the borough. Although this 12th century church is now deconsecrated, it was in its day a stopping point for pilgrims; visitors can see the remains of its original round tower. There is also a mass grave to the boys of the reformatory ship *Cornwall* who were drowned in an accident off Purfleet.

**Arena Essex Raceway** is the chief venue for motorsports in the area. Regular 'banger racing' takes place at the track in West Thurrock, near **Lakeside Shopping Centre** and Retail Park. The Centre attracts many millions of visitors a year, and boasts over 300 shops, a food court and multiplex cinema. The Retail Park features more shops, as well as restaurants, a cinema, a leisure bingo complex and a watersports centre at the lake.

## PURFLEET

**3 miles W of Grays off the M25/A13**

Fans of Bram Stoker's novel *Dracula* will know that in this book the famous vampire buys a house called 'Carfax' in Purfleet. The town's esteemed **Royal Hotel**, by the Thames, is said to have played host to Edward VII, while still Prince of Wales in the 1880s and 1890s, at which time the hotel was called Wingrove's. The **Purfleet Heritage and Military Centre** is a heritage and military museum featuring displays of many items of interest and memorabilia in the setting of the No 5 Gunpowder Magazine on Centurion Way. This remaining magazine was built in the 1770s for testing and issuing gun powder to the army and navy.

**Purfleet Conservation Area** includes several buildings which were part of a planned village built by the one-time owners of the chalk quarry, the Whitbread family.

## AVELEY

**3 miles NW of Grays off the M25/A13**

**Mardyke Valley** is an important wildlife corridor running from Ship Lane in Aveley to Orsett Fen. Many pleasant views can be had along the seven-mile stretch along footpaths and bridleways. Davy Down within Mardyke Valley consists of riverside meadows, ponds and wetland. The Visitors' Centre is in the well-preserved water pumping station on the B186 near South Ockendon.

Aveley's 12th century **St Michael's Church** features many Flemish brasses and other items of historical interest.

## SOUTH OCKENDON

**3 miles N of Grays off the A13/A1306**

**Belhus Woods Country Park** covers approximately 250 acres and contains an interesting variety of habitats, including woodland, two lakes and the remains of a pond designed by 'Capability' Brown. The Visitors' Centre to this superb park can be found at the main entrance off Romford Road. Belhus Park Golf Course is a well-established 18-hole course set within this beautiful parkland.

**Grangewaters Country Park**, also in South Ockendon, has two lakes. Managed by Thurrock Environmental and Outdoor Education Centre, it offers watersports such as windsurfing, sailing and canoeing, as well as off-road biking, climbing and other outdoor pursuits. **Brannetts Wood** is one of the oldest recorded ancient woodlands in South Essex. It can be reached from the Mardyke Way, or from South Road here in South Ockendon.

The village **Church of St Nicholas** has one of only six round church towers in Essex. This one was built in the 13th century and used to have a spire, which was sadly destroyed by lightning in the 17th century.

## HORNDON-ON-THE-HILL

**6 miles NE of Grays off the B1007/A13**

Listed in the *Domesday Book* as *Horninduna*, a name which also appears on a Saxon coin of Edward the Confessor (1042-1066), it is said to have once been the site of a Royal Anglo-Saxon mint. The town's 16th century **Woolmarket** indicates the importance of the wool trade to the region, and is one of the area's historical treasures. The upper room served as Horndon's manor courtroom, while the lower, open area was used for trading in woollen cloth.

The main entrance and Visitors' Centre for **Langdon Hills Conservation Centre and Nature Reserve** are located off the Lower Dunton Road north of Horndon-on-the-Hill. A bridleway and footpaths lead visitors to meadows, a pond and outstanding ancient woods. Also within the reserve is the **Plotlands Museum**, housed in an original 1930s plotland bungalow known as the Haven.

## LINFORD
**3 miles NE of Grays off the A13/A1013**

**Walton Hall Museum** on Walton Hall Road has a large collection of historic farm machinery in a 17th century barn. It affords visitors the opportunity to watch traditional craftsmen, such as a blacksmith, saddlemaker, printer and wheelwright, together with a printing shop, baker's, dairy and nursery.

## STANFORD-LE-HOPE
**4 miles NE of Grays off the A1014**

**Stanford Marshes** is an area to the south of Stanford-le-Hope, next to the Thames. The Marshes are home to a variety of wildlife and are an ideal location for birdwatching. **Grove House Wood** in Stanford-le-Hope is a nature reserve managed by Essex Wildlife Trust and the local Girl Guides. A footpath here leads to reed beds, a pond and a brook as well as an area of woodland.

The graveyard of St Margaret's Church has an unusual half-barrelled tomb, for

one James Adams (d. 1765), that is decorated with gruesome stone-carved symbols of death.

## CORRINGHAM
**7 miles NE of Grays off the A13/A1014**

Corringham has a picturesque cluster of timber-framed houses in the old village, leading up to its medieval church, which retains some Saxon and Norman features. **Langdon Hills Country Park** north of Corringham is 400 acres of ancient woodland and meadows. It has many rare trees and spectacular views of the Essex countryside.

## CANVEY ISLAND
**10 miles NE of Grays off the A130**

Canvey Island is a peaceful and picturesque stretch of land overlooking the Thames estuary with views to neighbouring Kent. The island boasts two unusual museums: **Dutch Cottage Museum** is an early 17th century eight-sided cottage built by Dutch workmen for Dutch workmen and boasting many traditional Flemish features. **Castle Point Transport Museum** is housed in a 1930s bus garage. It houses an interesting collection of historic and modern buses and coaches, mainly of East Anglian origin. The **Canvey Miniature Railway** at the Waterside Farm Centre has two steam miniature railways guaranteed to delight the child in all of us.

## WEST TILBURY
**3 miles E of Grays off the A1089**

West Tilbury was the site chosen for the Camp Royal in 1588, to prepare for the threatened Spanish invasion. Queen Elizabeth I visited the army here, and made her famous speech,

*'I know I have the body but of a weak and feeble woman: but I have the heart and stomach of a king, and a king of England too.'*

Hidden away in rural tranquillity overlooking the Thames estuary, West Tilbury remains unspoilt in spite of its proximity to busy, industrial Tilbury. The former local church (now a private dwelling) in this quaint little village is a nautical landmark used for navigation. The list of Rectors of the church, dating from 1279-1978, when the church was disestablished, can be seen in The Kings Head Pub.

## EAST TILBURY

### 5 miles E of Grays off the A13

**Coalhouse Fort** is considered to be one of the best surviving examples of a Victorian Casement fortress in the country. As such it is a protected Scheduled Ancient Monument. Built between 1861 and 1874 as a first line of defence to protect the Thames area against invasion, it stands on the site of other defensive works and fortifications dating back to around 1400. Even before the Middle Ages, this was an important site.

Part of the construction work on the Fort was overseen by Gordon of Khartoum. It was constructed to be a dedicated Artillery casement fortress, which meant that the guns were housed in large vaulted rooms with armour-plated frontages. Beneath these rooms lies an extensive magazine tunnel system to service the artillery.

Over the years many alterations were made to the Fort to accommodate new artillery. The Fort was manned during both World Wars, and is now owned by Thurrock Borough Council and administered by The Coalhouse Fort Project, a registered charity run entirely by volunteers. Open to the public, it contains reconstructions of period guns and other displays, and also houses the **Thameside Aviation Museum**, with a large collection of local finds and other aviation material. In the two parade grounds visitors will find various artillery pieces and military vehicles. One recent addition to the many pieces of historical military equipment is a Bofor Anti-Aircraft Gun of the Second World War. The site also offers visitors the chance to handle period equipment or try on a period uniform.

During the year the Fort hosts a range of shows, including an historic artillery rally when various big guns are fired by crews in the uniforms of the period, including a Second World War crew firing a 1940 25pdr field gun. A guided tour (included in the price of admission) allows visitors to see the magazine tunnels beneath the gun casements and offer a feel for the work and conditions of a Victorian gunner. The tour also takes in the roof of the Fort, from which you will be able to judge for yourself the value of a fortification at this point along the Thames. The view from here is outstanding, taking in the two sister forts in Kent and, on a clear day, Southend.

The Fort is set in a lovely riverside park with walks and a children's play area, as well as other items of military history including a Quick Fire Battery and Minefield Control box. You can also follow the old railway tracks from the Fort to the side of the old jetty, where many of the armaments and supplies for the fort were shipped in.

It is possible that East Tilbury's **St Catherine's** church occupies the site of one of the first Christian monasteries in the 7th century. Its half-built tower was constructed by the First World War Garrison of Coalhouse Fort.

**The Bata Estate** is a conservation area of architectural and historical interest. Established in 1933, the British Bata Shoe Company was the creation of Czech-born Thomas Bata, who also developed a housing estate for his workforce. This range of uniform flat-roofed houses can still be seen on site.

## Tilbury

**3 miles SE of Grays off the A1089**

**Tilbury Fort** is a well-preserved and unusual 17th century structure with double moat. The largest and best example of military engineering in England at that time, the fort also affords tremendous views of the Thames estuary. The most violent episode in the fort's history occurred in 1776, during a particularly vociferous cricket match which left three people dead. For a small fee visitors to the fort can fire a 1943 3.7mm anti-aircraft gun - a prospect most children and many adults find irresistible! Owned by English Heritage, the site was used for a military Block House during the reign of Henry VIII and was rebuilt in the 17th century. It remains one of Britain's finest examples of a star-shaped bastion fortress.

Extensions were made in the 18th and 19th centuries, and the Fort was still being used in the Second World War.

**Tilbury Festival** is held every year in July in the field near the fort, and features arena events, craft and food stalls, and living history re-enactments. **Tilbury Energy and Environment Centre** at Tilbury Power Station provides a nature reserve and study centre for schools and community education. There is a flat two-mile nature trail leading to and from the Centre.

# SOUTHEND-ON-SEA

Beside the sea in Southend-on-Sea there is always plenty to do and see, and many events throughout the year to ensure its continuing interest and popularity. The town is one of the best loved and most friendly resorts in Britain, featuring the very best ingredients for a break at the seaside. With seven miles of beaches and the only European Blue Flag award in Essex, this treasure trove boasts **Adventure Island** theme park, **Cliffs Bandstand**, **Cliffs Pavilion** (the largest purpose-built performing arts venue in Essex), a distinguished art gallery and several interesting museums.

**Southend Pier and Museum** brings to life the fascinating past of the longest Pleasure Pier in the world. The Pier itself is 1.33 miles long; visitors can either take a leisurely walk along its length or take advantage of the regular train service that plies up and down the pier.

**Central Museum, Planetarium and Discovery**

*Southend-on-Sea*

**Centre** on Victoria Avenue is the only planetarium in the southeast outside London, and also features local history exhibits, archaeology and wildlife exhibits. **Beecroft Art Gallery** boasts the work of four centuries of artistic endeavour, with some 2,000 works including those by Lear, Molenaer, Seago and Constable.

**Sealife Adventure** employs the most advanced technology to bring you incredibly close to the wonders of British marine life, offering fun ways of exploring life under the waves, with concave bubble windows helping to make it seem you're actually part of the sea-creatures' environment.

*Southend-on-Sea*

Another exhibit features a walk-through tunnel along a reconstructed seabed. The Shark Exhibition is not to be missed.

A floral trail guided tour around the parks and gardens will reveal why Southend has won the Britain in Bloom Awards every year since 1993, as well as medals at the Chelsea Flower Show.

**The Kursaal** on the Eastern Esplanade is an indoor entertainment complex, one of the largest in the country, with indoor bowling, synthetic ice and roller rink, a fun casino, children's play area, snooker and pool, arts and crafts, retail units and theme restaurants.

Boat trips in summer include occasional outings on a vintage paddle steamer. Ferry trips to Felixstowe are also available from Southend.

The **Southchurch Hall Museum** in

Park Lane is a delightful 13th to 14th century timber-framed manor house with various displays and landscaped gardens. Period room settings are among this museum's many delights.

**Prittlewell Priory Museum**, slightly north of Southend town centre in Priory Park, is a well-preserved 12th century Cluniac Priory set in lovely grounds and housing collections of the Priory's history, natural history and the Caten collection of radios and communications equipment.

# AROUND SOUTHEND-ON-SEA

## OLD LEIGH
### ½ mile W of Southend off the A13

The unspoilt fishing village of Old Leigh has a long and distinguished history. It is picturesque, with sea front houses and narrow winding alleys. It has also earned its place in history: The pilgrim ship *The Mayflower* restocked here en route to the New World of America back in the mid-17th century, and the Dunkirk rescue embarked from here, as commemorated in a framed poem on the wall of the local pub, The Crooked Billet.

## LEIGH-ON-SEA
### 2 miles W of Southend off the A13

Leigh-on-Sea has quite a distinct character to Southend, being more intimate and serene, with wood-clad buildings and shrimp boats in the working harbour. The shellfish stall on the harbourside is justly famous. The **Leigh Heritage Centre**, housed in a former ancient blacksmith's in the waterside High Street of the Old Town, now houses

historical artefacts including a photographic display of the history of Leigh-on-Sea.

## ROCHFORD
### 3 miles N of Southend off the B1013

**The Old House**, at 17 South Street, is an elegant, lovingly restored house originally built in 1270. The twisting corridors and handsome rooms of this fine structure offer a glimpse into the past; the building now houses some District Council offices, and is said to be haunted.

## HADLEIGH
### 5 miles NW of Southend off the A13

**Hadleigh Castle**, built originally for Edward III, is owned by English Heritage and once belonged to Anne of Cleves, Catherine of Aragon and Katherine Parr. The ruins were also immortalised in a painting by Constable. The remains of this once impressive castle can still be seen. The curtain walls towers, which survive almost to their full height, overlook the Essex marshes and the Thames estuary.

**Hadleigh Castle Country Park** offers a variety of woodland and coastal walks

*Hadleigh Guildhall*

in grounds overlooking the Thames estuary. A Guided Events programme runs throughout the year.

### HOCKLEY
**6 miles NW of Southend off the A129**

**Hockley Woods** is a 280-acre ancient woodland, managed for the benefit of wildlife and for the public. Traditional coppice management encourages a diverse array of flora and fauna, including the nationally rare Heath Fritillary butterfly.

**Volpaia** in Woodlands Road is a lily specialist's small but beautiful woodside garden, with rare collected species and own-bred hybrid lilies, shade-loving shrubs and plants for sale.

### RAYLEIGH
**6 miles NW of Southend off the A1016**

**Dutch Cottage** at Crown Hill in Rayleigh is a tiny traditional Flemish eight-sided cottage based on a 17th century design created by Dutch settlers.

**Rayleigh Mount** is a prominent landmark in this part of the county. Once a motte-and-bailey castle built in the 11th century, it was abandoned some 200 years later. **Rayleigh Windmill**, in Bellingham Lane close to Rayleigh Mount, was built around 1809; the tower mill houses a fascinating collection of

bygones mostly used in and around Rayleigh. Refreshments are available from the coffee shop adjacent to the Mill.

### HULLBRIDGE
**8 miles NW of Southend off the A132**

**Jakapeni Rare Breed Farm** at Burlington Gardens in Hullbridge is a pleasant small-holding set in 30 acres of rolling countryside. Specialising in sheep and pigs, with other pets and wildlife, there's also a fishing lake, country walk and pets corner. Snacks and light refreshments are available from the café, and there's an attractive shop.

## CHELMSFORD

Roman workmen cutting their great road linking London with Colchester built a fort at what is today called Chelmsford. Then called *Caesaromagus*, it stands at the confluence of the Rivers Chelmer and Can. The town has always been an important market centre and is now the bustling county town of Essex. It is also directly descended from a new town planned by the Bishop of London in 1199. At its centre are the principal inn, the **Royal Saracen's Head**, and the elegant **Shire Hall** of 1791. Three plaques situated high up on the eastern

**BOOKLEAF CAFÉ AND BOOKSHOP**

74 Springfield Road, Chelmsford, Essex CM2 6JY
Tel: 01245 252220

**Bookleaf Café and Bookshop** is a real find. The café boasts a fine selection of teas, coffees, hot and cold dishes, cakes and pastries, while the bookshop is nothing short of outstanding, with a collection of over 5,500 second-hand and rare books on everything from fiction and poetry to history (including a fine section on local history), biography, travel, cookery and more. Open Monday to Saturday from 9 – 5, this fine shop is well worth including in any visit to Chelmsford and the surrounding area.

face of the Hall overlooking the High Street represent Wisdom, Justice and Mercy. The building now houses the town magistrates court.

Christianity came to Essex with the Romans and again, later, with St Cedd (AD 654); in 1914 the diocese of Chelmsford was created. **Chelmsford Cathedral** in New Street dates from the 15th century and is built on the site of a church constructed 800 years ago. The cathedral is noted for the harmony and unity of its perpendicular architecture. It was John Johnson, the distinguished local architect who designed both the Shire Hall and the 18th century **Stone Bridge** over the River Can and who also rebuilt the Parish Church of St Mary when most of its 15th century tower fell down. The church became a cathedral when the new diocese of Chelmsford was created. Since then it has been enlarged

and re-organised inside. The cathedral boasts memorial windows dedicated to the USAAF airmen who were based in Essex from 1942-5.

The Marconi Company, pioneers in the manufacture of wireless equipment, set up the first radio company in the world here in Chelmsford, in 1899. Exhibits of those pioneering days of wireless can be seen in the **Chelmsford Museum** (see panel below) in Oaklands Park, Moulsham Street, as can interesting displays of Roman remains and local history. Fine and decorative arts (ceramics, costume, glass), coins, natural history (live beehive, animals, geological exhibits) rub shoulders with displays exploring the history of the distinguished Essex Regiment. The museum is set in a lovely park complete with children's play area.

Also in the town, at Parkway, is

---

## WATERFRONT PLACE

Wharf Road, Chelmsford, Essex CM2 6LU
Tel: 01245 252000  Fax: 01245 252048
e-mail: info@water-frontplace.co.uk
website: www.waterfront-place.co.uk

Chelmsford's premier conference and banqueting centre **Waterfront Place** is one of the region's most distinguished centres for dining, celebrating that special occasion or corporate presentations and entertainment.

Framed by the banks of the Blackwater Canal, this superb venue boasts an impressive range of facilities.

There are three eateries offering an appealing blend of European dishes with a distinct Italian accent – Vittorio (bookable Mon to Sat 6 – 10.30 p.m.; Sun 12 – 3), Italia Bar & Oven (Mon to Sat 11 – 10.30; Sun 12 – 4) and Canalside Espresso Bar & Terrace (Mon to Sat 11 – 10.30; Sun 12 – 4) – all of which have helped Waterfront Place earn its well-deserved reputation as one of the most exciting places to eat in Chelmsford. Stylish and contemporary, the venue also features amenities that will ensure the success of any business or festive event. The experienced, dedicated staff offer the very best in service and quality.

## RUE GAVARRET LTD

163 Main Road, Broomfield, Chelmsford, Essex
Tel: 01245 363977 (warehouse)  01245  444085 (shop)
e-mail: ruegavarret@aol.com   website: www.cottagecollectionantiques.co.uk

At **Rue Gavarret Ltd**, owner and craftsman Ian Honeywood has, over many years, built up a network of buyers throughout the UK and Europe who, on his behalf, source many hundreds of pieces of antique pine furniture which is then shipped to the warehouse. Whatever piece you may be looking for – everything from dining and occasional tables, chairs, chests, sideboards, wardrobes, cabinets, carts, wheels and scuttles, rocking cradles and more – can be found here. Awarded 'Most Friendly Antiques Shop' by readers of the BBC *Homes and Antiques* Magazine, the shop – and accompanying warehouse – are well worth seeking out. Ian deals in the finest specimens of English and Continental pine, and prides himself on selling only quality, genuine and original pieces from England, France, Germany, Denmark and the Netherlands. He is happy to search for individual pieces, and can e-mail customers pictures of items which may match what they're looking for. Just 25 minutes from the M25 and M11, this friendly shop is a must-stop for anyone interested in solid craftsmanship and genuine antique pine.

At the Cottage Collection warehouse at Seabrooks Farm, Church Lane, Little Leighs (telephone number as given above), furniture restoration is always underway. All painted furniture is pressure-stripped at 90 degrees and slowly dried using de-humidifiers. All

woodworm is treated, and each piece is carefully and sensitively restored using traditional methods on-site. Those in the antiques trade and members of the general public are equally welcome to peruse the warehouse.

Rue Gavarret's informative and easy-to-navigate website features many photos of the kind of work Ian and his expert staff do, and many samples of the kinds of pieces they have to offer. The website also features links to other useful sites and further information.

Moulsham Mill Business & Craft Centre, set in an early 18th century water mill that has been renovated and now houses a variety of craft workshops and businesses. Crafts featured include jewellery, pottery, flowers, lace-making, dolls houses and bears, and decoupage work. There is a charming picnic area nearby, and a good café.

Three modern technologies - electrical engineering, radio, and ball and roller bearings - began in Chelmsford. At the Engine House Project at Sandford Mill Waterworks, museum collections from the town's unique industrial story provide a fun and fascinating insight into the science of everyday things.

# AROUND CHELMSFORD

## GREAT BADDOW
**1 mile S of Chelmsford off the A12/A130**

Baddow Antiques Centre at The Bringy, Church Street, is one of the leading antiques centres in Essex. Here, 20 dealers offer a wide selection of silver, porcelain, glass, furniture, paintings and collectibles. There is also a collection of 300 Victorian brass and iron bedsteads on display.

## SANDON
**2 miles SE of Chelmsford off the A414**

The village green here in Sandon has

## CHELMSFORD MUSEUM & ESSEX REGIMENT MUSEUM

Oaklands Park, Moulsham Street, Chelmsford, Essex CVM2 9AQ
Tel: 01245 615100  Fax: 01245 611250
e-mail: oaklands@chelmsfordbc.gov.uk
website: www.chelmsfordbc.gov.uk/leisure/museums

Chelmsford Museum, founded in 1835, has since 1930 been located in a lovely Victorian mansion in a city-centre park. The history of Chelmsford and its people from prehistoric times right up to the present day is told through displays that include geology, natural history (with a live beehive!), costumes and coins. Fine and Decorative Arts are represented by works by Edward Bawden and other regionally based artists, the Tunstall Bequest of 18th century drinking glasses and flamboyant Victorian pieces from Castle Hedingham Pottery.

The Essex Regiment on the same site relates the story of the 44th and 56th Regiments from 1741 to the modern Royal Anglian Regiment. Among the many items on display are a tailcoat of 1785 with Pompadour purple collar and cuffs, a French eagle standard captured in battle in 1812, the Regimental silver and silver drums presented by the people of Essex, medals won by Essex men including four Victoria Cross winners, the Colours of the 44th Foot carried for 102 years, and an Essex Home Guard display. Regularly changing temporary exhibitions supplement the permanent displays at both Museums.

Also under the aegis of Chelmsford Borough Council is a developing Science and Industry project at Sandford Mill, Chelmer Village (Tel/Fax: 01245 475498) with visits by appointment or on open days and science weeks for local schools.

produced a notable Spanish oak tree, the biggest in the country, planted in the centre of the village green. This oak tree is remarkable not so much for its height as for the tremendous horizontal spread of its branches. Around the green are a fine church and a number of attractive old houses, some dating back to the 16th century when Henry VIII's Lord Chancellor, Cardinal Wolsey, was Lord of the Manor of Sandon.

## SOUTH HANNINGFIELD
**6 miles S of Chelmsford off the A130**

The placid waters of nearby **Hanningfield Reservoir** were created by damming Sandford Brook, and transformed the scattered rural settlement of Hanningfield into a lakeside village. Now on the shores of the lake, the 12th century village church's belfry has been a local landmark in the flat Essex countryside for centuries. Some of the timbers in the belfry are said to have come from Spanish galleons, wrecked in the aftermath of Sir Francis Drake's defeat of the Armada.

The Visitor Centre at the Reservoir overlooks the 870-acre reservoir and the gateway to the 100-acre woodland beyond. The Centre also offers refreshments, a gift shop and toilet.

## HIGHWOOD
**3 miles SW of Chelmsford off the A414**

**Hylands House** was built in 1728; this beautiful neo-Classical Grade II listed villa is set in over 500 acres of parkland landscaped by Repton. Rooms that are open to the public include the Blue Room, Entrance Hall, Library, Saloon, Boudoir and Drawing Room. Host to many outdoor events, including the annual 'V' concerts (V98 was a particularly great success) and the Chelmsford Spectacular, **Hylands Park** features lawns, rhododendron bushes,

woodland paths, ornamental ponds and Pleasure Gardens adjacent to the House.

## WRITTLE
**2 miles W of Chelmsford off the A414**

From a tucked-away corner of St John's Green in this village came Britain's first regular broadcasting service; an experimental 15-minute programme beamed out nightly by Marconi's engineers. Opposite the Green, the Cock and Bell is reputed to be haunted by a young woman who committed suicide on the railway. Further along this street is the Wheatsheaf, one of the smallest pubs in the country.

Writtle's parish church of St John features a cross of charred timbers, a reminder of the fire which gutted the chancel in 1974. Ducks swim on the pond of the larger and quite idyllic main village green, which is surrounded by lovely Tudor and Georgian houses.

## WITHAM
**6 miles NE of Chelmsford off the A12/B1018**

The River Brain flows through this delightful town; a continuous walk has been created along its length for a distance of about three miles. The settlement dates back to at least the 10th century; remains of a Roman temple have been found at Ivy Chimneys, off Hatfield Road. Blackwater Lane leads to Whetmead, a nature reserve of 25 acres between the rivers Blackwater and Brain.

The **Dorothy L Sayers Centre** in Newland Street houses a collection of books by and about Sayers, the theologian, Dante scholar and novelist/ creator of the Lord Peter Wimsey mysteries, who lived in Witham for many years.

## LITTLE BRAXTED
**6 miles NE of Chelmsford off the A12/B1018**

Little Braxted has been voted the best-

*Little Braxted Church*

kept village on a regular basis since 1973. St Mary's chapel was built in 1888, and can accommodate only 12 people at a time. Services are held every Wednesday. The village church of St Nicholas is mentioned in the *Domesday Book*, and is famous for its murals.

## LITTLE BADDOW
### 5 miles E of Chelmsford off the A414

**Blakes Wood** is a designated Site of Special Scientific Interest, an ancient woodland of hornbeam and sweet chestnut renowned for its bluebells. There is a good circular way-marked one-and-a-half mile walk.

Cruising along the **Chelmer and Blackwater Canal** provides the visitor with a unique view of this part of rural Essex. Chelmer Cruises & Canal Centre at Paper Mill Lock in Little Baddow offers the barge *Victoria* for group hire (seats

48). Individual day trips at weekends and bank holidays can also be arranged. There's also an island picnic area, lockside tea room, walks and fishing.

## DANBURY
### 5 miles E of Chelmsford off the A414

This village is said to take its name from the Danes who invaded this part of the country in the Dark Ages. In the fine church, under a rare 13$^{th}$ century carved effigy, a crusader knight was found when the tomb was opened in 1779, perfectly preserved in the pickle which filled his coffin. Fine carving is also a feature of the bench ends; the oldest among them have inspired modern craftsmen to continue the same style of carving on all the pews. In 1402, *'the devil appeared in the likeness of Firor Minor, who entered the church, raged insolently to the great terror of the parishioners ... the top of the steeple was broken down and half the chancel scattered abroad.'* And, in 1941, another harbinger of disaster, a 500-lb German bomb, reduced the east end to ruins.

At **Danbury Common**, acres of gorse flower in a blaze of golden colour for much of the year. Along with Lingwood Common, Danbury Common is at the highest point of the gravel ridge between Maldon and Chelmsford. There is evidence here of Napoleonic defences and old reservoirs. Circular nature trails make exploring the area easily accessible. To the west, **Danbury Country Park** offers another pleasant stretch of open country, boasting woodland, a lake and ornamental gardens. Guide available by appointment.

## WOODHAM WALTER
### 6 miles E of Chelmsford off the B1010

Woodham Walter is a small village which lies two and a half miles west of the ancient market town and coastal port of Maldon. It is rumoured that Henry VIII

hunted in Woodham
Walter during his reign.
During the troubled times
after Henry's death, Mary
Tudor was concealed in
Woodham Walter Hall,
from whence she was
planning to escape from
England in 1550. The
church in Woodham, **St
Michael's**, was
constructed in April 1564
and is said to be one of
the oldest still standing in
the world.

*Maldon Basin*

## MALDON

**10 miles E of Chelmsford on the A414**

Maldon's High Street has existed since
medieval times, and the alleys and mews
leading from it are full of intriguing
shops, welcoming old inns and good
places to eat. One of the most distinctive
features of the High Street is the **Moot
Hall**. Built in the 14th century for the
D'Arcy family, this building passed into
the hands of the town corporation and
was the seat of power in Maldon for over
400 years. The original brick spiral
staircase (the best-preserved of its kind in
England) and the 18th century courtroom
are of particular interest. Guided tours
are available on Saturdays in summer
and by appointment with Maldon Town

Council (01621 857373) at other times.

A colourful appliqued embroidery
made to commemorate the 1,000th
anniversary of the crucial Battle of
Maldon (see Northey Island on page 295)
is on display at the **Maeldune Heritage
Centre** (Maeldune being the Saxon name
for Maldon). The Centre is housed in the
Grade I listed St Peter's Building, erected
in the 17th century by a local benefactor
when the nave of the church that had
once stood on this site collapsed. It can
be found at the junction of the High
Street and the steep and architecturally
interesting Market Hill. The benefactor,
one Thomas Plume, erected the building
to house his collection of 6,000 books

and a school; **The Plume Library** in St Peter's Building is open to the public.

A few minutes' walk down one of the small roads leading from the High Street brings you to the waterfront, where the old wharves and quays are still active. Moored at **Hythe Quay** are several Thames sailing barges, all over 100 years old and still boasting their traditional rigging and distinctive tan sails. The barges and Quay are overlooked by two pubs, the Queen's Head and the Jolly Sailor. Maldon, famous for its sea salt, is the only place in England still making salt from sea water. Salt production in Maldon dates from Roman times, and from its current premises on the waterfront has continued uninterrupted since 1882.

**Promenade Park** lies adjacent to Hythe Quay. This attractive park next to the River Blackwater opened in 1895. The Edwardian-style gardens include a marine lake where children can paddle and a sandy play-space by the waterside. Also in the park are an adventure playground, picnic site, amusement centre, tennis courts and mini-golf. A varied programme of events takes place in the park throughout the year, including the Mad Maldon Mud Race and the RNLI Rowing Race, both held annually over the Christmas and New Year holidays.

Housed in what was originally the park-keeper's lodge, by the park gates, **Maldon District Museum** looks back on the colourful history of the town through permanent and changing displays of exhibits and objects associated with the area and the people of Maldon.

Ruins are all that remain of the **St Giles the Leper Hospital**, founded by King Henry II in the 12th century. As

with all monastic buildings, it fell into disuse after Henry VIII's Dissolution of the Monasteries, though it retained its roof and was used as a barn until the late 19th century. Many other buildings in the town, almost as old, fortunately remain - including two fine churches.

## GOLDHANGER

### 4 miles NE of Maldon off the B1026

**Maldon District Agricultural & Domestic Museum**, at 47 Church Street in Goldhanger, features a large collection of vintage farm tools and machinery manufactured locally, as well as printing machinery and domestic artefacts.

## TOLLESBURY

### 9 miles NE of Maldon on the B1023

Located at the mouth of the River Blackwater is the marshland village of Tollesbury. **Tollesbury Marina** has been designed as a family leisure centre for the crews and passengers of visiting yachts. The Marina, with its tennis courts, heated covered swimming pool, bar and restaurant is ideally located for exploring the Blackwater and the neighbouring estuaries of the Crouch, Colne, Stour and Orwell. Guests arriving by land are welcome to use some Cruising Club facilities.

## LANGFORD

### 2 miles NW of Maldon off the B1019

The **Museum of Power**, Hatfield Road, covers all aspects of power, from domestic batteries to the massive machines that powered British industry. It includes the steam-powered pumping-station machinery of the redundant waterworks in which the museum is housed.

## NORTHEY ISLAND

### 1 mile SE of Maldon off the B1018

This small island, comprising mainly salt-marsh, is owned by the National Trust. Access to this nature reserve is on foot via a causeway passable at low tide. It is a Site of Special Scientific Interest, important to over-wintering birds.

The sea-walls of the Island make for an interesting walk, and were used as the camp base for the Viking army in AD991, when Byrhtnoth led the Saxons against the invading army. A fierce three-day battle took place, with Byrhtnoth's head eventually being cut off and the Viking warriors retreating despite their victory, leaving the English King Ethelred the Unready to pay an annual tribute, 'danegold', to the Danes to prevent further incursions.

## HEYBRIDGE BASIN

**2 miles E of Maldon off the B1026**

Here the Chelmer and Blackwater Canal meets the tidal estuary. The busy sea lock and the activities of crafts of all sizes provide an endlessly changing scene. A café and a shop selling local crafts occupy an old chandlery, and two pleasant inns overlook the water.

## PURLEIGH

**3 miles SW of Maldon on the B1010**

The first recorded vineyard in Purleigh was planted in the early 12th century, only 400 yards from the site of New Hall Vineyards in Chelmsford Road. It covered three acres of land next to Purleigh Church, where first US president George Washington's great-great-grandfather was the rector - until the time he was removed from this office for sampling too much of the local brew! Purleigh Vineyard became Crown property in 1163; subsequently the wines produced were taken each year to London to be presented to the monarch.

## RETTENDON

**6 miles SW of Maldon off the A130**

The **Royal Horticultural Society Garden** at Hyde Hall (see panel on page 296) comprises eight acres of year-round hillside colour, with a woodland garden, large rose garden, ornamental ponds with lilies and fish, herbaceous borders, shrubs, trees, and national collections of malus and viburnum. Meals and snacks are available in the attractive thatched barn; there is also a plant centre. Fine views can be had from this attractively landscaped hilltop garden.

## SOUTH WOODHAM FERRERS

**5 miles SW of Maldon off the B1012**

The empty marshland of the Crouch estuary, a yachtsman's paradise, was chosen by Essex County Council as the site for one of its most attractive new town schemes. At its centre, this successful 20th century new town boasts a traditional market square surrounded by pleasant arcades and terraces built in the old Essex style with brick, tile and weatherboard.

**Marsh Farm Country Park** in Marsh Farm Road, South Woodham Ferrers, is a working farm and country park adjoining the River Crouch. Sheep, pigs, cattle and hens roam; visitors can also partake of the adventure play area, farm trail, Visitors' Centre, gift shop and tea rooms. Guided tours are available by prior arrangement. Special events are held throughout the year.

## BATTLESBRIDGE

**7 miles SW of Maldon off the A132**

**Battlesbridge Antiques Centre** at Hawk Hill in Battlesbridge is the largest in Essex. Housed in five period buildings, more than 70 dealers display and sell their wares. The heart of the Centre is Cromwell House, its ground floor dedicated to specialist dealers with individual units. They will advise, value and give an expert opinion free of charge. They offer a wide variety of old and interesting pieces and collectibles.

The Centre's Haybarn Cottages were constructed as dwellings, while, alongside, The Bridgebarn began life as a barn with thatched roof and dates from the 19th century, at which time there were lime kilns nearby. It was converted to its present tiled roof in the 1930s. The building retains some fine oak beamwork, and houses a small 'penny arcade' with working model roundabout, fortune teller, and 'What the Butler Saw' as well as a large collection of antiques for sale.

The Old Granary is nestled on the

## RHS GARDEN HYDE HALL

Buckhatch Lane, Rettendon,
Chelmsford, Essex CM3 8ET
Tel: 01245 400256  Fax: 01245 402100
website: www.rhs.org.uk

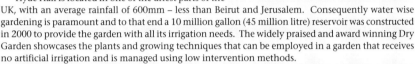

**RHS Garden Hyde Hall** is truly a garden of its time.  Set on a hilltop amongst rolling hills of arable crops, the garden combines environmental and sustainable practices with the high standards of horticulture for which the RHS gardens are renown.

Hyde Hall is located in one of the driest parts of the UK, with an average rainfall of 600mm – less than Beirut and Jerusalem.  Consequently water wise gardening is paramount and to that end a 10 million gallon (45 million litre) reservoir was constructed in 2000 to provide the garden with all its irrigation needs.  The widely praised and award winning Dry Garden showcases the plants and growing techniques that can be employed in a garden that receives no artificial irrigation and is managed using low intervention methods.

The garden has long been associated with roses, which thrive in the heavy clay soil and high light levels at the garden, and there are plenty of examples of the genus, from modern shrub roses through climbers, ramblers and old fashioned favourites.  One of the garden's best known sights is the shrub rose border, which during June is filled with up to 600 self sown *Eremurus robustus* (foxtail lily), held above the scented rose blooms.  The adjacent herbaceous borders demonstrate the art of ornamental horticulture to perfection and are crammed with colour throughout the season and include shrubs, tender perennials and annuals alongside the hardy perennials.  Work in the Queen Mother's Garden is continuing as the garden develops outward toward the Hillside Gardens, which now contain over 12,000 plants including species roses and naturalistic perennials.

Hyde Hall is managed with biodiversity in mind, and this has led to the creation of two wildflower meadows and, new for 2004, a model 'Garden for Wildlife' designed to demonstrate gardening for

wildlife – and people - on a domestic scale. The Wild Wood tree planting is another example of the environmental improvements being initiated at Hyde Hall, and eventually this planting will cover 75acres of former farmland, comprising 55,000 trees.

For a copy of the Events Programme and information on special events please contact the garden direct on 01245 400256. Now open all year round: January to March – 10am to dusk (or 5pm); April to September – 10am to 6pm; October to December 10am to dusk (or 5pm)

riverbank and houses five floors of dealers selling collectibles, reproductions, antiques and crafts, including specialists in old phones, clocks, furniture, cigarette cards, jewellery, fireplaces, interior design, dried flowers and much more. There are superb views from the top floor of the River Crouch and surrounding area, to be enjoyed as you take tea in the top-floor coffee shop.

This superb location is also the site of a

Classic Motor Cycle Museum, with displays evoking the history of motorcycling through the ages and some interesting memorabilia. Open on Sundays or by appointment. Three classic vehicle events are held annually.

### MUNDON

**3 miles SE of Maldon off the B1018**

Mundon and the surrounding area boast some excellent walking. The **St Peter's Way**, a long-distance path from Ongar to

St Peter's Chapel, Bradwell-on-Sea, leads through the village and past the disused Church of St Mary. This 14th century church is maintained by the Friends of Friendless Churches and is open to the public. Tolstoy is known to have visited the village.

## ALTHORNE

### 6 miles SE of Maldon on the B1012

The church of **St Andrew's**, some 600 years old, has a fine flint-and-stone tower, built in the perpendicular style. Inside the church there's a 15th century font which retains its original carvings of saints and angels. A brass plaque dated 1508 records that William Hyklott 'Paide for the werkemanship of the wall'; an inscription over the west door remembers John Wylson and John Hyll, who probably paid for the tower.

To the south, where Station Road meets Burnham Road, stands the villagers' own **War Memorial**. This solid structure of beams and tiles lends dignity and honour to the tragic roll-call of names listed on it.

To the north of the village is the golden-thatched and white-walled Huntsman and Hounds, an alehouse since around 1700.

## STEEPLE AND ST LAWRENCE

### 8 miles SE of Maldon off the B1021

Public footpaths lead down to the water from the village of Steeple; the houses of St Lawrence stand close to the water. Several sailing clubs and some waterside caravan and camping parks ensure that there is plenty of activity on the adjacent stretch of the River Blackwater. The **St Lawrence Rural Discovery Church**, on high ground further inland, overlooks the villages and the River Blackwater to

## WREKIN FARM FOODS

Burnham Road, Althorne, nr Burnham-on-Crouch, Essex CM3 6DT
Tel: 01621 786785 Fax: 01621 786697
e-mail: sales@wrekinfarmfoods.com
website: www.wrekinfarmfoods.com

There have been farmers and butchers at **Wrekin Farm Foods** for 75 years, in a beautiful part of Essex close to the marshes and estuaries. Beef and lamb reared on the farm, and local pork, are among the many delicacies sold here. Free-range turkeys and chickens, venison from Epping Forest, pigeon and game in season – pheasant, partridge, wild duck from the marshes – are

expertly prepared by the five butchers on site, ably assisted by three cooks who create pies, hot and cold meals, pates and more. Here they also cure bacon and hams, and offer a good variety of excellent seasonal vegetables and fruits.

All cuts of meat can be found here, and the staff are knowledgeable and helpful. In addition there's a good range of chutneys, jams and sauces. Mail order delivery to anywhere in the UK, in special ice-packed containers that can be transferred straight to your freezer and kept for any occasion. Hog Roasts a speciality for all occasions; see website for details.

*St Peter's on the Wall*

following centuries used at various times as a barn and a shipping beacon. Restored and re-consecrated in 1920, it is well worth the half-mile walk from the car park to reach it. It is the site of a pilgrimage each July.

There is an unusual war memorial marking the site of the Bradwell Bay Secret Airfield, used during the Second World War for aircraft unable to return to their original base.

the north; it also offers views over the River Crouch to the south. Exhibitions with local themes are held in the church during the summer months.

## BRADWELL-ON-SEA/BRADWELL WATERSIDE
### 12 miles E of Maldon off the B1021

A visit to Bradwell-on-Sea (the name derives from the Saxon words *brad pall*, meaning 'broad wall') is well worth the long drive for its sense of being right out on the edge of things – the timeless emptiness is if anything exaggerated by the distant views of buildings across the water on Mersea Island and the bulk of the nearby (now decommissioned) nuclear power station. A walk eastwards along the old Roman road across the marshes takes you to the site of their fort, 'Othona', on which the visitors of today will find the chapel of **St Peter's on the Wall**, built by St Cedd and his followers in AD654 using rubble from the ruined fort. In the 14th century the chapel was abandoned as a place of worship, and over the

**Bradwell Lodge**, in the village centre, is a part-Tudor former rectory that has known some famous visitors. Gainsborough, the Suffolk artist, used rooms as a studio, while the Irish writer Erskine Childers, who was shot by the Irish Free State in 1920 because he fought for the IRA, wrote *The Riddle of the Sands* here.

At Bradwell Waterside, a large marina has berths for 300 boats. The now-decommissioned nuclear power station has a visitor centre with an exhibition and high-tech audio-visual displays about electricity production and the

*Cottage in Bradwell*

decommissioning process. A nature trail is way-marked within the grounds of the station.

To the south of the village lie the remote marshes of the **Dengie Peninsula**, parts of which are important nature reserves The salty tang of sea air, brought inland on easterly winds, gives an exhilarating flavour to the marshlands. Like the Cambridgeshire and Lincolnshire fens, this once-waterlogged corner of Essex was reclaimed from the sea by 17<sup>th</sup> century Dutch engineers. The views across the marshes take in great sweeps of countryside inhabited only by wildfowl and seabirds.

## BURNHAM-ON-CROUCH

**12 miles SE of Maldon on the B1012**

Burnham-on-Crouch is attractively old-fashioned, and probably best known as a yachting venue. It is lively in summer, especially at the end of August when the town hosts one of England's premier regattas, Burnham Week. This week of racing and shore events attracts many visiting craft and landlubbers alike. In winter many yachts are left to ride at anchor offshore, and the sound of the wind in their rigging is ever-present.

Behind the gaily-coloured cottages along the Quay lies the High Street and the rest of the town, its streets lined with a delightful assortment of old cottages and Victorian and Georgian houses and shops.

In past times, working boats thronged the estuary where yachts now ply to and fro. Seafarers still come ashore to buy provisions, following a tradition that goes back to medieval times when Burnham was the market centre for the isolated inhabitants of Wallasea and Foulness Islands in the estuary. A ferry still links Burnham with Wallasea at weekends during the summer, and a programme of boat trips to see the seals on Foulness Sands operates from Burnham Quay.

Near the Yacht Harbour, west of the town and accessible along the sea-wall path is **Burnham Country Park**. Also alongside the river can be found the Millfield Recreation Ground and a sports centre.

**Burnham-on-Crouch & District Museum** on The Quay features agricultural, maritime and social history exhibits relating to the Dengie Hundred. There is also a small archaeological collection. Special exhibitions are mounted periodically.

**Mangapps Farm Railway Museum** on the edge of town offers an extensive collection of railway relics of all kinds, including steam and diesel locos, carriages and wagons, relocated railway buildings, one of the largest collections of signalling equipment open to the public, a complete country station and items of East Anglian railway history. Train rides are available when the museum is open, and Thomas the Tank Engine weekends are held several times a year.

**St Mary's Church** is constructed of Kentish ragstone that was transported to Burnham by sea. Construction was begun in the 12<sup>th</sup> century and was completed in the 14<sup>th</sup>, but since that time the nucleus of the town has moved closer to the waterfront. The arches and pillars are particularly fine examples of medieval craftsmanship, hence the church being known as 'The Cathedral of the Dengie'.

# LOCATOR MAP

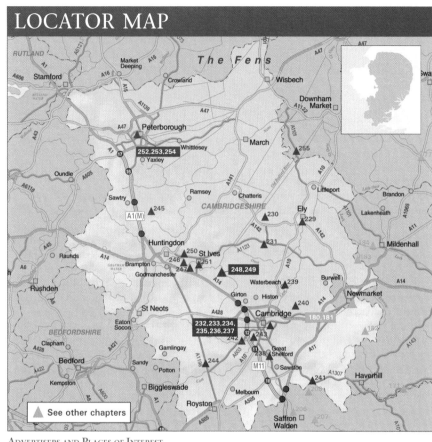

## ADVERTISERS AND PLACES OF INTEREST

229 Cloisters Antiques, Ely                          Page 303
230 The Hall, Witcham                                Page 305
231 Haddenham Galleries, Haddenham, Ely   Page 307
232 Powell & Bull, Cambridge                    Page 309
233 Hobbs Pavilion Restaurant, Cambridge  Page 310
234 The Cambridge Cheese Company,
      Cambridge                                         Page 311
235 Dream Jewellery, Cambridge               Page 311
236 Cambridge University Botanic Garden,
      Cambridge                                         Page 312
237 Cambridge & County Folk Museum,
      Cambridge                                         Page 313
238 Norfolk House, Great Shelford            Page 313
239 Farmland Museum & Denny Abbey,
      Waterbeach                                        Page 314
240 Anglesey Abbey, Gardens & Lode Mill,
      Lode                                                 Page 315
241 Chilford Hall Vineyard, Linton,
      Cambridge                                         Page 317

242 Burwash Manor Barns, Barton             Page 318
243 Honeysuckle Cottage, Grantchester     Page 319
244 Wimpole Estate, Arrington, Royston    Page 320
245 Country Working, Wood Walton,
      Huntingdon                                        Page 322
246 Axe & Compass, Hemingford Abbots,
      Huntingdon                                        Page 328
247 The Manor, Hemingford Grey,
      Huntingdon                                        Page 328
248 The White Horse Inn, Swavesey         Page 330
249 The Trinity Foot, Swavesey               Page 330
250 Houghton Mill, Houghton, Huntingdon Page 331
251 Metamorphosis, St Ives                     Page 332
252 Balagan Giftshop, Peterborough         Page 333
253 Railworld, Peterborough                    Page 335
254 Flag Fen, Peterborough                      Page 336
255 The Wildfowl & Wetlands Trust, Welney,
      Wisbech                                            Page 342

Far removed from the hustle and bustle of modern life, the Fens are like a breath of fresh air. Extending over much of Cambridgeshire from the Wash, these flat, fenland fields contain some of the richest soil in England. Villages such as Fordham and small towns like Ely rise out of the landscape on low hills.

Before the Fens were drained, this was a land of mist, marshes and bogs, of small islands inhabited by independent folk, their livelihood the fish and waterfowl of this eerie, watery place. The region is full of legends of web-footed people, ghosts and witchcraft. Today's landscape is the result of human ingenuity, with its constant desire to tame the wilderness and create farmland. This fascinating story spans the centuries from the earliest Roman and Anglo-Saxon times, when the first embankments and drains were constructed to lessen the frequency of flooding. Throughout the Middle Ages large areas were reclaimed, with much of the work being undertaken by the monasteries. The first straight cut bypassed the Great Ouse, allowing the water to run out to sea more quickly. After the Civil War, the **New Bedford River** was cut parallel to the first. These two still provide the basic drainage for much of Fenland. The significant influence of the Dutch lives on in some of the architecture and place names of the Fens. Over the years it became

*Wansford Riverside*

necessary to pump rainwater from the fields up into the rivers and, as in the Netherlands, windmills took on this task. They could not always cope with the height of the lift required, but fortunately the steam engine came along, to be replaced eventually by the electric pumps that can raise thousands of gallons of water a second to protect the land from the ever-present threat of rain and tide. The Fens offer unlimited opportunities for exploring on foot, by car, bicycle or by boat. Anglers are well catered for, and visitors with an interest in wildlife will be in their element.

Southeastern Cambridgeshire covers the area around the city of Cambridge and is rich in history, with a host of archaeological sites and monuments to visit, as well as many important museums. The area is fairly flat, so it makes for great walking and cycling tours, and offers a surprising variety of landscapes. The Romans planted vines here, and to this day the region is among the main producers of British wines. At the heart of it all is Cambridge

itself, one of the leading academic centres in the world and a city which deserves plenty of time to explore - on foot, by bicycle or by the gentler, more romantic option of a punt.

*Punting, Cambridge*

The old county of Huntingdonshire is the heartland of the rural heritage of Cambridgeshire. Here, the home of Oliver Cromwell beckons with a wealth of history and pleasing landscapes. Many motorists follow the **Cromwell Trail**, which guides tourists around the legacy of buildings and places in the area associated with the man. The natural start of the Trail is Huntingdon itself, where he was born the son of a country gentleman. Other main stopping places are covered in this chapter.

The **Ouse Valley Way** (26 miles long) follows the course of the Great Ouse through pretty villages and a variety of natural attractions. A gentle cruise along this area can fill a lazy day to perfection, but for those who prefer something more energetic on the water there are excellent, versatile facilities at Grafham Water. The Nene-Ouse Navigation Link, part of the Fenland Waterway, provides the opportunity for a relaxed look at a lovely part of the region. It travels from Stanground Lock near Peterborough to a lock at the small village of Salters Lode in the east, and the 28-mile journey passes through several Fenland towns and a rich variety of wildlife habitats.

# ELY

Ely is the jewel in the crown of the Fens, in whose history the majestic **Cathedral** and the Fens themselves have played major roles. The Fens' influence is apparent even in the name: Ely was once known as Elge or Elig ('eel island') because of the large number of eels which lived in the surrounding fenland.

Ely owes its existence to St Etheldreda, Queen of

*Ely Cathedral*

Northumbria, who in AD673 founded a monastery on the 'Isle of Ely', where she remained as abbess until her death in AD679. It was not until 1081 that work started on the present Cathedral, and in 1189 this remarkable example of Romanesque architecture was completed. The most outstanding feature in terms of both scale and beauty is the Octagon, built to replace the original Norman tower, which collapsed in 1322.

Alan of Walsingham was the inspired architect of this massive work, which took 30 years to complete and whose framework weighs an estimated 400 tons. Many other notable components include the 14th century Lady Chapel, the largest in England, the Prior's Door, the painted

nave ceiling and St Ovin's cross, the only piece of Saxon stonework in the building.

The Cathedral is set within the walls of the monastery, and many of the ancient buildings still stand as a tribute to the incredible skill and craftsmanship of their designers and builders. Particularly worth visiting among these are the monastic buildings in the College, the Great Hall and Queens Hall.

Just beside the Cathedral is the Almonry, in whose 12th-century vaulted undercroft visitors can take coffee, lunch or tea - outside in the garden if the weather permits. Two other attractions that should not be missed are the **Brass Rubbing Centre**, where visitors can

*Sunset at Ely*

shops and the riverside. That bustle is at its most fervent on Thursdays, when the largest general market in the area is held. Every Saturday there's a craft and collectibles market, and on the second and fourth Saturdays of the month Ely hosts a Farmers' Market.

At Babylon Gallery on Ely's Waterside, in a converted 18th century brewery warehouse, visitors will find an exciting collection of contemporary arts and crafts, in a programme of changing local and international exhibitions.

make their own rubbings from replica brasses, and the **Museum of Stained Glass**. The latter, housed in the south Triforium of the Cathedral, is the only museum of stained glass in the country and contains over 100 original panels from every period, tracing the complete history of stained glass.

Ely's **Tourist Information Centre** is itself a tourist attraction, since it is housed in a pretty black-and-white timbered building that was once the home of Oliver Cromwell. It is the only remaining house, apart from Hampton Court, where Oliver Cromwell and his family are known to have lived; parts of it trace back to the 13th century, and its varied history includes periods when it was used as a public house and, more recently, a vicarage. There are eight period rooms, exhibitions and videos to enjoy.

The Old Gaol, in Market Street, houses **Ely Museum**, with nine galleries telling the Ely story from the Ice Age to modern times. The tableaux of the condemned and debtors' cells are particularly fascinating and poignant.

Ely is not just the past, and its fine architecture and sense of history blend well with the bustle of the streets and

## AROUND ELY

### Prickwillow
**4 miles NE of Ely on the B1382**

On the village's main street is the **Prickwillow Drainage Engine Museum**, which houses a unique collection of large engines associated with the drainage of the Fens. The site had been in continuous use as a pumping station since 1831, and apart from the engines there are displays charting the history of Fens drainage, the effects on land levels and the workings of the modern drainage system.

### Littleport
**6 miles N of Ely on the A10**

**St George's Church**, with its very tall 15th century tower, is a notable landmark here in Littleport. Of particular interest are two stained-glass windows depicting St George slaying the dragon. Littleport was the scene of riots in 1861, when labourers from Ely and Littleport, faced with unemployment or low wages, and soaring food prices, attacked houses and people in this area, causing several deaths. Five of the rioters were hanged and buried in a common grave at St Mary's church. A plaque commemorating the event is attached to a wall at the back of the church.

## Little Downham

**3 miles N of Ely off the A10**

Little Downham's **Church of St Leonard** shows the change from Norman to Gothic in church building at the turn of the 13th century. The oldest parts are the Norman tower and the elaborately carved south door. Interior treasures include what is probably the largest royal coat of arms in the country. At the other end of the village are the remains (mainly the gatehouse and kitchen) of a 15th century palace built by a Bishop of Ely. The property is in private hands and part of it is an antiques centre.

## Coveney

**3 miles W of Ely off the A10**

A Fenland hamlet on the Bedford Level just above West Fen, Coveney's church of **St Peter-ad-Vincula** has several interesting features, including a colourful German screen dating from around 1500 and a painted Danish pulpit. Unusual figures on the bench ends and a fine brass chandelier add to the opulent feel of this atmospheric little church.

## Sutton

**6 miles W of Ely off the A142**

A very splendid 'pepperpot' tower with octagons, pinnacles and spire tops marks out Sutton's grand church of St Andrew. Inside, take time to look at the 15th century font and a fine modern stained-glass window.

The reconstruction of the church was largely the work of two Bishops of Ely, whose arms appear on the roof bosses. One of the Bishops was Thomas Arundel, appointed at the age of 21.

A mile further west, there's a great family attraction in the **Mepal Outdoor Centre**, an outdoor leisure centre with a children's playpark, an adventure play area and boat hire.

## Haddenham

**5 miles SW of Ely on the A1123**

More industrial splendour: **Haddenham Great Mill**, built in 1803 for a certain Daniel Cockle, is a glorious sight, and one definitely not to be missed. It has four sails and three sets of grinding stones, one of which is working. The mill last worked commercially in 1946 and was restored between 1992 and 1998. Open on the first Sunday of each month and by appointment.

# *Wardy Hill*

| | |
|---|---|
| **Distance:** | 5.5 miles (8.8 kilometres) |
| **Typical time:** | 120 mins |
| **Height gain:** | 0 metres |
| **Map:** | Explorer 228 |
| **Walk:** | www.walkingworld.com ID:1170 |
| **Contributor:** | Joy & Charles Boldero |

## Access Information:

For information about bus routes ring 0870 6082608. There is parking on the very wide grass verge at By-way sign on the edge of Wardy Hill village, by Beumont Farm fence line. Wardy Hill is situated on a minor road off the A142 4 miles west of Ely.

## Additional Information:

Wardy Hill is set on an island above the fens, on what is known as the Isle of Ely. Wardy Hill means 'look out'. In centuries past this was to watch for cattle raiders coming across the fens. It is thought it was a Bronze settlement as shields and swords have been found here.

The New Bedford River, or Hundred-Foot Drain as it is also called, was built after the Old Bedford River, built by the Dutchman, Vermuydrn in the 1600's, was found to be inadequate. The land between the two rivers is a flood plain and part of the R.S.P.B. famous

Welney Washes. To the left on the horizon Ely Cathedral can be seen.

The Three Pickerels pub at Mepal has an excellent menu. It is closed on Monday lunch times. It is open all day on Sundays.

## Description:

This walk is beside the New Bedford River to Mepal, then returning by tracks, footpaths which can be muddy after heavy rain and country lanes.

## Features:

River, Pub, Toilets, Wildlife, Birds, Flowers, Great Views, Butterflies

## Walk Directions:

**1** Go westwards through the village, ignoring all footpaths off the country lane. Continue along Jerusalem Drove to left hand bend.

**2** At bridleway sign go right along track passing Toll Cottage. Climb stile and cross to next one and climb it going up the bank.

**3** Turn left along river bank. Much further along go down bank to metal gate, climb stile. You can either continue along the track or climb the stile and go back onto bank. Climb stile.

**4** Turn right along road in Mepal, then almost immediately left to pub. Retrace steps to junction and turn right along pavement.

**5** Cross road by right hand bend and turn left along New Road. At end go around gate and cross field. Climb stile, cross second field, climb stile.

**6** Turn left along track then almost immediately right. Cross field and slippery bridge.

**7** Turn right along track. Cross road and continue along the track opposite. Cross track and continue along track. At fork either path can be used.

**8** Turn left at cross tracks.

**9** At T junction of tracks turn right.

**10** Turn left along country lane back to start of walk.

## HADDENHAM GALLERIES

20 High Street, Haddenham, Ely,
Cambridgeshire CB6 3XA
Tel: 01353 749188  Fax: 01353 740688

**The Creative Art Gallery** is set in the centre of Haddenham, with fine views across the fens, and with a natural meadow to be set out as a sculpture garden. The gallery holds ten selling exhibitions each year, exploring all aspects of Creative Art from a wide source of makers. Wherever possible it supports emerging artists, encourages new work and provides a valuable stepping stone in exhibiting affordable work to the public.

In conjunction with the exhibitions it runs workshops for local children and adults, and is regularly involved in regional arts events and working open days. Also there are eight studios let to local artists/craftsmen working in a variety of disciplines.

**The Ethnic Gallery** is adjoining through a 17th century carved doorway from Afghanistan. Alastair Hull, veteran traveller and writer, collects at source all the unusual and exciting items in this colourful gallery. He frequently travels through remote bazaars and villages within Central Asia and the East Indies Archipelago and has built up a unique collection and deep knowledge of the people, their culture and traditions.

The **Church of St Andrew** stands on a hillside in Haddenham. Look for the stained-glass window depicting two souls entering Heaven, and the memorial (perhaps the work of Grinling Gibbons) to Christopher Wren's sister, Anne Brunsell.

## STRETHAM

### 5 miles S of Ely off A10/A1123

The **Stretham Old Engine**, a fine example of a land-drainage steam engine, is housed in a restored, tall-chimneyed brick engine house. Dating from 1831, it is one of 90 steam pumping engines installed throughout the Fens to replace some 800 windmills. It is the last to survive, having worked until 1925 and still under restoration. During the great floods of 1919 it really earned its keep by working non-stop for 47 days and nights.

This unique insight into Fenland history and industrial archaeology is open to the public on summer weekends, and on certain dates the engine and its wooden scoop-wheel are rotated (by electricity, alas!). The adjacent stoker's cottage contains period furniture and photographs of fen drainage down the years.

**Downfield Windmill**, six miles southeast of Ely on the A142 bypass, was built in 1726 as a smock mill, destroyed by gales and rebuilt in 1890 as an octagonal tower mill. It still grinds corn and produces a range of flours and breads for sale (open Sundays and Bank Holidays).

## WICKEN

### 9 miles S of Ely off the A1123

Owned by the National Trust, **Wicken Fen** is the oldest nature reserve in the country, 600 acres of undrained fenland famous for its rich plant, insect and bird life and a delight for both naturalists and ramblers. Features include boardwalk and nature trails, hides and watchtowers, a cottage with 1930s furnishings, a working wind pump (the oldest in the country), a visitor centre and a shop. Open daily, dawn to dusk.

**St Lawrence's Church** is well worth a visit, small and secluded among trees. In the churchyard are buried Oliver Cromwell and several members of his family. One of Cromwell's many nicknames was 'Lord of the Fens': he defended the rights of the Fenmen against those who wanted to drain the land without providing adequate compensation.

**Wicken Windmill** is a fine and impressive smock windmill restored back to working order. One of only four smock windmills making flour by windmill in the UK, it is open the first weekend of every month and every Bank Holiday (except Christmas and Good Friday) from 11 a.m. until 5 p.m., and also over the National Mills Weekend the second week in May.

### FORDHAM

**10 miles SE of Ely off the A142/B1102**

A small village on the **Newmarket Cycle Way**, the poet James Withers spent most of his life in Fordham and is buried in the churchyard. A stained-glass window in the church is inscribed in his memory.

### ISLEHAM

**10 miles SE of Ely off the B1104**

The remains of a Benedictine priory, with a lovely Norman chapel under the care of English Heritage, are a great draw here in Isleham. Also well worth a visit is the Church of St Andrew, a 14th century cruciform building entered by a very fine

lychgate. The 17th century eagle lectern is the original of a similar lectern in Ely Cathedral.

### SNAILWELL

**12 miles SE of Ely off the A142**

Snailwell's pretty, mainly 14th century Church of St Peter on the banks of the River Snail boasts a 13th century chancel, a hammerbeam and tie beam nave roof, a 600-year-old font, pews with poppy heads and two medieval oak screens. The Norman round tower is unusual for Cambridgeshire.

# CAMBRIDGE

There are nearly 30 Cambridges spread around the globe, but this, the original, is the one that the whole world knows as one of the leading university cities. Cambridge was an important town many centuries before the scholars arrived, standing at the point where forest met fen, at the lowest fording point of the river. The Romans took over a site previously settled by an Iron Age Belgic tribe, to be followed in turn by the Saxons and the Normans.

Soon after the Norman Conquest, William I built a wooden motte-and-bailey castle; Edward I built a stone replacement: a mound still marks the spot. The town flourished as a market and river trading centre, and in 1209 a group of students fleeing the Oxford riots arrived.

The first College was **Peterhouse**, founded by the Bishop of Ely in 1284, and in the next century Clare, Pembroke, Gonville & Caius, Trinity Hall and Corpus Christi followed. The total is now 31, the latest being **Robinson College**, the gift of self-made millionaire David Robinson. The Colleges represent various architectural styles, the grandest and most beautiful being King's. Robinson has the look of a fortress; its concrete structure covered with a 'skin' of a million and a quarter hand-made red Dorset bricks.

The Colleges are all well worth a visit, but places that simply must not be missed include **King's College Chapel** with its breathtaking fan vaulting, glorious stained glass and Peter Paul Rubens' *Adoration of the Magi*; **Pepys Library**, including his diaries, in Magdalene College; and

*King's College Chapel*

Trinity's wonderful **Great Court**. A trip by punt along the 'Backs' of the Cam brings a unique view of many of the Colleges and passes under six bridges, including the **Bridge of Sighs** (St John's) and the extraordinary wooden **Mathematical Bridge** at Queens.

Cambridge has nurtured more Nobel Prize winners than most countries - 32 from Trinity alone - and the list of celebrated alumni covers every sphere of human endeavour and achievement: Byron, Tennyson, Milton and Wordsworth; Marlowe and Bacon;

## POWELL & BULL

31 Magdalene Street, Cambridge, Cambridgeshire CB3 0AF
Tel: 01223 462256  Fax: 01223 507931

**Powell & Bull**, located on Magdalene Bridge within view of Magdalene College and set in a row of medieval buildings, is a distinctive and distinguished jeweller's also selling a range of leather handbags, briefcases and wallets. Owned and run by Christopher Powell, a jeweller for the past 20 years, the shop boasts an exquisite range of necklaces, earrings, bracelets and more,

fashioned in gold, silver, titanium, stainless steel and acrylics, and all beautifully displayed in handsome cabinets and showcases.

Along with diamond and platinum rings - wedding rings can be specially commissioned - the shop also boasts a good selection of stainless steel and titanium pieces and jewellery with specialist finishes and modern designs, many created by Christopher on-site. There's also an exclusive range of Jane Hopkinson handmade leather bags, along with individual Italian handmade leatherware from small independent craftsmen, chosen for their quality and style.

Samuel Pepys; Sir Isaac Newton and Charles Darwin; Charles Babbage, Bertrand Russell and Ludwig Wittgenstein; actors Sir Ian McKellen, Sir Derek Jacobi and Stephen Fry; Lord Burghley; Harold Abrahams, who ran for England in the Olympics; and Burgess, Maclean, Philby and Blunt, who spied for Russia.

*Bridge of Sighs*

The Colleges apart, Cambridge is packed with interest for the visitor, with a wealth of grand buildings both religious and secular, and some of the country's leading museums, many of them run by the University. The **Fitzwilliam Museum** is renowned for its art collection, which includes works by Titian, Rembrandt, Gainsborough, Hogarth, Turner, Renoir, Picasso and Cezanne, and for its antiquities from Egypt, Greece and Rome. **Kettle's Yard** has a permanent display of 20$^{th}$ century art in a house maintained just as it was when the Ede family donated it, with the collection, to

## HOBBS PAVILION RESTAURANT

Parker's Piece, Cambridge,
Cambridgeshire CB1 1JH
Tel: 01223 367480/505760

**Hobbs Pavilion** is a superb restaurant set in a former cricket pavilion built in 1950 and named in honour of Cambridge-born Sir Jack Hobbs.

Located right in the centre of Cambridge, within five acres of former pitch, this popular and friendly restaurant has earned an enviable reputation for great food

and excellent, unobtrusive service, and has been favourably reviewed in *The Guardian, FHM* and other respected journals. Run by Mohammed Aktar, who is related to Ranjit Singh, another famous cricketer who came to Cambridge University before a distinguished career for India, here diners are spoilt for choice by the range of expertly prepared and presented dishes which include main courses such as roast duckling, Kashmir lamb, monkfish and sirloin steaks.

There are also vegetarian and vegan specials – which live up to Hobbs' claim to be one of the best venues for vegetarian food in Cambridge – and delectable puddings well worth leaving room for. The décor is modern and comfortable, and a new feature is the heated verandah, which gives the place a Mediterranean feel even in the depths of winter. *Open:* Monday to Saturday 11 a.m. – 10.30 p.m., Sundays 11 a.m. – 4 p.m. and 6 – 10 p.m.

the University in 1967. The **Museum of Classical Archaeology** has 500 plaster casts of Greek and Roman statues, and the **University Museum of Archaeology and Anthropology** covers worldwide prehistoric archaeology with special displays relating to Oceania and to the Cambridge area. The **Museum of Technology**, housed in a Victorian sewage pumping station,

*Trinity College*

features an impressive collection of steam, gas and electric pumping engines and examples great and small of local industrial technology. Anyone with an interest in fossils should make tracks for the **Sedgwick Museum of Earth Sciences**, while in the same street (Downing) the **Museum of Zoology** offers a comprehensive and spectacular survey of the animal kingdom. The **Whipple Museum of the History of Science** tells about science through instruments; the **Scott Polar Research Institute** has fascinating, often poignant exhibits relating to Arctic and Antarctic exploration; and the **University Botanic**

## CAMBRIDGE UNIVERSITY BOTANIC GARDEN

University of Cambridge, Cory Lodge, Bateman Street,
Cambridge CB2 1JF
Tel: 01223 336265 e-mail: enquiries@botanic.cam.ac.uk
Fax: 01223 336278  website: www.botanic.cam.ac.uk

The **Cambridge University Botanic Garden** is a 40-acre oasis of beautiful gardens and glasshouses located right in the heart of this historic city. The vision of Professor John Stevens Henslow, tutor and mentor to Charles Darwin, this Grade II* heritage landscape opened to the public in 1846 and now welcomes over 100,000 visitors each year.

Amongst many important collections held at the Botanic Garden, the national collections of species Tulips, Fritillaries and hardy Geraniums stand out. Landscape highlights include the renowned Winter Garden, which brings together vividly coloured stems, textured tree trunks, variegated foliage effect and the heady scent of winter flowers to create a beautiful garden even in the darkest months. To warm up, a visit to the Tropical Houses is recommended, where the luxuriant foliage of vines and mature trees is bejewelled with the flamboyant blooms of orchids and bromeliads. The Succulent and Cactus Houses offer contrast with displays of drought-adapted plants of wonderful form and crazy flowers.

The Woodland Garden combines an open and airy collection of decorative trees, including lime-tolerant Magnolias and maturing specimens of the Katsura and Dove trees, with a rich tapestry of herbaceous planting at its best in late spring. Close by, the newly renovated Bog Garden enjoys a sheltered microclimate where moisture-loving plants predominate.

The Limestone Rock Garden provides a wonderful vantage point over the Lake, which teems with birdlife. It is planted geographically, so it is possible to walk through the world's alpine flora from Australia via South Africa to North America. Rock garden plants are usually profuse and colourful flowerers - they need to show off to attract the few pollinators that live in desolate alpine habitats. The Limestone Rock Garden is at its most spectacular in June and July.

The Dry Garden is a model garden focusing on design and horticultural techniques that reduce the need for irrigation and yet create a bold and beautiful garden. The stunning plantings feature lots of grey-leaved, waxy-leaved and aromatic plants, giving a distinct Mediterranean feel that is encouraged by the newly-planted pergola and huge terracotta pots.

Perhaps most extraordinary at the Cambridge Botanic Garden are the Systematic Beds, designed in 1845 to reflect the standard 19th century plant textbook, written by Alphonse de Candolle. In his book, de Candolle sorted plants into two major groups: those with one seed leaf (monocotyledons) and those with two seed leaves (dicotyledons). The Systematic Beds thus present the monocotyledons in a central oval, surrounded by the dicotyledons. In all, the Systematic Beds today display about 1600 hardy, herbaceous species from 98 families, laid out in 157 beds, and you can still complete a circuit as if turning from the first to last pages of de Candolle's book.

The Cambridge University Botanic Garden, with its treasure trove of some 8,000 plant species set within the finest arboretum in East Anglia, is a must for plant lovers. It opens daily at 10am (closed 25 December - 1 January inclusive) and there is an admission charge.

Garden (see panel on page 312) boasts a plant collection that rivals those of Kew Gardens and Edinburgh.

The work and life of the people of Cambridge and the surrounding area are the subject of the **Cambridge and County Folk Museum** (see panel), housed in a 16th century building that for 300 years was the White Horse Inn. One of the city's greatest treasures is the **University Library**, one of the world's great research libraries with 6 million books, a million maps and 350,000 manuscripts.

Cambridge also has many fine churches, some of them used by the Colleges before they built their own chapels. Among the most notable are **St Andrew the Great** (note the memorial to Captain Cook); **St Andrew the Less**; **St Benet's** (its 11th century tower is the oldest in the county); **St Mary the Great**, a marvellous example of Late Perpendicular Gothic; and **St Peter Castle Hill**. This last is one of the smallest churches in the country, with a nave measuring just 25 feet by 16 feet. Originally much larger, the church was largely demolished in 1781 and rebuilt in its present diminished state using the old materials, including flint rubble and Roman bricks. The Church of the Holy

### CAMBRIDGE & COUNTY FOLK MUSEUM

2-3 Castle Street, Cambridge, Cambridgeshire CB3 0AQ
Tel: 01223 355159
website: www.folkmuseum.org.uk

Housed in a late 15th century timber-framed building that was formerly the White Horse Inn, the **Cambridge & County Folk Museum** takes a nostalgic, warm-hearted look at the everyday lives of people from Cambridge and the surrounding area from 1700 onwards. Topics include Crafts & Trades, Town & Gown, Witchbottles, Skating and Eels, and throughout the year themed talks and exhibitions take place. The Museum Shop stocks an interesting range of games and puzzles, books and many other items that make ideal Christmas stocking fillers, all with a nostalgic feel.

Sepulchre, always known as the **Round Church**, is one of only four surviving circular churches in England.

### NORFOLK HOUSE

2 Tunwells Lane, Great Shelford, Cambridgeshire CB2 5LJ
Tel: 01223 840287

**Norfolk House** is a distinctive Victorian residence lovingly restored in keeping with the period and set in the centre of Great Shelford. Spacious and handsomely decorated and furnished, the exterior boasts a delightful garden with pond and outdoor chess. With two twins and a double, this superior B&B is open all year round (except at Christmas). No smoking. Children over 10 welcome. Near Cambridge, the Imperial War Museum at Duxford, Ely Cathedral, Audley End and other sights and attractions, it makes an excellent touring base.

# AROUND CAMBRIDGE

## GIRTON
**3 miles NW of Cambridge off the A14**

The first Cambridge College for women was founded in 1869 in Hitchin, by Emily Davies. It moved here to Girton in 1873, to be *'near enough for male lecturers to visit but far enough away to discourage male students from doing the same'*. The problem went away when Girton became a mixed College in 1983.

## RAMPTON
**6 miles N of Cambridge off the B1049**

A charming village in its own right, with a tree-fringed village green, Rampton is also the site of one of the many archaeological sites in the area. This is **Giant's Hill**, a motte castle with part of an earlier medieval settlement.

## MILTON
**3 miles N of Cambridge off the A10**

**Milton Country Park** offers fine walking and exploring among acres of parkland, lakes and woods. There's a visitor centre, a picnic area and a place serving light refreshments.

## WATERBEACH
**6 miles NE of Cambridge on the B1102**

**Denny Abbey**, easily accessible on the A10, is an English Heritage Grade I listed Abbey with ancient earthworks. On the same site, and run as a joint attraction, is the **Farmland Museum** (see panel below). The history of Denny Abbey runs from the 12th century, when it was a Benedictine monastery. It was later home to the Knights Templar, Franciscan nuns and the Countess of Pembroke, and from the 16th century was a farmhouse. The old farm buildings have been splendidly

## FARMLAND MUSEUM & DENNY ABBEY

Ely Road, Waterbeach, Cambridgeshire CB5 9PQ
Tel/Fax: 01223 860489
e-mail: f.m.denny@tesco.net
website: www.dennyfarmlandmuseum.org.uk

Two thousand years of history are brought fascinatingly to life in a lovely rural setting on the A10 six miles north of Cambridge. The stone-built farmhouse at the heart of the site is actually the remains of a 12th century Benedictine Abbey which at different times was home to Benedictine monks, the Knights Templar and nuns of the Franciscan order, the Poor Clares. The superb Norman interior has been beautifully preserved and restored, and visitors can see the nuns' refectory and the rooms converted for their founder, the Countess of Pembrokeshire. Displays and children's activities tell the story of how Denny has evolved down the centuries.

On the same site, and run by English Heritage as a joint attraction, is the Farmland Museum. Old farm buildings have been splendidly renovated and converted to tell visitors about the rural history of Cambridgeshire from early days to modern times. The Museum is ideal for family visits, with specially designed activities for children, and among the top displays are a village shop, agricultural machinery, a magnificent 17th century stone barn, a traditional farmworker's cottage and the workshops, which include a basket maker and a blacksmith. Special weekend events, from buttermaking demonstrations to traditional building methods, are held regularly at the Museum, which is open from noon to 5pm April to October.

renovated and converted to tell the story of village life and Cambridgeshire farming up to modern times. The museum is ideal for family outings, with plenty of hands-on activities for children and a play area, gift shop and weekend tearoom.

## LODE

**6 miles NE of Cambridge on the B1102**

**Anglesey Abbey** (see panel below) dates from 1600 and was built on the site of an Augustinian priory, but the house and the 100-acre garden came together as a unit thanks to the vision of the 1st Lord Fairhaven. The garden, created in its present form from the 1930s, is a wonderful place for a stroll, with 98 acres of landscaped gardens including wide grassy walks, open lawns, a riverside walk, a working water mill and one of the finest collections of garden statuary in the country. There's also a plant centre, shop and restaurant. In the house itself is Lord Fairhaven's magnificent collection of paintings, sumptuous furnishings, tapestries and clocks.

## BOTTISHAM

**5 miles E of Cambridge on the A1303**

John Betjeman ventured that Bottisham's **Holy Trinity Church** was 'perhaps the best in the county', so time should certainly be made for a visit. Among the many interesting features are the 13th century porch, an 18th century

© NTPL

ANGLESEY ABBEY, GARDENS AND LODE MILL

Lode, Cambridgeshire, CB5 9EJ
Tel: 01223 810080

**Anglesey Abbey** estate is made up of 40 hectares (98 acres) of garden and parkland, a manor house in the Jacobean style and an eighteenth century watermill. The House is on the site of monastic buildings. There is little left now of the original as many alterations were made over the centuries.

What you see now was created by the first Lord Fairhaven and his brother from 1926 onwards. At the same time they started their collections to put in the house and gardens. There are sumptuous furnishings and rare works of art displayed as Lord Fairhaven intended; gardens within a garden display mythical beasts, lions, Roman emperors and Greek gods plus unusual trees, colour and interest for every season.

When the first Lord Fairhaven left Anglesey Abbey to the National Trust in the 1960s, he wanted the house and garden to be kept to 'represent an age and way of life that is quickly passing'.

His mother was American and his father English and what he left is a mixture of the two cultures. The house has been described as having 'something of a great Long Island interior'. The design of the garden is based on the eighteenth and nineteenth century English country garden.

monument to Sir Roger Jenyns and some exceptionally fine modern woodwork in Georgian style.

## SWAFFHAM PRIOR
### 8 miles NE of Cambridge on the B1102

Swaffham Prior gives double value to the visitor, with two churches in the same churchyard and two fine old windmills. The churches of **St Mary** and **St Cyriac** stand side by side, a remarkable and dramatic sight in the steeply rising churchyard. One of the mills, a restored 1850s tower mill, still produces flour and can be visited by appointment.

At **Swaffham Bulbeck**, a little way to the south, stands another church of St Mary, with a 13<sup>th</sup> century tower and 14<sup>th</sup> century arcades and chancel. Look for the fascinating carvings on the wooden benches and a 15<sup>th</sup> century cedarwood chest decorated with biblical scenes.

## BURWELL
### 10 miles NE of Cambridge on the B1102

Burwell is a village of many attractions with a history going back to Saxon times. **Burwell Museum** reflects many aspects of a village on the edge of the Fens up to the middle of the 20<sup>th</sup> century. A general store, model farm, local industries and children's toys are among the displays.

Next to the museum is the famous **Stephens Windmill**, built in 1820 and extensively restored.

The man who designed parts of King's College Chapel, Reginald Ely, is thought to have been responsible for the beautiful St Mary's church, which is built of locally quarried clunch stone and is one of the finest examples of the Perpendicular style. Notable internal features include a 15<sup>th</sup> century font, a medieval wall painting of St Christopher

*Stephens Windmill*

and roof carvings of elephants, while in the churchyard a gravestone marks the terrible night in 1727 when 78 Burwell folk died in a barn fire while watching a travelling *Punch & Judy* show.

Behind the church are the remains of **Burwell Castle**, started in the 12th century but never properly completed.

The **Devil's Dyke** runs through Burwell on its path from Reach to Woodditton. This amazing dyke, 30 yards wide, was built, it is thought, to halt Danish invaders.

## REACH
### 8 miles NE of Cambridge off the A4280

The charming village of Reach is home to the oldest fair in England, which celebrated its 800th anniversary on 1st May, 2000.

## LINTON

**10 miles SE of Cambridge on the B1052**

The village is best known for its zoo, but visitors will also find many handsome old buildings and the church of St Mary the Virgin, built mainly in Early English style.

A world of wildlife set in 16 acres of spectacular gardens, **Linton Zoo** is a major wildlife breeding centre and part of the inter-zoo breeding programme for endangered species. Collections include wild cats, birds, snakes and insects. For children there is a play area and, in summer, pony rides and a bouncy castle.

Chilford Hall Vineyard, on the B1052 between Linton and Balsham, comprises 18 acres of vines, with tours and wine-tastings available. Some two miles further off the A1307, **Bartlow Hills** are the site of the largest Roman burial site to be unearthed in Europe.

## DUXFORD

**8 miles S of Cambridge off A505 by J10 of the M11**

Part of the **Imperial War Museum**, Duxford Aviation Museum is probably the leader in its field in Europe, with an outstanding collection of over 150 historic aircraft from biplanes through Spitfires to supersonic jets.

The American Air Museum, where aircraft are suspended as if in flight, is part of this terrific place, which was built on a former RAF and US fighter base. Major air shows take place several times a year, and among the permanent features are a reconstructed wartime operations room, a hands-on exhibition for children and a dramatic land warfare hall with tanks, military vehicles and artillery. Everyone should take time to see this marvellous show - and it should be much more than a flying visit!

### CHILFORD HALL VINEYARD

Linton, Cambridge, Cambridgeshire CB1 6LE
Tel: 01223 895600  Fax: 01223 895605
e-mail: info@chilfordhall.co.uk
website: www.chilfordhall.co.uk

Established in 1972 and 'dedicated to making the difference', **Chilford Hall Vineyard** is an award-winning family-run concern just eight miles from Cambridge off the B1052 between Linton and Balsham, found by following the brown tourist signs from the A11 or A1307. Set in 40 acres of rolling countryside, it is a dedicated banqueting venue made up of a rich diversity of modern and period buildings set against the vineyard backdrop. With several distinct venues – the impressive Great Hall, with gleaming wood and an arched ceiling, dating from 1820;

The Pavilion, which is one of the largest event spaces in the region; the beautiful Gallery Hall, licensed for marriage ceremonies; the Coutyard, an informal area with its own bar; and the cosy timber-framed Linton Hall.

At the 18-acre vineyard, The Chilford Hall wine list boasts a comprehensive range of wines – including Muller-Thurgau, Ortega, Reichensteiner, Siegerrebe and an award-winning sparkling pink wine – to suit every taste and budget. Visitors can enjoy wine-tastings, winery tours, a vineyard trail and an extended walk. Open daily from 1st March to 1st November, the site also includes a Visitors' Centre, the Vineleaf Shop and the Vineleaf Café. The onsite Conference Centre can cater for up to 1,300 visitors.

## BURWASH MANOR BARNS

New Road, Barton, Cambridgeshire CB3 7AY
Tel: 01223 263423   Fax: 01223 264567

Michael and Susan Radford run Burwash Manor Farm, where a wide range of unique, interesting shops are located in converted stockyard buildings in the grounds of a moated manor house.

The Rocking Horse Toy Shop has new and nearly new high-quality, traditional, old-fashioned toys, from small wooden rattles to dolls' houses, wooden farms and rocking horses. The stock also includes books and games.

The Barn Tea Rooms offer a large selection of cakes, pastries and cooked-to-order lunches with a specials board supplementing the standard menu. It's a cosy, friendly place, with waitress service and, outside a seating and play area – children are always welcome. On the takeaway front, the Larder has for sale a range of foodstuffs prepared by people who care passionately about quality. The organic selection includes cheese, ice creams and rare-breed meats, as well as fruit and vegetables.

The Wine Cellar, in a converted dovecote, is a subtly-lit spot with an ever-changing range of personally chosen top-quality wines; tastings enable customers to create their own wine selection.

In the Summer House, an exciting range of textiles and soft furnishings showcases the best of English and Scandinavian styles, with many items – including made-to-measure curtains, blinds and items of clothing from jokey wellies to formal evening wear – designed and made in-house. Persian Tribal Rugs deal in rugs and kelims imported from nomadic tribes and Iranian villages for the wholesale and retail trade. The partners in Providence, located in a converted grain mill, moved to the UK from New England with a mission to spread the word on the Shaker philosophy on cabinets and interiors. Freestanding and built-in cabinets are the speciality, along with a full range of finishing paints, and the stock also includes handmade pottery and New England craft products.

The Secret Garden Christmas Shop – 'Christmas Wonderland in a marquee' – has a beautiful and exciting collection of unusual tree and room decorations and a range of personally selected freshly-cut trees, together with terrace garden furniture and statuary. Cambridge Learning is an independent software shop with a mail-order catalogue, specialising in selling mainly education and 'seriously fun' software to schools and homes, and operating a try-before-you-buy policy. The owners always keep an eye open for new products such as a mini-mouse for tiny hands. Bodyline Health offer various therapies in homely treatment rooms, with fully qualified therapists offering Swedish massage, aromatherapy, reflexology, homoeopathy, baby massage classes, head massage and sports and injury therapy.

Inside Out offers classic leisure clothing and footwear; Giftsmith is the place for all manner of unique hand-crafted gifts; Sterling Design features silverware gifts; Gosh offers a selection of modern designer clothing for children; Nursery Day has new and second-hand nursery equipment and clothes; Bagatelle sells decorative reproduction furniture and interiors; House of Fragrance is an emporium of fragranced gifts, essential oils and relaxation tapes and CDs.

At nearby **Hinxton**, a few miles further south, is another mill: a 17th century water mill that is grinding once more.

## SHEPRETH
**8 miles S of Cambridge off the A10**

A paradise for lovers of nature and gardens and a great starting point for country walks, **Shepreth L Moor Nature Reserve** is an L-shaped area of wet meadowland - now a rarity - that is home to birds and many rare plants. The nearby **Shepreth Wildlife Park** is a haven in natural surroundings to a wide variety of animals, which visitors can touch and feed. The 18th century **Docwra's Manor** is a series of enclosed gardens with multifarious plants that is worth a visit at any time of year. Fowlmere, on the other side of the A10, is another important nature reserve, with hides and trails for the serious bird-watcher.

## GRANTCHESTER
**2 miles SW of Cambridge off the A603**

A pleasant walk by the Cam, or a punt on it, brings visitors from the bustle of Cambridge to the famous village of Grantchester, where Rupert Brooke lived and Byron swam. The walk passes through **Paradise Nature Reserve**.

*'Stands the church clock at ten to three*
*And is there honey still for tea?'*

**The Orchard**, with its Brooke connections, is known the world over. Brooke spent two happy years in Grantchester, and immortalised afternoon tea in The Orchard in a poem he wrote while homesick in Berlin. Time should also be allowed for a look at the church of St Andrew and St Mary, in which the remains of a Norman church have been incorporated into the 1870s main structure.

## BARTON
**3 miles SW of Cambridge off the A603**

Looking south from this pleasant village you can see the impressive array of radio telescopes that are part of Cambridge University's Mullard Radio Astronomy Observatory.

## ARRINGTON
**11 miles SW of Cambridge off the A603**

Arrington's 18th century **Wimpole Hall** (see panel on page 320), owned by the National Trust, is probably the most spectacular country mansion in the whole county, and certainly the largest 18th century country house in Cambridgeshire. The lovely interiors are the work of several celebrated architects, and there's a fine collection of furniture and pictures. The magnificent formally laid-out grounds include a Victorian parterre, a rose garden and a walled garden.

---

## HONEYSUCKLE COTTAGE

38 High Street, Grantchester, Cambridgeshire CB3 9NF
Tel: 01223 845977   Mobile: 07974 767807

A former tithe cottage dating back to the 1800s, **Honeysuckle Cottage** is a charming and supremely comfortable bed and breakfast with three double ensuite bedrooms overlooking the lush garden. Quiet and secluded yet located in the centre of the historic village of Grantchester, near the handsome church, the house is within easy distance of several excellent pubs in close proximity, and just minutes from the Rupert Brooke tearooms, named for the village's most famous son. ETC 3 Diamonds. No children or pets.

## WIMPOLE ESTATE

Wimpole Hall & Home Farm, Arrington,
Royston, Cambs SG8 0BW
Tel: 01223 207257  Fax: 01223 207838

© NTPL

**Wimpole Hall**, the largest house in Cambridgeshire, dates back over 300 years and was bequeathed to The National Trust by Elsie Bambridge, daughter of Rudyard Kipling. The fine interior has an elegant Bookroom; a spectacular Yellow Drawing Room and an unusual Bath House designed by Sir John Soane. There is also an impressive Library designed by James Gibbs housing over 10,000 books and a Chapel magnificently painted by James Thornhill.

The gardens at Wimpole vary from the formal Victorian parterre and a Dutch garden to the Pleasure Grounds, with many unusual species of trees, plus a restored working Walled Garden, abundant with seasonal vegetables and flowers, overlooked by the Sir John Soane designed glasshouse.

Wimpole Park is the work of noted landscape designers of their day such as Charles Bridgeman, Humphry Repton, Sanderson Miller and 'Capability' Brown with extensive parkland, avenues of trees, serpentine lakes, woodland belts and a Gothic folly. Wimpole Home Farm was designed in 1792 by Sir John Soane, built as a model farm on the estate and all the buildings are centred around the farmyard: a large thatched barn; cart shed; stables and cattle stalls. The farm was restored in the 1980s and is now a working farm and centre for rare breeds, including White Park cattle and Tamworth pigs.

© NTPL

Landscaped **Wimpole Park**, with hills, woodland, lakes and a Chinese bridge, provides miles of wonderful walking and is perfect for anything from a gentle stroll to a strenuous hike.

A brilliant attraction for all the family is **Wimpole Home Farm**, a working farm that is the largest rare breeds centre in East Anglia. The animals include Bagot goats, Tamworth pigs, Soay sheep and Longhorn cattle, and there's also a pets corner and horse-drawn wagon ride. Children can spend hours with the animals or in the adventure playground.

### CAXTON
#### 6 miles W of Cambridge off the A1219B/A428

Caxton is home to Britain's oldest surviving postmill, and at **Little Gransden**, a couple of miles further southwest on the B1046, another venerable mill has been restored. A

scheduled ancient monument, it dates from the early 17th century and was worked well into the early years of the 20th century.

### MADINGLEY
#### 4 miles W of Cambridge on the A428

The **American Cemetery** is one of the loveliest, most peaceful and most moving places in the region, a place of pilgrimage for the families of the American servicemen who operated from the many wartime bases in the county. The cemetery commemorates 3,811 dead and 5,125 missing in action in the Second World War.

# HUNTINGDON

The former county town of Huntingdonshire is an ancient place first settled by the Romans. It boasts many grand Georgian buildings, including the handsome three-storeyed Town Hall.

Oliver Cromwell was born in Huntingdon in 1599 and attended Huntingdon Grammar School. The schoolhouse was originally part of the Hospital of St John the Baptist, founded during the reign of Henry II by David, Earl of Huntingdon. Samuel Pepys was also a pupil here.

Cromwell was MP for Huntingdon in the Parliament of 1629, was made a JP in 1630 and moved to St Ives in the following year. Rising to power as an extremely able military commander in the Civil War, he raised troops from the region and made his headquarters in the Falcon Inn.

Appointed Lord Protector in 1653, Cromwell was ruler of the country until his death in 1658. The school he attended is now the **Cromwell Museum**, located on Huntingdon High Street, housing the only public collection relating specifically to him, with exhibits that reflect many aspects of his political, social and religious life. The museum's exhibits include an extensive collection of Cromwell family portraits and personal objects, among them a hat and seal, contemporary coins and medals, an impressive Florentine cabinet - the gift of the Grand Duke of Tuscany - and a surgeon's chest made by Kolb of Augsburg. This fine collection helps visitors interpret the life and legacy of Cromwell and the Republican movement.

**All Saints** Church, opposite the Cromwell Museum, displays many architectural styles, from medieval to Victorian. One of the two surviving parish churches of Huntingdon, All Saints was considered to be the church of the Hinchingbrooke part of the Cromwell family, though no memorials survive to attest to this. The Cromwell family burial vault is contained within the church, however, and it is here that Oliver's father Robert and his grandfather Sir Henry are buried. The church has a fine chancel roof, a very lovely organ chamber, a truly impressive stained-glass window and the font in which Cromwell was baptised, as it's the old font from the destroyed St John's church, discovered in a local garden in 1927!

Huntingdon's other church, **St Mary's**, dates from Norman times but was almost completely rebuilt in the 1400s. It boasts a fine Perpendicular west tower, which partially collapsed in 1607. The damage was extensive, and the tower was not completely repaired until 1621. Oliver Cromwell's father Robert contributed to the cost of the repairs, as recorded on the stone plaque fixed to the east wall on the nave, north of the chancel arch.

**Cowper House** (No 29 High Street) has an impressive early 18th century frontage. A plaque commemorates the fact that the poet William Cowper (pronounced 'Cooper') lived here between 1765 and 1767.

Among Huntingdon's many fine former coaching inns is **The George Hotel**. Although badly damaged by fire in 1865, the north and west wings of the 17th century courtyard remain intact, as does its very rare wooden gallery. The inn was one of the most famous of all the posting houses on the old Great North Run. It is reputed that Dick Turpin used one of the rooms here. The medieval courtyard, gallery and open staircase are the scene of annual productions of Shakespeare.

Along the south side of the Market Square, the **Falcon Inn** dates back in parts to the 1500s. Oliver Cromwell is said to have used this as his headquarters during the Civil War.

About half a mile southwest of town stands **Hinchingbrooke House**, which today is a school but which has its origins in the Middle Ages, when it was a nunnery (ghostly nuns are said to haunt the building to this day). The remains of the Benedictine nunnery can still be seen. It was given to the Cromwell family by Henry VIII in 1538. Converted by the Cromwell family in the 16th century and later extended by the Earls of Sandwich, today's visitors can see examples of every period of English architecture from the 12th to early 20th centuries. King James I was a regular visitor, and Oliver Cromwell spent part of his childhood here. The 1st Earl of Sandwich was a central figure in the Civil War and subsequent Restoration, while the 4th Earl (inventor of the lunchtime favourite that bears his name) was one of the most flamboyant politicians of the 18th century. The House is open for guided tours, including lovely cream teas served in the Tudor kitchens.

**Hinchingbrooke Country Park** covers 180 acres of grassy meadows, mature woodland, ponds and lakes. There is a wide variety of wildlife including woodpeckers, herons, kestrels, butterflies and foxes. The network of paths makes exploring the park easy, and battery-powered wheelchairs are provided for less able visitors. The Visitors Centre serves refreshments at peak times.

Half a mile north, **Spring Common** offers another chance to enjoy some marvellous Cambridgeshire countryside. Covering 13 acres, its name comes from the natural spring that runs constantly and has long been a gathering place. The town developed around rather than within this area of rural tranquillity, which boasts a range of diverse habitats

## COUNTRY WORKING

An organic farm, home to a Caravan Club Site and Country Working
Red House Farm, Wood Walton, Huntingdon, Cambridgeshire  PE28 5YL
Tel: 01487 773297  Mobile: 07941 049843
e-mail: s_parsley@totalise.co.uk
website: www.countryworking.com

**The Caravan Club C.L. Site** is set between meadows and organic crops bordered by conservation hedgerows with the ancient Monks Wood across the field. The Wood Walton Fen Nature Reserve, Aversley and Brampton Woods are all close by. Electricity hook-ups are provided. The Farm is located between Cambridge and Peterborough, just 10 minutes drive from the A1 and A14.

**Country Working** was born to answer the demand for working/business premises away from crowded and congested city and suburban space. The brainchild of Stephen Parsley, who with his father farms the surrounding land, he has created premises in converted farm buildings and areas to provide work

places that offer a better quality of life than the norm.

Country Working  is now a group of farmers working together to provide businesses the opportunity to offer their workforce traffic-free commutes to work, free parking right outside the door, and office windows that overlook wildlife and countryside. This practical, smart-space ensures a superior solution to businesses looking for premises that are cost-effective, secure and -most important of all- supremely pleasant for staff.

including marsh, grassland, scrub and streams. Plant life abounds, providing food and shelter for a variety of animals, amphibians, birds and invertebrates.

# AROUND HUNTINGDON

### HARTFORD
½ mile N of Huntington off the B1514

At just half a mile from Hartford Marina, this lovely village offers plenty of excellent riverside walks.

### BARHAM
6 miles W of Huntingdon off the A1/A14

This delightful hamlet boasts 12 houses, 30 people and an ancient church with box pews, surrounded by undulating farmland. Nearby attractions include angling and sailing on Grafham Water, go-karting at Kimbolton and National Hunt racing at Huntingdon.

### WARBOYS
7 miles NE of Huntingdon off the B1040

An interesting walk to from Warboys to Ramsey takes in a wealth of history and pretty scenery. St Mary Magdalene's church has a tall, very splendid tower.

### RAMSEY
9 miles NE of Huntingdon on the B1040

A pleasant market town with a broad main street down which a river once ran, Ramsey is home to the medieval **Ramsey Abbey**, founded in AD969 by Earl Ailwyn as a Benedictine monastery. The Abbey became one of the most important in England in the 12th and 13th centuries, and as it prospered, so did Ramsey, so that by the 13th century it had become a town with a weekly market and an annual three-day festival at the time of the feast of St Benedict. After the

Dissolution of the Monasteries in 1539, the Abbey and its lands were sold to Sir Richard Williams, great-grandfather of Oliver Cromwell. Most of the buildings were then demolished, the stones being used to build Caius, King's and Trinity Colleges at Cambridge, the towers of Ramsey, Godmanchester and Holywell churches, the gate at Hinchingbrooke House and several local properties. In 1938 the house was converted for use as a school, which it remains to this day.

To the northwest are the ruins of the once magnificent stone gatehouse of the late 15th century - only the porter's lodge remains, but inside can be seen an unusual large carved effigy made of Purbeck marble and dating back to the 14th century. It is said to represent Earl Ailwyn, founder of the Abbey. The gatehouse, now in the care of the National Trust, can be visited daily from April to October.

The church of **St Thomas à Becket of Canterbury** forms an impressive vista at the end of the High Street. Dating back to about 1180, it is thought to have been built as a hospital or guesthouse for the Abbey. It was converted to a church to accommodate the many pilgrims who flocked to Ramsey in the 13th century. The church has what is reputed to be the finest nave in Huntingdonshire, dating back to the 12th century and consisting of seven bays. The church's other treasure is a 15th century carved oak lectern, thought to have come from the Abbey.

Most of **Ramsey Rural Museum** is housed in an 18th century farm building and several barns set in open countryside. Among the many fascinating things to see are a Victorian home and school, a village store, and restored farm equipment, machinery, carts and wagons. The wealth of traditional implements used by local craftsmen such as the farrier, wheelwright, thatcher, dairyman, animal husbandman and cobbler offer an insight into bygone days.

The unusual **Ramsey War Memorial** is a listed Grade II memorial consisting of a fine bronze statue of St George slaying the dragon atop a tall, octagonal pillar crafted of Portland stone.

## UPWOOD
### 8 miles NE of Huntingdon off the B1040

Upwood is a pleasant, scattered village in a very tranquil and picturesque setting. **Woodwalton Fen** nature reserve is a couple of minutes' drive to the west.

## SAWTRY
### 8 miles NW of Huntingdon on the A1

The main point of interest here has no point! **All Saints Church**, built in 1880, lacks both tower and steeple, and is topped instead by a bellcote. Inside the church are marvellous brasses and pieces from ancient Sawtry Abbey.

Just south of Sawtry, Aversley Wood is a conservation area with abundant birdlife and plants.

## HAMERTON
### 9 miles NW of Huntingdon off the A1

**Hamerton Zoological Park** has hundreds of animals from tortoises to tigers. Speically designed enclosures make for unrivalled views of the animals, and the park features meerkats, marmosets and mongooses, lemurs, gibbons, possums and sloths, snakes and even creepy-crawlies such as cockroaches!

## STILTON
### 12 miles NW of Huntingdon off the A1

Stilton has an interesting high street with many fine buildings, and is a good choice for the hungry or thirsty visitor, as it has been since the heyday of horse-drawn travel. Journeys were a little more dangerous then, and Dick Turpin is said to have hidden at the Bell Inn.

## ELLINGTON
### 4 miles W of Huntingdon off the A14

Ellington is a quiet village just south of the A14 and about a mile north of **Grafham Water**. Both Cromwell and Pepys visited, having relatives living in the village, and it was in Ellington that Pepys' sister Paulina found a husband, much to the relief of the diarist, who had written: '*We must find her one, for she grows old and ugly.*' All Saints church is magnificent, like so many in the area, and among its many fine features are the 15th century oak roof and the rich carvings in the nave and the aisles. The church and its tower were built independently.

## WOOLLEY
### 5 miles W of Huntingdon off the A1/A14

This quiet and secluded hamlet attracts a broad spectrum of visitors including anglers, golfers, walkers and riders, drawn by its lush and picturesque beauty and rural tranquillity.

## SPALDWICK
### 6 miles W of Huntingdon off the A14

A sizable village that was once the site of the Bishop of Lincoln's manor house, Spaldwick boasts the grand church of St James, which dates from the 12th century and has seen restoration in most centuries, including the 20th, when the spire had to be partly rebuilt after being struck by lightning. Two miles further west, **Catworth** is another charming village, regularly voted Best Kept Village in Cambridgeshire and well worth exploring.

## KEYSTON

**12 miles W of Huntingdon off the A14**

A delightful village with a pedigree that can be traced back to the days of the Vikings, Keyston has major attractions both sacred and secular: the church of **St John the Baptist** is impressive in its almost cathedral-like proportions, with one of the most magnificent spires in the whole county, while the Pheasant is a well-known and very distinguished pub-restaurants.

## BRAMPTON

**2 miles SW of Huntingdon off the A1**

Brampton is where **Huntingdon Racecourse** is situated. An average of 18 meetings (all jumping) are scheduled every year, including Bank Holiday fixtures (extra-special deals for families). In November, the Grade II Peterborough Chase is the feature race.

Brampton's less speculative attractions include the 13th century church of St Mary, and **Pepys House**, the home of Samuel's uncle who was a cousin of Lord Sandwich's and who got Samuel his job at the Admiralty.

## GRAFHAM

**5 miles SW of Huntingdon on the B661**

Created in the mid-1960s as a reservoir, **Grafham Water** offers a wide range of outdoor activities for visitors of all ages, with 1,500 acres of beautiful countryside, including the lake itself. The ten-mile perimeter track is great for jogging or cycling, and there's excellent sailing, windsurfing and fly-fishing.

The area is a Site of Special Scientific Interest, and an ample nature reserve at the western edge is run jointly by Anglian Water and the Wildlife Trust. There are nature trails, information boards, a wildlife garden and a dragonfly pond. Many species of waterfowl stay here at various times of the year, and bird-watchers have the use of six hides, three of them accessible to wheelchairs. An exhibition centre has displays and video presentations of the reservoir's history, a gift shop and a café.

## KIMBOLTON

**8 miles SW of Huntingdon on the B645**

History aplenty here, and a lengthy pause is in order to look at all the interesting buildings. St Andrew's Church would head the list were it not for **Kimbolton Castle** which, along with its gatehouse, dominates the village. Parts of the original Tudor building are still to be seen, but the appearance of the castle today owes much to the major remodelling carried out by Vanbrugh and Nicholas Hawksmoor in the first decade of the 18th century. The gatehouse was added by Robert Adam in 1764. Henry VIII's first wife Catherine of Aragon spent the last 18 months of her life imprisoned here, where she died in 1536. The castle is now a school, but can be visited on certain days in the summer (don't miss the Pellegrini murals).

## BUCKDEN

**4 miles SW of Huntingdon on the A1**

This historic village was an important coaching stop on the old Great North Road. It is known particularly as the site of **Buckden Towers**, the great palace built for the Bishops of Lincoln. In the splendid grounds are the 15th century gatehouse and the tower where Henry VIII imprisoned his first wife, Catherine of Aragon, in 1533 (open only on certain days of the year).

## ST NEOTS

**10 miles SW of Huntingdon off the A1**

St Neots dates back to the founding of a Saxon Priory, built on the outskirts of Eynesbury in AD974. Partially destroyed

*St Neots*

Cathedral of Huntingdonshire. It is an outstanding example of Late Medieval architecture. The gracious interior complements the 130-foot Somerset-style tower, with a finely carved oak altar, excellent Victorian stained-glass and a Holdich organ, built in 1855.

**St Neots Museum** - opened in 1995 - tells the story of the town and the surrounding area. Housed in the former magistrates' court and police station, it still has the original cells. Eye-catching displays trace local history from prehistoric times to the present day. Open Tuesday to Saturday.

by the Danes in 1010, it was re-established as a Benedictine Priory in about 1081 by St Anselm, Abbot of Bec and later Archbishop of Canterbury. For the next two centuries the Priory flourished. Charters were granted by Henry I to hold fairs and markets. The first bridge over the Great Ouse, comprising 73 timber arches, was built in 1180. The name of the town comes from the Cornish saint whose remains were interred in the Priory some time before the Norman Conquest. With the Dissolution of the Monasteries, the Priory was demolished. In the early 17th century the old bridge was replaced by a stone one. This was then the site of a battle between the Royalists and Roundheads in 1648 - an event sometimes re-enacted by Sealed Knot societies.

St Neots repays a visit on foot, since there are many interesting sites and old buildings tucked away. The famous **Market Square** is one of the largest and most ancient in the country. A market has been held here every Thursday since the 12th century. The magnificent parish **Church of St Mary the Virgin** is a very fine edifice, known locally as the

## LITTLE PAXTON
**2½ miles N of St Neots off the A1/A428**

Fewer than three miles north of St Neots at Little Paxton is **Paxton Pits Nature Reserve**. Created alongside gravel workings, the Reserve attracts thousands of water birds for visitors to observe from hides. The wealth of wildlife means that the area is an SSSI (Site of Special Scientific Interest) and ensures a plethora of colour and activity all year round. The site also features nature trails and a visitors' centre. It has thousands of visiting waterfowl, including one of the largest colonies of cormorants, and is particularly noted for its wintering wildfowl, nightingales in late spring and kingfishers. There are about four miles of walks, some suitable for wheelchairs. Spring and summer also bring a feast of wild flowers, butterflies and dragonflies.

Just north again is the Great Paxton church, originally a Saxon Minster.

## EYNESBURY

### 1 mile S of St Neots on the A428

Eynesbury is actually part of St Neots, with only a little stream separating the two. Note the 12th century **Church of St Mary** with its Norman tower. Rebuilt in the Early English period, it retains some well-preserved locally sculpted 14th century oak benches.

History has touched this quiet and lovely village from time to time: it was the home of the famous giant James Toller, who died in 1818 and is buried in the middle aisle of the church. Only 21 when he died, he measured some 8 feet tall - it is said he was buried here to escape the attention of body-snatchers, whose activities were widespread at the time. Eynesbury was also the birthplace of the Miles' Quads, the first-ever surviving quadruplets in Britain.

## BUSHMEAD

### 4 miles W of St Neots off the B660

The remains of **Bushmead Abbey**, once a thriving Augustinian community, are well worth a detour. The garden setting is delightful, and the surviving artefacts include some interesting stained-glass. Open weekends in July and August.

## GODMANCHESTER

### 2 miles SW of Huntingdon off the A1

Godmanchester is linked to Huntingdon by a 14th century bridge across the River Ouse. It was a Roman settlement and one that continued in importance down the years, as the number of handsome buildings testifies. One such is **Island Hall**, a mid-18th century mansion built for John Jackson, the Receiver General for Huntingdon; it contains many interesting pieces. This family home has lovely Georgian rooms, with fine period detail and fascinating possessions relating to the owners' ancestors since

their first occupation of the house in 1800. The tranquil riverside setting and formal gardens add to the peace and splendour - the house takes its name from the ornamental island that forms part of the grounds. Octavia Hill was sometimes a guest, and wrote effusively to her sister that Island Hall was 'the loveliest, dearest old house, I never was in such a one before.' Open only to pre-booked groups.

**Wood Green Animal Shelter** at Kings Bush Farm, Godmanchester is a purpose-built, 50-acre centre open to the public all year round. Cats, dogs, horses, donkeys, farm animals, guinea pigs, rabbits, llamas, wildfowl and pot-bellied pigs are among the many creatures for visitors to see, and there is a specially adapted nature trail and restaurant.

**St Mary's Church** is Perpendicular in style, though not totally in age, as the tower is a 17th century replacement of the 13th century original. A footpath leads from the famous Chinese Bridge (1827) to **Port Holme Meadow**, at 225 acres one of the largest in England and the site of Roman remains. It is a Site of Special Scientific Interest, with a huge diversity of botanical and bird species. Huntingdon racecourse was once situated here, and it was a training airfield during the First World War. Another site of considerable natural activity is Godmanchester Pits, accessed along the Ouse Valley Way and home to a great diversity of flora and fauna.

## PAPWORTH EVERARD

### 6 miles S of Huntingdon on the A1198

One of the most recent of the region's churches, St Peter's dates mainly from the mid-19th century. Neighbouring **Papworth St Agnes** has an older church in St John's, though parts of that, too, are Victorian. Just up the road at **Hilton**

## AXE & COMPASS

High Street, Hemingford Abbots, Huntingdon,
Cambridgeshire PE28 9AH
Tel: 01480 463605  Fax: 01480 463691
e-mail: enquiries@axeandcompass.co.uk
website: www.axeandcompass.co.uk

The **Axe & Compass** inn is truly charming, a thatched
16th century gem at the end of a row of thatched
cottages within view of the delicate church spire of
St Mary's. The picture-postcard exterior is adorned
with hanging baskets,

and to the rear there's a large lawned garden with picnic tables and a
fully-equipped safe children's play area.

The interior has an open-plan style and boasts original features such
as the stone floor and heavy beams, adding to the traditional and
welcoming ambience. Old photos of the pretty village and the pub itself
line the walls.

A perfect place to relax and enjoy a quiet drink or meal, this pub –
one of the best to be found in and around Cambridge - serves a good
selection of wines together with a range of beers, soft drinks and spirits
– including an excellent selection of malt whiskies.

Justly well known for its excellent food, the menu and specials board
offer up a variety of tempting home-cooked dishes every day at lunch
and dinner. Meals can be taken in the bar areas or the intimate, no-
smoking dining room.

## THE MANOR

Hemingford Grey, Huntingdon,
Cambridgeshire PE28 9BN
Tel: 01480 463134  Fax: 01480 465026
e-mail: diana_boston@hotmail.com
website: www.greenknowe.co.uk

Reputedly the oldest continuously inhabited
house in England, built around 1130, **The
Manor** is a distinguished and gracious home,
approached through a large, handsome garden
dotted with lush topiary. Open all year round
but strictly by appointment, most of the Norman
house remains virtually intact, despite changes over the past nine centuries. The original front of the
house is visible only to those venturing into the
fabulous hidden garden. Garden open daily 11am-5pm.

The Manor was made famous by the author Lucy
Boston, who re-created it as the house of Greene Knowe
in her series of classic books. The attic contains many
toys used by the fictional children of the past. As well
as writing, Lucy created exquisite patchworks, many
of which are on display throughout the house. She also
laid out the wonderful garden, planting nearly 300 roses
and a marvellous collection of irises. Visitors can buy
plants,  and can also enjoy guided tours and the gift
shop on-site.

is the famous **Hilton Turf Maze**, cut in 1660 to a popular medieval design.

### BOXWORTH

**7 miles SE of Huntingdon off the A14**

A village almost equidistant from Huntingdon and Cambridge, and a pleasant base for touring the area, Boxworth's **Church of St Peter** is unusual in being constructed of pebble rubble.

A mile south of Boxworth is **Overhall Grove**, one of the largest elm woods in the country and home to a variety of wildlife.

## THE GREAT OUSE VALLEY

### HEMINGFORD ABBOTS

**3 miles SE of Huntingdon off the A14**

Once part of the Ramsey Abbey Estate, Hemingford Abbots is set around the 13th century church of St Margaret, along the banks of the Great Ouse. Opportunities for angling and boating facilities, including rowing boats for hire, as well as swimming, country walks, golf and a recreation centre are all within a couple of miles. The village hosts a flower festival every two years.

Just to the east is **Hemingford Grey**, with its church on the banks of the Ouse. **The Manor** (see panel opposite) at Hemingford Grey is reputedly the oldest continuously inhabited house

in England, built around 1130. Visits (by appointment only) will reveal all the treasures in the house and garden.

### FENSTANTON

**7 miles SE of Huntingdon off the A14 bypass**

Lancelot 'Capability' Brown (1716 – 1783) was Lord of the Manor from 1768, and he, his wife and his son are buried in the medieval church. Born in Northumberland, Brown started his working life as a gardener's boy before moving on to Stowe, where he worked under William Kent. When Kent died, Brown set up as a garden designer and soon became the leading landscape artist in England, known for the natural, unplanned appearance of his designs. His nickname arose from his habit of remarking, when surveying new projects, that the place had 'capabilities'.

Any visit here should also take in the 17th century manor house and the red-brick Clock Tower.

### WYTON

**2 miles E of Huntington off the A1123**

Wyton is mentioned in the *Domesday Book*, and is thought to have been

*River Ouse, Hemingford Grey*

## THE WHITE HORSE INN

1 Market Street, Swavesey,
Cambridgeshire CB4 5QG
Tel: 01954 232470

Having seen service as an
auction house, a public health
office and a meeting place for
various societies since it was
built in the early 16<sup>th</sup> century,
**The White Horse Inn** in
Swavesey continues to play
many parts. First and foremost,
of course, it's a friendly village
pub, run by Pat and Will
Wright, who have a strong
interest in real ales and fine malt
whiskeys. Guest ales are always featured. Bar lunches are served Mondays to Saturdays, and there
are also tempting Sunday roast dinners, including a vegetarian option, and senior citizen specials
on Tuesdays.

Evening meals are available Monday through Saturday. Attractive and welcoming inside and out,
the bars are warm and welcoming, with open log fires and exposed oak beams. The public bar has bar
billiards and darts, and there's a separate pool room and a function room. Old photographs of this
handsome village share wall space with prints and drawings of Cambridge colleges. Outside there's a
patio dining area and safe children's play area. Various charities benefit from events organised here,
the most notable being the annual barrel-rolling contest revived by the publicans in 1997.

## THE TRINITY FOOT

Huntingdon Road, Swavesey, Cambridge,
Cambridgeshire CB4 5RD
Tel/Fax: 01954 230315
e-mail: info@trinityfoot.co.uk
website: www.trinityfoot.co.uk

With an accent on the freshest fish, **The Trinity
Foot** is a handsome and welcoming pub and
restaurant set in a five-and-a-half acre garden just
eight miles from Cambridge and Huntingdon.
Tastefully decorated and furnished, it always boasts
a relaxed and friendly ambience. Parrot fish, shark, John Dory, talipia, swordfish, gilt-headed bream
and more grace the menu, which also makes best use of the finest steaks, chicken, duck, gammon and

other traditional favourites in tempting dishes that will
please every palate. And to drink? A choice of over 20
varieites of wine, two real ales, 20 malt whiskies and more.

Adjoining this fine pub and restaurant is a wet fish
shop that supplies the restaurant and is also managed by
proprietor Robert Clarke, who together with his wife
Nicola has made The Trinity Foot a popular destination
for excellent food, drink and hospitality. Open: Monday
to Friday 11.00-15.00 & 18.00-23.00, Saturdays 11.00-
11.00. Sundays 12.00-21.00. Food is served Monday to
Friday 12.00-14.30 & 18.00-21.30, Saturdays 12.00-21.30,
Sundays 12.00-20.00.

founded in the 8<sup>th</sup> century. It is a popular tourist destination thanks to its proximity to **Houghton Mill** (see panel) and opportunities for riverside walks, as well as its charming thatched buildings and shops.

## HOUGHTON

**5 miles E of Huntingdon on the A1123**

**Houghton Meadows** is a Site of Special Scientific Interest with an abundance of hay meadow species. One of the most popular walks in the whole area links Houghton with St Ives.

## ST IVES

**6 miles E of Huntingdon off the A1123**

This is an ancient town on the banks of the Great Ouse which once held a huge annual fair and is named after St Ivo, said to be a Persian bishop who came here in the Dark Ages to spread a little light.

## HOUGHTON MILL

Houghton, Huntingdon,
Cambridgeshire PE28 2AZ
Tel: 01480 301494 Fax: 01480 469641
website: www.nationaltrust.org.uk/houghtonmill

The National Trust-owned **Houghton Mill** deserves its reputation as a popular tourist attraction. There has been a mill on this site for some 1,000 years. The present mill dates from the 18<sup>th</sup> century. This impressive five-story brick and clapboard structure stands on a tributary of the River Ouse midway between Huntingdon and St Ives.

The mill is one of the last and the most complete to survive in the area. As such it is the most important of the very few remaining mills. It has recently had its wheel restored, as part of a 1.2 million pound restoration project and is fully operational. This has provided improved facilities for visitors. Open days during the summer months offer visitors the chance to see the mill in action, and to appreciate the different forms of sustainable energy - a water turbine which generates electricity for the site and for other National Trust properties, and the waterwheel at work to produce stoneground flour. Milling takes place on Sundays and Bank Holiday Mondays, and the site also contains an art gallery, miniature millstones to turn by hand, and a tea room. In addition, the area to the north of the mill is an unusual survival of undeveloped Ouse riverbank, which the Trust intends to protect for its ecological interest and landscape value as an appropriate setting for this fine mill.

In the Middle Ages, kings bought cloth for their households at the village's great wool fairs and markets, and a market is still held every Monday. The Bank Holiday Monday markets are particularly lively affairs, and the Michaelmas fair fills the town centre for three days.

Seagoing barges once navigated up to the famous six-arched bridge that was built in the 15<sup>th</sup> century and has a most unusual two-storey chapel in its middle. Oliver Cromwell lived in St Ives in the 1630s; the statue of him on Market Hill, with its splendid hat, is one of the village's most familiar landmarks. It was made in bronze, with a Portland stone base, and was erected in 1901. It was originally designed for Huntingdon, but they wouldn't accept it!

The beautiful parish church in its churchyard beside the river is well worth a visit. The quayside provides a tranquil mooring for holidaymakers and there are wonderful walks by the riverside.

Clive Sinclair developed his tiny TVs and pocket calculators in the town, and another famous son of St Ives was the great Victorian rower John Goldie, whose name is remembered each year by the second Cambridge boat in the Boat Race.

The **Norris Museum**, in a delightful setting by the river, tells the story of Huntingdonshire for the past 175 million years or so, with everything from fossils, mammoth tusks and models of the great historic reptiles through flint tools, Roman artefacts and Civil War armour to lace-making and ice-skating displays, and contemporary works of art. A truly fascinating place that is open throughout the year, admission is free. Exhibitions include a life-size replica of a 160-million-year-old ichthyosaur. There are remains of woolly mammoths from the Ice Ages, tools and pottery from the Stone Age to Roman times and relics from the medieval castles and abbeys. Also on show are toys and models made by prisoners of the Napoleonic Wars.

*'As I was going to St Ives I met a man with seven wives.*

*Each wife had seven sacks, each sack had seven cats, each cat had seven kits.*

*Kits, cats, sacks and wives, how many were going to St Ives?'*

- None, of course, but today's visitors are certain to have a good time while they are here.

Just outside St Ives are **Wilthorn Meadow**, a Site of Natural History Interest where Canada geese are often to be seen, and **Holt Island Nature Reserve**, where high-quality willow is being grown to reintroduce the traditional craft of basket-making. Take some time for spotting the butterflies, dragonflies and kingfishers.

## METAMORPHOSIS

13 Market Hill, St Ives, Cambridgeshire PE27 5AL
Tel: 01480 356684  Fax: 01480 352530

Some 28 years ago, Cherry and Keith Durant began selling Keith's handmade leather goods at festivals and agricultural shows throughout the country. Over the years this business evolved, and **Metamorphosis** in the centre of St Ives is now the base for a fascinating and eclectic mix of world crafts and cultures.

This shop is the place to find Tibetan prayer wheels, Russian

matrioshkas, samples of Egyptian papyrus, Peruvian ocarinas and Native American rattles. The huge range is complemented by books and CDs on subjects such as Buddhism, reiki, tarot, crystals, alternative therapies, t'ai chi and folklore. Alongside the meditation and relaxation CDs there's an amazing diversity of world music. Together with all of this there's an impressive selection of chess sets from around the world, small pieces of Indian furniture and mirrors, beautiful silver jewellery and probably the best selection of body piercing jewellery in the area – together, of course, with Keith's leatherwork and a special corner devoted to the eccentric world of artist Simon Drew. *Open:* Mon-Sat 9.30-17.00 (also open Sundays in December).

## BLUNTISHAM

**3 miles NE of St Ives on the A1123**

There's an impressive church here in Bluntisham, with a unique 14th century chancel that ends in three sides. The rector in times past was the father of Dorothy L Sayers – creator of nobelman sleuth Lord Peter Wimsey - and Dorothy once lived in the large Georgian rectory on the main road.

## EARITH

**4 miles E of St Ives on the A1123**

The **Ouse Washes**, a special protection area, runs northeast from the village to Earith Pits, a well-known habitat for birds and crawling creatures; some of the pits are used for fishing. The Washes are a wetland of major international importance supporting such birds as ruffs, Bewick and Whooper swans, and hen harriers. The average bird population is around 20,000. Some of the meadows flood in winter, and ice-skating is popular when the temperature really drops. There's a great tradition of ice-skating in the Fens, and Fenmen were the national champions until the 1930s.

## SOMERSHAM

**4 miles NE of St Ives on the B1040/B1060**

The **Raptor Foundation** is found here, a major attraction where owls and other birds of prey find refuge. There are regular flying displays and falconry shows. Somersham once had a palace for the Bishops of Ely, and its splendid church of St John would have done them proud.

# PETERBOROUGH

The second city of Cambridgeshire has a long and interesting history that can be traced back to the Bronze Age, as can be seen in the archaeological site at Flag Fen. Although a cathedral city, it is also a New Town (designated in 1967), so modern development and expansion have vastly increased its facilities while retaining the quality of its historic heart.

*Peterborough Cathedral*

### BALAGAN GIFTSHOP

1 Cathedral Square, Peterborough, Cambridgeshire PE1 1XH
Tel: 01733 319606

Balagan is a modern gift shop located in the heart of Peterborough, just steps away from the Cathedral. This wonderful shop specialises in sterling silver jewellery with in-house ranges of swarovski crystal and diamond jewellery, together with designer watches from names such as Storm and Diesel. They also stock a wide range of giftware and gadgets from designers such as Alessi and Leatherman. Customers will be sure to find gifts for themselves or others from among the many unusual items for sale here.

*River Nene, Peterborough*

Railway, which operates 15-mile steam-hauled trips between Peterborough and its HQ and museum at Wansford. A feature on the main railway line at Peterborough is the historic Iron Bridge, part of the old Great Northern Railway and still virtually as built by Lewis Cubitt in 1852.

Just outside the city, by the river Nene, is **Thorpe Meadows Sculpture Park**, one of several open spaces in and around the city with absorbing collections of modern sculpture.

Peterborough's crowning glory is, of course, the Norman **Cathedral**, built in the 12th and 13th centuries on a site that had seen Christian worship since AD655. Henry VIII made the church a cathedral, and his first queen, Catherine of Aragon, is buried here, as for a while was Mary Queen of Scots after her execution at Fotheringay. Features to note are the huge (85-foot) arches of the West Front, the unique painted wooden nave ceiling, some exquisite late15th century fan vaulting, and the tomb of Catherine.

Though the best-known of the city's landmarks, the Cathedral is by no means the only one. The **Peterborough Museum and Art Gallery** covers all aspects of the history of Peterborough from the Jurassic period to Victorian times.

The Gildenburgh Gallery at 44 Broadway boasts a good collection of fine art from the 20th and 21st centuries and a design-led craft shop. The views of Peterborough to be had from the gallery are panoramic and impressive.

There are twin attractions for railway enthusiasts in the shape of **Railworld** (see panel opposite), a hands-on exhibition dealing with modern rail travel, and the wonderful **Nene Valley**

## AROUND PETERBOROUGH

### PEAKIRK
**7 miles N of Peterborough off the A15**

A charming little village, somewhat off the beaten track, Peakirk boasts a village church of Norman origin that is the only one in the country dedicated to St Pega, the remains of whose hermit cell can still be seen.

### CROWLAND
**10 miles NE of Peterborough off the A1073**

It is hard to imagine that this whole area was once entirely wetland and marshland, dotted with inhospitable islands. Crowland was one such island, then known as Croyland, and on it was established a small church and hermitage back in the 7th century, which was later to become one of the nation's most important monasteries. The town's impressive parish church was just part of the great edifice which once stood on the site. A wonderful exhibition can be

## RAILWORLD

Oundle Road, Peterborough,
Cambridgeshire PE2 9NR
Tel/Fax: 01733 344240
e-mail: mail@railworld.net
website: www.railworld.net

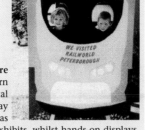

**Railworld Exhibition Centre
and Museum** highlights modern
train travel and environmental
challenges and its Model Railway
is most impressive. Railworld has
Hovertrains and 'Steam Age' exhibits, whilst hands-on displays
will delight children. There are also films, local railway history
and workers' database. Open Monday to Friday 11am-4pm. All
day free parking.

found in the **Abbey** at Crowland, open
all year round. The remains cover a third
of the Abbey's original extent.

Crowland's second gem is the unique
**Trinity Bridge** - set in the centre of town
on dry land! Built in the 14th century, it
has three arches built over one over-
arching structure. Before the draining of
the Fens, this bridge crossed the point
where the River Welland divided into
two streams.

## THORNEY

**8 miles E of Peterborough on the A47**

**Thorney Abbey**, the church of St Mary
and St Botolph, is the dominating
presence even though what now stands
is but a small part of what was once one
of the greatest of the Benedictine abbeys.
Gravestones in the churchyard are
evidence of a Huguenot colony that
settled here after fleeing France in the
wake of the St Bartholomew's Day
massacre of 1572 and to settle the
drained fenland at the request of
Oliver Cromwell.

The **Thorney Heritage Museum** is a
small, independently-run museum of
great fascination, describing the
development of the village from a Saxon
monastery, via Benedictine Abbey to a
model village built in the 19th century

by the Dukes of Bedford.
The main innovation was a
10,000-gallon water tank
that supplied the whole
village; other villages had to
use unfiltered river water.
Open Easter to the end
of September.

## WHITTLESEY

**5 miles E of Peterborough off
the A605**

The market town of
Whittlesey lies close to the
western edge of the Fens
and is part of one of the last
tracts to be drained. Brick-making was a
local speciality, and 180-foot brick
chimneys stand as a reminder of that
once-flourishing industry. The church of
**St Andrew** is mainly 14th century, with a
16th century tower; the chancel, chancel
chapels and naves still have their
original roofs.

A walk around this charming town
reveals an interesting variety of
buildings: brick, of course, and also some
stone, thatch on timber frames, and rare
thatched mud boundary walls.

**The Whittlesey Museum**, housed in
the grand 19th century Town Hall in
Market Street, features an archive of
displays on local archaeology,
agriculture, geology, brick-making and
more. Reconstructions include a 1950s
corner shop and post office, blacksmith's
forge and wheelwright's bench.

A highlight of Whittlesey's year is the
**Straw Bear Procession** that is part of a
four-day January festival. A man clad in
a suit of straw dances and prances
through the streets, calling at houses and
pubs to entertain the townspeople. The
origins are obscure: perhaps it stems
from pagan times when corn gods were
invoked to produce a good harvest;
perhaps it is linked with the wicker idols

used by the Druids; perhaps it derives from the performing bears which toured the villages until the 17th century. What is certain is that at the end of the jollities the straw suit is ceremoniously burned.

Whittlesey was the birthplace of the writer L P Hartley (*The Go-Between*) and of General Sir Harry Smith, hero of many 19th century campaigns in India. He died in 1860, and the south chapel off **St Mary's** church (note the beautiful spire) was restored and named after him.

## FLAG FEN

### 6 miles E of Peterborough signposted from the A47 and A1139

**Flag Fen Bronze Age Centre** (see panel below) comprises massive 3,000-year-old timbers that were part of a major settlement and have been preserved in peaty mud. The site includes a Roman road with its original surface, the oldest wheel in England, re-creations of a

Bronze Age settlement, a museum of artefacts, rare breed animals, and a visitor centre with a shop and restaurant. Ongoing excavations, open to the public, make this one of the most important and exciting sites of its kind.

## MARCH

### 14 miles E of Peterborough off the A141

March once occupied the second-largest 'island' in the great level of Fens. As the land was drained the town grew as a trading and religious centre, and in more recent times as a market town and major railway hub. **March and District Museum**, in the High Street, tells the story of the people and the history of March and the surrounding area, and includes a working forge and a reconstruction of a turn-of-the-century home.

**St Wendreda's** uniquely dedicated church, at Town End, is notable for its

---

## FLAG FEN

Britain's Bronze Age Centre, The Droveway, Northey Road, Peterborough PE6 7QJ
Tel: 91733 313414  Fax: 01733 349957
e-mail: office@flagfen.freeserve.co.uk
website: www.flagfen.com

**Flag Fen** is one of Europe's most important Bronze Age sites; this archaeological jewel is situated on the outskirts of the Cathedral City of Peterborough. This Bronze Age religious site pre-dates the Cathedral by nearly 2000 years. The Museum of the Bronze Age contains artefacts found on the site over the last 20 years of excavating.

The park is entered through a uniquely designed 21st Century roundhouse; this visitor centre is your portal to the past, with information boards, and pictures. Once out on the park you will be stepping back into the past, and have the chance to see how your ancestors used to live, as you explore the Bronze Age and Iron Age roundhouses in their landscape setting.

The Preservation Hall contains undercover archaeology, along with a 60 metre mural painting depicting life in the Bronze Age in the Fens. During the summer months, archaeologist's can often be seen at work, uncovering Peterborough's past.

Workshops and Lectures are among our full programme of events, which include Sword and Bronze Casting, Flint Knapping, Theatre in the Park, and our Annual big event, which attracts visitors from across the country. If you would like details please contact us.

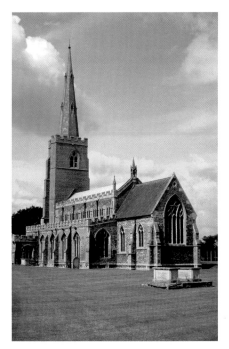

*St Wendreda's Church*

magnificent timber roof, a double hammerbeam with 120 carved angels, a fine font and some impressive gargoyles. John Betjeman declared the church to be 'worth cycling 40 miles into a headwind to see'.

The **Nene—Ouse Navigation Link** runs through the town, affording many attractive riverside walks and, just outside the town off the B1099, **Dunhams Wood** comprises four acres of woodland set among the fens. The site contains an enormous variety of trees, along with sculptures and a miniature railway.

### STONEA

**3 miles SE of March off the B1098**

**Stonea Camp** is the lowest 'hill'-fort in Britain. Built in the Iron Age, it proved unsuccessful against the Romans. A listed ancient monument whose banks and ditches were restored after excavations in 1991, the site is also an increasingly important habitat for wildlife.

### CHATTERIS

**8 miles S of March off the A141**

A friendly little market town, the **Chatteris Museum and Council Chamber** features a series of interesting displays on Fenland life and the development of the town. Themes include education, agriculture, transport and local trades, along with temporary exhibitions and local photographs, all housed in five galleries.

The church of St Peter and St Paul has some 14th century features but is mostly more modern in appearance, having been substantially restored in 1909.

### LONGTHORPE

**2 miles W of Peterborough off the A47**

**Longthorpe Tower**, part of a fortified manor house, is graced by some of the very finest 14th century domestic wall paintings in Europe, featuring scenes both sacred and secular: the Nativity, the Wheel of Life, King David, the Labours of the Months. The paintings were discovered during renovations after the Second World War.

### ELTON

**6 miles SW of Peterborough on the B671**

Elton is a lovely village on the river Nene, with stone-built houses and thatched roofs. **Elton Hall** is a mixture of styles, with a 15th century tower and chapel, and a major Gothic influence. The grandeur is slightly deceptive, as some of the battlements and turrets were built of wood to save money. The hall's sumptuous rooms are filled with art treasures (Gainsborough, Reynolds, Constable) and the library has a wonderful collection of antique tomes.

## THORNHAUGH
### 8 miles NW of Peterborough off the A1/A47

Hidden away in a quiet valley is **Sacrewell Farm and Country Centre**, whose centrepiece is a working watermill. All kinds of farming equipment are on display, and there's a collection of farm animals, along with gardens, nature trails and general interest trails, play areas, a gift shop and a restaurant serving light refreshments.

## BURGHLEY
### 14 miles NW of Peterborough off the A1

*"The largest and grandest house of the Elizabethan Age"*, **Burghley House** presents a dazzling spectacle with its domed towers, walls of cream coloured stone, and acres of windows. Clear glass was still ruinously expensive in the 1560s so Elizabethan grandees like Cecil flaunted their wealth by having windows that stretched almost from floor to ceiling. Burghley House also displays the Elizabethan obsession with symmetry - every tower, dome, pilaster and pinnacle has a corresponding partner.

Contemporaries called Burghley a "prodigy house", a title shared at that time with only one other stately home in England - Longleat in Wiltshire. Both houses were indeed prodigious in size and in cost. At Burghley, Cecil commissioned the most celebrated interior decorator of the age, Antonio Verrio, to create rooms of unparalleled splendour. In his "Heaven Room", Verrio excelled even himself, populating the lofty walls and ceiling with a dynamic gallery of mythological figures.

The eighteen State Rooms at Burghley house a vast treasury of great works of art. The walls are crowded with 17th century Italian paintings, Japanese ceramics and rare examples of European porcelain grace every table, alcove and mantelpiece, and the wood carvings of Grinling Gibbons and his followers add dignity to almost every room. Also on display are four magnificent State Beds along with important tapestries and textiles.

In the 18th century, Cecil's descendants commissioned the ubiquitous "Capability" Brown to landscape the 160 acres of parkland surrounding the house. These enchanting grounds are open to visitors and are also home to a large herd of fallow deer which was first established in Cecil's time. Brown also designed the elegant Orangery which is now a licensed restaurant overlooking rose beds and gardens.

A more recent addition to Burghley's attractions is the **Sculpture Garden**.

*Burghley House*

Twelve acres of scrub woodland have been reclaimed and planted with specimen trees and shrubs and now provide a sylvan setting for a number of dramatic artworks by contemporary sculptors.

Throughout the summer season, Burghley hosts a series of events of which the best known, the Burghley Horse Trials, takes place at the end of August.

# WISBECH

One of the largest of the Fenland towns, a port in medieval times and still enjoying shipping trade with Europe, Wisbech is at the centre of a thriving agricultural region. The 18th century in particular saw the building of rows of handsome houses, notably in North Brink and South Brink, which face each other across the river. The finest of all the properties is undoubtedly **Peckover House**, built in 1722 and bought at the end of the 18th century by Jonathan Peckover, a member of the Quaker banking family. The family gave the building to the National Trust in 1948. Behind its elegant façade are splendid panelled rooms, Georgian fireplaces with richly carved overmantels, and ornate plaster decorations. At the back of the house is a beautiful walled garden with summerhouses and an orangery.

No 1 South Brink Place is the birthplace of Octavia Hill (1838-1912), co-founder of the National Trust and a tireless worker for the cause of the poor, particularly in the sphere of housing. The house is now the **Octavia Hill Museum** with displays and exhibits commemorating her work.

More Georgian splendour is evident in the area where the Norman castle once stood. The castle was replaced by a bishop's palace in 1478, and in the 17th

*Peckover House*

century by a mansion built for Cromwell's Secretary of State, John Thurloe. Local builder Joseph Medworth built the present Regency villa in 1816; of the Thurloe mansion, only the gate piers remain.

The **Wisbech and Fenland Museum** is one of the oldest purpose-built museums in the country, and in charming Victorian surroundings visitors can view displays of porcelain, coins, rare geological specimens, Egyptian tomb treasures and several items of national importance, including the manuscript of Charles Dickens' *Great Expectations*, Napoleon's Sèvres breakfast set captured at Waterloo, and an ivory chess set that belonged to Louis XIV.

Wisbech is the stage for East Anglia's premier church **Flower Festival**, with flowers in four churches, strawberry teas, crafts, bric-a-brac, plants and a parade of floats. The event takes place at the beginning of July. The most important of the churches is the church of St Peter and St Paul, with two naves under one

## Wisbech

| | |
|---|---|
| **Distance:** | 3.1 miles (4.83 kilometres) |
| **Typical time:** | 120 mins |
| **Height gain:** | 5 metres |
| **Map:** | Explorer 235 |
| **Walk:** | www.walkingworld.com ID: 739 |
| **Contributor:** | Joy & Charles Boldero |

### Access Information:

Bus service: ring the Tourist Information Centre in Wisbech on 01945-583263. There are several free car parks in the town. The walk starts from the large Love Lane car park off Alexandria Road, near the church.

### Description:

Wisbech is an ancient port and has many historical buildings. There is a fine brass on the floor of St Peter and St Paul's Church of Thomas de Braustone, Constable of Wisbech Castle in the 1400s .

The Norman Castle was replaced by a Bishop's Palace in 1478 and in the 17th Century this was replaced by a mansion-house built for John Thurloe, who was Oliver Cromwell's Secretary of State. Later this was replaced by the Georgian Crescent in 1816. Along New Inn Yard on the left is one of the oldest timber-framed buildings in the town.

Along South Brink on the left is the house where Octavia Hill was born, now a museum. She was one of the founder members of the National Trust. Along North Brink there are many old historic houses including the 18th Century Peckover House, owned by the NT. Elgood's Brewery has a museum; the brewery has functioned for the last 200 years. The Wisbech and Fenland Museum has many interesting items including the manuscript of 'Great Expectations' by Charles Dickens.

### Features:

River, Pub, Toilets, Museum, Church, Castle, Stately Home, National Trust/NTS, Good for Wheelchairs

### Walk Directions:

**1** Turn right into Love Lane, going towards the church. At the church turn right , then left along the street that leads to the Market Place. Turn left into Market Street.

**2** At the T-junction turn left around The Crescent. Turn right along High Street, then left along the alley, New Inn Yard. Turn left along River Nene Quay to the statue. Cross the road and continue along Post Office Lane, crossing the road to the car park. Cross the car park, keeping to the right-hand side. Turn right from the car park, then left along Somers Road and continue along Coal Wharf Road.

**3** Turn right at T-junction along South Brink with the river on the left. Cross road at traffic-lights, turn left along North Brink. Cross two roads. At Elgood's Brewery retrace your steps, crossing one road.

**4** Turn left along Chapel Road. Turn right up Exchange Square, then left at road, left again along Old Market. Cross the road and continue along North Street. Go over the river bridge and keep right beside it for a short distance.

**5** Cross the road and turn left signed 'Pedestrian Zone'. Cross School Lane and turn right along Scrimshire's Passage. Turn left along Hall Street. Turn right by Boots the Chemist, cross the market square and go along Market Street opposite.

**6** Turn left, then left again going down steps. Turn right into Love Lane which leads to the car park.

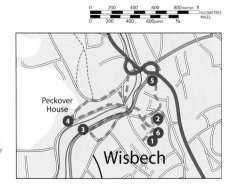

*Museum Square, Wisbech*

roof and an independent tower with a peal of ten bells. Note the royal arms of James I and the 17th century wall monuments in the chancel.

Other sights to see in Wisbech include Elgoods Brewery on North Brink and the impressive 68-foot limestone memorial to Thomas Clarkson, one of the earliest leaders of the abolitionist movement. The monument was designed by Sir George Gilbert Scott in Gothic style.

Still a lively commercial port, Wisbech boasts a restored **Marina** and new facilities for small craft that include floating pontoons with berths for 75 yachts. River trips are available from the yacht harbour.

**The Angles Theatre** – one of the oldest working theatre in Britain – is a vibrant centre for the arts located in a Georgian building with a history stretching back over 200 years. Some of the best talent in the nation, from poets and musicians to dance, comedy and theatrical troupes come to perform in the intimate 112-seat auditorium.

Wisbech's **Lilian Ream Photographic Gallery** is named for a daughter of

Wisbech born in the late 19th century who at the time of her death in 1961 had amassed a collection of over 1,000 photographs of Wisbech people, places and events, making for a unique and fascinating insight into the history and culture of the town. The gallery is housed in the Tourist Information Centre in Bridge Street, and offers changing exhibitions from this treasure trove of pictorial memorabilia.

## THE FENS AROUND WISBECH

### WEST WALTON AND WALTON HIGHWAY
**3 miles NE of Wisbech off the A47/B198**

Several attractions can be found here, notably the Church of St Mary the Virgin in West Walton with its magnificent 13th century detached tower that dominates the landscape. Walton Highway is home to the **Fenland and West Norfolk Aviation Museum**, whose exhibits include Rolls-Royce Merlin engines, a Lightning jet, a Vampire and a Jumbo jet cockpit simulator. The museum is open weekends in summer.

### LEVERINGTON
**1 mile NW of Wisbech off the A1101**

The tower and spire of the church of St Leonard date from the 13th and 14th centuries. The most exceptional feature of an exceptionally interesting church is the 15th century stained-glass Jesse window in the north aisle. There are many fine memorials in the churchyard. Oliver Goldsmith wrote *She Stoops to Conquer* while staying in Leverington.

## PARSON DROVE

### 6 miles W of Wisbech on the B1187

Parson Drove is a Fenland village which Samuel Pepys visited in 1663. He stayed at the village's **Swan Inn**, and mentions it in his diaries, though he was not complimentary. It was a centre of the woad industry until 1914, when the last remaining woad mill was demolished. Parson Drove is most certainly not the

*'heathen place'* once described by Pepys!

The **Parson Drove Visitors Centre** is set in the old Victorian lock-up on the village green, a building with an unusual 170-year history. Photographs and documents trace the story of this lovely Fens village.

## WELNEY

### 12 miles S of Wisbech off the A1101

The **Wildfowl & Wetlands Trust** (see panel below) in Welney is a nature reserve that attracts large numbers of swans and ducks in winter. Special floodlit 'swan evenings' are held, and there is also a wide range of wild plants and butterflies to be enjoyed.

## THE WILDFOWL & WETLANDS TRUST

Hundred Foot Bank, Welney, Wisbech, Cambridgeshire PE14 9TN
Tel/Fax: 01353 860711
e-mail: welney@wwt.org.uk  website: wwt.org.uk

**The Wildfowl & Wetland Trust Welney** is a wetland paradise of international importance with something to offer whatever the season. In winter, enjoy the magic of hundreds of Whooper and Bewick's Swans accompanied by flocks of thousands of ducks. During the day, carpets of Wigeon graze this precious wetland, while flocks of Pintail, Teal, Gadwall and Shoveler dabble in the pools and lagoons. Late afternoon is a special time as flocks of swans flight-in to claim their night roosting sites. Summer brings an atmosphere of peace and tranquillity broken only by the piping calls of waders, drumming Snipe and the chatter of warblers. Lush meadows are bordered by a dazzling display of Purple Loosestrife, Great Willowherb and Marsh Woundwort. Visitors can stroll along the boardwalks through rustling reedbeds, and spend a while pond-dipping for water beasts. The Visitor Centre houses displays, educational facilities and a well-stocked gift shop. WWT Welney also runs a packed programme of special events

# TOURIST INFORMATION CENTRES

## CAMBRIDGE

### CAMBRIDGE

Wheeler Street
Cambridge
Cambridgeshire
CB2 3QB
Tel: 0906 586 25 26
(premium rate number, calls charged
at 60p per min)
e-mail: tourism@cambridge.gov.uk
website: www.tourismcambridge.com

### ELY

Oliver Cromwell's House
29 St Mary's Street
Ely
Cambridgeshire
CB7 4HF
Tel: 01353 662062
Fax: 01353 668518
e-mail: tic@eastcambs.gov.uk

### HUNTINGDON

The Library
Princes Street
Huntingdon
Cambridgeshire
PE29 3PH
Tel: 01480 388588
Fax: 01480 388591
e-mail: hunts.tic@huntsdc.gov.uk
website: www.huntsdc.gov.uk

### PETERBOROUGH

3-5 Minster Precincts
Peterborough
Cambridgeshire
PE1 1XS
Tel: 01733 452336
Fax: 01733 452353
e-mail: tic@peterborough.gov.uk

### ST NEOTS

The Old Court
8 New Street
St Neots
Cambridgeshire
PE19 1AE
Tel: 01480 388788
Fax: 01480 388791
e-mail: stneots.tic@huntsdc.gov.uk
website: www.huntsdc.gov.uk

### WISBECH

2-3 Bridge Street
Wisbech
Cambridgeshire
PE13 1EW
Tel: 01945 583263
Fax: 01945 463078
website: www.fenland.gov.uk

## ESSEX

### BRAINTREE

Town Hall Centre
Market Place
Braintree
Essex
CM7 3YG
Tel: 01376 550066
Fax:01376 344345
e-mail: tic@bdctourism.demon.co.uk

### BRENTWOOD

44 High St
Brentwood
Essex
CM14 4AJ
Tel: 01277 200300
Fax: 01277 202375

## CHELMSFORD

County Hall
Market Road
Chelmsford
Essex
CM1 1GG
Tel: 01245 283400
Fax: 01245 430705
e-mail: chelmtic@essexcc.gov.uk

## CLACTON-ON-SEA

23 Pier Avenue
Clacton-on-Sea
Essex
CO15 1QD
Tel: 01255 423400
Fax: 01255 430906
e-mail: emorgan@tendringdc.gov.uk

## COLCHESTER

1 Queen Street
Colchester
Essex
CO1 2PG
Tel: 01206 282920
Fax: 01206 282924

## FLATFORD

Flatford Lane
"Flatford, East Bergholt"
Colchester
Essex
CO7 6UL
Tel: 01206 299460
e-mail: flatfordvic@babergh.gov.uk

## HARWICH

Iconfield Park
Parkeston
Harwich
Essex
CO12 4EN
Tel: 01255 506139
Fax: 01255 240570
e-mail: harwich@touristinformation
.fsnet.co.uk

## MALDON

Coach Lane
Maldon
Essex
CM9 4UH
Tel: 01621 856503
Fax: 01621 875873
e-mail: tic@maldon.gov.uk

## SAFFRON WALDEN

1 Market Place
Saffron Walden
Essex
CBIO 1HR
Tel: 01799 510444
Fax: 01799 510445
e-mail: tourism@uttlesford.gov.uk

## SOUTHEND

19 High Street
Southend-on-Sea
Essex
SS1 IJE
Tel: 01702 215120
Fax: 01702 431449
e-mail: shop@sbctic3.fsnet.co.uk

## THURROCK

Motorway Services
M25 Junction 30/31
Thurrock
Grays
Essex
RM16 3BG
Tel: 0870 225 4850
Fax: 0870 225 4851
e-mail: tourist.information@thurrock.gov.uk

## WALTHAM ABBEY

Unit B
2-4 Highbridge Street
Waltham Abbey
Essex
EN9 1DG
Tel: 01992 652295
Fax: 01992 716234
e-mail: townclerk@walthamabbey.org.uk

# NORFOLK

## AYLSHAM

Bure Valley Railway Station
Norwich Road
Aylsham
Norfolk
NR11 6BW
Tel: 01263 733903
Fax: 01263 733814
e-mail: aylsham.tic@broadland.gov.uk

## CROMER

Prince of Wales Road
Cromer
Norfolk
NR27 9HS
Tel: 01263 512497
Fax: 01263 513613
e-mail: jn@north-norfolk.gov.uk

## DISS

Meres Mouth
Mere Street
Diss
Norfolk
IP22 3AG
Tel: 01379 650523
Fax: 01379 650838
e-mail: disstic@dial.pipex.com

## DOWNHAM MARKET

The Priory Centre
78 Priory Road
Downham Market
Norfolk PE38 9JS
Tel: 01366 387440
Fax: 01366 385 042
e-mail: downham-market.tic@west-
norfolk.gov.uk

## GREAT YARMOUTH

Marine Parade
Great Yarmouth
Norfolk
NR31 8NE
Tel: 01493 842195
Fax: 01493 858588
e-mail: tourism@great-yarmouth.gov.uk

## HOVETON

Station Road
Hoveton
Norfolk
NR12 8UR
Tel: 01603 782281
Fax: 01603 782281

## HUNSTANTON

Town Hall
The Green
Hunstanton
Norfolk
PE36 6BQ
Tel: 01485 532610
Fax: 01485 533972
e-mail: hunstanton.tic@west-norfolk.gov.uk

## KING'S LYNN

The Custom House
Purfleet Quay
King's Lynn
Norfolk
PE30 1HP
Tel: 01553 763044
Fax: 01553 819441
e-mail: kings-lynn.tic@west-norfolk.gov.uk

## MUNDESLEY

2 Station Road
Mundesley
Norfolk
NR11 8JH
Tel: 01263 721070
Fax: 01263 722796
e-mail: jn@north-norfolk.gov.uk

## NORWICH

The Guildhall
Gaol Hill
Norwich
Norfolk
NR2 1NF
Tel: 01603 666071
Fax: 01603 765389
e-mail: tourism.norwich@gtnet.gov.uk

## SHERINGHAM

Station Approach
Sheringham
Norfolk
NR26 8RA
Tel: 01263 824329
Fax: 01263 821668
e-mail: jn@north-norfolk.gov.uk

## WELLS-NEXT-THE-SEA

Staithe Street
Wells-next-the-Sea
Norfolk
NR23 1AN
Tel: 01328 710885
Fax: 01328 711405
e-mail: jn@north-norfolk.gov.uk

# SUFFOLK

## ALDEBURGH

152 High Street
Aldeburgh
Suffolk
IP15 5AQ
Tel: 01728 453637
Fax: 01728 453637
e-mail: atic@suffolkcoastal.gov.uk

## BECCLES

The Quay
Fen Lane
Beccles
Suffolk
NR34 9BH
Tel: 01502 713196
Fax: 01502 713196

## BURY ST EDMUNDS

6 Angel Hill
Bury St Edmunds
Suffolk
IP33 1UZ
Tel: 01284 764667
Fax: 01284 757084
e-mail: tic@stedsbc.gov.uk

## FELIXSTOWE

The Seafront
Felixstowe
Suffolk
IP11 2AE
Tel: 01394 276770
Fax: 01394 277456
e-mail: tic@suffolkcoastal.gov.uk

## IPSWICH

St Stephens Church
St Stephens Lane
Ipswich
Suffolk
IP1 1DP
Tel: 01473 258070
Fax: 01473 432017
e-mail: tourist@ipswich.gov.uk

## LAVENHAM

Lady Street
Lavenham
Suffolk
CO10 9RA
Tel: 01787 248207
Fax: 01787 249459
e-mail: lavenhamtic@babergh.gov.uk

## LOWESTOFT

East Point Pavilion
Royal Plain
Lowestoft
Suffolk
NR33 OAP
Tel: 01502 533600
Fax: 01502 539023
e-mail: touristinfo@waveney.gov.uk

## NEWMARKET

Palace House
Palace Street
Newmarket
Suffolk
CB8 8EP
Tel: 01638 667200
Fax: 01638 660394
e-mail: newmarket.tic@forest-heath-dc.demon.co.uk

## SOUTHWOLD

69 High Street
Southwold
Suffolk
IP18 6DS
Tel: 01502 724729
Fax: 01502 722978
e-mail: southwoldtic@waveney.gov.uk

## STOWMARKET

Wilkes Way
Stowmarket
Suffolk
IP14 1DE
Tel: 01449 676800
Fax: 01449 614691
e-mail: info@tic.keme.co.uk

## SUDBURY

Town Hall
Market Hill
Sudbury
Suffolk
CO10 1TL
Tel: 01787 881320
Fax: 01787 242129
e-mail: sudburytic@babergh.gov.uk

## WOODBRIDGE

Station Buildings
Woodbridge
Suffolk
IP12 4AJ
Tel: 01394 382240
Fax: 01394 386337
e-mail: wtic@suffolkcoastal.gov.uk

# INDEX OF ADVERTISERS

## NUMBERS

152 Aldeburgh, Aldeburgh, Suffolk   137

## A

Abbey House, Monk Soham, Woodbridge, Suffolk   164

Alder Carr Farm Shop & Crafts, Creeting St Mary, Needham Market, Suffolk   158

Aldringham Arts & Crafts Market, Aldringham, Leiston, Suffolk   132

The Amber Shop & Museum, Southwold, Suffolk   120

The Angel Hotel, Bury St Edmunds, Suffolk   206

The Angel Inn, Wangford, Southwold, Suffolk   122

Anglesey Abbey, Gardens & Lode Mill, Lode, Cambridgeshire   315

Art - e - Fax, Holt , Norfolk   54

Artstop. Biz., Aylsham, Norfolk   16

Aspens Jewellers, Woodbridge, Suffolk   144

The Avocet Collection, Lavenham, Suffolk   194

Axe & Compass, Hemingford Abbots, Huntingdon, Cambridgeshire   328

## B

Balagan Giftshop, Peterborough, Cambridgeshire   333

Ballaglass, Stisted, Braintree, Essex   239

Baumanns Brasserie, Coggleshall, Essex   240

Baylham House Rare Breeds Farm, Baylham, Suffolk   159

Bear Restaurant & Bar, Stock, Chelmsford, Essex   278

Beards of Eye, Eye, Suffolk   171

Bed Bazaar, Framlingham, Suffolk   162

The Bell Inn, Walberswick, Southwold, Suffolk   123

Bizarre Alternative Gifts, Southend-on-Sea, Essex   284

Black Sheep Ltd, Aylsham, Norfolk   15

Blickling Hall, Blickling, Norfolk   17

Bolding Way Holiday Cottages, Weybourne, Holt, Norfolk   51

Bookleaf Café & Bookshop, Chelmsford, Essex   286

Braintree District Museum, Braintree, Essex   237

Bressingham Gardens, Bressingham, Norfolk   13

Bridge Nurseries, Dunwich, Saxmundham, Suffolk   127

British Wildflower Plants, North Burlingham, Norfolk   28

Broadland Wineries, Cawston, Norwich, Norfolk   22

The Brudenell Hotel, Aldeburgh, Suffolk   136

Bulmer Brick & Tile Co. Ltd., Bulmer, Sudbury, Suffolk   189

Bure Valley Railway, Aylsham, Norfolk   14

Burwash Manor Barns, Barton, Cambridgeshire   318

Butley Pottery, Gallery & Barn Café, Butley, Woodbridge, Suffolk   150

## C

The C21 Shop, Mundesley, Norfolk   43

Cambridge & County Folk Museum, Cambridge, Cambridgeshire   313

The Cambridge Cheese Company, Cambridge, Cambridgeshire   311

Cambridge University Botanic Garden, Cambridge, Cambridgeshire   312

The Chaff House, Littlebury Green, Saffron Walden, Essex   259

Chappel Galleries, Chappel, Colchester, Essex   234

Charles Matts, Thurgarton, Norwich, Norfolk   19

Chediston Pottery, Chediston, Halesworth, Suffolk   126

The Cheeseboard, Harleston, Norfolk   14

Chelmsford Museum & Essex Regiment Museum, Chelmsford, Essex   289

Chilford Hall Vineyard, Linton, Cambridge, Cambridgeshire   317

Chilli & Chives, Hintlesham, Ipswich, Suffolk   183

Church Farm, Kettleburgh, Framlingham, Suffolk   169

City of Norwich Aviation Museum, Norwich, Norfolk   9

Clare Castle Country Park, Clare, Suffolk   200

Clarice House Hotel & Spa, Bury St Edmunds, Suffolk   202

Cley Smokehouse, Cley-next-the-Sea, Holt, Norfolk   57

Clinton House & Cottage, Yaxham, Dereham, Norfolk   98

Clippesby Hall, Clippesby, Great Yarmouth, Norfolk   34

Cloisters Antiques, Ely , Cambridgeshire   303

Coffee & Co, Newmarket, Suffolk   217

Colchester Castle, Colchester, Essex   228

Corncraft and The Summer House, Monks Eleigh, Hadleigh, Suffolk   183

The Cotton Tree, Southwold, Suffolk   119

The Cotton Tree, Woodbridge, Suffolk   146

The Cotton Tree, Ipswich, Suffolk   177

The Country Shop, North Walsham, Norfolk   42

Country Working, Wood Walton, Huntingdon, Cambridgeshire   322

Countryside Cottages, Holt, Norfolk   53

Crispins Restaurant & Rooms, Messing, Tiptree, Essex   233

The Crockery Barn, Ashbocking, Ipswich, Suffolk   168

Cromer Museum, Cromer, Norfolk   45

Crowes, Sheringham, Norfolk   48

Crystal Waters Traditional Smokehouse, Lowestoft, Suffolk   110

**D**

Daphne Cooper at Millstone, East Rudham, Norfolk   93

Delicious Delicatessen, Great Dunmow, Essex   265

Doodle Pots, Holt, Norfolk   55

Doric Arts Gallery & Framing Workshop, King's Lynn, Norfolk   80

Dragon Hall, Norwich, Norfolk   8

Dream Jewellery, Cambridge, Cambridgeshire   311

Dutch Nursery, Coggleshall, Essex   241

Dyes House Gallery, Aylsham, Norfolk   16

**E**

East Anglian Railway Museum, Chappel, Colchester, Essex   234

Easton Farm Park, Easton, Woodbridge, Suffolk   166

Easton Farm Park Holiday Cottages, Easton, Woodbridge, Suffolk   166

Elm Tree Gallery, Woolpit, Bury St Edmunds, Suffolk   212

Emcy Garden & Leisure, Holt, Norfolk   56

Eric Bates & Sons Ltd, Hoveton, Wroxham, Norfolk   30

Essex Kilns, Tollesbury, Maldon, Essex   294

**F**

Fairhaven Woodland & Water Garden, South Walsham, Norwich, Norfolk   33

Farmland Museum & Denny Abbey, Waterbeach, Cambridgeshire   314

Felbrigg Hall, Felbrigg, Norwich, Norfolk   47

Fiddlesticks B&B, Pentlow, Clare, Suffolk   200

Fisks Restaurant, Lavenham, Suffolk   196

Flag Fen, Peterborough, Cambridgeshire   336

The Forge Café, Restaurant & Gift Shop, Thornham Magna, Eye, Suffolk   161

Friday Street Farm Shop & Tea Room, Farnham, Saxmundham, Suffolk   144

Fritton Lake Countryworld, Fritton, Great Yarmouth, Norfolk   26

**G**

Gainsborough's House, Sudbury, Suffolk   188

Gallery 48, Lavenham, Suffolk   195

Gaye Drummond Flowers, Dedham, Essex   236

The George, Cavendish, Sudbury, Suffolk   199

The Gin Trap Inn, Ringstead, Hunstanton, Norfolk   72

The Golden Boar Inn, Freckenham, Bury St Edmunds, Suffolk   221

Grange Farm, Dennington, Framlingham, Suffolk   165

The Great Escape Holiday Co.Ltd   Prelims

Green Island, Ardleigh, Colchester, Essex   235

Green Lawn Bonsai, Boxford, Sudbury, Suffolk   191

The Greyhound Inn, Pettistree , Wickham Market, Suffolk   148

The Griffin Inn, Yoxford, Suffolk   130

Grove Farm, Roughton, Norfolk   44

Grove Farm Gallery & Studio, Catfield, Great Yarmouth, Norfolk   34

The Guildhall, Lavenham, Lavenham, Suffolk   195

## H

Haddenham Galleries, Haddenham, Ely , Cambridgeshire   307

The Hall, Witcham, Cambridgeshire   305

Head Street Gallery, Halstead, Essex   244

Hedgerows Farm Shop & Nursery, Brent Eleigh, Lavenham, Suffolk   193

Hill Farm B&B, Kirtling, Newmarket, Suffolk   219

Hobbs Pavilion Restaurant, Cambridge, Cambridgeshire   310

Holiday Cottage, Orford, Suffolk   153

Holkham Hall & Bygones Museum, Wells-next-the-Sea, Norfolk   64

Holland House, Docking, Norfolk   71

Honeysuckle Cottage, Grantchester, Cambridgeshire   319

Houghton Mill, Houghton, Huntingdon, Cambridgeshire   331

House Bait II, Burnham Market, Norfolk   66

## I

Ingatestone Hall, Ingatestone, Essex   277

Ipswich Transport Museum, Ipswich, Suffolk   179

## J

Japanese Garden, Terrington St Clement, King's Lynn, Norfolk   83

## K

Kelvedon Hatch Secret Nuclear Bunker, Brentwood, Essex   274

Kims Coffee House, Saffron Walden, Essex   256

Kingfisher Lodge, Wroxham, Norwich, Norfolk   29

Kitty's Homestore, Wickham Market, Woodbridge, Suffolk   149

The Knot Garden, Wood Dalling, Norwich, Norfolk   23

## L

The Lord Nelson, Burnham Thorpe, Norfolk   67

Lowestoft Maritime Museum, Lowestoft, Suffolk   108

Lynford Hall Country House Hotel, Mundford, Thetford, Norfolk   104

## M

Maidens Barn, High Easter, Chelmsford, Essex   275

The Manor, Hemingford Grey, Huntingdon, Cambridgeshire   328

Manor Barn, Happisburgh, Norfolk   38

Meadow Dairies, Holt, Norfolk   56

The Meare Shop & Tearoom, Thorpeness, Aldeburgh, Suffolk   133

Melton Hall, Woodbridge, Suffolk   146

Mersea Island Vineyard, East Mersea, Colchester, Essex   252

Metamorphosis, St Ives, Cambridgeshire   332

Milden Hall Farmhouse, Milden, Lavenham, Suffolk   193

Mirabelle Restaurant & Bistro, West Runton, Cromer, Norfolk   45

Moor Farm Stable Cottages, Foxley, Dereham, Norfolk   100

Mountfitchet Castle & Norman Village, Stansted, Essex   263

The Muckleburgh Collection, Weybourne, Norfolk   52

Mulberry House, Maldon, Essex   292

Museum of East Anglian Life, Stowmarket, Suffolk   157

## N

National Horseracing Museum, Newmarket, Suffolk   218

The Needlecraft Shop, Beccles, Suffolk   113

Norfolk & Suffolk Aviation Musuem, Flixton, Bungay, Suffolk   116

Norfolk Barn, Docking, Norfolk   69

Norfolk House, Great Shelford, Cambridgeshire   313

The Norfolk Shire Horse Centre, West Runton, Cromer, Norfolk   46

North House Gallery, Manningtree, Essex   255

North Walsham Garden Centre, North Walsham, Norfolk   41

Northgate House, Bury St Edmunds, Suffolk    205

## O

Ocean House, Aldeburgh, Suffolk    136

The Old Chequers Restaurant, Friston, Aldeburgh, Suffolk    132

The Old House, Bocking, Braintree, Essex    238

The Old Vicarage, Wenhaston, Halesworth, Suffolk    125

Orlando's of Aldeburgh, Aldeburgh, Suffolk    138

Out of the Blue, Coggleshall, Essex    240

Oxburgh Hall, Oxburgh, King's Lynn, Norfolk    87

## P

P & R Antiques Ltd, Spexhall, Halesworth, Suffolk    126

Palmer & Burnett, Saxmundham, Suffolk    131

The Parish Lantern, Beccles, Suffolk    113

The Parish Lantern, Walberswick, Southwold, Suffolk    123

Park Farm B&B and Cottages, Sibton, Saxmundham, Suffolk    130

the passion of flowers, Holt, Norfolk    55

Paxton Dene, Brightlingsea, Essex    250

Peacock's Country Flower & Gift Store, White Roding, Essex    267

Pensthorpe Waterfowl Park & Nature Reserve, Pensthorpe, Fakenham, Norfolk    88

Peter Conoley & Son, Watton, Thetford, Norfolk    101

Pilgrims Reach Restaurant & Freehouse, Docking, Norfolk    70

The Plough Inn, Marsham, Norfolk    18

Poplar Hall, Frostenden, Southwold, Suffolk    118

Poplar Nurseries, Garden Centre & Restaurant, Markstey, Colchester, Essex    231

The Post House, Stocks Green, Castle Acre, Norfolk    97

Powell & Bull, Cambridge, Cambridgeshire    309

Pyramid Egyptian Arts & Crafts, Lowestoft, Suffolk    109

## R

Railworld, Peterborough, Cambridgeshire    335

Rare View B&B, Gosfield, Halstead, Essex    245

Redgates Farmhouse, Seward End, Saffron Walden, Essex    260

Redhouse Farm, Haughley, Stowmarket, Suffolk    157

The Residence at Sutherland House Restaurant, Southwold, Suffolk    120

RHS Garden Hyde Hall, Rettendon, Chelmsford, Essex    296

Richardson's Smokehouse, Orford, Suffolk    152

Ringstead Gallery, Ringstead, Hunstanton, Norfolk    73

The Romantic Garden Nursery, Swannington, Norwich, Norfolk    22

Romark Jewellers, Bury St Edmunds, Suffolk    203

Royal Gunpowder Mills, Waltham Abbey, Essex    271

Rue Gavaret, Broomfield, Essex    288

## S

Saffron Walden Antiques Centre, Saffron Walden, Essex    258

Salthouse Harbour Hotel, Ipswich, Suffolk    176

Sandringham House, Sandringham, Norfolk    76

Saseenos Holiday Cottage, Thorpeness, Suffolk    135

Sceptred Isle Food Company, Saffron Walden, Essex    257

Shawsgate Vineyard, Framlingham, Suffolk    162

The Ship Inn Dunwich, Dunwich, Saxmundham, Suffolk    128

Sleeping Partners, Framlingham, Suffolk    162

Snape Maltings, Snape, Aldeburgh, Suffolk    142

Sole Bay Pine Company, Blythburgh, Suffolk    125

Somerleyton Hall & Gardens, Lowestoft, Suffolk    112

Southwold Pier, Southwold, Suffolk    121

Spice Bar, Restaurant & Café, Woodbridge, Suffolk    145

St Edmunsbury Cathedral, Bury St Edmunds, Suffolk    204

The Stables, Holt, Norfolk    52

The Stables at Ivy Lodge Barn, Hoo, Woodbridge, Suffolk    167

Staithe Antiques, Brancaster Staithe, Norfolk    68

Step House, Wetheringsett, Stowmarket, Suffolk    160

Stiffkey Antiques, Stiffkey, Wells-next-the-Sea, Norfolk    61

Suffolk House Antiques, Yoxford, Suffolk    129

Sutton Hoo, Sutton Hoo, Woodbridge, Suffolk    148

Swaffham Museum, Swaffham, Norfolk   95

The Swan Inn, Barnby, Beccles, Suffolk   115

## T

Tannington Hall, Framlingham, Suffolk   163

The Thaxted Garden for Butterflies, Thaxted, Essex   265

Thetford Garden Centre, Kilverstone, Thetford, Norfolk   103

Thorpeness Country Club Apartments & Dolphin Inn, Thorpeness, Aldeburgh, Suffolk   134

The Thorpeness Hotel & Golf Club, Thorpeness, Aldeburgh, Suffolk   134

The Thursford Collection, Thursford, Fakenham, Norfolk   89

The Titchwell Manor Hotel, Brancaster, King's Lynn, Norfolk   69

Topsail Charters, Maldon, Essex   293

Tot Hill House, Tot Hill, Stowmarket, Suffolk   156

The Treasure Box, Hickling, Norwich, Norfolk   35

The Trinity Foot, Swavesey, Cambridgeshire   330

Tunstead Old Farm Cottages, Tunstead, Norwich, Norfolk   31

The Turks Head, Haskerton, Woodbridge, Suffolk   147

## V

Verandah House, Stowmarket, Suffolk   155

Very Nice Things, Reepham, Norfolk   22

Vintage Pink, Lavenham, Suffolk   195

## W

Walcot Green Farm Cottage, Diss, Norfolk   12

Walsingham Shirehall Museum & Abbey Grounds, Little Walsingham, Norfolk   91

Waterfront Place Restaurant, Chelmsford, Essex   287

The Wells Deli Company, Wells-next-the-Sea, Norfolk   62

The Wells Deli Company, Little Walsingham, Norfolk   90

Wentworth Hotel & Restaurant, Aldeburgh, Suffolk   139

West Stow Anglo-Saxon Village, West Stow, Bury St Edmunds, Suffolk   207

Westcliffe Gallery, Sheringham, Norfolk   48

Weston House Farm, Mendham, Harleston, Norfolk   117

Weybourne Forest Lodges, Weybourne, Holt, Norfolk   50

Wheldons Farm Shop & Pick Your Own, Newton, Sudbury, Suffolk   191

White Hall Plants, Worlingworth, Framlingham, Suffolk   164

The White Horse Inn, Swavesey, Cambridgeshire   330

The White Horse Pleshey, Pleshey, Chelmsford, Essex   268

The White Lion Hotel, Aldeburgh, Suffolk   138

Whitehall Farm, Burnham Thorpe, Norfolk   65

The Wildfowl & Wetlands Trust, Welney, Wisbech, Cambridgeshire   342

Wimpole Estate, Arrington, Royston, Cambridgeshire   320

Wood 'N' Things, Holt , Norfolk   54

Woodlands Farm, Brundish, Framlingham, Suffolk   165

Worlington House, Worlington, Suffolk   222

Wrekin Farmfoods, Althorne, Burnham-on-Crouch, Essex   297

Wyken Vineyard, Stanton, Bury St Edmunds, Suffolk   210

## Y

Yardleys, Orchard Pittle, Hadstock, Cambridgeshire   260

Ye Olde Bell & Steelyard, Woodbridge, Suffolk   145

| | Start | Distance | Time | Page |
|---|---|---|---|---|
| 1 | ALDERFORD COMMON<br>Alderford Common | 3.1 miles (4.8km) | 1½ hrs | 20 |
| 2 | LUDHAM MARSHES<br>Ludham Village | 3.5 miles (5.5km) | 1½ hrs | 32 |
| 3 | BACTON WOODS<br>Bacton Woods Picnic Site | 3.1 miles (4.8km) | 1½ hrs | 40 |
| 4 | BLAKENEY<br>Blakeney Main Street | 3.1 miles (4.8km) | 1½ hrs | 58 |
| 5 | SHOULDHAM WARREN<br>Shouldham Warren Forestry Car Park | 3.1 miles (4.8km) | 1½ hrs | 84 |
| 6 | NORTH COVE<br>North Cove Village | 5.0 miles (8.0km) | 3 hrs | 114 |
| 7 | IKEN CLIFF - RIVER ALDE - TUNSTALL FOREST - SNAPE<br>Iken Cliff Picnic Site | 5.3 miles (8.5km) | 2½ hrs | 140 |
| 8 | EYE<br>Pennings Picnic Site Car Park, nr Eye | 3.5 miles (5.5km) | 1½ hrs | 170 |
| 9 | GREAT WALDINGFIELD - LITTLE WALDINGFIELD - GREAT WALDINGFIELD<br>Great Waldingfield Church | 3.1 miles (4.8km) | 1 hr | 190 |
| 10 | LAYER BRETON - LAYER MARNEY - BIRCH - LAYER BRETON<br>Layer Breton Church Car Park | 4.0 miles (6.4km) | 1½ hrs | 232 |
| 11 | STANSTED MOUNTFITCHET - UGLEY GREEN - AUBREY BUXTON - STANSTED<br>Stansted Mountfitchet CAstle Car Park | 3.1 miles (4.8km) | 1 hr | 262 |
| 12 | WARDY HILL - MEPAL - WARDY HILL<br>Wardy Hill Village | 5.5 miles (8.8km) | 2 hrs | 306 |
| 13 | WISBECH<br>Love Lane Car Park, Wisbech | 3.1 miles (4.8km) | 2 hrs | 340 |

# *Looking for more walks?*

The walks in this book have been gleaned from Britain's largest online walking guide, to be found at *www.walkingworld.com*.

The site contains 300 walks across eastern England, so there is plenty more choice in this region alone. If you are heading further afield there are walks of every length and type across England, Scotland and Wales – ideal if you are taking a short break as you can plan your walks in advance.

Want more detail for the walks in this book? Next to every walk in this book you will see a Walk ID. You can enter this ID number on Walkingworld's 'Find a Walk' page and you will be taken straight to the details of that walk.

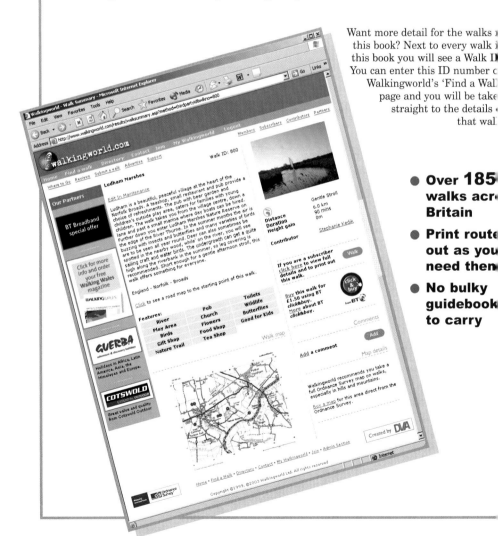

- Over **185** walks across Britain

- Print routes out as you need them

- No bulky guidebook to carry

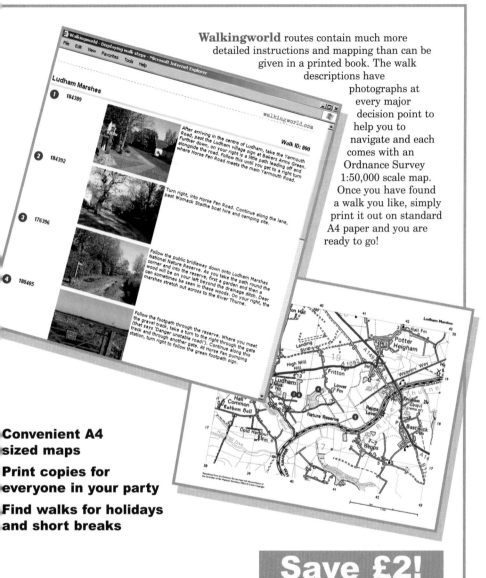

**Walkingworld** routes contain much more detailed instructions and mapping than can be given in a printed book. The walk descriptions have photographs at every major decision point to help you to navigate and each comes with an Ordnance Survey 1:50,000 scale map. Once you have found a walk you like, simply print it out on standard A4 paper and you are ready to go!

**Convenient A4 sized maps**

**Print copies for everyone in your party**

**Find walks for holidays and short breaks**

*A modest annual subscription gives you access to over 1850 walks, all in Walkingworld's easy to follow format. The database of walks is growing all the time and as a subscriber you gain access to new routes as soon as they are published.*

it the Walkingworld website at *www.walkingworld.com*

# *Travel Publishing*

| | |
|---|---|
| **The Hidden Places** | Regional and National guides to the less well-known places of interest and places to eat, stay and drink |
| **Hidden Inns** | Regional guides to traditional pubs and inns throughout the United Kingdom |
| **GOLFERS GUIDES** | Regional and National guides to 18 hole golf courses and local places to stay, eat and drink |
| **COUNTRY LIVING** MAGAZINE **RURAL GUIDES** | Regional and National guides to the traditional countryside of Britain and Ireland with easy to read facts on places to visit, stay, eat, drink and shop |

## *For more information:*

**Phone:** 0118 981 7777  **Fax:** 0118 982 0077
**e-mail:** adam@travelpublishing.co.uk  **website:** www.travelpublishing.co.u

# Easy-to-use, Informative
## Travel Guides on the British Isles

*Travel Publishing Limited*

7a Apollo House • Calleva Park • Aldermaston • Berkshire RG7 8TN

# ORDER FORM

To order any of our publications just fill in the payment details below and complete the order form. For orders of less than 4 copies please add £1 per book for postage and packing. Orders over 4 copies are P & P free.

**Please Complete Either:**

I enclose a cheque for £ [                    ] made payable to Travel Publishing Ltd

**Or:**

Card No: [                        ]    Expiry Date: [            ]

Signature: [                        ]

NAME: [                        ]

ADDRESS: [                        ]

TEL NO: [                        ]

**Please either send, telephone, fax or e-mail your order to:**

Travel Publishing Ltd, 7a Apollo House, Calleva Park, Aldermaston, Berkshire RG7 8TN
Tel: 0118 981 7777    Fax: 0118 982 0077    e-mail: info@travelpublishing.co.uk

| HIDDEN PLACES REGIONAL TITLES | PRICE | QUANTITY | HIDDEN INNS TITLES | PRICE | QUANTITY |
|---|---|---|---|---|---|
| Cambs & Lincolnshire | £8.99 | ............ | East Anglia | £7.99 | ............ |
| Chilterns | £8.99 | ............ | Heart of England | £7.99 | ............ |
| Cornwall | £8.99 | ............ | Lancashire & Cheshire | £7.99 | ............ |
| Derbyshire | £8.99 | ............ | North of England | £7.99 | ............ |
| Devon | £8.99 | ............ | South | £7.99 | ............ |
| Dorset, Hants & Isle of Wight | £8.99 | ............ | South East | £7.99 | ............ |
| East Anglia | £8.99 | ............ | South and Central Scotland | £7.99 | ............ |
| Gloucs, Wiltshire & Somerset | £8.99 | ............ | Wales | £7.99 | ............ |
| Heart of England | £8.99 | ............ | Welsh Borders | £7.99 | ............ |
| Hereford, Worcs & Shropshire | £8.99 | ............ | West Country | £7.99 | ............ |
| Kent | £8.99 | ............ | COUNTRY LIVING RURAL GUIDES | | |
| Lake District & Cumbria | £8.99 | ............ | East Anglia | £10.99 | ............ |
| Lancashire & Cheshire | £8.99 | ............ | Heart of England | £10.99 | ............ |
| Lincolnshire & Nottinghamshire | £8.99 | ............ | Ireland | £10.99 | ............ |
| Northumberland & Durham | £8.99 | ............ | North East of England | £10.99 | ............ |
| Sussex | £8.99 | ............ | North West of England | £10.99 | ............ |
| Yorkshire | £8.99 | ............ | Scotland | £10.99 | ............ |
| HIDDEN PLACES NATIONAL TITLES | | | South of England | £10.99 | ............ |
| England | £10.99 | ............ | South East of England | £10.99 | ............ |
| Ireland | £10.99 | ............ | Wales | £10.99 | ............ |
| Scotland | £10.99 | ............ | West Country | £10.99 | ............ |
| Wales | £10.99 | ............ | | | |

**Total Quantity** [            ]

**Total Value** [            ]

# READER REACTION FORM

The *Travel Publishing* research team would like to receive reader's comments on any visitor attractions or places reviewed in the book and also recommendations for suitable entries to be included in the next edition. This will help ensure that the *Country Living series of Rural Guides* continues to provide its readers with useful information on the more interesting, unusual or unique features of each attraction or place ensuring that their visit to the local area is an enjoyable and stimulating experience. To provide your comments or recommendations would you please complete the forms below and overleaf as indicated and send to:

The Research Department, Travel Publishing Ltd,

7a Apollo House, Calleva Park, Aldermaston, Reading, RG7 8TN.

Your Name:

Your Address:

Your Telephone Number:

Please tick as appropriate: Comments ☐ Recommendation ☐

Name of Establishment:

Address:

Telephone Number:

Name of Contact:

# READER REACTION FORM

*Comment or Reason for Recommendation:*

........................................................................................................

........................................................................................................

........................................................................................................

........................................................................................................

........................................................................................................

........................................................................................................

........................................................................................................

........................................................................................................

........................................................................................................

........................................................................................................

# READER REACTION FORM

The *Travel Publishing* research team would like to receive reader's comments on any visitor attractions or places reviewed in the book and also recommendations for suitable entries to be included in the next edition. This will help ensure that the *Country Living series of Rural Guides* continues to provide its readers with useful information on the more interesting, unusual or unique features of each attraction or place ensuring that their visit to the local area is an enjoyable and stimulating experience. To provide your comments or recommendations would you please complete the forms below and overleaf as indicated and send to:

The Research Department, Travel Publishing Ltd,

7a Apollo House, Calleva Park, Aldermaston, Reading, RG7 8TN.

Your Name:

Your Address:

Your Telephone Number:

Please tick as appropriate: Comments ☐     Recommendation ☐

Name of Establishment:

Address:

Telephone Number:

Name of Contact:

# READER REACTION FORM

*Comment or Reason for Recommendation:*

....................................................................................

....................................................................................

....................................................................................

....................................................................................

....................................................................................

....................................................................................

....................................................................................

....................................................................................

....................................................................................

....................................................................................

# READER REACTION FORM

The *Travel Publishing* research team would like to receive reader's comments on any visitor attractions or places reviewed in the book and also recommendations for suitable entries to be included in the next edition. This will help ensure that the *Country Living series of Rural Guides* continues to provide its readers with useful information on the more interesting, unusual or unique features of each attraction or place ensuring that their visit to the local area is an enjoyable and stimulating experience. To provide your comments or recommendations would you please complete the forms below and overleaf as indicated and send to:

The Research Department, Travel Publishing Ltd,

7a Apollo House, Calleva Park, Aldermaston, Reading, RG7 8TN.

Your Name:

Your Address:

Your Telephone Number:

Please tick as appropriate: Comments ☐ Recommendation ☐

Name of Establishment:

Address:

Telephone Number:

Name of Contact:

# READER REACTION FORM

*Comment or Reason for Recommendation:*

.........................................................................................

.........................................................................................

.........................................................................................

.........................................................................................

.........................................................................................

.........................................................................................

.........................................................................................

.........................................................................................

.........................................................................................

.........................................................................................

# INDEX TO TOWNS & PLACES OF INTEREST

## A

Abberton 231
  *Abberton Reservoir Nature Reserve 231*
  *Fingringhoe Wick Nature Reserve 231*
Abridge 272
  *BBC Essex Garden 272*
Acle 28
  *St Edmund 29*
Aldeburgh 135
  *Aldeburgh Festival 139*
  *Maltings at Snape 139*
  *Moot Hall 141*
  *St Peter and St Paul 141*
Aldham 233
  *Old Hill House 233*
Aldringham 133
  *Aldringham Craft Market 133*
Alpheton 214
  *St Peter and St Paul 214*
Althorne 297
  *St Andrew's 297*
  *War Memorial 297*
Ardleigh 235
  *Ardleigh Outdoor Education Centre 235*
  *Ardleigh Reservoir 235*
  *Butterfield Church 235*
  *Spring Valley Mill 235*
Arrington 319
  *Wimpole Hall 319*
  *Wimpole Home Farm 320*
  *Wimpole Park 320*
Attleborough 101
  *St Mary 101*
  *Tropical Butterfly Gardens and Bird Park 102*
Aveley 280
  *Mardyke Valley 280*
  *St Michael's Church 280*
Aylmerton 46
  *Felbrigg Hall 46*
Aylsham 15
  *Blickling Hall 17*
  *Bure Valley Railway 15*
  *Little Barningham 19*
  *Mannington 18*
  *Market Place 15*
  *Wolterton Park 18*
Aythorpe Roding 268
  *Aythorpe Roding Windmill 268*

## B

Banham 105
  *Banham Zoo 105*
Bardwell 209
Barham 323
Barking 158
Barningham 211
  *Knettishall Heath Country Park 211*
Bartlow 261
  *Bartlow Hills 261*
Barton 319
Battlesbridge 295
  *Battlesbridge Antiques Centre 295*
Bawdsey 153
Baylham 159
  *Baylham House Rare Breeds Farm 159*
Beauchamp Roding 275
  *Church of St Botolph 275*
Beaumont-cum-moze 248
  *St Leonard 248*
  *Trading Quay 248*
Beccles 113
  *Beccles and District Museum 115*
  *Roos Hall 115*
  *St Michael 115*
  *William Clowes Museum of Print 115*
Bildeston 183
Billericay 277
  *Barleylands Farm Museum and Visitors' Centre 279*
  *Norsey Wood 279*
  *The Chantry House 277*
Blake End 242
  *Blake House Craft Centre 242*
  *The Great Maze 242*
Blakeney 59
  *Guildhall 59*
Blakeney Point 59
Blundeston 111
Bluntisham 333
Blythburgh 124
  *Holy Trinity 124*
  *Toby's Walks 124*
Bobbingworth 274
  *Blake Hall Gardens 274*

Bodham 53
   *East Anglian Falconry Centre 53*
Bottisham 315
   *Holy Trinity Church 315*
Boxford 188
Boxworth 329
   *Church of St Peter 329*
   *Overhall Grove 329*
Bradwell-on-Sea/Bradwell Waterside 298
   *Bradwell Lodge 299*
   *Dengie Peninsula 299*
   *St Peter's on the Wall 298*
Braintree 237
   *Braintree District Museum 238*
   *Town Hall Centre 238*
Bramfield 126
   *St Andrew's 126*
Bramford 178
   *Suffolk Water Park 179*
Brampton 325
   *Huntingdon Racecourse 325*
   *Pepys House 325*
Brancaster Staithe 68
Brandeston 169
Brandon 223
   *Brandon Country Park 223*
   *Brandon Heritage Centre 223*
   *Breckland 223*
   *Grime's Graves 223*
   *High Lodge Forest Centre 223*
   *Thetford Forest 223*
Brantham 185
   *Cattawade Picnic Site 185*
Brent Eleigh 193
Brentwood 276
   *Brentwood Cathedral 276*
   *Brentwood Centre 276*
   *Brentwood Museum 277*
   *Thorndon Country Park 277*
Bressingham 12
   *Bressingham Gardens and Steam Museum 12*
   *The Fire Museum 12*
Brightlingsea 250
   *All Saints Church 250*
   *Brightlingsea Museum 251*
   *Brightlingsea Outdoor Education Centre 251*
   *Jacobes Hall 250*
   *Town Hard 250*
Brisley 99
Bromeswell 150

Broxbourne 272
   *Broxbourne Old Mill and Millpool 272*
Broxted 267
   *Church Hall Farm Antique and Craft Centre 267*
   *Church of St Mary the Virgin 267*
Bruisyard 131
   *Bruisyard Vineyard, Winery and Herb Centre 131*
Buckden 325
   *Buckden Towers 325*
Bungay 115
   *Bungay Museum 116*
   *Butter Cross 116*
   *Castle 115*
   *Holy Trinity 116*
   *St Mary 116*
Bures 189
Burgh Castle 28
Burghley 338
   *Burghley House 338*
   *Sculpture Garden 338*
Burnham Market 67
Burnham Thorpe 65
   *Creake Abbey 67*
Burnham-on-Crouch 299
   *Burnham Country Park 299*
   *Burnham-on-Crouch & District Museum 299*
   *Mangapps Farm Railway Museum 299*
   *St Mary's Church 299*
Burwell 316
   *Burwell Castle 316*
   *Burwell Museum 316*
   *Devil's Dyke 316*
   *Stephens Windmill 316*
Bury St Edmunds 202
   *Abbey Gardens 203*
   *Angel Hotel 204*
   *Bury St Edmunds Art Gallery 205*
   *Cupola House 204*
   *Greene King Brewery Museum and Shop 204*
   *Manor House Museum 204*
   *Moyse's Hall Museum 205*
   *Nowton Park 206*
   *Nutshell 204*
   *St Edmundsbury Cathedral 203*
   *St Mary's 203*
   *Theatre Royal 204*
   *Victorian Corn Exchange 204*
Bushmead 327
   *Bushmead Abbey 327*
Butley 151
   *Butley Priory 151*
   *Staverton Thicks 151*
Buxhall 157

## C

Caister-on-Sea 26
  *Caister Castle 26*
  *Thrigby Hall Wildlife Gardens 27*

Cambridge 308
  *Bridge of Sighs 309*
  *Cambridge and County Folk Museum 313*
  *Fitzwilliam Museum 310*
  *Great Court 309*
  *Kettle's Yard 310*
  *King's College Chapel 309*
  *Mathematical Bridge 309*
  *Museum of Classical Archaeology 311*
  *Museum of Technology 311*
  *Museum of Zoology 311*
  *Pepys Library 309*
  *Peterhouse 308*
  *Robinson College 308*
  *Round Church 313*
  *Scott Polar Research Institute 311*
  *Sedgwick Museum of Earth Sciences 311*
  *St Andrew the Great 313*
  *St Andrew the Less 313*
  *St Benet's 313*
  *St Mary the Great 313*
  *St Peter Castle Hill 313*
  *University Botanic Garden 311*
  *University Library 313*
  *University Museum of Archaeology and Anthropology 311*
  *Whipple Museum of the History of Science 311*

Campsea Ashe 150

Canvey Island 281
  *Castle Point Transport Museum 281*
  *Dutch Cottage Museum 281*

Capel St Mary 185

Carlton Colville 118
  *East Anglia Transport Museum 118*

Castle Acre 96
  *Castle Acre Priory 96*

Castle Hedingham 245
  *Castle 245*
  *Church of St Nicholas 246*
  *Colne Valley Farm Park 246*
  *Colne Valley Railway and Museum 246*

Castle Rising 82
  *Castle Keep 82*

Catworth 324

Cavendish 198
  *Cavendish Vineyards 198*
  *St Mary 198*
  *Sue Ryder Foundation Museum 198*

Cawston 23
  *Broadland Wineries 23*
  *St Agnes Church 23*

Caxton 320

Chappel 234
  *Chappel Viaduct 234*
  *East Anglian Railway Museum 234*

Charsfield 167

Chatteris 337
  *Chatteris Museum and Council Chamber 337*

Chelmondiston 182

Chelmsford 286
  *Chelmsford Cathedral 287*
  *Chelmsford Museum 287*
  *Engine House Project 289*
  *Moulsham Mill Business & Craft Centre 289*
  *Royal Saracen's Head 287*
  *Shire Hall 287*
  *Stone Bridge 287*

Chelsworth 192

Chickney 267

Chigwell 272
  *Hainault Forest Country Park 272*

Chillesford 151

Chingford 272
  *Queen Elizabeth Hunting Lodge 272*

Chipping Ongar 274
  *Church of St Martin of Tours 274*
  *Livingstone Cottages 274*

Clacton-on-Sea 246
  *Clacton Pavilion 247*
  *Clifftop Public Gardens 247*
  *Great Clacton 247*
  *Jaywick Sands 247*
  *Seaquarium and Reptile Safari 247*
  *The Pier 247*

Clare 199
  *Ancient House 199*
  *Boyton Vineyards 201*
  *Clare Castle 200*
  *Clare Castle Country Park 200*
  *Nethergate House 200*
  *Stoke-by-Clare 200*

Cley-next-the-Sea 57
  *Cley Mill 57*
  *St Mary's 57*

Cockfield 213
  *Old Rectory 213*

Coggeshall 239
  *Coggeshall Grange Barn 239*
  *Coggeshall Heritage Centre 239*

MarksHall 241
Paycocke's House 239
Colchester 227
  Bourne Mill 230
  Castle Museum 229
  Colchester Arts Centre 229
  Colchester Castle 228
  Colchester Zoo 230
  Dutch Quarter 229
  First Site 229
  High Woods Country Park 230
  Hollytrees Museum 229
  Mercury Theatre 229
  Natural History Museum 229
  Oyster Fisheries 230
  St Botolph's Priory 229
  Tymperleys Clock Museum 229
Coltishall 14
  Ancient Lime Kiln 14
  Redwings Horse Sanctuary 15
Copford 231
  Springfields at Copford 231
  St Mary the Virgin 231
  St Michael and All Angels 231
Corringham 281
  Langdon Hills Country Park 281
Cotton 160
  Mechanical Music Museum & Bygones 160
Covehithe 118
  St Andrew 119
Coveney 305
  St Peter-ad-Vincula 305
Cressing 239
  Cressing Temple Barns 239
Cretingham 169
Cromer 43
  Cromer Museum 44
  Cromer Pier 43
  Lifeboat Museum 43
  St Peter & St Paul 43
Crowland 334
  Abbey 335
  Trinity Bridge 335

**D**

Dalham 220
  Dalham Hall 221
  St Mary's 220
Danbury 291
  Danbury Common 291
  Danbury Country Park 291
Darsham 129
Debenham 164

Dedham 235
  Art & Craft Centre 236
  Castle House 236
  Dedham Vale Family Farm 235
  Marlborough Head 236
  Sir Alfred Munnings Art Museum 236
  Toy Museum 236
Dennington 164
Denver 85
  Denver Sluice 85
  Denver Windmill 86
  Great Denver Sluice 85
Dereham 97
  Bishop Bonner's Cottages 99
  Dumpling Green 99
Dersingham 75
  Dersingham Wood 75
Dillington 99
  Norfolk Herbs at Blackberry Farm 99
Diss 11
  Market Place 11
  Shambles 12
  St Mary's 11
  The Mere 11
Docking 69
Dovercourt 254
  Iron Lighthouse 254
Downham Market 85
  Clock Tower 85
  Collectors World 85
  Magical Dickens World 85
Dunwich 127
  Dunwich Forest 128
  Dunwich Heath 128
  Dunwich Museum 128
Duxford 317
  Imperial War Museum 317

**E**

Earith 333
  Ouse Washes 333
Earl Soham 164
Earl Stonham 159
Earsham 117
  Otter Trust 117
East Bergholt 186
  Constable Country Trail 186
  East Bergholt Place Garden 186
  Flatford Mill 186
  St Mary's 186
  Stour House 186
  Willy Lott's Cottage 186

East Harling 105
 Tomb of Robert Harling 105
 Tomb of Sir Thomas Lovell 105
East Raynham 94
 Raynham Hall 94
East Tilbury 282
 Coalhouse Fort 282
 St Catherine's 282
 Thameside Aviation Museum 282
 The Bata Estate 282
Easton 166
 Crinkle-Crankle Wall 166
Edwardstone 189
Ellington 324
 Grafham Water 324
Elmstead Market 251
 Beth Chatto Gardens 251
 Rolts Nursery Butterfly Farm 251
 St Anne and St Lawrence 251
Elmswell 156
 Great Ashfield 156
Elton 337
 Elton Hall 337
Elveden 223
 Elveden Hall 223
Ely 303
 Brass Rubbing Centre 303
 Cathedral 303
 Ely Museum 304
 Museum of Stained Glass 304
 Tourist Information Centre 304
Epping 272
 St John's Church 272
Erwarton 182
 Erwarton Hall 182
Euston 208
 Euston Hall 208
Exning 220
 St Martin 220
Eye 169
 St Peter and St Paul 169
Eynesbury 327
 Church of St Mary 327

**F**

Fairstead 238
 Church of St Mary and St Peter 238
Fakenham 88
 Museum of Gas & Local History 89
 Pensthorpe Waterfowl Park 89

Feering 242
 Feeringbury Manor 242
Felixstowe 180
 Felixstowe Ferry 181
 Felixstowe Water Clock 181
 Landguard Fort 181
 Landguard Point 181
 Pier 180
Fenstanton 329
Finchingfield 243
 Guildhall 243
 Spains Hall 243
 St John the Baptist 243
Flag Fen 336
 Flag Fen Bronze Age Centre 336
Flatford 235
 Bridge Cottage 235
Flempton 208
 Lark Valley Park 208
Flixton 117
 Norfolk and Suffolk Aviation Museum 117
Fordham 308
 Newmarket Cycle Way 308
Framlingham 161
 Castle 161
 Lanman Museum 163
 St Michael 163
Framsden 167
 Post Mill 167
Fressingfield 173
 Ufford Hall 173
Freston 181
 Freston Park 181
Frinton-on-Sea 248
 Church of Old St Mary 249
 Connaught Avenue 248
 Frinton Gates 249
 The Homestead 249
Friston 132
Fritton 27
 Fritton Lake Countryworld 27
Fyfield 274
 Fyfield Hall 274

**G**

Gestingthorp 246
 St Mary the Virgin 246
Girton 314
Glandford 59
 Glandford Shell Museum 59

*Letheringsett Watermill 59*
*Natural Surroundings Wild Flower Centre 59*
Glemsford  198
Godmanchester  327
*Island Hall 327*
*Port Holme Meadow 327*
*St Mary's Church 327*
*Wood Green Animal Shelter 327*
Goldhanger  294
*Maldon District Agricultural & Domestic Museum 294*
Good Easter  275
Gosfield  243
*Gosfield Lake Leisure Resort 243*
Grafham  325
*Grafham Water 325*
Grantchester  319
*Paradise Nature Reserve 319*
*The Orchard 319*
Grays  279
*Thameside Theatre 279*
*Thurrock Museum 279*
Great and Little Thurlow  201
Great Baddow  289
*Baddow Antiques Centre 289*
Great Bardfield  243
*Great Bardfield Museum 243*
*St Mary the Virgin 243*
Great Bentley  251
Great Bircham  74
*Great Bircham Windmill 74*
Great Bradley  201
Great Dunmow  265
*Brick House 266*
*Doctor's Pond 266*
*Great Dunmow Maltings 266*
*The Flitch Way 266*
Great Easton  267
Great Saling  242
*Saling Hall Garden 242*
Great Snoring  90
Great Walsingham  92
*St Peter's 92*
Great Warley  279
*Warley Place 279*
Great Welnetham  214
Great Witchingham  21
*Dinosaur Adventure Park 21*
*Norfolk Wildlife Centre & Country Park 21*
*Weston Longville 21*
*Wings Raptor 21*

Great Yarmouth  24
*Amazonia 24*
*Anna Sewell House 25*
*Elizabethan House Museum 24*
*Merrivale Model Village 24*
*Nelson's Monument 24*
*Norfolk Nelson Museum 24*
*Old Merchant's House 24*
*Pleasure Beach 24*
*St Nicholas' 25*
*The Quay 25*
*The Rows 25*
*The Sealife Centre 24*
*The Tollhouse 24*
*Town Hall 25*
Greensted  276
*St Andrew's 276*
Gressenhall  99
*Roots of Norfolk at Gressenhall 99*

**H**

Haddenham  305
*Church of St Andrew 307*
*Haddenham Great Mill 305*
Hadleigh  191, 285
*Clock Bell 192*
*Guildhall 191*
*Hadleigh Castle 285*
*Hadleigh Castle Country Park 286*
*Toppesfield Bridg 192*
*Wolves Wood 192*
Hadstock  260
*Church of St Botolph 260*
*Linton Zoo 261*
Halesworth  125
*Halesworth and District Museum 126*
Halstead  244
*Townsford Mill 244*
Hamerton  324
*Hamerton Zoological Park 324*
Happisburgh  39
*St Mary's 39*
Harleston  13, 157
Harlow  273
*Gibberd Collection 273*
*Gibberd Gardens 273*
*Harlow Museum 273*
*Harlow Study and Visitors Centre 273*
*Mark Hall Cycle Museum and Gardens 273*
*Parndon Wood Nature Reserve 273*
Hartest  215
*Gifford's Hall 215*
*Hartest stone 215*

Hartford 323

Harwich 253
   *Electric Palace Cinema 254*
   *Guildhall 254*
   *Ha'penny Pier Visitor Centre 253*
   *High Lighthouse 253*
   *Lifeboat Museum 253*
   *Low Lighthouse 253*
   *Maritime Museum 253*
   *National Vintage Wireless and Television Museum 253*
   *The Redoubt 254*
   *Treadwell Crane 254*

Hatfield Broad Oak 268
   *Hatfield Forest 268*

Haughley 156
   *Haughley Park 156*

Haverhill 201
   *Anne of Cleves House 201*
   *East Town Park 201*
   *Haverhill Local History Centre 201*

Hawkedon 214

Heacham 74
   *Heacham Park Fishery 74*
   *Norfolk Lavender 74*

Helmingham 167

Hemingford Abbots 329

Hemingford Grey 329
   *The Manor 329*

Hempstead 261

Hengrave 208
   *Hengrave Hall 208*

Herringfleet 112
   *Herringfleet Windmill 112*

Hessett 212

Heybridge Basin 295

High Easter 275
   *Aythorpe Post Mill 275*

Highwood 290
   *Hylands House 290*
   *Hylands Park 290*

Hilgay 86

Hilton 327
   *Hilton Turf Maze 329*

Hintlesham 182

Hinxton 319

Hockley 286
   *Hockley Woods 286*
   *Volpaia 286*

Hoddesdon 272
   *Rye House Gatehouse 272*

Holkham 63
   *Holkham Hall 63*

Holland-on-Sea 248
   *Holland Haven Country Park 248*

Hollesley 153

Holme-next-the-Sea 71
   *Peddar's Way 71*

Holt 53
   *Gresham's School 55*
   *Home Place 56*

Honington 211

Horham 172

Horndon-on-the-Hill 281
   *Langdon Hills Conservation Centre and Nature Reser 281*
   *Plotlands Museum 281*
   *Woolmarket 281*

Horning 33

Horringer 215
   *Ickworth House 216*

Houghton 331
   *Houghton Meadows 331*

Hoxne 172

Hullbridge 286
   *Jakapeni Rare Breed Farm 286*

Hunstanton 61
   *Sea Life Sanctuary 62*

Huntingdon 320
   *All Saints 321*
   *Cowper House 321*
   *Cromwell Museum 321*
   *Falcon Inn 321*
   *Hinchingbrooke Country Park 322*
   *Hinchingbrooke House 322*
   *Spring Common 322*
   *St Mary's 321*
   *The George Hotel 321*

## I

Icklingham 206
   *Rampart Field 207*

Ingatestone 277
   *Ingatestone Hall 277*

Ipswich 176
   *Christchurch Mansion 177*
   *Ipswich Museum 178*
   *Ipswich Transport Museum 178*
   *Old Custom House 177*
   *Orwell Country Park 178*
   *Tolly Cobbold 177*

Isleham 308

Ixworth 209

**K**

Kedington 201
St Peter and St Paul 201
Kelvedon 242
Feering and Kelvedon Museum 242
Kelvedon Hatch 275
Kelvedon Secret Nuclear Bunker 275
Kentford 220
Gypsy Boy's Grave 220
Kersey 192
Water Splash 192
Kessingland 118
Suffolk Wildlife Park 118
Keyston 325
St John the Baptist 325
Kimbolton 325
Kimbolton Castle 325
King's Lynn 80
Caithness Crystal 82
Custom House 81
Greenland Fishery Building 81
Guildhall of St George 81
Guildhall of the Holy Trinity 81
Hanseatic Warehouse 81
King's Lynn Arts Centre 81
Museum of Lynn Life 81
Saturday Market Place 81
South Gate 81
St Margaret 80
Kirby-le-Soken 249

**L**

Lackford 208
Langford 294
Museum of Power 294
Langham 60
Langham Glass & Rural Crafts 60
Langmere 13
100th Bomb Group Memorial Museum 13
Lavenham 193
Guildhall 194
Little Hall 195
The Priory 196
Lawshall 215
Wishing Well 215
Laxfield 173
Heveningham Hall 173
Laxfield & District Museum 173
Layer Breton 231
Stamps and Crows 231

Layer Marney 233
Layer Marney Tower 233
Leigh-on-Sea 285
Leigh Heritage Centre 285
Leiston 132
Leiston Abbey 132
Long Shop Museum 132
Lessingham 39
Broadlands Museum 39
Sutton Windmill 39
Leverington 341
Levington 180
Trimley Marshes 180
Linford 281
Walton Hall Museum 281
Linton 317
Bartlow Hills 317
Linton Zoo 317
Litcham 97
Village Museum 97
Little Baddow 291
Blakes Wood 291
Chelmer and Blackwater Canal 291
Little Braxted 291
Little Clacton 247
Jubilee Oak 247
Oakwood Crafts Resource Centre 247
St James 247
Little Downham 305
Church of St Leonard 305
Little Easton 266
Barn Theatre 266
Church 266
Little Gransden 320
Little Paxton 326
Paxton Pits Nature Reserve 326
Little Walsingham 90
Augustinian Priory 91
Clink in Common Plac 92
East Barsham Hall 91
Franciscan Friary 92
Holy House 91
Shire Hall 92
Shrine of Our Lady of Walsingham 91
Slipper Chapel 92
Littleport 304
St George's Church 304
Lode 315
Anglesey Abbey 315
Long Melford 196
Holy Trinity Church 196

*Kentwell Hall 198*
*Melford Hall 197*

Longthorpe 337
*Longthorpe Tower 337*

Loughton 272
*Corbett Theatre 272*
*Epping Forest 272*

Lound 111
*St John the Baptist 111*

Lowestoft 108
*Claremont Pier 109*
*ISCA Maritime Museum 111*
*Lifeboat Station 109*
*Lowestoft & East Suffolk Maritime Museum 109*
*Lowestoft Museum 111*
*Oulton Broad 110*
*Pleasurewood Hill 110*
*Royal Naval Patrol Museum 109*
*Royal Norfolk & Suffolk Yacht Club 109*
*War Memorial Museum 109*

**M**

Madingley 320
*American Cemetery 320*

Maldon 292
*Hythe Quay 293*
*Maeldune Heritage Centre 292*
*Maldon District Museum 293*
*Moot Hall 292*
*Promenade Park 293*
*St Giles the Leper Hospital 294*
*The Plume Library 293*

Manningtree 255
*Manningtree Museum 255*
*The Walls 255*

March 336
*Dunhams Wood 337*
*March and District Museum 336*
*Nene—Ouse Navigation Link 337*
*St Wendreda's 336*

Mendham 117

Mendlesham 159

Mersea Island 252
*Cudmore Grove Country Park 252*
*National Nature Reserve 252*

Mildenhall 221
*Mildenhall & District Museum 222*
*St Mary's 222*

Milton 314
*Milton Country Park 314*

Mistley 254
*Mistley Place Park Environmental & Animal Rescue Centre 254*

*Mistley Quay Workshops 254*
*Mistley Towers 254*

Monks Eleigh 183

Morston 60

Moulton 220
*Packhorse Bridge 220*

Mountnessing 277
*Mountnessing Post Mill 277*

Mundesley 42

Mundford 105

Mundon 297
*St Peter's Way 297*

**N**

Nacton 179
*Nacton Picnic Site 179*
*Orwell Park House 179*

Nayland 186

Needham Market 158
*St John the Baptist 158*

Newbourne 180

Newmarket 216
*Animal Health Trust 219*
*British Racing School 219*
*National Horseracing Museum 219*
*National Stud 219*
*Nell Gwynn's House 219*
*Palace House 219*
*Rowley Mile 217*
*St Agnes 220*
*St Mary and All Saints 220*
*Tattersalls 219*
*The Jockey Club 218*

North Elmham 100

North Walsham 39
*Alby Crafts & Gardens 42*
*Market Cross 39*
*Paston School 41*

North Weald 276
*North Weald Airfield Museum and Memorial 276*

Northey Island 294

Norwich 4
*Atrium 6*
*Bridewell Museum 5*
*Bridge 6*
*Bulwer and Miller 5*
*Castle 4*
*Castle Museum and Art Gallery 5*
*Cathedral 6*
*Cathedral Close 7*
*City Hall 5*
*City of Norwich Aviation Museum 9*

*Cow Tower 7*
*Dragon Hall 8*
*Elm Hill 8*
*Erpingham Gate 7*
*Guildhall 5*
*Inspire Discovery Centre 8*
*Norfolk & Norwich Millennium Library 6*
*Norwich Castle Museum 9*
*Pull's Ferry 7*
*Royal Arcade 5*
*Sainsbury Centre for Visual Arts 9*
*Samson and Hercules House 7*
*Saxon Bishop's Throne 6*
*St Peter Hungate 8*
*St Peter Mancroft 8*
*The Assembly House 6*
*The Forum 6*
*The Mustard Shop 6*
*University of East Anglia 9*
*Venta Icenorum 9*

## O

Old Hunstanton 74
*Norfolk Coastal Footpath 74*
Old Leigh 285
Orford 151
*Havergate Island 152*
*Orford Ness 152*
*St Bartholomew's Church 152*
Otley 167
*Moated Hall 167*
Oxborough 86
*Oxburgh Hall 86*
*St John the Evangelist 86*

## P

Pakenham 209
*Nether Hall 209*
*Newe House 209*
*Watermill 209*
*Windmill 209*
Papworth Everard 327
Papworth St Agnes 327
Parham 166
*Parham Airfield 166*
Parson Drove 342
*Parson Drove Visitors Centre 342*
*Swan Inn 342*
Paston 42
Peakirk 334
Peasenhall 131
*Woolhall 131*

Peterborough 333
*Cathedral 334*
*Nene Valley Railway 334*
*Peterborough Museum and Art Gallery 334*
*Railworld 334*
*Thorpe Meadows Sculpture Park 334*
Pleshey 268
Point Clear 251
*East Essex Aviation Society & Museum 251*
Polstead 187
Poringland 10
*The Playbarn 10*
Potter Heigham 35
*Horsey Mere 35*
*Horsey Windpump 35*
*Museum of the Broads 35*
Prickwillow 304
*Prickwillow Drainage Engine Museum 304*
Purfleet 280
*Purfleet Conservation Area 280*
*Purfleet Heritage and Military Centre 280*
*Royal Hotel 280*
Purleigh 295

## R

Radwinter 260
Rampton 314
*Giant's Hill 314*
Ramsey 323
*Ramsey Abbey 323*
*Ramsey Rural Museum 323*
*Ramsey War Memorial 324*
*St Thomas à Becket of Canterbury 323*
Ramsholt 153
Ranworth 31
*Broadland Conservation Centre 33*
*St Helen's 31*
Rayleigh 286
*Dutch Cottage 286*
*Rayleigh Mount 286*
*Rayleigh Windmill 286*
Reach 316
Redgrave 211
Reedham 28
Reepham 23
*Marriott's Way 23*
Rendlesham 150
*Rendlesham Forest 150*
*St Gregory the Great 150*
Rettendon 295
*Royal Horticultural Society Garden 295*

Rickinghall  212
Ringstead  71
  *Ringstead Downs 74*
Rochford  285
  *The Old House 285*

## S

Saffron Walden  256
  *Anglo-American War Memorial 258*
  *Audley End House 258*
  *Bridge End Gardens 258*
  *Common 257*
  *Fry Public Art Gallery 258*
  *Old Sun Inn 256*
  *Saffron Walden Museu 256*
Sandon  290
Sandringham  75
  *Sandringham Country Park 75*
  *Sandringham House 75*
Sawtry  324
  *All Saints Church 324*
Saxmundham  131
Saxtead Green  163
  *18th-century mill 163*
Scole  13
Shepreth  319
  *Docwra's Manor 319*
  *Shepreth L Moor Nature Reserve 319*
  *Shepreth Wildlife Park 319*
Sheringham  47
  *North Norfolk Railway 49*
  *Pretty Corner 51*
  *Sheringham Park 51*
  *The Poppy Line 49*
Shimpling  215
  *Faint House 215*
Shotley  182
Sible Hedingham  246
Sibton  131
Sizewell  133
Snailwell  308
Snape  143
  *Blaxhall Stone 143*
  *Snape Maltings Riverside Centre 143*
Snettisham  75
  *RSPB Bird Sanctuary 75*
Somerleyton  111
  *Fritton Lake Countryworld 111*
  *Somerleyton Hall 111*

Somersham  333
  *Raptor Foundation 333*
South Hanningfield  290
  *Hanningfield Reservoir 290*
South Ockendon  280
  *Belhus Woods Country Park 280*
  *Brannetts Wood 280*
  *Church of St Nicholas 280*
  *Grangewaters Country Park 280*
South Walsham  31
  *Fairhaven Woodland and Water Garden 31*
  *South Walsham Inner Broad 31*
  *St Benet's Abbey 31*
South Weald  279
  *Old Macdonald's Educational Farm Park 279*
  *Weald Country Park 279*
South Woodham Ferrers  295
  *Marsh Farm Country Park 295*
Southend-on-Sea  283
  *Adventure Island 283*
  *Beecroft Art Gallery 284*
  *Central Museum, Planetarium and Discovery Centre 284*
  *Cliffs Bandstand 283*
  *Cliffs Pavilion 283*
  *Prittlewell Priory Museum 285*
  *Sealife Adventure 284*
  *Southchurch Hall Museum 285*
  *Southend Pier and Museum 283*
  *The Kursaal 284*
Southwold  119
  *Buckenham House 119*
  *Museum 122*
  *Sole Bay Inn 121*
  *Southwold Lifeboat Museum 122*
  *Southwold Sailors' Reading Room 122*
  *St Edmund King and Martyr 123*
Spaldwick  324
St Ives  331
  *Holt Island Nature Reserve 332*
  *Norris Museum 332*
  *Wilthorn Meadow 332*
St Neots  325
  *Church of St Mary the Virgin 326*
  *Market Square 326*
  *St Neots Museum 326*
St Osyth  252
  *St Osyth Priory 252*
  *St Peter and St Paul 252*
Stanford-le-Hope  281
  *Grove House Wood 281*
  *Stanford Marshes 281*

Stansted Mountfichet 261
  Mountfichet Castle 261
  Norman Village 261
  Stansted Airport 261
  Stansted Windmill 264
  The House on the Hill Museum Adventure 263
Stanton 211
  Wyken Vineyards 211
Steeple and St Lawrence 298
  St Lawrence Rural Discovery Church 298
Stiffkey 60
  Binham Priory 61
  Stiffkey Salt Marshes 61
Stilton 324
Stock 279
Stoke by Nayland 187
  Church of St Mary 187
Stonea 337
  Stonea Camp 337
Stonham Aspal 159
  British Birds of Prey and Nature Centre 159
Stow Bardolph 85
  Holy Trinity 85
Stowmarket 155
  Gipping Valley River Park 156
  Museum of East Anglian Life 155
Stratford St Mary 187
  Ancient House 187
  Priest's House 187
Stretham 307
  Downfield Windmill 307
  Stretham Old Engine 307
Stutton 182
Sudbury 189
  Gainsborough's House 189
  Quay Theatre 191
  Salter's Hall 191
  Victorian Corn Exchange 191
Sutton 305
  Mepal Outdoor Centre 305
Sutton Hoo 147
Swaffham 94
  Assembly Room 94
  Butter Cross 94
  Cockley Cley Iceni Village and Museums 96
  EcoTech Discovery Centre 96
  St Peter & St Paul 94
  Swaffham Museum 96
Swaffham Bulbeck 316
Swaffham Prior 316
  St Cyriac 316
  St Mary 316

Swannington 21
  Swannington Manor 21

T

Takeley 267
  Stane Street 267
Tatterford 92
  Houghton Hall 92
  Tatterford Common 92
Tattingstone 181
  Tattingstone Wonder 181
Tendring 248
  St Edmund 248
Terrington St Clement 83
  African Violet Centre 83
  Cathedral of the Marshland 83
Thaxted 264
  Almshouses 264
  Guildhall 264
  Thaxted Church 264
  Thaxted Garden for Butterflies 265
  Tower Windmill 264
The Bradfields 213
  Bradfield Woods 213
The Broads 27
Thelnetham 212
Thetford 102
  Ancient House 102
  Boudica's Palace 102
  Burrell Steam Museum 102
  Castle 102
  Cluniac Priory 102
  Grimes Graves 103
  The King's House 103
  Thetford Forest 103
  Thetford Warren Lodge 103
Thompson 101
  The Peddars Way 101
  Thompson Water 101
Thorney 335
  Thorney Abbey 335
  Thorney Heritage Museum 335
Thornham Magna & Parva 160
  Thornham Walks and Field Centre 160
Thornhaugh 338
  Sacrewell Farm and Country Centre 338
Thorpe Morieux 214
Thorpeness 133
  House in the Clouds 135
Thorrington 251
  China Maroc Bonsai 251
  Thorrington Tide Mill 251

Thursford Green  89
 *The Thursford Collection Sight and Sound Spectacul 89*
Tilbury  283
 *Tilbury Energy and Environment Centre 283*
 *Tilbury Festival 283*
 *Tilbury Fort 283*
Tiptree  233
 *Wilkin and Son Ltd 233*
Titchwell  69
 *St Mary 69*
 *Titchwell Marsh 69*
Tollesbury  294
 *Tollesbury Marina 294*
Trimley St Martin  180
Trimley St Mary  180
 *Trimley Marshes 180*

**U**

Ufford  149
 *Church of the Assumption 149*
Upwood  324
 *Woodwalton Fen 324*

**W**

Walberswick  123
 *Walberswick & Westleton Heaths 124*
Waldringfield  180
Walsham-le-Willows  211
 *St Mary's 211*
Waltham Abbey  269
 *Dragonfly Sanctuary 269*
 *Epping Forest District Museum 269*
 *Hayes Hill 271*
 *Holyfield Hall 271*
 *Lee Navigation Canal 270*
 *Lee Valley Park Farms 271*
 *Lee Valley Regional Park 270*
 *Myddleton House Gardens 271*
 *Royal Gunpowder Mills 270*
 *The House Mill 271*
 *Town Hall 270*
Walton Highway  341
 *Fenland and West Norfolk Aviation Museum 341*
Walton-on-the-Naze  249
 *Marine Parade 249*
 *Naze Tower 250*
 *Old Lifeboat House Museum 250*
 *The Backwaters 249*
 *The Naze 249*
 *The Pier 249*
Wangford  123

Warboys  323
Waterbeach  314
 *Denny Abbey 314*
 *Farmland Museum 314*
Watton  100
 *Clock Tower 101*
 *Griston Hall 100*
 *Wayland Wood 100*
Weeley  248
 *St Andrew's 248*
Wells-next-the-Sea  62
 *Harbour Railway 62*
 *Holkham Meals 63*
 *Wells—Walsingham Light Railway 62*
Welney  342
 *Wildfowl & Wetlands Trust 342*
Wenhaston  125
 *St Peter 125*
West Runton  45
 *Beacon Hill 45*
 *Norfolk Shire Horse Centre 46*
West Stow  207
 *Anglo-Saxon Village 207*
 *West Stow Country Park 207*
West Thurrock  279
 *Arena Essex Raceway 280*
 *Lakeside Shopping Centre 280*
 *St Clement's Church 279*
West Tilbury  281
West Walton  341
Westleton  129
 *Minsmere Bird Sanctuary 129*
 *Suffolk Coastal Path 129*
Wetheringsett  160
 *Mid-Suffolk Light Railway Museum 160*
Wethersfield  242
 *Boydells Dairy Farm 242*
Weybourne  51
 *The Muckleburgh Collection 53*
 *Weybourne Hope 51*
Whittlesey  335
 *St Andrew 335*
 *St Mary's 336*
 *Straw Bear Procession 335*
 *The Whittlesey Museum 335*
Wicken  307
 *St Lawrence's Church 308*
 *Wicken Fen 307*
 *Wicken Windmill 308*
Wickham Market  149
Wickhambrook  214

Widdington 261
  Mole Hall Wildlife Park 261
  Priors Hall Barn 261
Wighton 92
Willingale 274
  St Andrew's 274
  St Christopher's 274
Wingfield 172
  Wingfield College 172
Wisbech 339
  Flower Festival 339
  Lilian Ream Photographic Gallery 341
  Marina 341
  Octavia Hill Museum 339
  Peckover House 339
  The Angles Theatre 341
  Wisbech and Fenland Museum 339
Witham 290
  Dorothy L Sayers Centre 290
Wivenhoe 230
  Nottage Institute 230
Woodbridge 145
  Buttrum's Mill 147
  Suffolk Punch Heavy Horse Museum 146
  Tide Mill 147
  Woodbridge Museum 146
Woodham Walter 291
  St Michael's 292
Woolley 324
Woolpit 212
  Lady's Well 213
  Museum 212
Woolverstone 181
  Cat House 181
  Woolverstone House 181
Worlington 223
  Wamil Hall 223
Worlingworth 172
Worstead 35
  St Mary 35
Writtle 290
Wroxham 29
  Bure Valley Railway 30
  Cangate 30
  Hoveton Hall Gardens 30
  Willow Farm Flowers 30
  Wroxham Barns 30
  Wroxham Broad 30
Wymondham 10
  Becket's Chapel 11
  Market Place 11
  Railway Station 11

The Bridewell 11
Wymondham Abbey 10
Wymondham Heritage Museum 11
Wyton 329
  Houghton Mill 331

Y

Yaxley 161
  St Mary 161
Yoxford 129